The International Judge

The International Judge

An Introduction to the Men and Women Who Decide the World's Cases

Daniel Terris, Cesare P. R. Romano, and Leigh Swigart

Brandeis University Press
Waltham, Massachusetts

PUBLISHED BY UNIVERSITY PRESS OF NEW ENGLAND
HANOVER AND LONDON

Brandeis University Press
Published by University Press of New England,
One Court Street, Lebanon, NH 03766
www.upne.com
© 2007 by Brandeis University Press
Printed in the United States of America

5 4 3 2 1

Library of Congress Cataloging-in-Publication Data
Terris, Daniel.
  The international judge : an introduction to the men and women who decide the world's cases / Daniel Terris, Cesare P.R. Romano, and Leigh Swigart.
     p.   cm.
  Includes bibliographical references and index.
  ISBN-13: 978-1-58465-666-1 (cloth : alk. paper)
  ISBN-10: 1-58465-666-2 (cloth : alk. paper)
    1. Judges. 2. International courts. 3. Justice, Administration of.
  I. Romano, Cesare (Cesare P. R.) II. Swigart, Leigh. III. Title.
  K2146.T47 2007
  341.5'5—dc22   2007030206

To all our children:
Emma and Leo
Alex and Marcus
Ben, Eli, Theo, and Sam

Contents

Photograph gallery follows page 140.

Foreword

Sonia Sotomayor

A proposed bill in Congress to prohibit the citation of foreign law in federal judicial decisions gave rise in recent years to a heated and extensive dialogue among American judges, academics, and commentators on the appropriate role that foreign and international law should play in American constitutional adjudication. But the question of how much we have to learn from foreign law and the international community when interpreting our Constitution is not the only one worth posing. As *The International Judge* makes clear, we should also question how much we have to learn from international courts and from their male and female judges about the process of judging and the factors outside of the law that influence our decisions. This book makes an invaluable contribution to the efforts to answer that question by laying bare the institutional, political, moral, ethical, and legal concerns that animate the work of international courts and their judges.

Daniel Terris, Cesare P. R. Romano, and Leigh Swigart deftly identify the many challenges confronting international judges that national judges do not face. The authors, however, also identify the many ways in which international judges address and confront the same issues that my colleagues and I do on the United States Courts of Appeals. Like Judge Cecilia Medina Quiroga of the Inter-American Court of Human Rights, all judges have cases that touch our passions deeply, but we all struggle constantly with remaining impartial and "let[ting] reason speak." Like Judge Navanethem Pillay of the International Criminal Tribunal for Rwanda, all judges believe that "the test of our accomplishment is in the jurisprudence produced." But we are also acutely aware of the other dimensions of our roles as judges and, like Judge Pillay, we struggle to find ways to convince colleagues of our views and to accommodate the needs—and respect the powers—of the other branches of government.

Terris, Romano, and Swigart describe international courts as bold, cacophonous places where the halls resonate with a chorus of disparate

Sonia Sotomayor is a United States Circuit Court Judge for the Second Circuit Court of Appeals. Alan Schoenfeld, a law clerk to Judge Sotomayor, assisted in the preparation of this foreword.

voices, all oriented toward the common goal of pronouncing justice. While my colleagues on American courts of appeals rarely confront linguistic challenges among ourselves, we certainly speak to each other in different idioms. On my court, former prosecutors, district court judges, commercial lawyers in private practice, elected politicians, and academics dispute and reach consensus on a wildly divergent array of cases and controversies. *The International Judge* reveals the extent to which all courts, no matter what their provenance or jurisdiction, are in large part the product of their membership and their judges' ability to think through and across their own intellectual and professional backgrounds, to reach some juncture of consensus and cooperation in which a common language is used to articulate the rules and norms that bind their communities. In the end, despite our different legal cultures—civil or common law-based, as discussed by the authors—we are all trying to achieve justice.

Perhaps the most important contribution this book makes is its unique view of the dynamics of institution-building in the singular context of young international courts. Rare is the opportunity to view such important institutions in their parturition and to hear the voices of their founding mothers and fathers, who have and will shape the paths of those institutions. International tribunals are of relatively recent vintage, at least in comparison to the formal legal systems of many countries. But there are other young legal systems throughout the world where pioneering judges—like those of the international courts—are trying to cultivate the rule of law in the wake of revolutions and other political upheavals. This book provides a nuanced roadmap for those judges, as well as for judges from established legal systems, while we all attempt to cobble together a culture of justice-seeking in a changed world.

All this talk about the utility of this book for American judges and academics is not meant to suggest that it is anything less than important reading for those whose concerns lay elsewhere from American law and judicial politics. Rather, it merely reflects my particular point of view as a federal appellate judge. This book stands strongly on its own terms as an illuminating discussion of the politics and pragmatics of developing an international rule of law and of institution-building and offers some captivating portraits of the pioneers who work tirelessly to bring these institutions from their incipience to their maturity.

Introduction

What Is an International Judge?

Over the last century, international law, once reserved for arcane matters of diplomacy and trade, has come to encompass a broad range of human experience and activity. In the wake of major historical developments, the nations of the world have created a new set of legal institutions designed to resolve disputes between global actors, to settle conflicts that might otherwise play out on the battlefield, and to offer the promise of justice to those who cannot find it within their own countries. The success of these institutions rests ultimately on the shoulders of just over two hundred men and women who serve in a role unheard-of less than a hundred years ago: the international judge.

International judges serve on courts and tribunals established by global or regional bodies to address issues of justice that cross national borders. Within the United States, one sometimes hears the term "international judge" applied to any judge working outside of the United States, but this is a misnomer. A criminal court judge in Argentina or a member of the Constitutional Court of Germany is a "national judge," working within the legal system of his or her country. An international judge serves on a body whose jurisdiction includes more than one sovereign nation or on a body established by an international organization to deliver justice in a country where the legal structure is deemed insufficient to address a severe situation, such as the aftermath of ethnic cleansing or genocide.

International judges sit on fewer than twenty international judicial bodies, located in cities around the world, including The Hague (the Netherlands), Arusha (Tanzania), and San José (Costa Rica). In their professional capacity, their allegiance is to a body of international law that has developed through treaties, custom, and the evolution of general legal principles. They are usually nominated for their positions by their own governments, but often they are elected or appointed through a regional or international organization like the European Community, the Organization of American States, or the United Nations.

The courts that international judges serve on vary considerably in their jurisdictions, the types of cases they hear, and the impact of their judgments. Some international courts have jurisdiction across the globe; others have jurisdiction in specific continents or regions. In every case, however, these judges serve alongside peers from different countries. Their mission compels them to work across boundaries of geography, background, culture, training, and experience to forge law and render justice that will earn the respect of citizens of countries worldwide.

Many writings have taken note of the growth of international courts and have analyzed the developments in international law and in these courts as institutions.[1] In this book, we take a close look at the people who are the most visible representatives of these institutions, the judges charged with the important task of deciding the world's cases.

Why Are International Judges Important?

Their names may be unfamiliar, their judgments sometimes obscure, but the work of international judges has changed the character of the world we inhabit. Consider their role in the major developments of our time.

Globalization. The explosive growth of international trade and commerce rests on a foundation of rules. International judges preside over regional and global institutions that enforce those rules and that persuade and sometimes compel national governments to change their own laws to comply with transnational norms. These courts have played a key part in accelerating the global economic engine.

A check on globalization. At the same time, the work of international judges has provided a forum for those who have felt disempowered by the process of globalization, by providing a means by which small countries can confront larger ones and by which individuals can confront governments. International courts adjudicate issues of human rights, unfair trade practices, and (to some extent) the global environment, offering the possibility of correctives to unfettered growth.

Human rights. Men and women around the world have embraced the idea of international human rights, and the laws protecting those rights are enforced in international courts and tribunals. The work of international judges represents an avenue of hope for millions of individuals whose own governments may fail or abuse them.

Ending impunity. International judges have convicted and sentenced the perpetrators of some of the most horrific and extensive crimes of our time. There is an open debate about whether the presence of international criminal courts will deter future violence. But, building on the legacy of the Nuremberg and Tokyo trials, the nations of the world have created legal institutions where the perpetrators of genocide and other crimes against humanity can now be held accountable.

Regional integration and identity. It is scarcely an exaggeration to say that international judges have made possible the new Europe, with its ongoing integration of economy, law, and politics. The European Court of Justice and the European Court of Human Rights have issued rulings that have changed the face of the continent. To a lesser extent, international courts have played a role in developing regional cooperation in the Americas and in Africa.

New developments in law and justice. Working in a transnational environment, international judges have melded different systems and traditions, forging new vocabularies and methods that at their best permit law to flourish in place of chaos and unchecked power. The growth of international courts has also stimulated deeper thought about the interplay that must take place between legal institutions and other actors (such as governments and civil society) if justice is to be secured.

Creating alternatives to war and violence. As technology increases the potential for human self-destructiveness, the search for peaceful means to resolving conflict and quelling violence becomes more urgent. International courts are not a panacea, but they represent a crucial building block in the process of creating confidence in transnational cooperation.

Surveying these developments, some people have concluded that international judges have become too powerful. At stake, critics say, are the concepts of sovereignty and freedom. The debate has been especially heated in the United States, where senior figures have charged that international courts are a venue for politically motivated action against U.S. leaders, personnel, and interests. Critics have portrayed international judges as cosmopolitan radicals riding roughshod over unwilling nations and peoples in their rush to impose an ill-defined set of "global values." In Europe, too, some fear that transnational courts are sacrificing national character and prerogative on the altar of continental identity.[2]

At the same time, others fret openly about whether international judges are powerful *enough*. In many cases, courts depend on countries to submit themselves willingly to their jurisdiction and to enforce their judgments. Compliance with their orders varies widely, and strong countries have a tendency to follow the courts only when they believe that their interests are being served. When the criminal courts address issues of mass violence, they have the resources to bring to justice only a tiny fraction of the perpetrators, leaving many victims frustrated and angry. For all of their reach, the effectiveness of international judges depends ultimately on the faith and trust of powerful nations, leaving courts vulnerable to the vagaries of international politics.

Generalizations will not suffice. International judges are neither omnipotent nor toothless. They are, instead, engaged in a process of building institutions, a process that by definition involves moments of strength and moments of weakness, progress and regression, triumph and defeat. International courts and tribunals are not abstractions; they are profoundly human enterprises. This means, of course, that these institutions are far from perfect. International judges sometimes display serious flaws: pride, inconsistency, self-interest, and occasionally just plain incompetence.

Yet international judges more often embody the human virtues of intellectual acumen, creativity, dedication, and even compassion. Most importantly, their humanness endows their professional homes—international courts and tribunals—with the institutional capacity to learn, to experiment, to grow, to mature. They have accomplished a great deal in a comparatively short segment of human history, but they are only at the beginning of an era. This book is an attempt to capture a sense of individual achievement and perspective in a time of institutional innovation.

Behind This Book

This book builds on the work of two academic undertakings: the Brandeis Institute for International Judges and the Project on International Courts and Tribunals.

The Brandeis Institute for International Judges (BIIJ) was established in 2002 as the first ongoing gathering for judges serving across the broad spectrum of international courts and tribunals. The BIIJ, alternating meeting places in its early years between the United States, Europe, and Africa, has provided international judges with the opportunity to share concerns and ideas and to develop channels of communication and cooperation that foster judicial dialogue. These sessions have both revealed and helped to nurture a sense of community among the tiny, far-flung group of men and women who make up the international judiciary. Daniel Terris founded the BIIJ, and Leigh Swigart has served as one of its principal conveners since 2003.[3]

The Project on International Courts and Tribunals (PICT) was jointly established in 1997 by the Center on International Cooperation (CIC), at New York University, and the Foundation for International Environmental Law and Development (FIELD), at the School of Oriental and African Studies, University of London. In 2002, PICT moved its United Kingdom base to University College London as part of the establishment at the Faculty of Laws of the Centre for International Courts and Tribunals. In

2006, Cesare Romano, the manager of PICT at NYU since its inception, joined the Loyola Law School in Los Angeles.[4]

PICT's mission is to address the legal, institutional, and financial issues arising from the multiplication of international courts and tribunals and other dispute settlement bodies as well as from the increased willingness of members of the international community to have recourse to such bodies. PICT couples academic research with concrete action aimed at facilitating the work of international courts and tribunals. Among its activities one can mention the work done with the International Law Association to develop the Burgh House Principles, a pathbreaking template for protecting the independence and integrity of international judges, and the ongoing project on process and legitimacy in the nomination, election, and appointment of international judges.[5]

As we spoke to colleagues and to our projects' larger constituencies about our study of the international judiciary, we came to realize that relatively few people have had an opportunity to understand the development of international courts and tribunals through the perspective of judges themselves. This book emerged from our conviction that both experts in the field and outside observers of international law and adjudication could benefit from an examination of the individual men and women who sit on these courts, the members of a small but influential new professional group.

We bring to this book three distinct disciplinary perspectives. Daniel Terris is trained as a historian, whose most recent writing has focused on ethics and organizational history. Cesare Romano is a scholar of international law, whose decade-long management of PICT has given him the opportunity to write extensively on international courts, in particular on the legal and political aspects of their work. Leigh Swigart is an anthropologist who has written on the intersection of language and culture in West Africa and other regions. By combining the perspectives of law, international relations, history, and anthropology, we hope to illuminate not only the contributions that judges are making to international law, but also to show the ways that they are enmeshed in their institutions. Any understanding of their work, we argue, needs to go beyond legal documents and judgments and to consider the ways that judges participate in larger historical trends and act as members of complex human institutions whose inner dynamics and personal relationships shape their work.[6]

Methodology

This book is designed to be accessible to readers who are curious about international law and its adjudicative institutions but new to its study.

We have tried to be fair to the perspectives and opinions of the judges and transparent about our own ideas, while at the same time providing a sufficient context for informed readers to draw their own conclusions about the nature and direction of these courts.

At the same time, we believe that this volume will be useful to experts, too. While some of the contextual material will be familiar to those readers immersed in international law, the voices of the judges themselves have been relatively absent from the academic literature.[7] We hope that this book will encourage scholars of international law to undertake new research, using as a starting point this foundation of knowledge about international judges and the human complexities involved in their work, thereby adding new perspectives to well-developed narratives in the field. Perhaps this volume will also stimulate historians, anthropologists, and other social scientists to examine legal institutions as they seek to understand trends in the development of global institutions and ideas.

While designed to be of use to people around the world whose lives are affected by international courts, this book has a specific purpose in the context of the United States. American attitudes about international courts have often been colored by ambivalence, sometimes moving toward outright hostility. In many cases, the resistance of U.S. politicians, lawyers, and members of the public to international courts has been based on misinformation about these courts, their purpose, and their methods. We entertain a special hope that this book will contribute to the broader public discourse about the interplay between the United States Constitution and international law, as well as between the United States and international institutions more generally.

The heart of our primary research was a series of interviews, ranging from one to three hours in length, with judges from most of the courts and tribunals addressed in this volume.[8] These interviews, conducted from 2004 to 2006, covered a wide variety of topics, including the judges' own backgrounds and career developments, the processes by which they were nominated and elected or appointed to the courts, the routines of their work, their relationships among colleagues, their thoughts on key cases decided by their courts, the ways judgments are crafted, the relationship between law and politics, and issues of character and ethics. Most of our interviewees were sitting judges at the time that we spoke with them. All but one of the interviews were tape-recorded, with the understanding that we would quote directly but without attribution to any individual.[9] We developed an interview protocol, which we shared in advance with the interviewees, and we used it as a roadmap during our interviews, although we made no effort to ask everyone interviewed exactly the same questions and in the same order. We preferred to follow the flow of the interviewee's reasoning and steer him or her with questions from the protocol to areas that we thought might yield useful insights.

Our sample of thirty-two represents approximately one out of every seven sitting international judges.[10] We did not employ any statistical methodology in selecting whom to interview. As far as possible, we tried to select a sample that is representative of the current international judiciary, including both men and women, both judges and presidents of courts. We gave preference to those who were sitting judges at the time that we spoke with them. This made it possible to get a better look at international courts from the trenches, but it had the obvious disadvantage that judges are sometimes reluctant to talk openly about their lives at the courts while they are still serving on them. To compensate for that, we included in the group some recently retired judges.

The voices of judges from most of the major international courts are present here. Although numerically there are more regional than global courts, this book contains more voices from the latter than the former. We privileged visibility and impact, and we tried to include all courts that at some point have received world media attention. Some regional courts outside of the main world judicial centers, like the Andean Court of Justice, based in Quito, Ecuador, or the Caribbean Court of Justice, based in Port of Spain, Trinidad and Tobago, are not represented in our sample, though we tried to include any available information on these courts, too. Our interview sample is also geographically uneven; Asia, a region of the world that provides a disproportionately small share of international judges, receives relatively little attention in this study.[11]

We also spoke on a less formal basis with a variety of other people observing international courts, including individuals who plead before judges and work with them out of such offices as the registry and the office of the prosecutor. We did not attempt to interview people working in governmental positions. Undoubtedly, governmental representatives play a fundamental role in international courts. It is, after all, states that decide to create international courts, diplomats who draft their legal instruments, and in many cases government representatives who appear before them and eventually decide the fate of international judicial bodies. This subject is worthy of a book in itself. We chose a particular angle from which we would like to look at international courts—that of international judges—and we intentionally left other possible approaches for future scholars to develop.

Likewise, it is arguable that arbitrators play a role as important as judges of standing tribunals in "deciding the world's cases." Arbitration still plays a major role in international dispute settlement, and has a story in some ways richer and longer than that of international courts.[12] However, arbitrators are a substantially different subject than international judges. As they are "judges for hire," who get together to decide a specific case and then disband, they tend to form less structured, permanent, and cohesive communities than judges. Granted, these two categories of adjudicators have much in common, and it is often the case that exceptional individuals are simultaneously international judges and arbitrators. Still, it seems to us that the phenomena are different enough to be distinguishable.

This volume draws upon the expanding scholarly literature on international courts and tribunals, but we have chosen to limit our direct engagement with the scholarship in the service of providing an accessible portrait of international judges and the environments in which they work. In certain chapters, the words of judges take clear priority over already published works as we attempt to paint the insider's view of the experience of international judges. We provide, at the end of this book, an extensive bibliography for the benefit of those doing further research in this area. We make only passing reference, and only when strictly needed, to the main theories of international judging. This book captures something those theories and large analyses do not: the impact of individual experience on institutional behavior. We did not aim to write the ultimate book on international judges, nor to articulate the ultimate theory of international adjudication. We have a more modest goal. We hope to signal to scholars, in a variety of fields, that international courts and tribunals are a still largely uncharted territory, rich with possible opportunities for further research.

Finally, in trying to preserve the readability of the book, we have adopted several conventions that require explanation. First, we use the term "international courts" as a catch-all term to describe a set of institutions that might more precisely be described as "international judicial bodies."[13] Second, at the time of our writing, an international judge is more than four times more likely to be a man than a woman, so we use the third person masculine ("he") when referring to a generic international judge, rather than succumbing to the confusing practice of switching genders in these instances. Third, we use the terms "states" and "governments" interchangeably when referring to countries nominating judicial candidates or coming before international courts as parties to a case.

We should also make all those who have a legal education in domestic systems aware that in the world of international courts, some terms might have a different meaning than what they are used to. For instance, in the Anglo-American legal tradition, the word "chambers" refers literally to a judge's private workspace (e.g., office, library, everything but his public courtroom) and metaphorically to the judge's staff (e.g., law clerks, deputies, etc.). A decision taken "in chambers" would be one issued without a public hearing, perhaps based on written submissions. In the world of international courts, the word "chambers" is used to describe either the entire judicial branch of a court or the multi-judge subunits of a court that are delegated to hear particular cases (in American courts these are called "panels"). As far as possible, we have tried to explain ambiguous terms, but the reader should be aware that many differences do exist.

The International Judge: A Road Map

This book traces the growth in importance of the work of international judges, but it does not suggest that there is an inexorable line of development for international courts. What we emphasize instead is that the judges who serve on these bodies are working both as guardians of the law and as builders of legal institutions and that these roles are not always in harmony with each other. Furthermore, we argue that relationships *between* international courts matter. Whether or not there is an emerging "system" of international law, one important factor in the effectiveness of individual courts is the nature of the relationships between international courts and between international courts and domestic courts. With these elements—the construction of new institutions and the relationships between them—in mind, three principal themes have emerged from our research.

First, international judges, taken collectively, comprise a *community of knowledge-based experts* where similarities across the group are more important than differences. It is true, of course, that international judges are a diverse lot, coming from many countries around the globe, a variety of professional backgrounds, and legal systems with different rules and traditions. Nevertheless, the judges tend to share similar backgrounds in terms of education and experience in the international community, which lead to considerable harmony in matters of judicial temperament, outlook, and style. A shared understanding of the judicial function, and what it entails, binds them together. This common temperament, cutting across many different courts, leads to mutual respect and deference, and it makes judges and courts more predictable and the interpretation of law more stable than it might otherwise be. This community, however, is neither uniform nor necessarily benign. International judges can be parochial about defending their turf, and there is a keen competition between courts for attention and authority in an informal hierarchy of international law. Furthermore, an overdeveloped sense of community among judges can lead to a form of "corporate solidarity" that deflects constructive criticism and stifles new thinking.

Second, in their role as interpreters of the law, international judges are *reluctant radicals*. Faced with the challenges of creating new legal institutions, working in an uncertain political environment, and trying to establish the credibility and legitimacy of their courts, international judges have frequently forged new paths in law in situations where there have been no road maps. By and large, however, they are not adventurers by temperament. They are more likely to see themselves as compelled to break new ground by circumstance, rather than seeking opportunities to make their mark by developing new law. These tendencies have led to remarkable advances in international law, but they also have the potential to undermine the stability and legitimacy of the international courts if states begin to feel that the judges have overstepped their bounds.

Third, international judges are keenly aware that while their rulings can be sweeping and influential, they work in *fragile institutions*. Judges cannot afford to ignore the larger circumstances in which their courts are situated, which subject them to pressures from competing loyalties, inadequate funding, public expectations, and the currents of politics. External circumstances have created subtle but significant threats to the cornerstone of an international judge's work, his independence from outside influences. But judges themselves also play a large part in contributing to both the strength and the fragility of international judicial bodies. With the public credibility of their courts at stake, international judges work, as one observer puts it, "under a microscope," so their mistakes are correspondingly magnified. Furthermore, imperfect processes for choosing international judges and for monitoring their performance on the job leave the courts vulnerable to potential lapses of integrity and competence among the members of their benches.

We have organized the volume to begin with a global portrait of the institutions and a profile of international judges as a group, moving from there toward consideration of specific aspects of their lives and work.

Chapter 1, "International Courts: An Overview," presents the array of international courts and tribunals that exist today, from their establishment in the aftermath of devastating wars to their recent expansion in number and jurisdiction in the late twentieth century. It also highlights the limits to the expansion of the international judiciary and the dangers of excessive expectations about what international courts can achieve.

Chapter 2, "International Judges: Who Are They and How Do They Get on the Courts?" offers a group profile of the men and women serving on the international bench. Despite their geographic, cultural, and professional diversity, international judges tend to emerge from similar backgrounds in terms of education, training, and career development. The selection process for international judges, while varying considerably from court to court, often involves nominees in undignified electioneering at the national level, the international level, or both. Yet this process, with all its flaws, has been surprisingly successful at putting a diverse and well-qualified group of judges onto the bench of international courts.

"Inside the Courts," the third chapter, shows international judges in their working environment in the various courts around the world. The challenge of working in multiple languages and with varying cultural assumptions, the intricate nature of bureaucratic hierarchies, the interdependence of the judges with the administrative arms of the courts—these and other issues have a profound effect on the nature of the judges' work. Sometimes these interactions bring new levels of understanding to their process and decisions; at other times, the complexities of working in underfunded or understaffed international institutions create obstacles to their effectiveness.

The challenges of interpreting the law in the fluid circumstances of international courts are tackled in chapter 4, "International Judges and International Law." The debate between conservative and progressive interpretations of the law is common to all legal systems. In the absence of clear-cut constitutional structures around them, and cognizant of the need to meld different legal systems in transnational settings, international judges have often been forced to enter the dangerous territory of "making" law through their interpretation of treaties, custom, and general principles. The balancing act between applying the law as it is and filling the lacunae and dispelling uncertainties about international law is an exercise in diplomacy, both inside and outside the courts. International judges perform it daily, often with positive results, but sometimes attracting vigorous criticism.

Chapter 5, "Between Law and Politics," shows that the work of international courts can never be entirely divorced from the world of international politics. Potential threats to judicial independence lurk in the selection process, the funding mechanisms, and the inherent tension between national loyalty and professional responsibility. Rather than pretending that these threats do not exist, international judges have tackled political challenges transparently, shrewdly balancing their responsibilities as interpreters of the law with their responsibilities as global professionals.

The final chapter, "Tests of Character," confronts the difficulties of establishing and maintaining standards of ethics and integrity in an international system where the rules are new and the conditions constantly changing. There have indeed been well-documented transgressions by members of the international bench, but these individual lapses have not undermined the basic integrity of the courts as a whole. Nevertheless, in a system where judicial ethics is monitored primarily by judges themselves, the dangers of "corporate solidarity" leave the courts vulnerable to potential problems of injustice and loss of credibility.

Interspersed between these six thematic chapters are five profiles of individual international judges, which provide a more in-depth look at the experiences and choices of veterans on the bench. These profiles are intended to give the reader direct access to the stories of these men and women, told in their own voices and highlighting what is important to them about their lives and work.[14] We have chosen to present these profiles in a way that allows the judges by and large to speak for themselves, reserving our commentary and arguments for the body of the chapters.

It is a truism of the law that "justice must not only be done, but must be seen to be done." This famous phrase is usually invoked to emphasize the responsibility of judges to comport themselves in a manner beyond public reproach. But if justice is indeed to be "seen," then the public, too, has a responsibility to take an active role to *do* the seeing: to be attentive to the work of the judiciary, to ask searching questions, to embrace the institutions of the law as its own. We offer this volume as an invitation to "see" the work of international judges and, through insight, to contribute to the ultimate "doing" of justice.

Abbreviations

AB	Appellate Body (shorthand for World Trade Organization Appellate Body)
BIIJ	Brandeis Institute for International Judeges
CARICOM	Caribbean Community
CCJ	Caribbean Court of Justice
CJAC	Court of Justice of the Andean Community
EC	European Community/Communities
ECHR	European Court of Human Rights
ECJ	Court of Justice of the European Communities (along with the Court of First Instance)
EFTA	European Free Trade Area Court of Justice
EU	European Union
GATT	General Agreement on Tariffs and Trade
IACHR	Inter-American Court of Human Rights
ICC	International Criminal Court
ICJ	International Court of Justice
ICTR	International Criminal Tribunal for Rwanda
ICTY	International Criminal Tribunal for the former Yugoslavia
ILC	International Law Commission
ILM	*International Legal Materials*
ITLOS	International Tribunal for the Law of the Sea
NATO	North Atlantic Treaty Organization
NGO	Nongovernmental organization
OTP	Office of the Prosecutor
PCA	Permanent Court of Arbitration
PCIJ	Permanent Court of International Justice
PICT	Project on International Courts and Tribunals
SCSL	Special Court for Sierra Leone
UN	United Nations
UNCSW	United Nations Commission on the Status of Women
UNTS	*United Nations Treaty Series*
WTO	World Trade Organization
WTO AB	World Trade Organization Appellate Body

The International Judge

1 ⁀ International Courts
An Overview

A Brief History of International Adjudication

The expansion of the number and power of international courts since the end of the Cold War seems to point toward an increasing role not only for law in general but for judges in particular. The process is not a recent one, however; it has a history of more than three hundred years. Its development is, furthermore, neither linear nor inevitable.

There are essentially three milestones in the history of international courts. The first is the advent of modern arbitration. Many of both the powers and constraints of contemporary international courts have their roots in this practice. Arbitration is a peaceful method of settling disputes by way of legally binding decisions. The parties to a dispute themselves choose arbitrators, usually from among a known pool of highly respected and knowledgeable individuals. Each of the parties appoints an arbitrator and the two arbitrators together choose a third arbitrator, who usually chairs the panel.[1] The parties not only pick the arbitrators but also decide how the panel will go about deciding the case (that is to say, the "rules of procedure") and what law they will apply in doing so (also known as the "substantive law"). The decision of the arbitral panel, called "the award," is legally binding for the parties. Noncompliance with the award triggers legal responsibility. The binding nature of the outcome is one of the elements that arbitration shares with judicial settlement (that is to say, settlement reached by way of courts). Both arbitration and judicial settlement, also known collectively as "adjudication," are distinct from nonbinding means to settle disputes, such as consultation, mediation, conciliation, and good offices. The outcome of these latter processes (usually called "diplomatic means") is a nonbinding recommendation that the parties have a duty to consider in good faith but remain free to implement or disregard.

Although arbitration has been practiced for centuries and in many societies, its use between sovereigns and states was discontinued for long stretches during the Middle Ages and Renaissance. The resurgence of international arbitration in modern times coincided with the Enlightenment. Great Britain and the United States took the first concrete steps toward its reestablishment in the late eighteenth century. The fact that the superpower of that age and the superpower of the future were the forerunners of the arbitration process should not come as a surprise. In both countries, unlike in most of the rest of the world, the rule of law was already a long-established tradition, even at that time. To many citizens of those countries, it seemed only logical that what had been achieved domestically might also be applied internationally. There was also in both countries a numerically small but disproportionately influential tradition of pacifism, mostly religiously inspired, which played an important part in the quest for alternatives to war.

In 1794, the United States and Great Britain concluded the so-called Jay Treaty, named after the U.S. secretary of state and chief justice John Jay, to resolve outstanding issues in the aftermath of the American War of Independence.[2] The treaty set up three claims commissions, composed of British and American representatives, which successfully adjudicated some 536 claims, relating mostly to maritime seizures, and fixed the boundary between the United States and what is today Canada. The successful Jay Treaty model was quickly replicated by the United States in several more treaties as well as by other countries.

In 1871, the United States and Great Britain successfully resorted again to a law-based and binding process to settle claims arising out of the U.S. Civil War, claims created principally by the failure of Great Britain to observe its duties as a neutral power.[3] Unlike the mixed commissions under the Jay Treaty, in the so-called *Alabama* cases foreigners were invited to participate in deciding the cases. A five-member collegial body rendered the awards; the United States and Great Britain appointed one member each, and the other three were appointed by the king of Italy, the emperor of Brazil, and the president of the Swiss Confederation. All future international courts would later follow the practice of relying on benches or panels composed primarily of foreigners.

The *Alabama* settlement became a model for the benefits of resorting to law-based, impartial, and binding methods to resolve international disputes. Arbitration increased considerably afterward, eventually leading to its institutionalization. In 1899, the Hague Peace Conference adopted the Convention on the Pacific Settlement of International Disputes, creating the Permanent Court of Arbitration (PCA). The novelty of the PCA was that it provided states with a readily available list of eminent jurists (designated by states themselves) to be chosen as arbitrators, a ready-made procedure, and a permanent secretariat to assist proceedings. Despite its name, the PCA was not a quantum leap from the ad hoc arbitration that took place before, as it was neither permanent (there was no designated body that sat regularly) nor a court (as its members were not independent of the parties that appointed them). The PCA, which still exists in The Hague, had its golden age in the period between the beginning of the twentieth century and World War II. Since the late 1990s, it has reawakened, riding the general surge in international adjudication, but because its work is arbitration and not judicial settlement, it falls outside the taxonomy of international courts.

The transition from arbitration to judicial settlement—the second milestone—began with the establishment of the Permanent Court of International Justice (PCIJ) in 1922 in The Hague. The PCIJ was the first permanent, and truly global, international court of general jurisdiction, and it largely became the template for all future international courts.[4] The PCIJ consisted of a group of fifteen judges, elected periodically by the assembly and the council of the League of Nations—the universal organization of that era—in such a way as to "represent the main forms of civilization and the principal legal systems of the world."[5] The idea that the bench of an international court should be representative of the membership of the organization of which the court is an organ is still a fundamental feature of all contemporary international courts.

The PCIJ could hear disputes between two states on any international legal matter or give nonbinding advisory opinions on any dispute referred to it by the council or the assembly of the League of Nations. States could only appear before the PCIJ provided they had accepted the court's jurisdiction. This acceptance of jurisdiction could be *ante hoc* (where states agreed in advance that certain types of disputes would be settled by the PCIJ) or *ad hoc* (where states agreed on a case-by-case basis regarding which disputes to submit to the court). The provision for ante hoc jurisdiction was, arguably, an innovation as contrasted to the à la carte justice provided by arbitration. States could provide for judicial settlement before the emergence of any dispute by inserting into a treaty a clause that might read, "In the event of a dispute between the parties to this agreement, the dispute shall be submitted, at the request of any party, to the PCIJ"; or they could make open-ended unilateral declarations accepting the court's jurisdiction on any future dispute with any other state that had made corresponding declarations. This latter was the biggest innovation of all, as it was a radical departure from previous practice, moving away from ad hoc procedures and toward generalized acceptance of the jurisdiction of international judicial bodies.

The PCIJ disappeared with the demise of the League of Nations at the outbreak of World War II, to be reestablished, with only marginal changes, at the war's end as the International Court of Justice (ICJ), the "principal judicial organ" of the United Nations.[6] The continuity between the PCIJ and the ICJ, and also their preeminence in the pantheon of international courts, is highlighted by the fact that the term "World Court" generally refers to the combined history of the two institutions.

The third milestone in this history is the transformation of international courts from mere settlers of disputes between sovereign states to what could be called "agents of international justice," opening the courtroom doors to entities other than governments, such as individuals, corporations, and international organizations. In the decades that followed World War II, international courts underwent several mutations, branching out into different families and genera.

Definitions

There is no clear-cut, universally accepted definition of an international court. As in the taxonomy of living creatures or plants, it depends on the criteria of classification. Five basic elements, however, characterize the international courts and tribunals that have the broadest and most sustained impact.[7] Those courts:

1. Are permanent, or at least long-standing;[8]
2. Have been established by an international legal instrument;[9]
3. Use international law to decide cases;[10]
4. Decide cases on the basis of rules of procedure which pre-exist the case and usually cannot be modified by the parties;[11] and
5. Issue judgments that are legally binding on the parties to the dispute.[12]

In 2006, seventeen courts met these criteria and operated with a certain regularity:

1. International Court of Justice (ICJ)
2. International Tribunal for the Law of the Sea (ITLOS)
3. International Criminal Tribunal for the former Yugoslavia (ICTY)
4. International Criminal Tribunal for Rwanda (ICTR)
5. International Criminal Court (ICC)
6. Special Court for Sierra Leone (SCSL)
7. European Court of Human Rights (ECHR)
8. Inter-American Court of Human Rights (IACHR)
9. World Trade Organization dispute settlement system, and, in particular, the Appellate Body (WTO AB)
10. Court of Justice of the European Communities (along with the Court of First Instance) (ECJ)
11. European Free Trade Area Court of Justice (EFTA Court)
12. Court of Justice of the Andean Community
13. Caribbean Court of Justice (CCJ)

14. Permanent Review Court of the Mercosur
15. Common Court of Justice and Arbitration of the Organization for the Harmonization of Corporate Law in Africa
16. Court of Justice of the Economic Community of West African States
17. Court of Justice of the Economic and Monetary Community of Central Africa

The first thirteen courts on this list are the most active and consequential institutions, and they constitute our focus, although we were able to carry out interviews with judges serving on only the first eleven.[13]

Several other courts around the globe do meet the five criteria above, but they are not yet operational, operate intermittently, have been dormant for a period of time, or their impact is marginal. These include such bodies as the Central American Court of Justice, the Economic Court of the Commonwealth of Independent States, the Arab Maghreb Union Judicial Authority, and the African Court of Justice. Two new institutions, the African Court of Human and Peoples' Rights and the Extraordinary Chambers in the Courts of Cambodia, are recently established as of 2006, but they are not yet fully functioning and it is too early to count them among the active international courts.[14]

This accounting by no means includes all international or regional bodies that carry out quasi-judicial or dispute settlement functions. A plethora of other bodies, numbering several dozen, exercises judicial or quasi-judicial functions, including arbitral tribunals (the Permanent Court of Arbitration), administrative tribunals (the World Bank Administrative Tribunal or the European Union Civil Service Tribunal), and treaty-monitoring bodies with compliance-review functions (the Committee against Torture).[15] These bodies settle important disputes and rule on important questions, but do not meet one or more of the above set criteria; for instance, because their decisions are not binding on the parties, or because the parties pick and choose those who will decide the case, the applicable laws, and the procedure.

Even among the thirteen principal international courts and tribunals, the diversity and complexity of these bodies make generalizations difficult. There is a strong tendency to approach international courts as separate universes. Each international court is, after all, the product of particular historical, political, and legal circumstances. Each derives powers from different sources, most have been created by different groups of states, and all have a distinct jurisdiction. Some have a geographical jurisdiction limited to a certain region of the globe (what lawyers call "jurisdiction *ratione loci*"), while others have no limits per se (the so-called universal courts). Jurisdiction can also be limited to particular issues (*ratione materiae*), subjects (*ratione personae*), and time periods (*ratione temporis*).

Still, international courts *do* have enough commonalities to be approached as a "class" or "order" of their own within the larger "kingdom" of international organizations, although there is a fundamental difference between international courts and international organizations more generally. States have been cooperating to achieve common goals through permanent institutions for almost 150 years. These international organizations provide various services, including facilitating the settlement of disputes between members. However, dispute settlement within or by international organizations is a political process that takes place according to the long-established rules of diplomacy, where power relations usually dictate the outcome.

International courts, conversely, make legal determinations. To be precise, they determine whether certain acts are congruous with certain norms, in particular with the norms of international law. It is dispute settlement "under the shadow of the law."[16] Since the end of World War II, through the signing of an array of treaties and the delegation of decision-making powers to international agencies, states have accepted a growing number of international legal obligations, with three key characteristics. First, states' behavior is increasingly subject to scrutiny under the general rules, procedures, and discourse of international law (and often domestic law as well). Second, these rules are increasingly precise in the conduct they require, authorize, or proscribe. Third, the authority to implement, interpret, and apply those rules, and to create further rules and/or settle disputes arising out of their implementation, is often delegated. These three phenomena (obligation, precision, and delegation) are the "three dimensions" of the commonly termed "legalization of world politics."[17] International courts are a specific aspect of the larger phenomenon of the legalization of world politics, a phenomenon that could be called the "judicialization of world politics," one characterized by a high degree of delegation, which eventually might make obligations become more precise and perhaps even more binding.

To summarize, in our own time there are four basic genera of international courts, listed in the order in which they emerged:

1. **Classical state-only courts,** like the International Court of Justice. To this genus belongs also the more recent International Tribunal for the Law of the Sea and the World Trade Organization dispute settlement system, where the judicial institution is the World Trade Organization Appellate Body.

2. **Human rights courts,** such as the European Court of Human Rights, the Inter-American Court of Human Rights, and the African Court of Human and Peoples' Rights.

3. **Courts of regional economic and/or political integration agreements,** such as the European Court of Justice, the judicial organ of

the European Communities/European Union; the Court of the European Free Trade Agreement; and the Caribbean Court of Justice.[18]

4. **International criminal courts,** such as the International Criminal Court, the International Criminal Tribunal for the former Yugoslavia, and the International Criminal Tribunal for Rwanda. A specific subgenus is that of the so-called hybrid or internationalized criminal courts, such as the Special Court for Sierra Leone, the Extraordinary Chambers in the Courts of Cambodia, the Special Panels for Serious Crimes in East Timor, or the proposed "Hariri Tribunal" to try the murderers of the former Lebanese prime minister.[19]

Courts of the first genus can only hear cases between sovereign states.[20] As there are fewer than two hundred sovereign states in the world, they serve a numerically small community and, accordingly, their caseloads tend to range from a few to several dozen per year. In these courts, diplomacy and sovereignty play important roles. These are the courts where the arbitral heritage and the original mission of dispute settlement are most evident.

Human rights courts have been created to provide redress to individuals whose human rights have been violated, usually by their own states. Individuals can submit to these courts—directly (in Europe) or indirectly through specific organs of international organizations called "commissions" (in the Americas and Africa)—cases concerning the violation of their rights, as provided for in the respective basic regional human rights agreements. The range of issues these courts address is considerable and in many regards is similar to that addressed by national supreme courts. The spectrum of cases includes hard-core human rights topics like the death penalty, extrajudicial killings, conditions of detention, and fair trials; issues of discrimination, freedom of expression, participation in political life, and relationships within the family; and matters involving rights to housing, health, and sexual identity. These courts tend to have large dockets—sometimes thousands of cases per year—as potential plaintiffs number in the hundreds of millions.

The third genus is that of courts of regional economic integration agreements. Numerically, this is the largest genus; there are about a dozen of these courts around the globe. These courts commonly handle requests of interpretation of community law from national courts; for example, a court in Denmark may ask the European Court of Justice to rule on an interpretation of European Community law relevant to a specific Danish case. They also decide disputes between member states on the content and implementation of community laws, disputes between organs of the community in question and member states, and disputes between individuals or corporations and community organs or member states. The ECJ, the principal judicial body of the European Community/European Union, the first and arguably most successful of all regional economic (and, in this case, also political) integration agreements, has provided the template for most other courts in this group.

Finally, international criminal courts are the latest genus to develop, all in the years since 1993. Their mission is to rule on international crimes (war crimes, crimes against humanity, crimes of genocide) through trials and, eventually, to determine criminal sanctions, like detention. Most of these criminal courts are ad hoc—they have a limited lifespan—and have jurisdictions limited to a specific period and region (such as the former Yugoslavia, Rwanda, or Sierra Leone).[21] They are also usually geared toward the prosecution of high-level political and military leaders. Of these, the only permanent court is the International Criminal Court, which also, at least potentially, has no particular temporal (at least from 1 July 2002 onward) or geographic restrictions. In these international courts, individuals are always the defendants (never states), and the burden of the prosecution is shouldered by the office of the prosecutor, an organ of an international organization, in the name of humankind. The United Nations, to different degrees, has a connection with all of these criminal bodies.[22]

Overall, the most interesting, and also perplexing, aspect of the multiplication of international jurisdictions in recent years is the fact that not only the successes but also the failures of experiments in international justice have provided reasons to establish even more international courts.[23] In looking at the history of the development of these courts, it is evident that the success of the European courts, like the ECJ and ECHR, has led to attempts to replicate them in other regions of the globe (e.g., the Andean Court of Justice and the African Court of Human and Peoples' Rights). Conversely, the rise of many international criminal bodies created after the ICTY/ICTR "twin courts" can be explained partly in terms of attempts to address the shortcomings of those early and temporary templates. At the same time, these courts' success in making international criminal justice look indispensable, if not a human right, has also been inspirational. Other international courts have been created either because those existing could not do the job or because they could not do it satisfactorily. Thus, for instance, the International Tribunal for the Law of the Sea was invented at a time when dissatisfaction with the ICJ, particularly among developing countries, was at its peak. In addition, as the ICJ is a generalist court, certain highly technical and self-contained legal regimes, like the international trade regime of the GATT/WTO agreements, called for specialized bodies. Finally, as the ICJ is a "civil court" and only states can appear before it, using it to hold criminal trials was not an option.

In the News

The framers of the Permanent Court of International Justice could hardly have anticipated, in 1922, the widespread impact of international courts by the beginning of the twenty-first century. Momentous issues of torture, genocide, and crimes against humanity are played out in their court-rooms, as well as less dramatic issues like border disputes, trade agreements, and even such mundane matters as the nomenclature of cheese. The actions of these courts reverberate around the globe, as a small sample of news headlines from the period from 2004 to 2006 can illustrate.

"ICJ to Israel: Drop dead!" blared the headline in one of Israel's leading papers, the *Jerusalem Post,* in the summer of 2004.[24] The International Court of Justice had found that the route of the wall built between Israel and the occupied Palestinian territory violated various international obligations incumbent upon Israel, and that according to international law Israel should both dismantle sections of the wall and make reparation for any damage caused. This case involved a nonbinding advisory opinion,[25] so there was no immediate impact, but in the tense atmosphere of Middle East politics, the court's opinion unleashed a world media maelstrom. The furor created by the "Wall case" overshadowed the larger role played by the so-called World Court in its more regular work of adjudicating disputes. While pundits were busy commenting about the Wall opinion, Costa Rica submitted a border dispute with Nicaragua to the ICJ, possibly averting a prickly escalation, while in West Africa, Nigeria and Cameroon were arguing over the implementation of the ICJ ruling assigning the oil-rich Bakassi peninsula to Cameroon.

"Ottawa vows to appeal the WTO decision upholding duties on imports from Canada," reported the *Los Angeles Times* in August 2005. Disputes before the World Trade Organization that year included cases involving lumber, textiles, and passenger airplanes. "Japan ends restrictions on U.S. apple imports," the *Sacramento Bee* announced in September; the WTO ruling ended a dispute that had gone on for twenty years.

In 2004 and 2005, the trial of Slobodan Milosevic, the former Yugoslavian president, was slowly proceeding before the International Criminal Tribunal for the former Yugoslavia. Outside the courtroom, the ICTY cast a long shadow on European politics. The news in May 2005 that the tribunal's prosecutor suspected that General Ante Gotovina, a popular Croatian hero of the war, was hiding in a Franciscan convent in Croatia triggered a headline from the Associated Press: "The hunt for Croatia's fugitive war crimes suspect triggers tales, jokes."[26] Gotovina was arrested in December 2005 ("Croatian suspect in war crimes is arrested in Canary Isles," said the *New York Times*) and transferred to The Hague to stand trial.[27]

On opposite sides of the globe, hybrid international criminal tribunals were in the spotlight. "Cambodians hope justice will close dark chapter," *USA Today* declared in March 2005, as the creation of a special court to try former Khmer Rouge leaders in Cambodia, responsible for the genocide carried out during Pol Pot's regime, was advancing.[28] The next year, the Special Court for Sierra Leone scored a major triumph. "Liberia's Taylor flown to The Hague to face war crimes charges," proclaimed the *Washington Post,* three months after the capture of the notorious former Liberian president Charles Taylor in March 2006.[29]

When the European Court of Justice upheld Greece's exclusive right to use the name "feta" in October 2005, the headline writers had a field day. "Cheese law a feta accompli," one paper announced, though another journal in far away Australia warned that "Protecting feta won't make it betta."[30] That same year, fans of the sport that Americans know as "soccer" but the rest of the world calls "football" found their interest consumed by a different case before the ECJ, as several European clubs claimed their right to demand compensation for their players lent to national teams to play in the Euro and World Cups.[31] A case brought by the British retailer Marks & Spencer got the attention of governments across Europe when the company claimed its right under European Community law to offset losses made by its former European subsidiaries in France, Germany, and Belgium against UK profits when calculating its tax liability. A nuanced ruling by the ECJ avoided the worst-case scenario for governments worried about the loss of revenue. "M&S wins EU tax verdict—European Court of Justice attaches significant qualifications—Ruling likely to cost tax authorities millions rather than billions," the *Financial Times* reported in December 2005.[32]

"Celebrities have a right to be left alone" was the verdict of the *International Herald Tribune* in July 2004, when Princess Caroline of Monaco, a favorite target of paparazzi, won a landmark case against Germany at the European Court of Human Rights.[33] The German Constitutional Court had previously ruled that the applicant, who was undeniably a contemporary "public figure," had to tolerate the publication of photographs of herself in a public place, even if they showed her in scenes from her daily life rather than engaged in her official duties. The princess, claiming that her human rights had been violated, took her case to the ECHR, which ruled differently, sending a chill down the collective spine of tabloid editors throughout Europe.

A more momentous ECHR decision, that the trial of Kurdish guerrilla leader Abdullah Öcalan by a Turkish court had been improper, sent political seismic waves across the continent and beyond. "European court rules Kurd's trial was unfair; Turkey stuck between E.U., nationalists," noted the *Washington Post* in May 2005.[34] At stake was, among other things, Turkey's application to become a member of the European Union.[35]

The Inter-American Court of Human Rights made headlines in the United States when it heard the case of Lori Berenson, a U.S. citizen currently serving a twenty-year prison term in Peru for collaborating with the terrorist organization Túpac Amaru Revolutionary Movement. Berenson had been tried twice in Peru. In November 2004, the IAHCR, while condemning the military court that originally tried her, ruled that she had received a fair trial the second time around.

This small sampling illustrates that international courts make news. The judges who pen those decisions, however, remain largely in the shadows. In contrast to the United States, where the views and personalities of individual judges—at least those of the Supreme Court and other key institutions—are a part of the public discourse, very rarely, if ever, do the media try to put a name and a face on international justice. This is, as we shall see, partly a matter of international legal culture and partly a matter of judicial temperament, but it is striking how little attention is bestowed on the authors of decisions that pull countries back from the brink of war, punish the world's worst criminals, and redistribute billions of dollars.

The Limits of the Judicialization of World Relations

The expansion of international courts and the range of their cases may, however, produce a false impression. The judicialization of world relations can be overstated and blown out of proportion. Linear narrations tend to create the impression of a world on a long, steady march away from chaos and lawlessness toward the rule of law guaranteed by the oversight of international judges. In other words, the march might seem unidirectional and the destiny of humanity scripted. In reality, this journey has many false steps and wrong turns, and the future is far from clear.

First, we should recognize that legalization and judicialization have disproportionately affected certain areas of international law and relations. Economic agreements have proven to be particularly fertile ground. It seems that the more that states move toward economic integration or harmonization of legislation, the greater the need for the guarantee of third-party dispute settlement. Human rights is another area that has been increasingly legalized and judicialized, as individuals seek redress for violations of their rights by their own governments before an impartial and internationally based body and as states wish to demonstrate their membership in the community of democratic nations by upholding various human rights treaties.[36] Similarly, in the criminal field, the remarkable growth of international criminal tribunals is a reaction to the fact that, for years, perpetrators of war crimes or crimes against humanity escaped prosecution by being able to benefit from the protection of their own governments or other complicit powers.

There are, however, many areas of international relations that, while showing increasing degrees of legalization, have not been judicialized. There is no "Court of the International Monetary Fund" and no "NATO High Tribunal." There is no "International Court of the Environment" that might decide, for example, whether a state violated the Kyoto Protocol to the United Nations Framework Convention on Climate Change.[37] In the fields of international financial relations, the protection of the environment, military and security affairs, telecommunications, the regulation of transcontinental migrations, and cooperation in the sphere of health, the predominant role is still played by diplomatic bargaining. These are issues where collective, day-to-day management and flexibility are seen as more important than giving the chance to any given government to bring instances of violations of the letter of the agreements before a third-party impartial body. States are believed to need more leeway in these fields than in others. They should be able to respond to a financial and monetary crisis by temporarily breaking the rules, they need to be encouraged to progress in the reduction of greenhouse gases rather than being fined for noncompliance, and they need to have the last word about where their military personnel are and what they do.

What is more, the penchant toward international courts and tribunals varies greatly across societies. Democracies are more likely to support, establish, and submit to the jurisdiction of international courts and tribunals than nondemocratic regimes.[38] Major powers tend to be more reluctant to submit to third-party judicial scrutiny than smaller states, the major exception to this being the United Kingdom. The United States, a democracy and the hyperpower of this age, has an ambivalent attitude toward international judicial bodies. In general, it tends to conceive international courts more as a constraint than a tool through which it can achieve its foreign policy goals. It tends to favor judicialization in certain areas, like trade, where power alone will not be enough to hold sway, as it is vulnerable to retaliation, but it tends to oppose international criminal courts because of the possibility—albeit often only theoretical—that its use of military power might come under foreign judicial scrutiny.

Smaller states seem to prefer international judicial bodies, as these fora provide them with tools to achieve goals that would otherwise be beyond their capabilities, such as leveling the playing field with major powers. Without the International Court of Justice, Djibouti would have had a much more difficult time raising the issue of alleged violation of its politicians' diplomatic immunities by French magistrates,[39] and Mexico could not have called attention to the rights of its nationals detained on death row in the United States.[40] Equally, without the World Trade Organization dispute settlement system, Guatemala could not object to the European Community's regime for the importation, sale, and distribution of bananas,[41] nor could Antigua do the same regarding U.S. measures affecting Internet gambling.[42]

Different regions of the world are also judicializing at varying degrees and paces. After the devastations suffered during World War II, Europeans seem to have had an epiphany, launching a continentwide quest for peace, security, and prosperity that rests on two main judicial pillars, the European Court of Justice and the European Court of Human Rights. Africa, in the struggle to achieve a certain degree of stability and prosperity, has also given birth to a large number of international judicial institutions. But the fact that many African institutions have either been non-starters or foundered after a few years for lack of resources or political support also indicates that the commitment to independent, third-party adjudication might be, at least for the political elites of these countries, a matter of lip service.[43]

International courts are rare sightings in Asia and the Pacific region, which cover about two-thirds of the planet and contain more than half of the human population. The limited exceptions are the Serious Crimes Unit/Panel in East Timor, which ended its work in 2005, and the Extraordinary Chambers in the Courts of Cambodia, which was still in the process of formation in 2006. Asia lacks a strong regional organization that can provide the necessary subsoil for international courts to take root, probably because the continent is simply too large and diverse to allow for a regional organization of continental scale. The paucity of international judicial bodies in Asia is surely not due to a lack of commitment to the rule of law in many countries in the region, nor to a cultural preference for agreement and harmony over legal conflict, as has sometimes been suggested. Asian countries participate actively in litigation in such fora as the International Court of Justice or the WTO Appellate Body with a frequency not significantly lower than countries from other regions. Asia has also sent many first-rate judges to international courts.

While several states have accepted the jurisdiction of multiple international judicial bodies, most are subject to the jurisdiction of only one or two. As for individuals, the overwhelming majority in the world do not have the opportunity to submit their cases to the scrutiny of an international judicial body. Forty-six European states, including most of the states of the former Soviet Union, are subject to the ECHR jurisdiction. In the Americas, only twenty-four out of a total of thirty-five states of the Organization of American States have accepted the jurisdiction of the Inter-American Court of Human Rights, and the United States is not among them. As of 2006, just over half the countries of the world (102) have accepted the jurisdiction of the ICC, although the Security Council can refer alleged crimes for investigation by the court regardless of the given state's consent.[44] Each ad hoc criminal tribunal has jurisdiction only over the territory of the former Republic of Yugoslavia or over that of Rwanda, respectively. The same applies in the case of Sierra Leone, although the effects of this court have also been felt in neighboring Liberia. Still, for a Chinese, a Fijian, or a Zimbabwean—or, for that matter, a citizen of the United States—protection of her or his human rights by way of an international judicial body is not, as yet, an option.

The process of judicialization is neither unidirectional nor irreversible. There are already signs that the world has reached its limit on international judicial bodies, as the breakneck pace of the 1990s gives way to smaller and less dramatic developments. In the areas that have made headlines in the drive toward judicialization, like international trade, some critics have argued that governments should limit the scope of courts by bringing politics back to the center of the debate.[45]

Finally, the judicialization of world affairs is limited by the weaknesses of the existing international courts themselves. Although their expansion has alarmed some critics, they remain small and fragile institutions, subject to the cooperation and the pressures of powerful actors on the world stage.

2 ✎ International Judges
Who Are They and How Do They Get on the Courts?

The effectiveness of international courts depends, for a start, on the quality of the men and women who ascend to the bench. Yet ensuring that international courts are staffed by the best and brightest is a significant challenge.

First, there is a general problem of scarcity of individuals who possess the many and exacting qualities required from a good international judge. The fact that, at the same time, there is a high and rising demand to staff an increasing number of international courts compounds the problem. Second, the procedures used to identify, vet, and select candidates are often scattered and haphazard and, more crucially, these procedures are in many ways flawed.

Generalizations about the selection process for international judges are difficult to form because every court has a different procedure to recruit international judges, and sometimes huge variations exist in the way individual governments approach the challenge. In addition, while the formal outlines of the process are public, relatively little information is available about the inside machinations leading to international judicial appointments. No systematic and comprehensive study of this process has yet been carried out.[1] While some countries are more thorough than others in documenting the process, many others never release the information about the process to the public. In any case, as in any political matter, the heart of the story often lies in handshakes and conversations that are off the official record.

Be that as it may, the route to an international judicial appointment almost invariably starts with being chosen by one's own government as the national nominee. The nomination process is often shrouded in mystery, since information about the decision making has traditionally been restricted to governing elites (politicians, senior civil servants, and, very occasionally, members of the bench, bar, and academia). Although the basic legal instruments of international courts provide for certain minimal requirements that judges should meet, it is not always clear how governments assess candidates. If the court in question is composed of fewer judges than the number of nominating states, an election will decide who is chosen; otherwise, the national pick will be appointed, sometimes after some level of institutional vetting.

Elections are particularly complex moments, where a number of considerations—like states' national interests, prestige and power politics, and the need to ensure representativeness—interact to eventually determine the result. Significantly, and as contrasted to national processes of judicial appointment, politics seems to have a more limited scope. Major powers do not necessarily control the process and, in recent years, nonstate actors have started playing a role in reshuffling orders of priority and undermining well-established equilibria.

Despite the imperfections of these procedures, the nations of the world have by and large elevated a strong and experienced cadre of professionals to these important positions. Significant vulnerabilities remain, however, which threaten to undermine both the effectiveness of the courts and public confidence in their work. As we shall see, most judges and close observers agree that the essence of the current system cannot be changed: governments must recruit and appoint international judges, and alternative procedures involving either public participation or appointment by an executive would merely create a different set of problems. However, several signs indicate that the problem of ensuring that international courts have competent personnel is spurring reconsideration of national and international practices.

Before turning to the selection process, a "snapshot" of international judges at a single moment in time may illuminate the general characteristics of the international bench as a group and the challenges in selecting and electing qualified candidates.

A Group Portrait

A group portrait, in the manner of Rembrandt's *Night Watch,* of today's international judges would strike the viewer first with the diversity of the figures on the canvas. The ethnic diversity would be obvious; it would be up to the skill of the artist to hint at the range of countries of origin, languages spoken, and professional backgrounds. Yet a closer examination would reveal patterns and similarities beyond the common garb of the judicial robes.[2] Despite their many differences, the men and women on the international bench embody patterns of education and experience that form the basis of a global community.

Where Do They Hail From?

In January 2006, 215 men and women were serving as permanent members of the bench of the thirteen major international courts and tribunals. They hailed from 86 different countries from every inhabited corner of the globe.[3] By region, Europeans were dominant, with nearly two-thirds of the group (137). The United Kingdom had the highest number of nationals on international benches (9), followed by France, Italy, and Germany (7 each). There were 37 citizens of the Americas, including 3 U.S. citizens,[4] 20 Africans, and 5 from the Pacific/Oceania region. Asia, representing more than half of the world's total population, comprised just under 8 percent of the judges on these courts (16).

These considerable variations across the globe derive principally from the inclination or disinclination of states to create and subject themselves to the jurisdiction of international courts. The judicial pillars of the European area alone employ 99 judges,[5] a reflection of the continent's historical leadership and commitment to the development of transnational legal institutions. The Asian nations, by contrast, have not created regional courts to address economic or human rights issues, so their presence on the international bench is limited to courts with global representation. Africa's share would be larger if the survey included the judges of the several dormant or not yet active international courts on that continent.

Education

One of the distinguishing features of the international courts is the challenge of melding the two main legal systems of the world: the civil law system (essentially the legal system of the Roman Empire), and the common law system (developed first in England and spread around the world through the British Empire).[6] Of the 215 judges serving in January 2006, 63 percent (136) were from civil law countries, a figure that reflects the large number from continental Europe. Another 14 percent (30) hailed from common law countries, such as the United Kingdom or the United States. The remaining 49 judges came from countries that either have a mix of the common law/civil law systems (such as Cyprus or South Africa), or have Islamic law and/or local customary law blended to varying degrees with civil law (Tunisia) or common law (Pakistan).

Typically, international judges have studied law in the leading universities of their native countries. While their legal training focused initially on their own countries' domestic law, many also studied international law, which is not common law or civil law or a blend of the two—it is a system of law unto itself. Only a small number of the 215 judges did not have a formal law degree, and most of those had studied international law in an academic program outside of a law school, for instance in a program in international relations or political science.[7]

The large majority of international judges also have graduate or doctoral degrees, most typically in international law, international relations, and/or international economics. In many instances, these advanced degrees have been obtained abroad, from a handful of the world's elite universities. Using data as of January 2006, at least thirty-nine had degrees from universities in the United Kingdom and at least twenty-nine from institutions in the United States,[8] a fact that suggests that many of those from civil law countries gained direct knowledge and experience of the common law outlook at some point in their training. The world's most prestigious schools could boast of several international judges among their alumni: in the United States, Columbia and Harvard had seven each, well ahead of the next, Yale, with three.[9] In the United Kingdom, Cambridge and the University of London topped the charts with fourteen and eleven respectively, ahead of Oxford, with eight.[10] In France, the University of Paris (in its various articulations) had the lion's share, with eleven alumni serving on international courts.[11] Among judges from countries that used to be in the Soviet sphere of influence, many studied at the University of Moscow or other top schools in former Eastern bloc countries. The fact that many judges have degrees from a handful of the world's elite schools means that, at least in large courts, it is not uncommon to find a minimum of two judges who have studied in the same institution. It also means that a significant part of the international judiciary studied largely with the same professors and in many cases even the same textbooks. Still, international judges have an educational background much more heterogeneous than that found among judges of most national high courts. As a comparison, of the nine U.S. Supreme Court justices of the current bench (2006), five studied law at Harvard, two at Yale, and the remaining two at Northwestern and Columbia.

Gender

The viewer of the portrait of international judges would notice one fact almost instantly: the group is overwhelmingly male. Women are absent from or underrepresented in all courts, although it seems that in the past few years the situation has slowly started to improve. Just 21 percent (forty-five) of the judges on the thirteen courts were women in January 2006. Nearly a decade after its formation, no woman had ever served among the twenty-one members of the International Tribunal for the Law of the Sea. There was only one woman on the International Court of Justice; Rosalyn Higgins had been elected in 1995, the first woman to be elected in the court's forty-nine-year history.[12] The first woman to be elected to the WTO Appellate Body was Merit Janow in 2003. Both Higgins and Janow remain the only women in their respective courts.

The European Court of Justice had two women judges among its twenty-five members, but its Court of First Instance, a more "junior" group, had a more balanced group of nine women out of twenty-five judges on its bench. Comparatively, the Andean Court of Justice and the Caribbean Court of Justice have a greater ratio of female representation, with one woman each out of, respectively, benches of four and seven judges.[13]

Women's representation tends to be slightly better in the case of human rights and humanitarian law bodies, but there are significant differences from body to body and region to region. At the Inter-American Court of Human Rights, Cecilia Medina Quiroga, the only female judge in 2006, was only the second woman in its twenty-five-year history ever to serve on the court.[14] The European Court of Human Rights showed more balance, but it did not come close to gender equality (twelve female judges out of forty-five judges altogether). On the ad hoc international criminal tribunals, the number of women judges remained low. At the ICTY there was one woman trial judge, and three at the ICTR (out of nine), while in the Appeals Chamber shared by the two tribunals there were but two (out of seven). The Special Court for Sierra Leone had three women judges (out of ten).

A striking exception in January 2006 was the strong representation of women on the International Criminal Court—seven of eighteen members. At the Rome Conference that gave birth to the ICC in 1998, delegates had noted the scarce presence of women in the ad hoc tribunals and the excellent performance of those few who had served there. Lobbying by nongovernmental organizations and the support of sympathetic states helped bring about the article in the Rome Statute that requires states to take into account the "fair representation of women" when choosing the court's judges. At the time of the first and second elections of the judges, several NGOs made extensive efforts to bring forward the names of women who met the election requirements, particularly from those countries that had little diplomatic leverage to get one of their nationals elected. Once some of these women were nominated, NGOs vigorously lobbied states to elect them, which eventually resulted in an international bench with the highest female participation of all international courts: more than one-third of the bench.[15]

Professional Background

It is difficult to provide reliable aggregate data about the professional background of international judges. As they are invariably people with several decades of work experience, many of them have lengthy curricula and many have had career changes. Few can be labeled as belonging clearly to a particular profession. A rich and diversified career seems to be the one trait common to most international judges.

International judges have principally had three kinds of careers: the national judiciary, academia, or civil service (either in international organizations or in the service of their own governments, in a variety of capacities, including diplomacy). Some have had significant legal practices as private attorneys, rising to the top of their respective law firms. A few might even have had political experience, but it is rare that career politicians become members of the international judiciary.[16] Again, the blend varies from court to court, and it is not uncommon for some judges to have had more than one of those careers.

To provide some approximate figures, *grosso modo:* out of 215 judges one can count about 85 who have significant academic credentials (tenured or associate, but not counting visiting and adjunct positions); 70 who can claim to be professional national judges; and about 60 who mostly had a career as civil servants. This last figure can be broken down further: about 40 served in international organizations and approximately 20 for their own government.[17] Finally, about 10 can be labeled as practicing attorneys.

While none of the three principal careers (judge, academia, civil service) provides a clear majority of judges in any particular court, some seem to provide a generally larger share of international judges than others. In the early days of international dispute settlement, most judges and arbitrators were drawn from the halls of universities. Because of their profession, international law professors were likely to have written a fundamental opus on a relevant topic, and their former students had often become legal advisers and diplomats for countries or organizations. In recent years, however, it seems academics have been losing their edge, if not in absolute numbers then at least in relation to the other recruitment pools, which have widened. As governments grow increasingly concerned about judicial activism and international judges who take control of the making of international law, an extensive record of publication may provide the basis of opposition to an academic's candidacy for the position of international judge.

Especially since the advent of international criminal tribunals, the number of national judges serving on international benches has considerably increased. Courtroom management skills are a valuable asset when handling high-profile criminal trials, so it should be no surprise that the statute of the ICC tends to favor those with competence in criminal law and procedure, as well as the necessary relevant experience as judge, prosecutor, advocate, or in another, similar capacity in criminal proceedings. The statute provides that the bench will have no less than nine judges with this type of experience, on a bench of eighteen. Those with expertise in relevant areas of international law, such as international humanitarian law and the law of human rights, and experience in a professional legal capacity of relevance to the judicial work of the court have only five "reserved" seats.[18] In adopting this balance, negotiators of the ICC statute were probably taking into account the criticism that the first benches of the Yugoslavia and Rwanda tribunals were too "academic" and therefore responsible for the slow pace of their first trials.

Civil service, and in particular work in legal affairs, whether for a national government and/or an international organization, is another principal recruitment pool. Legal advisors of an international organization to which the court is attached occasionally make the transition to the bench: Allan Rosas, currently judge of the ECJ, was previously the principal legal adviser of the European Commission. It is not uncommon to find on the bench of newly created international courts some of the diplomats who have negotiated its creation; a large number of the judges of the ITLOS were at some point involved in the negotiations leading to the adoption of the Law of the Sea Convention. The same is true in the case of some judges of the International Criminal Court, whose president, Philippe Kirsch, a Canadian diplomat by background, was a principal figure in the Rome Conference that created the court. Having reached the apex of service domestically or internationally, a civil servant can end his career in a very dignified way by serving as an international judge. Because of their connections both within their countries and in the international community, many senior diplomats have an inside track in the nomination and election processes.[19]

International Judges Wanted: The Job Market

As in every market, there are two sides in the international judge job market: supply and demand. Demand may not, on the face of it, seem very high. International judges have fixed terms of service ranging from three to nine years, so perhaps one-third of the total number of seats turns over every four years. In some cases, judges are reappointed or reelected; nevertheless, considering the overall size of the "international judiciary," there is a need for an average of approximately ten qualified individuals per year to serve as international judges, and a corresponding need for at least three times that number of qualified candidates. This may appear to be few, in comparison to the number of lawyers in the world.

Supply, however, is surprisingly low. Many observers agree that in the world in general, as well as in some countries in particular, the pool of individuals who are informed about the vacancies, supported by their government, and sufficiently qualified, available, and willing to relocate (in many cases), is limited and can hardly fill all the vacancies. As one veteran international judge puts it, "When creating an international tribunal, you go through the names. There are no more than, I would say, a hundred names you will go through in order to see what to catch."[20] The result is that in recent years the quality of candidates and recruited judges has become an issue in some international courts.

Several factors limit the pool of suitable candidates. To start with, the international judicial profession is still not really one for which one can be trained in advance. "You cannot create a profession because you don't have a career," one judge explained. "I mean in domestic law, you have a branch of government called the judiciary, and you start from a very low level, as an assistant district attorney, or something like that, and you grow up in that system. At the international level you don't have a centralized system of justice, hence you don't have intermediate steps below it. There is no step one; it starts at step twenty."[21]

In addition, exacting qualifications are required. Besides high moral character and a reputation of impartiality and integrity, a good candidate needs to have the "right" nationality, extensive professional experience in specific fields, and command of one or more languages beyond his native tongue. People with these characteristics are rarely unemployed, which means that candidates must be lured away from high-profile and/or highly paid jobs, such as top-level national judicial appointments, careers in government, or private practice. For the great majority, service on the international bench entails relocation abroad, sometimes to court seats thousands of miles from home. Because the system is set up to ensure geographical diversity on the benches of international courts, between one-half and two-thirds of the judges are nationals of developing countries, which have rather small pools of suitable candidates due to more general problems of access to higher education.

The difficulties encountered in finding a sufficient number of suitable nominees for the elections of the new African Court of Human and Peoples' Rights provide a graphic illustration. Following the coming into force of the protocol establishing the court on January 25, 2004, the African Union called on states parties to put forward nominations to fill the eleven seats of the court.[22] At first, too few nominees had been proposed (fifteen), and many did not meet the statutory criteria. The initial date of June 2004 for the election of judges was therefore postponed until January 2006 and the list for nominations reopened. Out of fifty-three member states of the African Union, only twenty-one had ratified the protocol creating the court and thus could put forward nominations and vote. By the time the election was held, two of the candidates on the original list had withdrawn and one had been murdered, apparently at the behest of her husband for reasons unrelated to her job. Other nominations came in, bringing the total number of nominees to twenty-one, from sixteen states. While the protocol entitles states to nominate up to three candidates each, almost none put forward multiple names and many declined to put forward anyone at all.[23]

Selecting Nominees

In general, one cannot apply to become an international judge.[24] Most of the time one is called. It is not only a matter of having the right skills and experience, but most of all a matter of being on the radar screen of, and appreciated by, one's own government, particularly by some key civil servants. Much as in the case of the U.S. Supreme Court, where the president can nominate anyone whom he thinks fit for the job, national governments have total control over who will be put forward for an international judicial position and who will not. It is only in the case of the hybrid criminal courts for Sierra Leone and Cambodia that the UN Secretary General is charged with the task of identifying and putting forward nominations to fill the slots reserved for international judges in those bodies (seven for Sierra Leone and five for Cambodia). Still, even in those cases, governmental connections are crucial, as the Secretary General does not advertise the positions in, say, the *Economist,* but rather solicits and receives suggestions from UN members. The support of one's government (and in the case of the WTO, the European Community) and also the absence of any major objection by the foreign voting governments are essential if one is to become an international judge.[25]

The success or failure of an international court ultimately depends on whether those in national governments who select nominees make a good faith effort to provide the court with the best possible judges and have the court's best interests in mind, or whether they are instead motivated by less altruistic considerations. The choice of nominees at the national level is the most crucial link in the chain, and it is potentially the weakest, since it depends on the competence and integrity of the government. If the process at the national level produces unsuitable nominees, often there is little (and sometimes nothing) that can be done at the international level to correct the situation. For reasons of political delicacy, governments are loath to question one another's nominees.

In general, states that have a high level of accountability for public officials, transparency, and judicial independence tend to strive for transparent and reasonably open selection practices, but these states are in the minority. Where the political structure is corrupt or autocratic, states are unlikely to become suddenly virtuous when it comes to international judicial appointments, and these states *do* nominate and elect international judges. It is undeniable that the principle of judicial independence—and more importantly, the perception of judicial independence—is jeopardized by the fact that procedures are, with very limited exceptions, neither open nor accountable.

Undoubtedly, governments often work hard to exercise control over the selection of their own nominees (and also to influence the selection of nominees of other countries), but this does not mean that it would be either wise or feasible to exclude national governments from this nomination process. The selection of candidates by executives does not necessarily produce bad candidates. Very often, governments are in the best position to make a good pick, since they have direct knowledge of many of those potential candidates who have the necessary skills to become international judges. After all, governments closely monitor at least two of the three pools from which nominees are recruited traditionally—civil service and the national judiciary—and in some countries the leading professors are government employees as well. It is also possible that highly public and transparent processes involving domestic constituencies might lead to unnecessarily high levels of politicization. Anyone familiar with the process of selecting U.S. Supreme Court justices knows that the affair can lead to unsavory mud-slinging. Nevertheless, even if governments continue to drive the nomination process, the adoption of uniform practices and standards for raising the bar could go a long way toward ensuring better benches and increasing the overall legitimacy of the process.

How governments single out nominees is largely a function of domestic customs and practice. In many cases, governments are given little or no guidance other than the general and sometime imprecise guidelines on qualifications of candidates. In most states, nominees are simply sought through informal networks by the head of the executive branch (the prime minister and/or president), the minister of foreign affairs, sometimes in consultation with the minister of justice, or by the legal adviser of the ministry of foreign affairs. Civil servants play a crucial role, as they have the ears of the ultimate decision makers. Personal acquaintance is often the decisive criterion in deciding which nominee is going to be presented. In the absence of a formal application procedure, the process is initiated within the government ministries, and not all governments are even so kind as to ask potential nominees whether they would be interested in the position in advance. Some judges confess that they learned that they had been chosen as national nominees only once the decision had already been made, or that they accepted only after undergoing considerable pressure.

"It was pretty accidental that I got here, because I had not taken a prior decision to become [an international] judge," one member of a criminal court recalls. One of this judge's countrymen had resigned his position on the court before his term of service was complete, and the government very much wanted to retain its hold on the seat. "They nominated me for the position before they had consulted with me!" Eventually he was asked about his wishes, but not before he had received an invitation from the Secretary General to come to New York to discuss the matter.

Another criminal court judge found her entrée through her involvement in the International Association of Women Judges. Meeting people from around the world at the organization's conferences, she found herself encouraged to put herself forward for the International Criminal Court, since the new bench very much needed candidates from her region and female ones. The association supported her nomination by writing a letter directly to her ministry of foreign affairs. "Clearly it worked," she recalls, because the next thing she knew she was reading in her local newspaper that she was her country's nominee.

In the absence of meaningful guidance and standards, procedures inevitably vary from country to country. Some governments advertise vacancies, sometimes in the specialized press, less often in the national press. Usually, there is a deadline to submit the application, and then some or all applicants, depending on numbers, are invited to a meeting with a panel, which might be composed of a mix of governmental officials involved in legal affairs, national judges, and current or former judges of international courts. Depending on the number of nominees, the interview might last for about one hour and it is usually at this stage that linguistic skills of the nominee are verified. Finally, the panel's recommendation is forwarded to the government, which might (usually) or might not (rarely) follow the advice.[26] The increasing difficulty that governments have when identifying suitable nominees to meet a swelling demand, as well as pressure from within the courts to address the decreasing levels of quality nominees, has induced several states to either adopt spontaneously or at least consider more formal procedures for the national selection of nominees. In recent years several countries, such as the United Kingdom, Ireland, Finland, Latvia, the Netherlands, Slovenia, and Belgium, have taken these steps. Unsurprisingly, most of the cases are in Europe, where the problem is more urgent because that region has the highest density of international judicial bodies.

Some pressures for changes in the nomination process at the national level have come from the regional organizations that founded the courts. In 1998, for example, the Parliamentary Assembly of the Council of Europe recommended that governments advertise vacancies in the specialized press, ensure that nominees have experience in the field of human rights and fluency in one of the court's working languages, avoid expressing any particular preference for one of the three nominees they are mandated to present, and select nominees of both sexes.[27] The recommendation was transmitted to the ECHR itself, which expressed an opinion on it.[28] The judges considered valid the Parliamentary Assembly's concerns to ensure that the appointment of judges be as fair as possible "the product of a genuine and informed election from among the candidates who are fully qualified to discharge the complex and sensitive duties involved in the office," and they agreed that "the importance of the composition of the lists of the candidates by governments" should be stressed.[29] The council's Committee of Ministers, however, composed of governmental representatives, made it clear in their reply that they resented any intrusions upon executive prerogative: "The details of the procedures chosen by states in order to nominate candidates for election to the Court," the ministers wrote, "are a matter for sovereign national decision."[30] Further, while the committee agreed that advertising judicial vacancies in the press would be one way of satisfying the criteria of transparency and fairness, it stated that "there are other ways through which it can be achieved."[31]

Requirements

States receive little guidance regarding the criteria for nominees. Typically, the statutes of an international court specify little more than does the founding document of the International Court of Justice, which declares that "the Court shall be composed of a body of independent judges, elected regardless of their nationality from among persons of high moral character, who possess the qualifications required in their respective countries for appointment to the highest judicial offices, or are jurisconsults of recognized competence in international law."[32] It is clear that, in addition to "high moral character," two factors are essential: professional competence and the "right" nationality.

Although high moral character is undoubtedly the first and minimum requirement for any judicial office, it is not entirely clear how governments make such an assessment, or how they could. Indeed, statutes of international courts do not specify what "high moral character" is, and of all requirements it is probably the one that is the most difficult to objectify. To Manley Hudson, the American judge of the PCIJ between 1936 and 1942, the criterion embraces "more than ordinary fidelity and honesty, more than patent impartiality. It includes a measure of freedom from prepossessions, a willingness to face consequences of views which may not be shared, a devotion to judicial processes, a willingness to make the sacrifices which the performance of judicial duties may involve."[33]

A judge of the ICJ probably wrote the best line on the subject. With a perfect blend of candor, cynicism, and wit, T. O. Elias of Nigeria once noted that the requirement of moral integrity is "probably the equivalent of an unimpeachable conduct as a public figure; in other words, the candidate need not be an angel, though he must not be only a little better than a rascal."[34]

The vagueness of language about the character requirement could lead to abuse in a counterintuitive way. In at least one instance, a government explained the omission of the name of a sitting judge from those to be elected and reelected by asserting that he no longer lived up to the standards of "high moral character."[35] The allegations made against the judge were widely considered baseless and an ill-disguised excuse by that government to get rid of a judge who had proven to be too independent for its taste, but the state in question naturally maintained that it was merely upholding its obligations under the court's statute by excluding him from the list.[36]

The second standard requirement for nominees is competence. This is more easily assessed, and statutes often provide guidance by specifying the need for certain kinds of backgrounds or expertise in a particular area of international law.[37] We have already discussed the background of international judges. What can be added now is that some states traditionally prefer nominees with certain careers over others. Since time immemorial, the tradition in France has been to propose the legal adviser of the Ministry of Foreign Affairs for the seat on the World Court. In Portugal and Italy, academics occupy the highest position in the ladder of prestige in the legal profession, and therefore international judges are usually drafted from this pool.

One might expect to find judges with a military background in international criminal tribunals, which decide on war crimes. After all, for centuries soldiers have been judged by soldiers, not civilians. Yet only a few judges sitting on the international criminal courts in 2006 had a professional background in the military.[38] Even if one enlarged the scope to include all international judges since the resurgence of international criminal law in the aftermath of the end of the Cold War, those with a military background would remain a rare sighting. The "civilianization" of international criminal law started gradually. The judges of the Nuremberg trials were about half military and half civilians, while in the Tokyo trials civilians were the majority. Several countries in the world have started adopting the practice of having the military appear before ordinary civilian courts.[39] Granted, having a military background is no formal bar to being an international judge. However, considering the glaring absence of judges with such background on international benches despite the fact that many states around the world have well-developed military judicial branches that could offer plenty of competent nominees, it seems either that having professional military experience on one's curriculum vitae is a minus, or that this professional group fails to get sufficient political support to be nominated for such positions.

There is a third requirement that is probably even more crucial than character and competence to become an international judge: the right nationality. Prima facie, the nationality of an international judicial nominee is irrelevant. After all, judges are supposed to be independent and have no allegiance toward their own governments, so nationality should not really matter. Yet nationality *does* matter, as is borne out by the nomination and election/appointment process for international judges.

States are usually free to propose nominees who are not their nationals, and quite a few states have done so. The Costa Rican Elizabeth Odio Benito was proposed by Panama for the ICC, as she had lost the support of her own government. In some cases, governments may simply not have enough suitable internal candidates and will therefore look for candidates in friendly countries. Liechtenstein has such a tradition. For example, Lucius Caflisch and Carl Baudenbacher are both Swiss nationals nominated by Liechtenstein to the ECHR and EFTA Court, respectively. On the ECHR bench, Caflisch replaced Ronald St. John Macdonald, who was a Canadian and the first and only non-European to serve on the European Court of Human Rights (1980–1998). Another notable exception is David Hayton, a judge of the Caribbean Court of Justice who does not come from the Caribbean region—he is a highly respected former British law professor who taught at the University of London.

These exceptions aside, sometimes statutes are more specific. In the case of the Inter-American Court of Human Rights or the International Criminal Court, for example, the establishing statute requires that the nominee be a citizen of a member of the Organization of American States or a state party to the Rome Statute, respectively, meaning that a Swiss cannot be a judge at the IACHR and that a Russian or an American cannot be a judge at the ICC. But, nothing would prevent Colombia, which is both an OAS member and a party to the Rome Statute, from nominating an American to the IACHR and a Jordanian to the ICC.[40] Still, it is rare that statutes impose restrictions on states about the nationality of their nominees for judicial positions.

Also, the relative flexibility of the question of nationality reflects practice in many parts of the world. For example, in Africa it is not uncommon for judges qualified to sit on the highest courts to serve in multiple countries during their career. Emmanuel Ayoola, a Nigerian national who now serves on the Special Court for Sierra Leone, had previously served as a justice of the Supreme Court of Nigeria, chief justice of the Supreme Court of The Gambia, and president of the Republic of Seychelles Court of Appeal. Even in the United States, there is no constitutional requirement that federal judges, including Supreme Court justices, be citizens of the United States (in contrast to qualifications for the president and members of Congress), although there appears to be no instance of a noncitizen's being appointed as a judge to a U.S. federal court.

Overwhelming evidence suggests that the nationality of judges *does* matter.[41] First, governments go a long way toward controlling the composition of international courts, as will be explained below when discussing elections and appointments, and they hold on very tightly to their seats. In some courts, very carefully crafted formulas and "gentlemen's agreements" determine the distribution of seats by nationality to various regions of the globe. In others, the bench includes one national for each country that is a party to the court. Major powers are de facto permanent members on the bench of certain international courts. Whenever a standing judge from a major power resigns or passes away, the customary practice is to replace him with another national of that same state. One international judge explains, "When filling a vacancy for an unexpired term, the country will retain the seat, unless they put up somebody that is totally unacceptable for some other reason. We always joke that unless the person had two heads or something like that, it is going to go through." Moreover, statutes invariably provide that there cannot be more than one judge with the same nationality at any given time on the bench, and governments prefer to nominate their own nationals.

A final requirement for nomination to an international judicial position is fluency in at least one of the working languages of the court in question. Except in some regional courts in Latin America, the working language of most courts is either English or French and often both. Language is thus a factor that contributes to the limited pool of suitable candidates for international judgeships, more so in some countries than others. For native speakers of English and French, after all, it is a matter of being fluent in just one other language. For all other nominees, particularly those whose native tongues are not Indo-European languages, the hurdle to functioning as a judge in a foreign language might be substantial.

As with the other requirements, the determination of whether a candidate is sufficiently fluent in a court's working languages is essentially left to the national government. There is no formal examination, nor are certificates or diplomas required, and it is uncommon for candidates to be put into a situation where they need to display linguistic competence at a realistic work level. Nevertheless, international judges generally seem to be fairly proficient in at least in one of the languages of the courts where they work, although, according to many judges, levels of proficiency vary significantly, sometimes reaching problematic lows.[42]

Besides these formal requirements—high moral character, competence, nationality, and linguistic ability—many other factors are taken into consideration by governments when choosing their nominees. For instance, previous experience as an international judge is not a formal requirement but is probably a plus.[43] Figures are still too small to detect any meaningful professional flow-patterns between courts. When the boundary of the European Community expanded eastward in May 2004, several Eastern European countries gained the right to propose judges for the European Court of Justice. These countries had had representation for more than a decade at the European Court of Human Rights, by virtue of their membership in the Council of Europe, so it was natural that in choosing judges for the ECJ they should look to candidates who had already distinguished themselves on the bench of the ECHR. The ad hoc criminal tribunals have provided a pool of nominees for other subsequent courts, like the ICC, obviously, but also, in one instance, the WTO Appellate Body.[44] If any pattern is to be predicted, it is likely that, in the future, former ICC judges might be nominated to serve in hybrid or ad hoc criminal courts, and that the exchange between the ECHR and ECJ will continue.

As of 2006, however, only twenty sitting international judges had served on other international courts.[45] Some judges believe that it would be desirable to have a larger number of international judges with experience in multiple international courts.[46] This might not only help to foster a sense of community between the judges across the spectrum of courts, which is desirable in terms of the unity of international law, but it also might have more immediately tangible effects by diffusing best judicial practices across the system. The president of the ICJ, Rosalyn Higgins, finds it helpful to have a former president of another international court on the bench. "I think it's really useful for us to have on our court the former president of another court [Thomas Buergenthal, former president of the IACHR]. There's a real-life experience there that I think is valuable for us."

There are potential drawbacks to judicial migration across international courts. Ethics issues may arise as judges bring inside information from one institution to another. There are also advantages to bringing new voices and ideas into the international justice system, rather than relying on the recirculation of talent. Movement across courts might also threaten the cherished autonomy of individual courts. Yet the advantages in terms of coherence of rulings between the various bodies, the prospect of increasing efficiency, and the benefits of shared experience might outweigh these considerations.

"Vetting" Candidates

Some courts provide for a procedure to assess the qualifications of nominees and potential nominees for seats on the international bench. This "vetting" is sometimes part of the nomination process, when certain selection procedures aimed at structuring decision making at the national level and ensuring transparency and accountability are recommended or mandated. In other cases the vetting takes place after the nomination stage, which allows for consideration of the candidates by a regional or international body. The quality and depth of these vetting procedures vary considerably. In general, these procedures involve soliciting the advice of high-ranking lawyers from the country submitting the nomination. The International Court of Justice and the European Court of Human Rights have the most elaborate mechanisms. While these processes can be quite complex and may serve to discourage governments from putting forward nominees of inferior quality, the vetting procedures themselves generally are not determining factors in appointments to the bench.

In two other cases, an intermediary vetting step is in place, not so much to ensure transparency and fairness, but rather to give greater control of the electoral process to certain key states. Under the statutes of the ad hoc tribunals for Yugoslavia and Rwanda, the Security Council selects between twenty-eight and forty-two nominees from among all put forward by states, taking into account the adequate representation of the principal legal systems of the world.[47] While it has been rare in practice that at any given election, except the first, there have been more than forty-two national candidatures, the Security Council has the right to filter out unsuitable candidates or candidates put forward by countries whose judges might have an inherent conflict of interest, like those involved in the Yugoslavian conflict with respect to the ICTY. In practice, this gives the permanent members of the Security Council an enhanced role when it comes to vetting candidates for the ad hoc tribunals.

The other procedure is more intrusive and more regularly used. At the WTO, candidates for the Appellate Body are vetted by a selection committee composed of the director general and the chairs of the General Council, Dispute Settlement Body, Council for Trade in Goods, Council for Trade in Services, and the Trade-Related Aspects of Intellectual Property Rights (TRIPS) Council. The European Community and the United States have enjoyed de facto special privileges at this stage, having the ability to object to candidates. The U.S. trade representative office carefully vets each candidate, reading his or her past work and/or judicial decisions, and interviews each in Washington, D.C., or Geneva prior to deciding whether to endorse the candidacy. This unilateral de facto veto power is believed to be used routinely.[48]

Election or Appointment

Once nominees have been selected (with or without prior vetting), the next phase is election or appointment. Elections are held in the case of those courts, such as the International Court of Justice, where there are many more member states than seats on the bench.[49] In other cases, like the Andean Court of Justice or the EFTA Court, the number of judges is equal to the number of states and therefore there is no need for elections.[50] This is notably the case in the major European courts; each state party to both the European Court of Justice and the European Court of Human Rights is guaranteed by statute to have a judge on the bench. National choices are ratified by states collectively, and judges are appointed.

Inevitably, elections raise a number of issues. First, there is the problem of how to ensure that the composition of the court reflects the composition of the larger organization. In the case of international courts, statutes usually require that, when voting, the electors bear in mind not only the qualifications of the nominees (or, more rarely, their gender), but also that the body as a whole broadly represents the membership of the organization.[51] The statute of certain courts is more precise, requiring a particular blend reflecting equitable geographical distribution and representation of the principal legal systems of the world, but there is little evidence that the latter is really an issue. There is a notable exception, though. In the case of the Caribbean Court of Justice, achieving wide geographic representation seemingly is not a goal. Currently, Guyana and Trinidad and Tobago have two nationals on the bench each, whereas other member states are not represented at all.

Operatively, formulas and more or less tacit understandings reflecting underlying political, economic, and social equilibria determine the ultimate composition of a court. In the case of the International Court of Justice, a series of informal, but strictly observed, understandings determines the eventual "national" composition of the court. The distribution among the principal regional groupings at the UN closely shadows that of the Security Council (which is made of fifteen members, like the ICJ). In UN history, the five permanent members of the Security Council have always had their nominee elected.[52] The other ten seats have been held in rotation, with certain influential states, like India, Japan, Germany, Italy, and Egypt, having judges on the bench more often than others.

The same criteria and groupings are used in the distribution of judges at the International Criminal Court and the International Tribunal of the Law of the Sea, taking into account the fact that not all UN members have ratified the treaties instituting these bodies. At the ICC, the 2002 "Resolution on the Procedure for the Election of Judges to the ICC," which is binding, requires states to vote for at least three nominees from each regional grouping (Africa, Asia, Eastern Europe, Latin America, and "Western Europe and Others"). The result is that the eighteen seats of the ICC are currently distributed in about the same proportions as those of the ICJ: seven to the West, three to Latin America and the Caribbean, three to Africa, and Eastern Europe and Asia receive two each. The ICC is still too recent a creation to be able to discern any significant trends or claim that certain states are de facto permanent members of the bench.

At the Law of the Sea Tribunal, developing countries and small states seem to enjoy a relatively better position, and geopolitics seems to weigh less decisively. At the same time, the ITLOS exhibits several anomalies. Greece, a major power in maritime transport, has never had a judge elected, while Tanzania, hardly a power in maritime affairs, has had two judges consecutively elected since 1996. Strangest of all, the United Kingdom, once the world's preeminent maritime power, lost its seat in 2005 to a candidate from the landlocked nation of Austria.

In the WTO Appellate Body, as we have seen, the United States and the European Community seem, by virtue of a tacit understanding between the member states, not only to have permanent seats but also to enjoy a veto over the assignment of other seats. So far Japan has consistently had a national among the members, while the other seats have been distributed, one each, to Latin America, Asia, Africa, and the "Old Commonwealth."

In theory, the ad hoc tribunals for Yugoslavia and Rwanda also aspire to representativeness as subsidiary organs of the United Nations. But here political pragmatism outweighs "the blend" more conspicuously than in other courts. As already described, the Security Council plays a key role in filtering out judicial nominees from countries that might be too close to or involved in the incidents being investigated and tried. The very existence of this filter already deters certain countries from putting forward nominees. Thus, Russia, a permanent member of the Security Council but also a political ally of Serbia because of common ties to the Orthodox Church, has never had a judge on the ICTY bench. Albania, Romania, Bulgaria, and Greece, southern neighbors of the former Yugoslavia, have also never had a judge at the ICTY. Of the Eastern European countries, only Ukraine and Hungary (twice) have been represented, in those cases not by permanent judges but by ad litem members (serving only for a given case) of the bench. Likewise, Burundi, Rwanda's neighbor, a country rocked by the same ethnic tensions between Tutsis and Hutus but which did not experience a genocide, has never had a judge at the ICTR. All considered, and as compared to other courts, Western countries are probably overrepresented at the ICTY and ICTR, both numerically and in terms of key positions such as the presidency and prosecutor's office, but this reflects the commitment—military, financial and diplomatic—of those nations to the pacification and reconstruction of the regions in those courts' jurisdictions.

This tacit system of quotas and reserved seats heightens the importance of selecting good nominees nationally. The major powers enjoy de facto permanent representation on the benches of international courts, so if they put forward inferior candidates, the quality of the benches will suffer. In addition, competition for some seats does not take place globally, but only within the various groupings. Hence, if a region has, say, three seats assigned and only three states from that region have nominees, those nominees are virtually automatically elected as well.

At the United Nations, where several elections for different positions are held every year, diplomats tend to treat seats on various bodies as fungible. The goal is to ensure some degree of participation in important UN posts, and states are often indifferent as to which seats they win. Some positions are more coveted than others (like taking a turn on the Security Council); most, including seats on the international bench of the ICJ, ICTY, ICTR, or ITLOS, are frequently regarded as bargaining chips in the diplomatic process. Although UN elections are by secret ballot, governments have ample opportunities to collude and trade votes. A state might agree to vote for another state's candidate in exchange for that state's vote in an election for another organ it covets more. Considering the plethora of bodies that exist within the United Nations, the possibilities for this kind of "horse trading" are almost endless. One end result is that some courts suffer from shortages of good candidates more than others, as, inevitably, there is an implicit order of preference whereby certain high-prestige courts are the first choice of good candidates.

Then there are issues in relation to the way elections take place. The electors are, again, governments, acting through their ambassadors in the cities where elections are held—New York,[53] Geneva,[54] and Washington, D.C.[55] Nominees are often required to travel to the cities where elections are held to meet informally with the electors at parties and events organized by their national ambassadors.

In some cases, states are given the opportunity to present more than one nominee.[56] The rationale is that if states do so, the practice enlarges the pool of nominees from which judges are chosen, thus increasing chances that unsuitable picks can be filtered out and ensuring greater diversity on the resulting bench. However, this also makes elections less predictable and encourages governments to scheme to steer elections. For instance, it is very rare that governments pit two of their own nationals against each other, since in most courts there cannot be two judges of the same nationality.[57] When they do, it might spell failure for both nominees, regardless of their qualifications. Typically, states put forward one national nominee, on whom their electioneering efforts are concentrated, and add nationals of other countries to the pool. The governments of these "foreign" nominees will return the favor, thus mutually reinforcing national candidatures, but also restricting the list of nominees on which voting needs to take place. In other words, country A nominates *a,* its own national, along with *b* and *c,* nationals of countries B and C. Country B nominates *b,* its own national, but also *a,* and *c;* and so on. Hence, a successful candidate will often be nominated not only by his own country, but by a number of other countries as well. Sometimes, governments cooperate on "joint candidates," as in the case of the Croatian Budislav Vukas, who was backed by Austria as well as his native country in the ITLOS elections.

It is not uncommon for governments to try to steer an election by putting forward a strong candidate alongside one or two deliberately weaker choices. This happens even in the case of the European Court of Human Rights, where in principle there should be no electioneering, since each country has a guaranteed seat on the bench; it is not uncommon for a government to campaign to convince the Council of Europe to select the government's own favorite nominee, to the detriment of the other two candidates whose names it is required to submit.

Those states with sufficiently large missions in the cities where elections take place (particularly New York) usually dedicate one or more diplomats solely to keeping track of elections and promoting national nominees. Some missions have deployed highly professional marketing efforts to promote their nominees, including producing glossy color brochures that describe the virtues of their nominee and make the case for his being given a seat at the court.[58] The only campaign paraphernalia not yet spotted in New York for judicial elections are buttons and stickers![59]

Regardless of how casual or structured the scrutiny of nominees, those who vote rarely have adequate independent information to assess the nominees. The ECHR takes the unique step of putting the résumés of nominees into a standard format to facilitate comparison between them.[60] The standardized curricula vitae and the recommendation of the subcommittee are all the information members of the Parliamentary Assembly have before them when voting. The International Criminal Court has no formal mechanism to scrutinize nominees, no standardized curricula vitae, no interviews with committees. However, during the first two rounds of elections that have taken place to date, nongovernmental organizations played a vigorous role in trying to call states' attention to particularly unqualified nominees and to promote candidates with strong human rights and humanitarian law records, particularly women.

The lack of verification and validation of the curricular histories of nominees to international judicial positions is perplexing. Anyone who has hired someone knows that a curriculum vitae needs to be read with care and a healthy degree of skepticism. Very rarely are nominees for the international bench such public figures that information about their past activities can be easily found in the public domain. Even claims of linguistic competence, a part of the curriculum vitae that should be the easiest to verify, are rarely checked, and if an attempt is made it is often extremely delicate. One international judge recalls a meeting at the UN Secretary

General's office where the question *"Est-ce-que vous parlez français?"* was answered by the Anglophone nominee with a hesitant *"Oui,"* at which point the conversation reverted immediately to English.

Curricula vitae and information about nominees are very rarely made available to the general public through the Internet before elections take place. If information *is* available, it is because of the initiative taken by nongovernmental organizations working in the domain of international justice and not by the courts themselves. Even in the case of sitting judges, information provided is sometimes scant or incomplete, if not completely lacking (as was the case at the European Court of Human Rights until 2005). However, there is no legitimate reason why such information should not be available.

The Quest for Representativeness

No society has found the definitive solution to the dilemma of ensuring that a court is made of the best and most competent judges and, at the same time, fully represents the society, in all its complexity, in whose name it has to administer justice. Even in advanced democracies, with centuries of judicial tradition, the discussion of how judges should be chosen is far from settled.

How well or badly does the system of selection and election of international judges work? It is the general feeling that most international courts, as well as most of their judges, are up to the task with which they are charged. Some courts are better than others, but none can be singled out for having a particularly weak and inexpert bench.

This is probably because the level of qualifications required is notably high. It is unlikely that incompetence gets rewarded at the highest levels of a national judiciary, civil service, or academia, which are the areas from which most candidates are drawn. Moreover, despite the shortcomings of the nomination process, most governments make a good faith effort to put forward the best nominees, since international judges, though independent and serving in their own capacity, still somehow represent their national country in a highly visible context. Pushing unfit individuals onto an international bench might have serious costs to the reputation of a country, as it might signal lack of commitment toward the institution or be interpreted as an outright attempt at sabotage.

Yet the fundamental reason why international courts remain viable despite the flaws in the way judges are chosen is that, unlike with regard to domestic courts, the qualities of the individual judge matter less. Because international judges operate most of the time in teams, sometimes significantly large ones, and all decisions are taken collectively by majority, the

ensemble of a bench can offset a few judges who might be below par. Domestically, at most levels of jurisdiction, most cases are brought before a
single judge. When cases are heard en banc, it is usually before a limited
number of judges. Granted there are cases of major international courts
where important decisions are taken by small groups, like the WTO Appellate Body, where three members decide appeals, but they still consult
with the other four members before deliberating. Yet, at the end of the
day, what really matters in international courts is the quality of the bench
as a whole: the careful mixing of skills, competences, and, inevitably,
weaknesses, rather than the individual elements. What matters is the
group rather than a particular judge. As in every recipe, it is all about the
quality of the ingredients and their skillful blending. Certain blends are
better than others, but overall it is difficult to single out a court where
things have gone awfully awry.

This is no reason, of course, to be less rigorous in the process of selection and election of international judges. As with everything else in the
administration of justice, the result is not the only important thing—the
legitimacy of the process itself is essential. As long as the mechanics and
the actors at play remain shrouded in mystery, the public will not develop
a sense of confidence in and connection to international courts. Philippe
Sands, professor of international law at the University College London
and an active lawyer before many international courts, points out that
this sense of confidence is closely aligned with what public expectations
are for the courts. "If we are happy to have international courts fulfill political functions that tie them closely to international organizations,"
Sands writes, "then perhaps we should not get too exercised about how
judges are appointed. If, however, we see international courts and tribunals as exercising judicial functions analogous to those we expect of our
national courts, then it is right to focus our attention on who the judges
are and how they attain their offices."[61]

In the end, there seems to be a consensus that the very essence of the
process in which international judges are selected cannot be altered, at
least while sovereign states remain the building blocks of the international community.

First, the nationality of judges will keep on mattering. The world is
still several generations away from the day where the passport is irrelevant, even in those areas of the globe that have made greater strides toward integration, like Europe. Assigning seats on benches based upon
nationality is an attempt to ensure representativeness, but it is also
often a way to grant the powerful a permanent handle on their privileged positions. No one would suggest that the bench of the U.S. Supreme Court should represent all fifty states, or that California should
always have a judge on it, or that affirmative action criteria should be

employed to determine its membership. Clearly, representativeness of international bodies is desirable, but if pushed too hard, it might create a trade-off with competence, since in practice only a few countries have sufficiently large pools of suitable candidates to cover all the various international judicial appointments.

The first step to offset the problems created by a high demand and low supply of potential international judges may be to look better and harder for candidates. Greater publicity of international judicial vacancies, coupled with open and transparent national selection mechanisms, would go a long way toward ensuring that national human resources are tapped to their full and best potential. Leaving it to governments to adopt these procedures seems to be desirable, as it would allow greater respect for national traditions. At the same time, however, the adoption of minimum standards at the international level would help raise the bar for all. The courts appear to be moving in this direction—human rights and criminal courts more so than others, for no obvious reason.

Second, selection and election of international judges are and should remain tasks of governments since all other alternatives (e.g., entrusting these efforts to an international agency or direct election) are either not viable or, prima facie, not likely to produce better results. "The main responsibility is for the states to come up with good candidates," argues one court president. "And I do not want to criticize the judges who have been elected, neither previously nor now. I consider them all very qualified and I feel that we have an excellent team. Even if elections are a strange process, they can end up with a good result. And what is the alternative? There *is* no alternative."

Navanethem Pillay,
South Africa

*Judge of the International
Criminal Court*

The Beginning

When she was only six years old, Navanethem Pillay was called to testify in a trial in a South African court concerning the robbery of her father. This was her first courtroom experience and it proved to be influential in the path her life subsequently took. She has spent a good part of her adult life in courtrooms, although the roles she has played there are perhaps different from anything she could have imagined as a child growing up in apartheid South Africa.[1]

Pillay served as a judge on the International Criminal Tribunal for Rwanda from 1995 to 2003. For more than four of those years, she acted as the tribunal's president. Based upon this international judicial experience, she was nominated to serve as a judge on the historic first bench of the International Criminal Court.

The story of Pillay's path to the international judiciary is a remarkable one. She was born in Durban and grew up in a household where there was not even a newspaper to read. Her father was a bus driver, and her mother, like many Indian women, had never been to school, as her parents did not see the need for a daughter's education. Pillay observed of her situation as a young South African of color:

> *You were aware that you got secondhand books handed down from the white school. You were aware that you couldn't enter a park or a beach reserved for whites only. We grew up thinking there*

must be rights out there, and we've got to learn from the rest of the world. We were inspired by student movements outside South Africa. The Harvard student protest against apartheid caught our attention. As we went to high school, police would come and question us, search us, students with pamphlets protesting some terrible law or something else. At the university the police fired on students, and also at the university we were forcibly put into segregated camps. Everything was a struggle.

These experiences led Pillay to the study of law. She reminisced about how she came to read the Nuremberg court cases during her first year at Natal University, when she was twenty years of age:

Law courses were scheduled to suit the white students who were working in law firms. I would go early in the morning, since the first lecture was seven to eight in the morning and the next was seven to eight at night. I had the whole day, and I didn't have bus fare to go home and come back. I just sat in the library and read these Nuremberg cases.

Upon finishing her Bachelor of Law degree, Pillay had to decide how to pursue the legal profession despite multiple constraints.

I started off as a lawyer, and I always say I was trebly disadvantaged. I was black, I was a woman, and I was of a poor class. When I applied for positions at law firms, I was told: "We can't have our white secretaries take dictations from a black person. What if you fall pregnant? Is your father a lawyer or a business man?" And that's why I started a law practice on my own. I became the first woman to open her own law practice in Natal. Some male colleagues said that I was being presumptuous.[2]

Pillay found that as a beginning lawyer, she had to take any kind of work she could find, including defending her colleagues who were banned, put under house arrest, or charged under the Suppression of Communism Act. This was work she had no experience in, but she gained it quickly on the job. She also learned a great deal about South African courts in the apartheid era:

You learned that the courts often served as a tool of the apartheid system to keep "order and security." As I defended cases of racial discrimination, I realized that I had to learn international humanitarian law so we could raise international legal norms as standards for justice in the courtroom. In cases under the Terrorism Act, the state would detain hundreds, torture them, and bring them to court as witnesses. We had no access to those witnesses. We needed to know the rights of defendants and victims under conventions such as the International Convention on Civil and Political Rights, the Geneva Convention, and the Torture Convention. We tried to raise these arguments in the courts, and the courts would say, "We have our own laws, we are not interested in international law or the decisions of foreign courts." That's what motivated me to learn about international law and human rights.

Pillay found a notice in the newspaper about scholarships to Harvard Law School, applied to the Master of Laws Program, and was accepted. This experience was to be transformative for her. Not only did she study international law, but she also met many students who were supportive of the anti-apartheid struggle in her country. Two years after returning to South Africa, she headed once again for Harvard, where she received her doctorate in law. Pillay reports that her South African colleagues were baffled by all this study. Would it allow her to come back and charge higher fees? they asked. She wondered herself sometimes about the point of all this hard work. But, Pillay notes, the usefulness of her studies was to be proven later on. "I didn't realize that one day all this would come in handy, but it did. It qualified me to be an international judge."

First, however, Pillay served as judge in her home country in the post-apartheid era, when nonwhites were finally allowed to occupy such positions. In 1995, she became the first woman of color to be appointed acting judge of the Supreme Court of South Africa.

I had never entered a judges' room before; there had been no black judges when Mandela made me an acting judge. He called me himself to say the appointment gave him great personal joy. When news of the appointment was reported in the press, some white members of the Bar Counsel called a meeting and took a decision to monitor whether I was competent to serve as a judge. The president of the Bar Counsel came into my courtroom to observe me. The white judges whom I had just joined could have treated me similarly. Instead they supported me, if only for the reason that they objected to the notion that judges could be monitored.

Being a black judge in the new South Africa held some unique challenges. Pillay was very familiar with criminal cases since that was what she had been handling as a lawyer for years. But civil cases were largely outside her experience, especially commercial and corporate work, which had all gone to white lawyers in the past. She reports that none of the black law students in her class, for instance, had ever personally handled a check, yet some of their cases revolved around the misuse of negotiable instruments. Pillay tackled these cases involving property and commercial disputes but admits to having been happier when judicial resources were focused more on the protection of human rights.

It was during her time as a judge in South Africa that Pillay was approached by human rights organizations outside the country about the International Criminal Tribunal for Rwanda that was being set up in Arusha, Tanzania, in the aftermath of the genocide. Pillay confesses to having known little at the time about recent events in Rwanda. "We were in the euphoria of our own elections when it all happened. So we missed it! I had no real sense of the atrocities committed."

Pillay was encouraged to stand for election to the first bench of the Rwandan tribunal, being told that the bench needed a woman and an African. But Pillay was reluctant to leave South Africa, which had just entered an exciting era.

> I left home very grudgingly but was persuaded by supporters, who said, "Look, if you don't like it, you can resign after a year." But in the end, I spent eight and a half years at the International Criminal Tribunal for Rwanda in Arusha. Any personal discomfort I might have felt paled in comparison to the suffering of Rwandans and their need for justice.

From South Africa to Tanzania

Navi Pillay arrived at the International Criminal Tribunal for Rwanda in 1995. The early days of the tribunal were frustrating, Pillay reports:

> I felt like we were set up for failure. There were no courtrooms, offices, or library for the first two years. It was a logistical nightmare to be based in a remote town, declared a hardship area by the UN. But there was the determination to make it work. And for me it was much more. We believed that an international court could be hosted in Africa.

The mix of judges that Pillay found on the ICTR bench made for interesting professional challenges. There were six judges on the bench from as many countries, later increased to eighteen. They represented a wide gamut of cultures, languages, training, and past professional experience. And this past experience did not, in many cases, include that of judge in criminal jurisdictions. Pillay's own experience was primarily that of a defense counsel, one who was an advocate for the underdog and an activist. She describes her first reactions to being an international judge:

> First I thought, "How is this going to work?" Each of us was trained in our own law and our own procedure. And we were each

*somewhat territorial and defensive about our own systems. But we
had to put in place an international system of justice not tied to any
one national system. We learned to respect each other's suggestions
about procedures and rules for the court. Sometimes we would debate and debate the alternative procedures, from civil and common
law systems, and then realize, in the end, that the procedures might
be different but the principle was the same.*

*I felt inadequate when I started as I thought the other judges
would all be more experienced, as international judges or international lawyers. It's when I sat in courtroom that I realized that my
criminal law background actually gave me an advantage. The
ICTR statute provides for an adversarial system of criminal trials.
And I was in a criminal courtroom, which is what I had been doing
day in and day out as defense counsel. I soon got over the feeling of
inadequacy when I realized that, actually, most of my colleagues
had even less international court experience than I had. It was,
after all, new to all of us.*

*As judges, we were careful to exercise independence and impar-
tiality at all times. However, it was not easy to remain neutral or
impassive to the evidence of killings, torture, and sexual violence
perpetrated upon hundreds of thousands of people. The personal
accounts of suffering that I listened to for the eight years I was at
the ICTR still remain with me. Witnesses told us that they had
waited for the day when they could see justice done in court.*

After four years, Pillay was elected to replace the first ICTR president,
the Senegalese judge Laity Kama. She took over the presidency at a time
when the tribunal was coming under frequent criticism, both from the
United Nations and the greater public, for the slowness of trials, the cost of
maintaining of the court, and the small number of defendants. At the same
time, there were serious tensions between the ICTR chambers and registry,
two sections of the tribunal that function autonomously and not always in
tandem. One of Pillay's achievements as president, according to her, was to
secure proper administrative support for the judicial function, by appealing
to the UN Secretary General to effect changes in the registry. At one point,
she made a request for such changes before the General Assembly itself.
This took a lot of courage—or perhaps naiveté, says Pillay—but in the end
she was successful. Despite the tensions within the court that such actions
created, Pillay was reelected as ICTR president by her peers.[3]

Pillay sat on some very influential cases while serving as a trial judge
with the ICTR, some of which have contributed powerfully to recent developments in international criminal and human rights law. In *Prosecutor
v. Jean-Paul Akayesu,*[4] she and her colleagues rendered a judgment

against the mayor of the Taba commune in Rwanda, finding him guilty of genocide through the use of rape. This case is groundbreaking in that the ICTR recognized that rape and sexual violence can constitute genocide when they are committed with the intention of destroying in whole or in part a particular group. Pillay also presided over the so-called Media Case,[5] a high-profile trial that sentenced two Rwandan journalists to life and a third for thirty-five years on charges of inciting Hutu soldiers, militia, and civilians to murder hundreds of thousands of Tutsi and moderate Hutu. For the first time since the Nuremberg trials, an international court convicted journalists of inciting genocide. This landmark judgment of the international court carefully differentiates between illicit hate speech and legitimate political discourse.[6]

Women judges are often thought by the public to have a particular interest in gender crimes and their prosecution. Certainly, the extent and nature of gender crimes in the Balkans and in Rwanda, as well as the participation of women on both the prosecutorial and judicial staff of the ICTY and ICTR, served to advance the consideration of gender crimes and the development of jurisprudence to address them. Pillay found herself in a delicate position vis-à-vis gender crimes in Rwanda when she became the tribunal president. On the one hand, she did not feel that it was her position to push for the prosecution of gender crimes since such crimes were not part of the charges outlined in the indictments. On the other hand, she was called upon to answer questions by both the General Assembly and civil society about the blatant lack of charges of genocide in ICTR indictments.

> *Normally, we would say that judges—especially criminal judges— are supposed to sit back and not give any directions on how the prosecution should go. You do not go beyond that indictment, you just focus on the specific allegations against the individual. Two women judges in the ICTY, Elizabeth Odio Benito and Gabrielle MacDonald, asked the prosecutor whether rape counts had been investigated when they were hearing applications for the confirmation of indictments. I had read the expert group's report on which the Security Council based the decision to set up the ICTR. And that expert group documented sexual violence. We had taken judicial notice of that document. With this in mind, I and other judges directed questions to witnesses on rape and sexual violence that they had witnessed.*
>
> *I was delivering the human rights address at the United Nations on December 10, 1998, when questions were directed to me about why there were no rape charges. National judges are sheltered from public scrutiny to some extent by the sub judice rule.[7] But*

international judges are far more exposed to the glare of interna-
tional scrutiny and made accountable. The eyes of the interna-
tional public are on you. I discovered the public was watching and
questioning us. The question put to me by a representative from an
NGO was, "Why, out of twenty-one indictments issued to date, is
there no charge of rape?" The question deserved a serious re-
sponse, which only the prosecutor could make, not a judge.

The questions alerted me, during the course of court testimony
from a doctor from Médecins san Frontières when we were hearing
evidence, to ask whether he had seen any evidence of sexual vio-
lence or rape on the bodies of victims who were injured or killed.
Later, that intervention was one of the grounds for appeal—that I
had asked this question in early days, showing a bias. When wit-
nesses volunteered evidence of sexual violence, in the Akayesu case,
the three judges questioned them for more information.

NGOs were thus instrumental in bringing certain issues, like gender
crimes, to the attention of ICTR judges.

It is not only civil society that has played a central role in connecting
international criminal tribunals with the concerns of the greater public,
however. The press has played an equally powerful role in this regard.
The courts depend upon the press to disseminate information about their
decisions and major accomplishments; without this publicity, the full impact of their work in bringing about justice, and even reconciliation, cannot be felt. At the same time, a court staff often feels that the press does
not report on their work accurately, which can ultimately harm the reputation of the institution. Pillay speaks of a junior journalist who visited
the ICTR while there happened not to be any trials in session. This was
subsequently reported as "These judges are doing nothing!" in a half
dozen papers, without any fact checking. A full account of the work of
the tribunal is available on the court Web site, provided and maintained
by the outreach office. "The public has access to it," says Pillay. "But the
media is not interested in it. You don't sell papers with that kind of information. You need something sensational."[8]

Despite challenging moments in the life of the ICTR, Pillay feels that
the tribunal has had a major impact in Rwanda. Its judicial proceedings
have allowed Rwandans to turn their attention to a lower level of accused perpetrator, leaving the complex prosecution of those believed to
be most responsible for the genocide to the international community.
Ordinary Rwandans have willingly agreed to testify at the court and
traveled a long distance to do so. Other African nations have cooperated
in the tribunal's work, transferring suspects to Arusha and accepting convicted criminals to serve out sentences in their prisons. Basing the tribunal

in Africa was an important part of the legitimacy that it has earned. Pillay recognizes, however, that the mandate of the ICTR was hard for many Rwandans to accept.

> There are sovereignty issues. "Who is this other body that can impose its system of justice over us?" It's unheard-of. You only respect your own. I don't think South Africa would have liked it if apartheid perpetrators had been put on trial somewhere else, by some other people. We would have really developed an attitude against these so-called judges. "Who are they? What's their qualification?"
>
> But I think that the two ad hoc tribunals have gained credibility and acceptance from the international community. The outside world has seen that international criminal justice can be a reality. Even I didn't think it was possible, because each one of us was trained in our own system. But the test of our accomplishment is in the jurisprudence produced. Were the judgments just political, or did the judges really have the reasons and evidence to convict? It is telling that they have acquitted some of the defendants.

Just as in the Nuremberg trials, the fact that some individuals indicted for crimes against humanity have been exonerated demonstrates that justice is being pursued fairly. This is a point of pride among a number of ICTR judges.

From Ad Hoc Tribunal to Permanent Court

In 2003, Pillay was ready to step down from her position at the ICTR and return to South Africa. Her time as judge and then president had been stressful and exhausting and she was ready to give up the work of international justice. She told her government that she would not stand for reelection at the ICTR. Pillay reminisced:

> I thought eight years was long service. I wanted to go back home and retire. Justice Albie Sachs [of the South African Constitutional Court] told me, "You won't last seventy-two hours here! After that you will be totally bored!"

Around that same time, nominations were being made for the new bench of the International Criminal Court. Pillay's name was put forward, and she finally acquiesced to being considered for a judgeship. She confessed to being moved that people had noticed the work she had accomplished in Arusha, a corner of the world that was not always on the international radar screen.

International courts have often been criticized for the overly political nature of their judicial elections, and the ICC is no exception. By visiting the United Nations and its various missions in New York wearing the hat of ICTR president, Pillay was able to avoid much of the aggressive campaigning that is normally done to garner the necessary votes for election.[9] Instead of promoting her own election to the ICC, she visited diplomats and officials on behalf of ICTR judges up for election and kept discussion of herself to a minimum. She was asked difficult questions as a candidate for the ICC bench, however, which she answered frankly.

"Do you think the ICC will be able to avoid the mistakes made by the ad hoc tribunals?" I answered, "No, there will be the same mistakes again." "Will the ICC be less expensive?" "No," I replied, "it's going to be just as expensive if not more."

Despite what might be considered unpopular answers to such questions, Pillay was elected in the first of thirty-three rounds of highly public and sometimes contentious voting. She was elected for a term of six years and currently sits on a bench of eighteen judges.

Pillay does believe that some lessons have been learned from the ICTY and ICTR experiences, however. This is particularly true in the way that the ICC interacts with both civil society and victims of the crimes being prosecuted. The prominence of gender crimes in the trials of the ad hoc tribunals has made practitioners of international justice very aware of how these issues should be approached in the new permanent criminal court. More generally, NGOs have been instrumental both in the establishment of the ICC and in the formulation of its rules and procedures. Pillay noted:

I think there are lessons learned in the way that the ICC has been set up. The prosecutor works very closely with civil society. He relies on civil society to bring complaints to his notice. And we have had experts on victims' reparation address the judges.

Gender is an issue not just in the crimes that the ICC will deal with but also in the very composition of the court itself. The ICC is the first international judicial institution that has striven for a gender balance on the bench. With her now long experience in international judicial institutions, Pillay finds herself serving as an inspiration and source of advice for other women judges.

Not only women judges from international courts but also from national courts get together to exchange views on issues pertinent to them. I support the participation of women judges. Not because I think women judges decide in a particular way and men judges

*decide in a different way, but because of the principle of equality.
You can't keep 50 percent of the population out of the decision-
making process. Then you have skewed justice.*

*And yet I do think women come with a particular sensitivity and
understanding about what happens to people who are raped. You
know, we understand when we are told that it's like getting a death
sentence. And we understand when the witness says, "I'll be sick
for the rest of my life." She means she has been rendered HIV positive. I think the world is understanding better now after the huge
incidence of rape of men and boys in the Balkans, that it is a gender
crime of violence.*

*Had it not been for the NGO movement in civil society having
such an influence over the structure of the ICC election process, I
don't think we would have gotten the seven women on our bench.
And to illustrate that, we look at the ICJ—how long have they been
in operation and they still only have a single woman? This is like
most courts in the world. It's a hot issue in South Africa right now
about promoting more women to the high court bench. What I
hear most from women judges in South Africa who reach out to me
is, "But you know, we are in the minority here. We just can't make
a difference. I'm only one of two or we're only three out of eighteen
or whatever. The bench is dominated by men and we can't make a
difference." That's the main complaint.*

*And yet I assure you, amongst colleagues, it doesn't mean
women support other women judges in decision making or in personal differences. It's really an equality issue. Courts have got to be
seen to be equal.*

As of 2006, the ICC had yet to conduct a full-blown trial. Since the
court started work in 2003, the prosecutorial division has taken on a
number of investigations and issued several indictments. The three divisions of the ICC judiciary—the pretrial, trial, and appeal chambers—
have been involved in numerous activities, including the development of
rules and procedures, decision making on various motions, confirmation
of indictments, formulation of professional development plans, and the
creation of an ICC judicial code of ethics, a process in which Navi Pillay
has taken a leading role.[10]

The path from Durban to The Hague was long and hard and full of unexpected turns, leading to a destination that Navanethem Pillay could not
have envisaged—as a girl growing up in apartheid South Africa, as a law
student, or even as a newly elected ICTR judge. She now occupies a position with the potential to set the development of law in new directions.

3 ✍ Inside the Courts

A Sketch of the Courts

International courts and tribunals are complex institutions, with judges constituting a single element among many. In addition to the bench, international courts have administrative arms, often known as the registry, and, if they are criminal tribunals, a prosecutorial unit as well. These various branches of international courts are designed to work together in moving along the process of justice in the most effective manner. Courts are also staffed by large numbers of people who represent diverse nationalities, language and cultural groups, legal traditions, social systems, political ideologies, and worldviews. Some courts may furthermore consider cases that come from a wide range of geographic areas and deal with many different substantive issues. The resulting multiplicity of functions and perspectives and needs that make up these multifaceted institutions must be integrated into a single working system that can function productively and satisfy the scrutiny of its constituents and the larger public.

It is clear, then, that international judges do not work in a vacuum. While their primary task is to consider the facts and substantive points of the cases before them in accordance with the law, they do so in the context of a complex bureaucratic system. Judges necessarily become part of personal and professional networks within their institutions, which must, in turn, shape the way they perform their work. This chapter will describe how international courts look and feel to judges and others from the inside. It will explore how judges carry out their daily work and interrelate with their peers and colleagues, the tensions and opportunities that derive from the diverse backgrounds and training of judges and other staff, the cultural and linguistic issues that may arise both in the cases they address and within the courts themselves, the way that the various branches interact with and view one another, and the kinds of relations that judges have with their peers in other courts.

Despite possessing a heterogeneity that might be seen as antithetical to a sense of unity, judicial institutions tend to be animated by a strong collective identity on the part of their judges, an identity that can be harnessed in the service of justice. Judges must sometimes consciously strive to create it, however, in the face of not only individual diversity but also the sheer complexity of the international justice endeavor and the many difficulties that the courts routinely face. Members of the bench are the source both of the collective spirit that can effectively draw their courts together and also, perhaps inevitably, of the centrifugal forces that could pull them apart.

In order to provide a picture of how the work of an international judge appears from the inside, it may be helpful first to sketch out how some international courts appear from the outside, at least upon first glance. The physical traits of two judicial institutions in The Hague both influence and reflect the style of work and the human interactions that take place within them.

Various historic events and decisions, along with the unfailing support of the Dutch government, have turned this rather ordinary town into the recognized "capital of international justice." It is here that one finds the International Court of Justice, the oldest continuously operating international judicial institution, created in the atmosphere of guilt and earnestness produced by the events of World War II. It is located in the center of The Hague in the Peace Palace, an early-twentieth-century architectural whimsy financed by Andrew Carnegie and still maintained by the foundation that bears his name. The palace also houses the Permanent Court of Arbitration, The Hague Academy of International Law, and the Peace Palace Library. The palace is adorned with a hodgepodge of gifts offered by various states over the years—a bronze replica of the South American Christ *of the Andes graces the lobby, a large jasper vase from Tsar Nicholas II of Russia dominates the anteroom, mounted elephant tusks from the Kingdom of Siam are found in the Japanese Room, and a fountain with polar bears and seals, an unlikely offering of the Danish government, stands in the palace's inner courtyard garden. On the basement level is the "refectorium," a rather pompous name for the very ordinary cafeteria that serves visitors. Despite these and other peculiarities, the monumental building still manages to look the part of an institution devoted to the pursuit of justice.*

Although most phases of judicial proceedings at the ICJ are closed to the public, observers may be present during oral pleadings by the parties before the court or when a final judgment is read aloud. After passing inspection at the main gate, visitors enter the palace through a grand entrance and find themselves in the lofty foyer; they may proceed into the courtroom by passing first through large doors and then heavy draperies. The counsel and advisors to the parties are aligned on different sides of the courtroom, many of them wearing the traditional dress of their own country's judicial system. Barristers from around the British Commonwealth sport the inevitable white horsehair wigs. A court official enters the courtroom, indicates to all that they should stand, announces formally, "Mesdames, messieurs, la Cour!" and the members of the ICJ bench file in, resplendent in their black robes and ruffled collars. The president of the court is seated in the center of this impressive lineup. The language used by counsel when they address the court is polite, elegant, and highly deferential.

If the courtroom is not one's destination, one can head across the well-maintained Peace Palace gardens toward a more modern annex that houses the offices of ICJ judges. Built in the 1970s by the government of the Netherlands, this building exhibits some of the most regretful features of that era's forward-looking architecture. The atmosphere of the annex is calm, even sleepy. There are few staff in sight and no sense of hurry. It would not be immediately obvious what purpose the building served if one did not already know. The judges have large and comfortable offices, lined with bookcases and with large windows overlooking the garden. Accommodating secretaries are only a short call away. The atmosphere of the ICJ projects an overall sense of solemnity, order, and self-importance.

The International Criminal Tribunal for the former Yugoslavia is an easy thirty-minute walk from the ICJ, located next to a well-used park and easily accessible by bicycle, the preferred mode of transportation for many residents of The Hague. The tribunal is housed in what was once a large insurance building, and it retains the unassuming countenance of an institution devoted to extracting regular profit from the unpredictability of life. If one does not look closely, it is hard to find signs indicating that this is now a court of law, much less one that deals with some of the most heinous crimes that have been committed in recent history.

But then one notices that there is a security checkpoint blocking the entrance to the building and that the guards are wearing uniforms emblazoned with "United Nations." After inspection of one's possessions and questions about reasons for visiting the court, visitors are allowed to enter the foyer, where they are then required to turn over their passports in return for a badge. At this point, those wishing to observe the trial in progress that day may enter a small seating area separated from the main players of the courtroom—defendant, prosecuting attorneys, defense attorneys, judges, witnesses, along with several dozen clerks, court documenters, assistants, and interpreters—by an imposing sheet of bullet-proof glass. A decision must then be made about which language to hear the proceedings in through the headset attached to each chair—English? French? Albanian? BCS (the shorthand term for the cluster of mutually intelligible dialects known individually as Bosnian, Croatian, and Serbian)?

If one is not visiting the court to observe the trial, a phone call is made from the foyer to somewhere in the depths of the ICTY complex, and a secretary is dispatched to escort the visitors through a series of locked doors, which will only open when an official badge is waved before an electronic eye, and finally into the inner sanctum where judges have their offices. There is a bustle in the corridors, lined with efficient and no-nonsense rooms, as judges and court staff move quickly from place to place, a sense of purpose in their eyes. Afterward, one is similarly escorted out of the complex, and passports are retrieved before the visitor leaves the building. Once again, one is on the serene streets of The Hague.

The ICJ and the ICTY represent, perhaps, the two ends of the spectrum in terms of the physical premises they occupy. It is not uncommon for international courts to take over spaces designed for other uses. The International Criminal Tribunal for Rwanda, in Arusha, Tanzania, has carved out a convoluted space in the Arusha Conference Centre, which it shares with various organizations, businesses, and the headquarters of the East African Community. It has four courtrooms, which are in almost constant use. The fourth one was recently constructed, with funds from the Norwegian and British governments, in order for the tribunal to complete the maximum number of cases on its docket before it closes its doors in 2008, its anticipated completion date for trials. The International Criminal Court is temporarily housed in what was once an office building on the outskirts of The Hague, awaiting the construction of its own premises, which will be complete with courtrooms and a detention facility. The ICC has, for the moment, three courtrooms, the smallest of which looks, according to one observer, like it was outfitted from an Ikea catalogue, complete with blond, Scandinavian-style woodwork. The Law of the Sea Tribunal in Hamburg, on the other hand, has a modern and functional building, including an imposing courtroom, constructed specifically for its use by the German government.

The European Court of Human Rights, in Strasbourg, France, is similarly housed in an architecturally innovative building, financed and built by the Council of Europe. With the expansion of the court since the building was constructed, the ECHR appears already to have exhausted its ability to provide even a modest working space to each of its attorneys and legal assistants. The problematic acoustics in the largest courtroom, the Grand Chamber, often compel participants and spectators alike to listen to proceedings through translation headsets, even if the language being spoken is their native tongue. San José (Costa Rica), Geneva (Switzerland), and Luxembourg all host international judicial institutions as well, each occupying a space characterized by various advantages, drawbacks, and peculiarities.

The physical premises in which judges carry out their work thus differ as much as the work carried out within their walls. Along with the complex array of sociological factors discussed below, these physical conditions create the judges' working environment, the stage upon which a large cast of actors plays out the drama of international justice on a daily basis.

Everyday Work

What do international judges actually *do*? How much do they work? How are their days organized? In what activities do they spend their time? Who assists them in their work, if anyone? The answers to these questions are as varied as the institutions in which international judges serve. Courts have particular mandates and jurisdictions, as described in chapter 1, which in turn result in varying caseloads, patterns of work, and levels of logistical and legal support.

A distinction was drawn earlier between international courts that are permanent—that is, established as ongoing institutions—and those that will close when their mandated work is completed, the so-called ad hoc courts. International courts and tribunals can also be distinguished by whether they have full-time or part-time benches. One might assume that the status of judges' employment is a reflection of the caseload of a court—that is, that part-time benches are created because there is not much work to be performed and full-time benches exist in the busiest of courts. This assumption holds true in some cases. For example, the Law of the Sea Tribunal has part-time judges who deal with a very small number of cases. Only the court president is full time and resides permanently in Hamburg.[1] The other twenty members of the bench travel to the court twice a year from their countries of residence for plenary sessions, hearings, and deliberations on any cases the court might have on the docket. The European Court of Human Rights finds itself at the other end of the spectrum, with a crushing caseload, including a backlog of tens of thousands cases; its forty-six judges logically have full-time positions.[2] The

European Court of Justice similarly has full-time judges and a large case-load, although its caseload is lighter than that of its human rights counterpart.[3] The Caribbean Court of Justice maintains a full-time bench of seven judges, regardless of caseload, though the full bench does not hear every case; the new African Court of Human and Peoples' Rights, whose judges were elected and sworn in during 2006, has opted to have a full-time president and vice president, with the remaining nine members of the bench serving part time.[4] It is not yet clear what their caseload will be like, although the number of charges against states that come before the African Commission of Human and Peoples' Rights suggests that it might well be heavy.

However, a logical relationship does not always exist between the employment status of judges and how many cases are on a court's docket. The WTO Appellate Body "members" (they are not called judges) are available at all times and on short notice to meet in Geneva, at the headquarters of the World Trade Organization, to hold hearings and deliberate on cases.[5] The increasing number of cases submitted to the Appellate Body has begun to make the part-time status of its members problematic. The Inter-American Court of Human Rights meets several times a year in San José, Costa Rica, the court's seat for hearings and deliberations on multiple cases.[6] Between these long and very full working sessions, most judges pursue full-time employment in other domains, many as law professors in their home countries. The members of the bench of the International Court of Justice, on the other hand, are full time; although they have had an increasing number of cases in recent years, their caseload is still quite small compared to those of many international courts.[7]

The ad hoc criminal tribunals for the former Yugoslavia and Rwanda similarly have full-time benches.[8] Their caseloads are very high and they operate under constant pressure from the United Nations to bring their work to a close. The ICC had little work for its full-time judges as of 2006, since the first cases were still under investigation and few indictments had as yet been issued. While there was some work being carried out by the pretrial chamber, other judges were engaged in support work during these first years of the institution's life, such as developing judicial education plans and researching the question of reparations for victims.

The daily work of international judges is less a function of their part-time or full-time status than of the kind of court on which they serve. The cases of interstate courts, human rights courts, and courts of regional economic integration agreements require careful consideration of written texts, with oral hearings often playing a secondary or supporting role. This is especially true of courts that operate as courts of last instance and thus deal with points of law rather than fact. Thus, much of these courts' work may be done individually by judges and, for part-time judges, often at a distance from the seat of the court. A human rights judge gave this account of his typical day: "It is nearly always just reading documents. For example, the first thing I'll be doing when I get in at 8:00 tomorrow morning to my desk is to start reading the papers for a meeting, which I haven't yet read, and which are sitting on the desk and waiting for me. In many ways my work system—I suppose it comes from being a barrister, where you get briefed a lot of times at the last minute—is that I really prefer to read my documents just before I'm going to do something."[9] Judges of the International Court of Justice also spend more time outside of the courtroom than in, going over written submissions by the parties, researching the ways in which the issues before their court have been treated in other judicial forums, and preparing notes.

Appeals judges on criminal tribunals similarly do a lot of individual and text-based work on the cases under their consideration before coming together with the fellow members of their chamber for discussion and deliberation. Even though the appeals judges of the Special Court for Sierra Leone are full time, they spend little time at the seat of the court in Freetown. Instead, they work mostly in their home countries, communicating via e-mail with one another and the court staff. "We've been able to minimize the cost of running the court," says an appeals judge of the SCSL. "We download the records for appeal and we study them and then one person prepares the draft. Then we exchange opinions on the Internet. So far it has worked, but when the matter is complete, we need to be together, to visit oral arguments and discuss. Then we find ways of going to Sierra Leone or going to England to hold conferences."

The ad hoc criminal tribunals for Yugoslavia and Rwanda share an appeals chamber of seven judges, all of them residing in The Hague and making occasional trips to Arusha. The chamber may work on up to fifteen cases at once, each case being carefully considered individually and then taking perhaps several days to decide in consultation with fellow appeals judges. A trial judge at the ad hoc tribunals, on the other hand, may sit in a chamber of only three judges on a limited number of cases. These cases may last many months or longer, with thirty or more hours of court sessions per week. An ICTY appeals judge characterizes the different daily routines of the two kinds of judges like this: "A trial judge will basically work all the day or most of it in the courtroom. An appeals judge has a very limited courtroom activity because a case will be heard in one, two, three days. In a way, trial judges have very limited contact with others because, except in a bench of three, they don't have anything to do with the other judges as a group. Appeals judges have much more contact because there are seven of us and we have to work on almost all the cases together."

Not only is there variation in the way that the judges' daily work is organized, but the amount of support that they receive in this important work also differs substantially from institution to institution, possibly having a direct impact on judges' efficiency and output. In most courts, judges have secretaries, although they might share them with other judges. The availability of research or legal assistants, however, is less standard across courts. Former ICTY trial judge Patricia Wald believes that international judges need at least as much support as domestic judges, if not more: "The murkiness of much international law, its multiple sources embedded in different languages, the lack of judicial precedent for its varied applications, the melding of widely disparate rules of procedure and evidence found in the common law and civil law systems all make the international judge's task more difficult. Plainly put, the international judges need astute assistants."[10] Such assistants are not, however, a given.

Despite the heavy caseload of the ECHR, for instance, its bench has limited help in preparing cases. A lawyer will be assigned to assist on a case—to deal with related correspondence or to request further documents from the applicant—or several may be assigned if the case is particularly important. "Would I like to have a legal assistant? Would I ever!" one judge exclaims. Another ECHR judge explains, "Our infrastructure is not sufficient. We don't have the personal assistants or clerks that are well known in lots of other courts, national and international. But the fact is we sometimes really need them. You have forty-six very different states. Say you wanted to know something about the past history and the breakup of the Soviet Union or Yugoslavia and how that happened, and the consequences that this may have in a case before us. If you want to do additional research you've got to do it yourself. No, we are not spoiled!" This level of support can be contrasted, for example, with that of the U.S. Supreme Court, whose justices have three or four clerks each and a much smaller caseload than the judges of the ECHR.[11]

Criminal court judges have perhaps the most assistance among the courts considered here. These institutions are well staffed by legal assistants, often young lawyers who see working with an international court as a rewarding professional interlude. The judges of the Sierra Leone, Yugoslavia, and Rwanda courts thus all have a large cadre of legal officers who help them in myriad aspects of case preparation. While the judges at the SCSL do not have personal assistants assigned to them, the appeals chamber and two trial chambers each have at least five legal officers of varying rank working on specific cases, in addition to a number of interns. In contrast, each ICTY judge has his or her own law clerk, and each chamber—there are three trial chambers plus an appeals chamber—has a senior legal officer. In addition, there are "floating" legal officers who are assigned to follow specific cases. A number of judges at the ad hoc tribunals have, however, expressed frustration at the limited control they have in picking their own assistants, given the strict hiring regulations in force at the United Nations and the need for personnel to mirror the national makeup of the parent organization. "The registry and the prosecution," says one ICTR judge, "should be allowed to hire their own teams. The chambers should also be allowed, with much less bureaucracy, to hire their own teams. There wouldn't be any nepotism or unfairness there! The UN system is sometimes not flexible enough to see the specific needs of the court."

Yet the high level of support available to the judges at the ad hoc criminal tribunals might be envied by those at other international courts. An ICTR judge describes the system at his court: "Each judge has a legal officer. So you'll probably find that if you have a judicial panel, you have three judges, you have a trial coordinator, and you have three legal officers. But they are also working in a collective unit where each judicial chamber has a chamber coordinator. And then there are other legal officers working around the chamber coordinator, who also reports to a head of legal chambers. So for example, a draft judgment, once it passes through the judicial process, apparently is seen by six or seven legal officers before the managing judge actually gets into the act of editing it and putting his own signature on it. I'd never worked in an environment before where I had somebody else writing." Such a practice is not uncommon, however, in judicial institutions; U.S. judges routinely have their clerks draft legal opinions, even at the level of the Supreme Court.[12]

This issue of having legal assistants at international courts involved in judgment writing is somewhat controversial. Judges of the ICJ are particularly critical about this practice. "I am happy to have some help in research," one ICJ judge declares, "but only in research. I am very much against the system that is used, for instance, in international criminal courts, in which judges are sitting the whole day listening to witnesses and the clerks are making the judgments. I would never allow anybody else than myself to draw up the judgment." A clerk of the Caribbean Court of Justice reports that while the seven judges enjoy personal secretaries, extensive library resources, and the assistance of two highly qualified, full-time judicial researchers, it is the judges themselves who write all judgments. It is perhaps natural that the pace of work at the criminal courts, especially those that are finishing up their temporary mandates, makes certain practices the norm and allows for a speedier delivery of justice. But some ICJ judges forego any assistance at all, even in matters of research, believing that they should take on all aspects of the court's cases themselves. When it comes to legal assistants, says one ICJ judge, "we have a couple of judges who are against the whole idea and don't use them. The rest of us do. Some use them primarily for extra research, and things they think are not yet fully covered in the pleadings. I do that sometimes, but the thing I honestly find most useful is to use my clerk as I used to use a solicitor, to keep all the papers in order, to know what document is where."

How judges of all courts use the support staff at their disposal is highly individual and has as much to do with their former experience and background as with the work they have before them. While some international judges could well benefit from increased support, even those who are most burdened with work exhibit a surprisingly calm demeanor when discussing their profession. Being an international judge, however demanding, apparently provides many compensating satisfactions.

Deliberations and Judgment Writing

However different the daily routines of interstate dispute resolution bodies may be from criminal courts or human rights courts, all judicial institutions produce judgments on the cases that come before them, which at their best are well-argued and persuasive texts that lay out the reasoning for the judges' decisions. These judgments are the results not only of written and oral pleadings, hearings, testimony, and cross-examination—depending on the type of court—but they are also the product of complex deliberations that take place among judges themselves. Each court approaches this important process differently.

The way in which the International Court of Justice carries out deliberations and judgment writing is unique.[13] After written submissions by the parties have been studied carefully, judges meet briefly to summarize the principal elements of the case. Oral proceedings are then held, where parties plead their cases before the court. Each member of the bench then retreats in order to write a "note"—that is, a draft judgment—individually conceived. "As for the judge's note," one ICJ member explains, "you normally get about three to four weeks at the end of a case, where you go and wrap the proverbial towel around your head, and do more or less a draft judgment, but not drafted in such a polished way, not necessarily in sequence as you would do a judgment. But by the time that you've done that, it's three to four weeks, and then it's translated, because we work in French and English, and everything has to finish up in two languages. And then you've read each other's notes, and we're often talking about forty-, fifty-page things, and fifteen colleagues. You can see, seven weeks have gone by."

Judges of the ICJ differ about the usefulness of the note-writing process. It is clear that it takes an inordinate amount of time, which contributes to the generally acknowledged slow pace of work. Another judge arrived at the court believing that the process was cumbersome, but upon observing its benefits, he changed his mind. Given the delicate nature of many cases before the ICJ, the process of note writing ensures that every judge has really studied the material. "Otherwise, on a court like this," one judge says, "with all the political implications of cases, people will just vote; they walk in and they vote. And then they vote politics."

Although the process of writing notes may sound very solitary, ICJ judges point out that there is often informal discussion about the case among colleagues during the weeks devoted to this activity; for example, over coffee or lunch. Judges of the bench then have the opportunity to read each other's notes before meeting for their initial deliberations, which may last for up to a week for a complex case. All deliberations are done in plenary sessions with all fifteen members of the bench, which presents a challenge of organization. One judge notes that during these sessions, "there is a good dialogue, a very good dialogue. Quite stimulating, and because of personalities, sometimes quite fierce." The court president plays an important role during these first deliberations, calling upon judges—in inverse order of seniority on the bench—to declare their views, and then summarizing the general trend of thought articulated in the various individual notes. A drafting committee is then appointed, always chaired by the president.[14] One judge emphasizes the connection between drafting a judgment and thinking out the issues of a case: "There was an English judge in a domestic court who said, 'I don't think with my head, I think with my hand.' And it's true. It's when you draft that you see the problems and you try to solve them." Judges then participate in further deliberations as a judgment approaches its final version.

The European Court of Human Rights has a very different way of approaching the process of deliberations and judgment, one that fits the large number of cases processed by the court annually.[15] The forty-six-member bench is divided into five sections of nine or ten judges each. These sections, composed with an eye to balancing legal systems, language, and gender, remain relatively stable. Sections are allocated a certain number of applications to the court. Applications that appear clearly inadmissible are handled by a committee of three judges, who, acting unanimously, may strike out the case. Among the reasons for such strike-outs are the failure to exhaust domestic remedies, application to the court outside the six-month time limit, or any of the other grounds provided by Article 35 of the European Convention of Human Rights.[16] There is no appeal from the decision of a committee.

Applications that are admissible are considered by a chamber of seven judges, chosen from among the section members. The registry of the court is "absolutely critical to the operation of the European court," declares one of its judges. Cases for the chamber will be referred by the registry lawyer dealing with them to the judges nominated to be *rapporteurs* for those cases.[17] Following consultation between the judge/*rapporteur* and the registry lawyer, a proposal will be prepared for the chamber. This could be to communicate the case to the government for its observations or, if this has already been done, to make a finding of admissibility and possibly a provisional finding of a violation of human rights. This proposal will typically set out the details of the parties, the facts, the domestic law involved, and the relevant international law. It will specify the complaint made and, where communication of the complaint has already been made to the government, the government's response. Where admissibility and merits are dealt with together, as is frequently the case, the proposal will set out a provisional decision.

Members of the chamber are now ready to deliberate on the case. This is done in weekly section meetings, where members might deal with up to fifty new cases. While most cases are very straightforward, each agenda will contain some cases of a more complex nature. The chamber president will ask the *rapporteur* to introduce the case if it is a complex one. Otherwise, the group proceeds directly to discussing both the factual and legal aspects of the case, as presented in the case materials. The registry lawyer handling the case is present, as is a representative of the research division, whose role it is to assist in the standardization of jurisprudence across the court's sections. The chamber then votes on whether the case is admissible and, sometimes, on the merits as well. On those occasions when there appear to be grounds, the chamber may take a provisional vote concerning the violation of a particular article or articles of the European Convention of Human Rights. This alerts the registry to what the chamber's decision is likely to be, and, where appropriate, it may approach the parties with a view to encouraging a friendly settlement of the case. If no such settlement is forthcoming, then the registry prepares the final judgment based upon the chamber discussions. Complex cases or disagreement in the chamber may call for the appointment of a committee of judges to prepare the draft judgment. This draft will finally be brought to the chamber and examined paragraph by paragraph before being adopted.

The WTO Appellate Body, which operates with seven part-time members, has organized the process of deliberations and judgment writing with an emphasis on efficiency. As the name suggests, the AB only hears appeals of reports made by dispute settlement panels, ad hoc arbitral bodies that constitute the first level of jurisdiction of the WTO dispute settlement system. Cases are assigned randomly to a division of three Appellate Body members. For approximately the first month, the division reads the panel report, along with the background materials and the written pleadings of the parties. Each member then makes his own profile of the case before meeting with the others. With the help of members of the

AB's secretariat, a long list of questions about the case is then compiled for the oral hearing.

The oral hearing usually lasts two days, with pleadings only lasting about twenty to thirty minutes for each party and five to ten minutes for third parties. Parties are then questioned by division members on points that need to be clarified, and their answers become part of the case record. As one AB member puts it, "It is a really grueling exercise and I would not like to be on the receiving side of it! But the parties are on their toes." After the oral hearing, there is a phase of deliberation called the "exchange of views." The remaining four AB members, who have been given the case file to review, spend several days with the original division of three for a discussion about the various issues that have been raised in the case. An AB member characterizes the exchange of views as "a very innovative and distinguished aspect of our procedure," and adds that sometimes division members will change their opinions on a case as a result of discussion with their colleagues.

On the basis of these discussions, a draft judgment or "report" is prepared. After further deliberations and discussion, the report is given to the secretariat to be put into its final form. The Appellate Body can uphold, modify, or reverse the original legal findings and conclusions of the first panel's report. The Dispute Resolution Body has thirty days in which to accept or reject the appeal's report, the latter only by consensus.

The process of deliberation and judgment writing at the Rwanda tribunal differs from that of the courts considered above, along a number of dimensions. A criminal trial is centered on the indictment issued against a defendant by the prosecution, and all phases of the ensuing activities—pretrial procedures, trial, deliberations, and judgment writing—make reference to the initial charges found in this main accusatory instrument. Before the commencement of the trial, the indictment and all pretrial documents filed by the parties are carefully analyzed by the trial chamber to determine the factual and legal issues at stake. The judges sitting on that trial will then prepare a draft outline of a provisional judgment. Throughout the trial, the indictment continues to be considered in light of the factual and legal issues raised during the presentation of evidence. On the basis of this information, the draft outline of the judgment will be updated at the end of the trial.

After the trial is completed—and it may have lasted for many months or even more than a year—deliberations can begin. An ICTR judge emphasizes that "the deliberations phase is certainly the most important phase from which an ICTR judgment—its reasoning and verdict—will result." The judges sitting on the trial discuss in private a number of matters. First, they assess the evidence adduced. This assessment will include consideration of any internal discrepancies in witnesses' testimony, relationship between the accused and a witness, previous criminal record of the witness, the impact of trauma on a witness's memory, discrepancies in translation, and social and cultural factors. Second, they determine the weight to be attached to the evidence presented. This depends upon whether it is from an eyewitness, a hearsay witness, or an uncorroborated witness, as well as the source of the evidence (for written documents). Third, they discuss the crimes, as supported by the evidence. For example, does the testimony point to genocide, crimes against humanity, or a violation of the Geneva Conventions? Is the mode of liability that of a perpetrator, accomplice, or a person with superior responsibility? These discussions take place in reference to both the definitions of the ICTR statute and the tribunal's own case law. Fourth, they discuss the appropriate sentence for the person found guilty. This is considered in light of aggravating circumstances and the sentencing practices of both the ICTR and national courts in Rwanda.

After deliberation on all of these elements, a draft judgment is prepared. A final judgment is then drafted under the judges' instructions, being subject to many reviews and to an ongoing writing process. The nature of deliberations, another ICTR judge stresses, is very much dependent upon the presiding judge. "Some judges prefer a cooperative approach, others more of an individual approach. With cooperative thinking you have discussions. In the individual approach, it becomes a matter of mathematics because you add the individual opinions and see how, or whether, you have a majority." When agreed upon by the judges, the final judgment will be signed and then delivered at a public hearing.

The procedures outlined above represent something of an ideal scenario for deliberations and judgment writing. Judges are not, of course, always in agreement on a case or about how a judgment should be presented.[18] Overall, however, it would appear that the benches of international courts generally operate on a principle of "collegiality," whereby judges "are willing to listen, persuade, and be persuaded, all in an atmosphere of civility and respect."[19] This principle is particularly important in courts that are, by definition, diverse in nature.

Culture and the Courts

Each person working for an international court carries a sense of how best to accomplish the job of justice, a sense created through long experiences in his home country surrounded by others with a similar understanding of the world or, alternatively, in the expatriate or diplomatic circles in which he grew up or served professionally before joining the court. In the judicial institutions studied here, tensions related to different worldviews may arise, not only inside the courts themselves, which are characterized by alliances and hierarchies like other large institutions, but also in relation to the work they perform and the constituencies they serve. Within these tensions, however, there exists an enormous potential for forging new and powerful collective approaches to justice that can still honor the multiplicity of cultural understandings found both inside the courts and around the world at large.

International courts are without a doubt more heterogeneous than their national counterparts. This is simultaneously their greatest weakness and greatest strength. It is a weakness, obviously, because great efforts have to be made to bridge differences among judges. It is a strength because this same heterogeneity provides a range of skills, competences, and backgrounds much wider than any domestic court could ever exhibit, a range which is furthermore necessary to tackle the kinds of problems international courts deal with on a daily basis. To be effective, the bench of an international court needs to achieve a balance between prioritizing collective endeavor and appreciating and benefiting from individual diversity.

Although achieving such a balance might seem nearly impossible, international courts clearly are, in fact, relatively successful at doing just this. Working as an international judge can create a powerful common mindset. The members of this community tend to see each other not as servants or representatives of a particular polity, but instead as fellow professionals in a common judicial enterprise that transcends national borders. They are bound together because they face common substantive and institutional problems, they pay attention to one another's judgments beyond what might formally be mandated by any legal principle or judicial structures, and they learn from one another's experience and reasoning.[20]

International judges can be seen as forming what some social scientists have termed an "epistemic community," that is to say, a group of people who, while different in many regards, are animated by common ideas, sets of values, or aims.[21] Members of an epistemic community are a "network of knowledge-based experts," held together by the members' "shared belief or faith in the verity and the applicability of particular forms of knowledge or specific truths."[22] The judges who serve on international courts share a belief in the aims of international justice and the value of international law. This allows them to transcend personal differences—or, very often, to *use* these personal differences—to carry out the work of their institutions.[23]

The development of this epistemic community—for, indeed, it is still in a formative stage—is facilitated by certain preexisting similarities among international judges, the common patterns of training and professional background.[24] Yet despite these patterns, the wide array of perspectives that judges bring to bear on the work of an international court strikes a contrast with work in a national context. One judge was surprised by the difference. "I always thought that I understood international organizations because I had worked with them a lot," he says, "but I didn't. Being in one is completely different. You realize how homogenous a government is, instinctively. A government is basically monolithic, and people may have their differences, but they don't challenge the basics. In an international organization, everyone challenges the basics all the time." In many cases, judges see the mix of professional backgrounds as an asset to their institutions. One European judge calls it "great fun to work with people from very different backgrounds—not just national backgrounds, but actually almost more important here are the professional backgrounds of the people. Professors tend to be interested in solving juridical problems. Former administrators tend to be interested in getting a practical solution to work on the ground. Judges tend to be preoccupied with getting through a caseload and not keeping everyone waiting."

There thus seems to be general agreement between judges and observers that, because international courts tackle very different sets of international and transnational problems in various legal and political contexts, a bench made of a blend of people with different backgrounds is a crucial asset. Indeed, each of the three basic pools from which candidates are drawn contributes uniquely to the blend. Diplomats provide the understanding of the larger political framework within which the case is embedded, as well as potential ramifications of judgments. They often provide the essential reality check in the deliberations. Academics are able to connect the judgment to the larger construction of international law, providing the formal correctness and consistency necessary to buttress the legitimacy of the ruling. National judges know, obviously, how to judge; that is to say, they know how to deliberate and reach consensus, how to run a courtroom, and how to assess evidence correctly and give proper weight and consideration to both parties' arguments. Each group naturally has weaknesses as well. Diplomats tend to be too deferential to governmental and systemic interests and often argue for the status quo. Academics are often accused of being incapable of participating in a consensus, of being too abstract, and of being "maximalists" who are disinclined to make the necessary compromises of judicial work. National judges might have too little understanding and appreciation of international law and may not be as worldly as those in the other groups. Some exceptional individuals have all of these skills necessary to be a judge and more, but they are rare beasts indeed.

The president of a criminal court paints a less rosy view, however, of the professional mix in his institution. "When you look at what the judges actually were before," he says, "you see many differences. Some are former international judges, some are former national judges, some are former lawyers, some are former law professors, and some are former diplomats. Well, you put that together, you shake, and it explodes." Different backgrounds contribute significantly to different practical approaches to problem solving. "I found the national judges extremely rigid in the way they were approaching things, and the diplomats tended to see everything like, 'This is something that should be fixed.' Neither approach works. So, at the beginning, certainly, the cultural differences based on all these different factors were very pronounced. But, over time, I think there has really been a tightening of the judicial culture here."

Judges in international courts seem to be relatively successful in creating a collective identity for themselves, one that allows them to pull together and work toward a common goal. This is very obvious in a court like the European Court of Justice, where dissenting or separate opinions cannot be made. One ECJ member remarks that "a judge coming from a national system who was appointed to the court, and who continued to see everything in terms of his own national legal system, looking at it through 'national spectacles,' would come up with a completely different viewpoint on all of the questions. And if all the judges were free to do that, then you would not actually manage to forge a community rule at all. You would have a collection of national viewpoints. The fact that the judges are obliged to pool their perspectives, and obliged to reach some kind of common view, is, I think, one of the main reasons why the court has succeeded." Several ECJ judges observe that not only is it possible for a large group of judges from different professional, national, and linguistic backgrounds to agree in the process of writing a judgment, it is not even particularly difficult. This can perhaps be explained by the fact that the judges appointed to the court have already demonstrated that they have gone beyond a narrow nationalism and participate in a larger European identity. Even for a body like the International Criminal Court, with a virtually worldwide jurisdiction and judges from around the globe, the mission of the institution seems to be so compelling that judges are able to put aside their differences and, in the words of one ICC judge, "start working together and reconcile their differences in order to form a united approach to justice."

This "united approach to justice"—the new judicial culture that is beginning to characterize the international system—is something that may not be familiar, however, to new international judges. It is something that may very well have to be absorbed through experience and learned by trial and error. And despite the newness of this profession, there is little formalized training or mentoring about the practical aspects of being an international judge for those who are just coming onto the job. Novice judges are mostly left alone to figure out how things work in their court, posing questions to colleagues for clarification as they go. Only one court seems to have made a more formal attempt to help incoming judges learn the ropes of their institution: the creation of a "godfather system" between new and experienced judges at the European Court of Justice. But this scheme was, in the end, more an idea than a reality. Several judges from various courts note that support staff at their courts—experienced legal officers and secretaries—were the most helpful in providing guidance upon their arrival and helping them to make a smooth transition onto the bench.

International judges do not simply encounter a series of new duties and procedures in joining a court, however. They also become members of a complex community, made up of fellow judges, support staff, and administrators. Across this spectrum, judges inevitably end up allying themselves with like-minded individuals, in both professional and social contexts. Some judges confess to being drawn to colleagues with whom they share a language or training. For others, however, worldview and ideology are more significant as a foundation for friendship and collegiality. "I think there are natural alignments," comments one member of the International Court of Justice, "and I don't think they are related to nationality, geography, gender, or language. I really profoundly believe this from my experience. It's just where your mindsets are similar. You have similar views on important questions like ethics, and the right way to go about things. You might expect it to be about whether you are on the conservative or the liberal end of the spectrum. But I don't believe it's any of the criteria you might imagine." A European Court of Justice judge similarly notes that there are some differences between judges who are more conservative and those who are more activist. "That you have in any court. There are people who want to be more cautious than others. But then, in my view, it's a sliding scale, and somebody who might want to be very cautious in a certain type of situation tends to be much more bold in other situations." Thus, it is difficult to predict with whom judges will feel the most solidarity or sympathy among the members of their bench.

International benches are also characterized by certain hierarchies. A judge of the European Court of Human Rights acknowledges this frankly. "Do we have a hierarchy? Well, you have persons who have a particularly good knowledge of the case law and, of course, their arguments will be strong. You have persons who are known as being either very eloquent but maybe far-reaching, or you have persons who are more the consensus builders. It's like that in every court." One court administrator uses stronger language in referring to hierarchy, characterizing court presidents as "alpha males": "When someone is elected president, it's for some reason. Not only because of geographical representation but, in most cases, it's also because of personality." A judge with experience of various international courts concurs that personality traits are important, but he distinguishes intellectual leadership from an ability to lead in a more pragmatic sense. "There are people who, by their personality, wisdom, knowledge, et cetera, impose themselves. Sometimes there are leaders and dissenters within the institutions, but everybody respects them because they have a vision. They have intellectual power and vision. That is one type of leadership. There is another type of leadership, which uses savoir-faire—these leaders are the consensus-getters, who are very persuasive but not necessarily strong on substance."

The size of a court may also influence its institutional culture, especially in regard to the flexibility of its procedures and the relative formality of its atmosphere. Large benches that work mostly in the plenary format may necessitate specific rules for taking the floor, simply to limit the amount of time spent in discussion. Judges who work in smaller chambers of three or five may operate with fewer constraints. The European Court of Justice is an interesting test case due to its expansion in 2004 from fifteen to twenty-five judges.[25] Several members of the court note that the increased size has changed the dynamics of interaction among judges, partly because of the need to introduce technology. "It is a very different court in many ways," says one judge who experienced the transition. "I mean it's a different court socially, for a start. We don't know each other as well as we used to. It's also a different court in terms of the organization. We still meet as the full court, but we now have microphones—you press a button if you want to speak, and that changes the nature of discussion. And I'm sure it changes the nature of the deliberations when there are a lot of judges around the table as well." Perhaps paradoxically, notes a fellow ECJ judge, the increased size of the bench has not led to more-drawn-out plenary sessions. "Interestingly enough, this has also led meetings to be much shorter because the threshold for taking the floor is much higher. There's a microphone, and everybody's thinking, 'What is he going to say?'" This added formality has apparently discouraged judges from speaking "off the cuff."

As for tensions that may exist among members of the bench, most international judges refrain from speaking too openly about less-than-ideal relations with their peers. Both off-the-record comments by judges and observations by other staff members of courts reveal, however, that there are sometimes enormous tensions and bitter disagreements—even outright feuds—among judges serving on the same court. The existence of such tensions makes international courts and tribunals no different from any other workplace. The need, however, for judges to maintain the appearance of integrity and dispassion in order to promote public confidence in their performance places particular constraints on the expression of professional or personal frustration by disgruntled members of the bench. Such matters are better left for the pages of memoirs, written after retirement from the bench, and perhaps not even then.

International courts face an additional challenge unknown to most national judiciaries: their benches are composed of judges trained in distinct legal traditions. Most judges have either a common or civil law training, depending upon the country where they studied. Countries of the postcolonial world generally inherited the system of their colonizer; thus, judges from the United Kingdom, Nigeria, St. Kitts and Nevis, and India will all have a common law training, while their peers from France, Mali, Algeria, and Vietnam will have a civil law training. In some countries, judges might also use customary or Islamic law alongside common or civil law. One might say that international judges have learned to speak the language of law using not only different vocabularies but also different grammars.[26]

Judges necessarily bring their training with them to the courts on which they serve, which, as institutions, have found various and unique ways of blending the different systems, especially in terms of their rules of procedure and evidence. As a judge of the European Court of Justice explains, "European Union law is a kind of mosaic system, a mixture of common law and continental systems," and the same mosaic effect exists in all international courts to a greater or lesser degree. On the Caribbean Court of Justice, judges with a civil law perspective work in tandem with experts in common law. Says one former clerk of the court, "This collaboration allows highly accomplished judges to learn from each other and benefit from each other's experiences." One judge who was instrumental in the development of the rules of procedure and evidence for the Yugoslavia tribunal describes the accomplishment of "the first real code of criminal procedure on the international level" as "a synthesis of three things. First, a synthesis between the civil and the common law. And the statute was made on the basis of common law, but we managed to inject a good part of civil law—at least permitting a more active role of the bench in the cases. Secondly, we had to inject into it all the codes of human rights that were developed in the UN. And then, thirdly, we had to adapt it to the conditions of the international legal system, which is a different environment, particularly in its access to persons and to evidence and to territory. So, it was very complicated!"

International judges disagree about how significant an impact the different training of judges actually has on the work of their courts. Many would agree, however, that the impact is less about substantive law and more about the habits and procedures that directly shape the outlines of judicial work. It has been noted that common law judges are clearly more comfortable with oral hearings than their civil law peers. One member of the European Court of Justice remarks on how this plays out in day-to-day work.

"There is a different attitude among members of the court toward hearings," he says. "Some think that oral hearings are not very important, because they have this notion that it is the court that knows the law and there's no purpose in having a hearing. Because *we* know the law. That's very much in the French legal tradition. Why do we need the parties to come and tell us the law? We don't have anything to gain by having to sit here for three hours listening to the parties. And so you will see that many times they will not even ask any questions. And then you have other members who actually use hearings not only to promote discussion of the facts but also to clarify some elements of the law. I think it's a reflection of the nature of this court where you have quite different legal traditions. It makes it interesting, but sometimes it also creates certain tensions, this different approach to defining judicial function and the search for the legal truth." Another ECJ judge observes that attorneys from civil law countries are often stymied when asked by the bench to answer questions extemporaneously, expecting to simply read their statement aloud to the court. Barristers from common law countries, on the other hand, are experienced with such requests and handle them with great skill.

The procedural differences between common and civil law traditions become even more visible in the context of an international criminal court. Civil law judges and attorneys may not be familiar with the cross-examination of witnesses or the notion of the inadmissibility of hearsay evidence. Their common law colleagues may find communication between judges and counsel outside the formal setting of the courtroom to be not only unfamiliar but, to their minds, a breach of ethics. A common law judge on a criminal tribunal admits to discomfort with the role of written evidence in trial proceedings, preferring the common law insistence on oral testimony by witnesses: "The big fight is between written and oral evidence. [Civil law judges] say a lot of things can come in by written evidence. You don't have to have the person who saw it or heard it and that sort of thing. Now, I do not feel myself capable of assessing a written document by a presumed witness unless it's on its face incredible or contradictory. But if somebody tells a straight story and I never see the person or never have a chance to cross-examine them, I don't feel that I can evaluate it. The civil law folks say, well, you have juries, and those are lay people and so that's why you need to have the actual witness, because they are not capable of evaluating written evidence, but judges are. Well, I think that's baloney! We are no more capable of looking at a piece of paper and knowing whether it's truthful unless we know a lot more about the situation in which it was written." But this same judge has experienced some of the civil law procedures of the international court as liberating. "I especially liked the fact that, more so than in [common law domestic] courtrooms, the rules permit the judges to ask questions. Usually you try not to interrupt the flow of the testimony, but as you listen to it, you're compiling in your own mind what you think they haven't covered. And it's perfectly allowable at the end of the testimony for the judges to ask those questions. In several instances, I felt those questions were very useful. And I felt like I was in the process, I was an active player."

The Rwanda tribunal also struggles with its mix of civil and common law procedures. It was suggested by some that certain common law procedures might even be considered the culprit when it comes to the tribunal's long and drawn-out trials. "I find the common law approach struggles quite a bit about the admission of documents," one judge notes with exasperation. "That's quite a waste of time, sometimes. There, I prefer the civil law or mixed law approach, simply to say that we take it in as much as possible and we weigh it on the merits at the end of the day. In my courtroom, I deliberately try to avoid any procedural discussions. Procedural discussions are just sand in the machinery. The point is to get rid of the question, in a fair way, balancing the interests, but not to allow discussions just for the sake of it."

Another key challenge in international justice is the interface between particular cultural and historical experiences, and standards of international justice and human rights. While already an issue in Europe—especially with the expansion of the Council of Europe to include the former Soviet Union—it may become even more complex when one moves out of the Western world. How do populations in Africa, for example, a continent that is currently the site of numerous international justice processes and investigations, perceive the aims and activities of courts and tribunals established by the United Nations or other international organizations? Can different views on how justice should be carried out be successfully reconciled?

The former UN undersecretary general for legal affairs, Hans Corell, recounts the meeting he had with the president of Rwanda in November 1994 to discuss the imminent establishment of the ICTR: "We got into a very animated discussion about the death penalty. I mean, not an unpleasant but an animated discussion. And he said to me, 'Look Mr. Corell, don't come here with your European ideas. This is Africa and here we apply the death penalty.' And I said, 'With all due respect, Mr. President, if you maintain that this court should have the right to apply the death penalty, it's inconceivable that the United Nations will set it up for the simple reason that there are permanent members of the Security Council who refuse to apply this penalty. And if you want to apply it in Rwanda and we don't have this UN court, you won't see these criminals because they have fled the country and no one is going to extradite them to Rwanda to a sure death. So why not cooperate with the tribunal and then these people might be put in prison for life, if found guilty?'" Ultimately, the ICTR was established and, indeed, the maximum sentence it applies is life in prison.[27] But some ICTR judges themselves come from countries where the death penalty is not considered an excessive punishment, and they have had to adjust their own expectations on this count. A member of the bench recounted of a colleague: "He was an experienced judge, but where did he get his experience? In a small locality in Tanzania. In one of my first meetings with him, I asked if he had ever passed a death sentence. And he said, 'Yes! Countless times. You know, if we don't, the people will lynch the accused and kill him anyway.'"

One of the interesting aspects of international judicial institutions is that persons with local perceptions of justice—which, as in the practice of the death penalty, are not always in harmony with international norms – work in close contact with those who may have a very different outlook. Such contact is often eye-opening and can be beneficial all around. If the international legal order is to serve global interests, some would argue, then both local and more widespread understandings of justice should be taken into consideration.[28] One ICTR judge, also a national judge from a small developing country, comments on the ultimate benefits of local and international justice systems brushing shoulders: "I'm not in the school of thought that feels that there's an incompatibility with respect for local customs and the application of advanced standards of discipline. I think that there is room for both concepts to coexist. I personally think that international standards have a legitimacy that can embrace the world, anticipating local developments, and I think you can say that the purpose of having international standards is to nudge noncompliers nearer to them."

The Challenges of Linguistic Diversity

"Language issues bedevil all international courts!" So speaks a judge of the European Court of Human Rights about the challenges he sees confronting those who work not only in his own court but also in the international justice system more generally. With a jurisdiction covering the forty-six states of the Council of Europe and a judge representing each one of them, language problems are perhaps particularly pronounced at the ECHR. Yet all courts experience to some degree the challenges that accompany the linguistic diversity not only of its staff but also of the parties appearing before the court.

All languages are not equal, however. The most common pattern followed by international courts, and historically by other international institutions as well, is to elevate one or more languages to the status of "working language." All court personnel are required to speak at least one working language, and official documents are produced in only those languages. English and French are the most common working languages, reflecting the global predominance of the first in the contemporary world and the historic centrality of the second to the development of international law and institutions. The ECHR pairs English and French, as do all the UN's courts. The International Criminal Court has followed suit. The Rwanda tribunal has gone further and made efforts to make Kinyarwanda, the language of most of the Rwandan population, a quasi–working language of the court. Courts with regional jurisdiction generally operate in the languages that make sense in their geographic zone: the Inter-American Court of Human Rights uses Spanish, with English serving as a secondary language; the Serious Crimes Investigation Unit in East Timor had English, Portuguese, Tetum, and Bahasa Indonesian as working languages, although English played a very significant role among judges and staff; the Caribbean Court of Justice has three official languages, English, French, and Dutch, although the latter is little used compared to the others; and the African Court of Human and Peoples' Rights has adopted the languages that have official status in the countries of the African continent—English, French, Portuguese, and Arabic. Only one court, the European Court of Justice, uses French as its sole working language.

The decreased role of the French language in international courts parallels its declining importance on the world scene over the past century. Although equal in status as a working language in many courts, it is rarely spoken by as many judges or court staff as English. This may leave the Francophones feeling frustrated or marginalized, especially in courts where the Anglo-Saxon presence, both linguistic and legal, is dominant. In a court like the European Court of Human Rights, where most judges come from countries where neither working language is spoken, English is clearly the priority language to learn, despite the fact that the court is located in Strasbourg, France. An ECHR judge comments, "It's very frustrating when, like myself, you're coming here trying to get your French up to the standard and every time you open your mouth in French, someone responds in English. And when you are in a deliberation and somebody is speaking in English, hardly anyone is listening on the interpretation, sometimes no one. But when someone is speaking in French, then you will always see two, three, or four of the judges listening to the translation."

The dominance of English over French is also noted by judges of the WTO Appellate Body, the Law of the Sea Tribunal, and the International Criminal Court, all of which use both as working languages. One ICC judge observes that despite the possible tension that could arise from this language "competition," the court staff does not necessarily divide up into Francophone and Anglophone groups: "English obviously dominates here, as it dominates any other international organization. The reason why I've said there's no Anglophone group is that the English-speaking world is no longer Anglo-Saxon—it's much bigger than that now." Indeed, another ICC judge, noting that she and many other judges speak English as a third or fourth or fifth language, claims that the *real* language of the ICC is "broken English."

This natural evolution toward a single working language in courts may appear beneficial, as it might eventually reduce the need for translation altogether, at least among judges. Many judges point out, however, that those who have English as a native language find themselves in an advantageous position in relation to their peers. Only native speakers have the full range of lexicon and usage that allows them to express complex legal ideas with the greatest subtlety and skill. "If somebody from China takes the floor in English," observes a judge of the Law of the Sea Tribunal, "even if he is an expert and had been at the Law of the Sea Conference, he will never leave the same impression from his ideas as somebody whose mother tongue is English." A judge whose native language is Arabic notes, "There is always an advantage for someone who speaks his own language, especially in law. I mean, I've spent my whole life working in two languages that are not my own. And that's a great handicap. I might have been much better had I been able to use my own language! And even between the two foreign ones, I get a little bit confused sometimes. So I think the linguistic advantage is important. But it is over-weighed sometimes by the intellectual advantage. I mean, someone who is not very articulate in a particular language . . . still, if he has a certain force of reasoning, he can impose his way in spite of this small handicap."

Despite the obvious primacy of English in most international courts and tribunals, many judges concur that the ideal scenario is for courts to have members who are proficient in multiple working languages. Those with the greatest linguistic skills often end up taking the lead in deliberations. A judge of the European Court of Human Rights observes that "people who have facility in one or other or both of the working languages—and by that I mean practically speaking them like a native—have an enormous advantage. And I think that their influence is proportionately increased in that regard. It's noticeable that at the top level of the court, the people are multilingual." A judge of the International Court of Justice speaks admiringly of colleagues whose knowledge of both English and French is so impeccable that they can look at versions of court judgments in both languages, see where the translators have not quite gotten it right, and make an alternative suggestion for phrasing or terminology. A judge on the Rwanda tribunal from an English-speaking country discovered, upon taking up his post, that speaking French would facilitate his work immensely. He immediately undertook to study it, despite his already crushing workload. Many international judges similarly add language study to their already long list of professional activities, and often the court administration facilitates such efforts. For example, the Caribbean Court of Justice has instituted weekly Dutch classes aimed at allowing members of the court to serve citizens of Surinam with greater ease.

Several judges, and perhaps not surprisingly those who are multilingual themselves, have suggested that candidates for the position of international judge be evaluated, at least partially, on their language skills. A member of the Rwanda tribunal bench, who has neither French nor English as a native tongue, insists on the need for broad language competency: "We all speak with our accents, but judges should certainly be fluent in at least one and, hopefully, in *both* languages of the court. I think that what we should strive for in the future, at the international level, is a situation where we have *bilingual* judges. I speak English and French and I find that it is a *huge* advantage." A former Yugoslavia tribunal judge and native English speaker suggests, as an alternative, that courts try to have more bilingual legal assistants and other staff. That way, judges could be assisted in their work on documents in languages that they do not speak. However, an ICTY colleague—once again a non-native English-speaking polyglot—argues that asking for judicial candidates who speak two working languages is not overly demanding, and, furthermore, he notes the disadvantages of depending on legal assistants for such aid: "When you have *two* languages only, you should select candidates who have at least a good basic knowledge of both, otherwise it can't work. Sometimes, for judges who speak just one language, I have the impression that they are maybe led to a certain extent by their bilingual assistants."

Despite recognizing the obvious advantages of international courts having multilingual benches, many in the field of international law fear that requiring extensive language skills for the position of international judge would further limit an already small pool of qualified candidates. Linguistic competence, as noted in chapter 2, tends to receive only a cursory examination during the election process for international judges. For the time being, professional experience and legal knowledge would seem to trump linguistic skill as qualifications.

Where there is a diversity of languages, there is translation. Indeed, the work of international courts and tribunals could not take place without the support of a veritable army of both document translators and simultaneous interpreters. But the ubiquity of translation in the international justice system does not keep judges and other staff from feeling ambivalent about the impact of this process upon both the proceedings of their courts and their overstressed budgets. Having judges who are not fluent in the working languages of their courts is just one of a whole range of issues that must be solved through the rendering of documents and speech from an original to another language.

The European Court of Human Rights, with a jurisdiction of forty-six states—which have, between them, no fewer than forty-four official tongues—receives documents relevant to cases in dozens of different languages. Only the essential ones can be translated between French and English in-house, with most translations into other languages sent out to freelancers. Oral pleadings by states before the court are similarly done in either French or English. As for the eventual judgments by the ECHR, one judge reports that "one of our big problems" is that "our judgments are not translated automatically into the language of the country from which they came. Somebody has to do that in-country. This is a real public relations failure for the court. It's like the loop is never closed."

The problems of translation take on another dimension in the context of a criminal tribunal, where witnesses testify in a number of different languages, all of which need to be interpreted for judges and other courtroom staff, into both English and French. "Translators rule the courtroom," one ICTY judge declares. "My impression is that the translators were very good. But how could I possibly know whether their translation of Bosnian or Serbian was accurate? I just had to go on the fact that they seemed to know what they were doing and everybody else thought they knew what they were doing. There is no way to second-guess a translation."

At the ICTR, courtroom interpretation is even more arduous. Most Rwandan witnesses testify in the national language, Kinyarwanda. During the first trials, there were no interpreters trained in simultaneous interpretation from this language into French and English. The procedure was thus for a witness to make a statement in Kinyarwanda, which was translated consecutively into French, during which time a simultaneous interpreter rendered it into English. This procedure added days onto testimony in trials for which the prosecution and defense together sometimes called well over a hundred witnesses. The ICTR also experiences long delays for the translation of all documents into the necessary languages. "It is impossible for all documents to be translated into both working languages in a timely fashion," one trial judge notes. "Even though the registry has expressed a policy of doing it, they just don't have the personnel to do it. So they have a system of establishing priorities, which also means that the issues at the low level never get translated, because they have all these emergency matters that are cropping up. And it creates legal problems that you have to adjudicate. For example, if you have a motion that's filed by the prosecution in English with supporting material in English, and the defense team has two Francophone lawyers, they need to wait for the French translation to make their comments. These are practical problems that affect the trial."

While judges may wish to assume that the courtroom interpreters are doing their work competently, several have noted moments when linguistic confusion has had the potential to alter the direction of justice. This may be particularly true in the context of criminal courts. An ICTY judge recalls a debate over correct translation in an important case, where "a certain word in Serbo-Croatian affected the question of when the handover went from one military leader to another. They'd sent out some document to us and a Bosnian word was translated into English as 'heretofore.' And the question was, did 'heretofore' mean that up to that minute the old general was in charge or not? Or could it mean that he had been replaced some days earlier?"

Courtroom interpretation is, not surprisingly, an enterprise fraught with difficulties not experienced by interpreters in other contexts. These interpreters are called upon to translate technical language in a wide variety of subject matters; they need to know terms relevant to different legal orders and generally handle the lexically and syntactically complex language of legal practitioners; and, during deliberations, they have to follow and translate the arguments of judges who often refer to the specificities of their own national legal traditions and jurisprudence. If they are interpreting testimony, interpreters are often required to jump from one linguistic "register" to another—from, for example, the simple speech of a rural dweller to the technical jargon of a ballistics expert. Furthermore, it is crucial that interpreters accurately convey not only the meaning and content of witness testimony but also all the "non-linguistic cues" exhibited by the speaker, as these are part of the evidence itself.[29] As one expert in courtroom interpretation puts it, interpreted testimony should include "all of the pauses, hedges, self-corrections, hesitations, and emotion as they are conveyed through tone of voice, word choice and intonation."[30] All of these cues may have an impact on how a judge evaluates the testimony of a witness and thus on the process of justice itself.[31]

Difficulties may also arise from the compounding of linguistic *and* cultural differences during testimony, and these are even trickier than purely linguistic ones to recognize and rectify. At the ICTR, Rwandan witnesses may be deemed "not credible" by defense or prosecuting attorneys because of inconsistencies in their testimony, recorded at different times. For example, a witness may variably describe the car of an accused as blue or green, thus suggesting a faulty memory. Attorneys and judges may not realize that Kinyarwanda, like many other languages in the world, uses a single term to cover that particular range of the color spectrum, and that native Kinyarwanda speakers tend consequently to translate the term into French as *bleu* or *vert* indiscriminately. Witnesses may also describe someone as a "brother," and then later as a "cousin" or "uncle," which would not be unusual for someone in a society with extended and flexible kinship relationships but may sound unreliable to someone for whom these kinship categories are quite distinct.

The interaction of language and culture may be significant not only in the context of courtroom proceedings but also in conceptions of the law itself. Many judges refer to differences between common and civil law concepts and how they are expressed through terms that may not be directly translatable between English and French. A judge of the International Court of Justice speaks of the great advantage of his court having two working languages, but he also points out some of the dangers: "We do not deliberate on a draft judgment in French or in English. We actually deliberate on a judgment which is already in two languages, and which is read to the court in the two languages. And at that stage, you find it's very interesting that if you draft in your mother tongue, you sometimes use language that looks convincing, but which translated means nothing. And that's true for English to French as well as from French to English. Now the disadvantage, of course, is that you have to work more, and it's not always easy because the concepts are not the same. When you say *'compétence'* in French, and 'jurisdiction' in English, it does not have the same meaning. When you say *'recevabilité'* in French, and 'admissibility' in English, it also does not have the same meaning. Thus, there is obviously a danger in not saying exactly the same thing in the two languages. But at the same time, there is the advantage of trying to control what you are saying in a more precise way. I think it's a risk, but the advantage is greater than the risk."

A former legal advisor at the WTO Appellate Body agrees that the positive aspects of multilingualism in international courts should not be dismissed simply because they create an inconvenient need for translation and interpretation. "If you want to celebrate the diversity of the backgrounds, origins, and perspectives of international judges, the diversity of their languages must be included. I believe that although there are costs and delays associated with translation, there are more advantages than disadvantages in having many languages on board, both in terms of the worldwide legitimacy of international institutions it creates but also in terms of the precision of legal language." She points out that sometimes only in the translation process is a term or expression discovered to be vague or ambiguous. Translators act as the "first public" of the judgments and statements of international courts; they are the first test of their clarity and precision. In the case of the WTO AB, each judgment is issued in three authoritative versions: English, French, and Spanish. This can be compared to other courts that are less punctilious about linguistic issues. Writes former ICTY judge Patrica Wald, "Decisions—interim and final—at the ICTY are issued in both English and French, but only one is the authoritative version and I am told that there are often not insubstantial variations in the two versions."[32]

Several judges of the European Court of Justice, the only court to use French as its sole working language, comment on the connection that exists between a language and the way legal reasoning is performed. "This court operates in the French language so, automatically, French is there in the structure of notions and in the style of argumentation," one ECJ judge explains. "This style and the notions are different, because each legal system is based on a language. A lawyer working in his own legal system is not confronted with this difference. He thinks legal notions and associations are natural. But they are *not* natural." His colleague on the bench puts it this way: "It's not just a question of language, it's a question of formulation and thinking. The French tradition is much more abstract than the tradition of some other countries, so the tradition of this court is to formulate things at a high level of abstraction."

It is difficult to assess the loss that the declining use of the French language may represent for the international legal system overall. What is clear is that the dominant use of English brings with it a certain conception of the law. One international legal expert observes that so many lawyers from the United States are now taking part in international litigation that their legal culture is percolating into the courts where they appear. "It's the prevalence of English and the dearth of French in pleadings that is bringing this about. English has become the conveyor belt, if you will, of American legal culture to the international level." This culture includes not only a certain penchant for "adversarial legalism," but also the increasing use of advocacy-oriented amici curiae and the presence of private practitioners and law firms in international litigation.[33]

Differences in legal thinking may be exacerbated when judges from far-flung countries suddenly find themselves working side by side. A judge of the European Court of Human Rights admits that the expansion of the Council of Europe to include most of the former Soviet Union has been eye-opening. "The more we take in judges from new countries, the more we have problems about judges who have had their training in Russian, or in another local language, but neither in English nor in French. And this is not only a linguistic issue, it is also an issue of approach and the kind of argument you use and the kind of civility that you use in your argument." The expansion of the European Court of Justice to twenty-five countries has had a similar effect. "Until the last enlargement," observes one judge of that court, "I think many of the members could cope with at least quite a few of the European languages. I mean we couldn't read Finnish or Greek, but if you had to look at a text of a particular article, you could probably even struggle with the Dutch text if you know a little bit of German and so on, whereas now it's impossible even to suppose that you could have a grasp of any significant majority of the languages." The recent ECJ enlargement even brought up the question of whether the working language of the court might be changed from French to English, the latter being a more frequently studied language in the countries of

Eastern Europe. But in the end, French has been preserved as the official language of the ECJ.

International courts will always have the practical challenges associated with language diversity; translation and interpretation will necessarily be the principal tools for bridging linguistic gaps, which will in turn keep the process of international justice moving at a slow pace. But as investigations by the International Criminal Court begin in a number of different countries, it is clear that dealing with the question of a court's working languages is just the tip of the iceberg. "The language question is crucial," emphasizes a UN official who was instrumental in the development of the Rome Statute. "Every time you hear a case through interpreters, you are a bit nervous that the nuances are not properly conveyed." An ICC trial judge notes that the court will also need to handle the translation of victims' and witnesses' testimony from a huge variety of languages—for which there may not exist trained translators—so that the documents in English and French versions can become part of the official trial record. The enormity and complexity of this task are perhaps more reasons that it is preferable when possible to dispense criminal justice at the local level and in national judiciaries, as spelled out by the ICC principle of complementarity.

The Pace of Justice

It has often been pointed out that the international justice system proceeds at an almost glacial pace. Given the time-consuming activities of preparing both oral and written presentation of facts to the bench, the complication of translation, and the sometimes painstaking processes of deliberations and judgment writing, it is no wonder that cases sometimes take years to be decided in international courts. This slowness worries not only outside observers but many judges and court staff as well, who will often cite the famous dictum that "justice delayed is justice denied."[34] Criminal courts have come under particular attack on the issue of drawn-out trials, as many people feel that victims of war crimes need the psychological benefits that come with seeing those responsible for their suffering tried and sentenced. When asked what he would change about his court if he had the power to, one judge from a developing country on the Rwanda tribunal confesses, "I've had real astonishment on the issue of delay! That is the issue I would tackle first here, because I think that it is possible to establish standards and to measure those standards and to manage their application. Where I come from, we don't have a lot of money to spend. I don't accept the issue of resources as a handicap in reducing problems of this nature."

The International Court of Justice is also well-known for the length of its proceedings. It has a relatively limited docket of cases, but they can take several years to move through the phases of written and oral pleadings by the parties, and then deliberations and judgment writing by the bench.[35] Some of the delays are due to the parties themselves, who may drag their feet in order to give diplomacy a chance to resolve the dispute first. While ICJ judges perform much solitary work, their collective sessions are almost always done in plenary fashion, with all fifteen judges in attendance. Some movement has occurred, however, toward trying to change the time-honored way of doing things at the ICJ, although resistance exists as well. "There is a tension within the court on this," one judge comments. "I think an emergent majority is now very concerned about these things. There are still those who feel that the overall thing is quality, and I, of course, agree completely." It is imperative, this judge continues, that members of the international community "understand that we need the proper time to do all of this. . . . The two cardinal things that are absolutely nonnegotiable in this court are quality and the representative, collegial nature of our work. Provided you can keep those, there are always improvements that can be made." This same judge was quick to point out that the ICJ acts very quickly under some circumstances: "We do advisory opinions fast. We try to give priority to cases when people are killing each other, even if they're not the earliest on the docket." As a result, "some other cases then get left behind." Another ICJ judge suggests that the slowness of work at the court is due to the plenary nature of most sessions: "Fifteen judges is a lot. Thus I think the solution is in chambers. The problem with chambers, of course, is that in our statute, we must get the agreement of both states concerned to have a case heard in chambers. And states are always a little reluctant because they are afraid that the composition of the chamber may be in their disfavor."

The European Court of Justice also has long delays in processing its cases and even in responding to requests by national courts for preliminary rulings on questions of European Community law. One ECJ judge asserts that his colleagues previously "only had eyes for their national law. They simply didn't see a 'Euro' perspective. Now, they have begun to see that all sorts of things are arguable which previously they had not thought of as arguable." He points out that the court has cut its average time for handling a case from twenty-five months to twenty, though "we have to improve on that." But improvements will go only so far. "This is a situation where the convoy moves at the speed of the slowest ship. It only requires somebody to be held up back in the country for everything to be held up."

The European Court of Human Rights is the institution with both the greatest volume and the greatest backlog of cases: forty-five thousand applications to the court came in during 2005 alone.[36] While most of them will ultimately not be deemed admissible, the court needs to treat them with respect. "For most of those cases, we can't do anything," one member of the court concedes. "But there's a person, a human being behind each one—a drama for them, perhaps the big drama of their life. So we have the obligation to give them an answer within a reasonable time. That's the symbolic function of the European Human Rights Convention, that, outside the national legal system, every person in Europe—and it's not just citizens, because it's open to noncitizens, it's open to stateless persons even—anyone within the jurisdiction of a state can apply to Strasbourg. It's a kind of declaration by states that they've opened their windows and their doors and they say, 'We're transparent; for anyone not pleased with what goes on at the national level, who feels they haven't had a fair deal from the national authorities, there is this independent international machinery which we take part in, and you can go there.'"

Only one court among those considered here does not have a problem of delays and backlog—the WTO Appellate Body. By statute, the Appellate Body must resolve cases within ninety days.[37] This gives the court legitimacy, according to one judge, but it also pushes members, who work on a part-time basis, to decide their cases in record time. One judge refers to working under "pressure-cooker conditions," and declares that a bit more time would benefit the decisions rendered by the Appellate Body. "We usually meet for, three, four, five days to finalize a report. And I would have liked to have another meeting, to take a week off to digest the report and then meet again. Although the results are not bad, they could be much better turned out, technically and intellectually, if each one of us had more time to reflect on the final product in the penultimate phase."

International justice is not alone in the pace of its proceedings; many domestic courts also dispense justice slowly. The reason that Italy is so often called before the ECHR is precisely for its violation of the article of the European Human Rights Convention which guarantees the right to a speedy trial.[38] It can sometimes take years for a important case to work its way from the trial phase to the Supreme Court in the United States, and complex criminal cases can spend years in the courts.[39] Once again, the fact that international courts operate so much in the public eye and often on high-profile cases makes them particularly vulnerable to scrutiny. "There will always be some criticism," says an ICTR judge, "and some of it is based on previous sins and some of it is based on a lack of understanding of international criminal justice. And the main criticism will probably be that we are too expensive and too slow. But I will invite any of those who are criticizing us to come and sit in the courtroom and hear these genocide cases and see if he or she will be able to speed things up!"

The Other Side of the Bench

While judges in many ways are the most visible symbols of international courts and tribunals, they represent just one division of a judicial institution. The functioning of courts is overseen by a registry or other administrative organ, which is responsible for myriad aspects of the institutions' daily work, including applications to the court by parties, record keeping, budgetary issues, translation and interpretation, outreach to the public, security, information technology, court library and archives, and audiovisual services. The administrative branch of criminal courts will furthermore oversee such other critical elements of the court system as the defense unit, detention unit, witness assistance and protection, and issues surrounding the service of sentence by those found guilty. In addition, criminal courts have a prosecutorial organ, often referred to as the office of the prosecutor, or OTP. These various organs need to work in a cooperative and synchronized manner in order for courts to carry out their work with optimal success.

Registries play somewhat varying roles in different types of courts. In the European Court of Human Rights, the registry is critical in assessing the prima facie admissibility of applications to the court and thus determining which cases are brought before judges. One ECHR judge remarks gratefully about the registry that "we have a terrific cadre of lawyers. It's really the reason why the court has been so successful. They have fantastic qualifications; most of them could get jobs almost anywhere." An ICTR judge is similarly impressed by the diverse functions carried out by his court's registry, recognizing that it provides "a network of services that support the judicial function." These include translation and interpretation, management of files, the appointment of defense lawyers, the relationship between the accused and their attorneys, and witness management.

At the same time, there may exist tensions between a court's bench and its registry, especially in courts where the statutes leave the relative authority of the various organs open to interpretation or where they have some overlapping functions. Such tensions may slow down the efficiency of international courts or create an atmosphere that is not entirely conducive to their best performance. One UN official notes with consternation that sometimes judges have been known to raise themselves up above other court staff in UN judicial bodies: "There was a certain tendency at a particular period in time when judges didn't seem to recognize that the registrar has a special role in the courts. Because the registrar is a UN official! And the registrar is the one who is responsible for the budget. So it goes without saying that he has to have a decision in these matters. The judges aren't above the law. And it is for the registrar to make decisions here, because obviously the judges are going to be decision makers in their own matters." Some judges respond to such a view by pointing out that it is customary for registrars to be under the supervision of court presidents or chief justices in national systems. Says one ICTR judge, "We accept that the registrar is the person in charge of the budget and administration, but judges should be consulted on matters relating to judicial work, such as adequate resources, and staff and facilities for defense, as these factors impact the pace of trials. It is instructive that the states parties to the Rome Statute redressed this by making the registrar accountable to the president of the ICC." Conflict between the chambers and the registry were perhaps the worst in the early days of the Rwanda tribunal, when complaints by the president and other staff members of the court about the registrar's performance, and an ensuing in-house investigation, eventually led to his resignation and replacement.[40]

Some tensions also exist at the ICTR between the presidency and the office of the prosecutor concerning which organ is most appropriate to take on certain tasks. Some feel that the fundamental necessity for a judge, including the president, to maintain an unquestioned appearance of impartiality should preclude him from performing various public functions. A member of the Rwanda tribunal's OTP emphasizes that it is the nature of the prosecutor's job to outline public plans and strategies, as he works on getting member states to cooperate with investigations. "There is a limit," he says, "to which the judges, particularly the president, can speak on some aspects of this matter without it impinging on their judicial impartiality. I mean, I wouldn't like the president, who is a judge, to negotiate with a country about witness protection, witness relocation, protection of witnesses, et cetera. These are the responsibilities of the prosecutor."

The International Criminal Court, from its earliest days, has likewise seen some tensions among the various organs of the court. The presidency has necessarily taken on some administrative functions as the court starts its work, functions that might ordinarily be overseen solely by the registry. The chief prosecutor, as he begins investigations in a number of different cases, has become a public face of the court, along with the president. Given the different ways that the court's organs tend to view their work and the court more generally, the public has received some mixed messages from the leadership of the court. To preempt some of the problems that might arise due to this overlap of functions, the ICC has created what it calls the "coordination council," a body that brings together the president, the chief prosecutor, and the registrar for regular meetings and that has now been formalized in the regulations of the court. As one ICC judge reflects, "We want to have one court, a court that is perceived as one force, not as a series of centrifugal forces."

At the same time, it is very important in criminal courts that the chambers and the prosecution not be seen as *too* close or cooperative, that they be perceived as independent of one another so that trials are perceived as fair. An ICTY judge mentions the care that he takes not to recruit legal assistants who have previously worked in the OTP, for fear that they might have been involved in investigations leading to cases assigned to his appeals chamber. He also recounts that his own legal assistant decided, after several years, to take a job with the ICTY prosecution for a change of pace. While bidding him goodbye, his former assistant said it was a shame that they could no longer see each other, or at least they could not socialize openly. He contradicted her: "No, we *can* see each other, but only with *everybody* seeing us. Otherwise we shouldn't meet." At the International Criminal Court, the parts of the building that house the judges are locked off from the prosecution, allowing no casual wandering from one to the other, which might result in inappropriate interactions. Proximity among different types of judges might be seen as problematic as well. "We have pretrial judges, trial judges, and appeal judges on the same floors," one judge observes. "I would think that in the future we should be separated." The fact that many international courts are housed in buildings designed for other purposes may make such a separation hard to achieve.

International judges have much to say about the counsel who appear before their benches, representing either states or individuals. The bench of the International Court of Justice often sees the same advocates appearing in its courtroom case after case, as they are drawn from a core of recognized international lawyers who are "for hire" by any state that wishes to retain them. Alain Pellet, a legal scholar and himself a member of what he terms the "invisible bar" of the ICJ, estimates that the same fourteen advocates pleaded three cases or more each in the twenty cases decided by the ICJ between 1986 and 1997. Some of these counsel, including Pellet himself, pleaded in over nine.[41] Many of these repeat advocates hail from Western Europe and, in more recent years, from North America, even when the parties before the court are African or Latin American states.[42] One ICJ judge comments that occasionally one party will retain "the old guard" while the other party will call in some new legal power, "the bright young things," for their representation, "and that's interesting to see."

As the oldest international judicial institution, and one heavily dictated by tradition, the ICJ tends to see only the most capable of lawyers in its courtroom, with an occasional exception. Other courts do not have the same experience. There is, in fact, a general feeling that advocates for parties before international courts often leave much to be desired—they are simply not up to the task before them. This can be frustrating for judges, whose work is facilitated by the two sides of a case being presented with equal skill. A judge of the European Court of Justice comments that there are some excellent lawyers who regularly appear before his court. "Then on the other end, you have some poor lawyer who's coming from a small town and who has taken a case before a national court of first instance and has no experience of European Community law. And then, maybe even against his own preference, the judge of that national court decides to ask us for a preliminary ruling, and then the poor guy has to come here. And then for some reason he doesn't even bother to find out exactly what customarily happens, so he comes here with a long speech, which repeats what he already said in writing. That's the other extreme. And we have everything in between." The European Court of Human Rights sees a similar unevenness in the quality of advocates for both states and applicants. "Generally the standard of advocacy is not good in our court," says a member of the ECHR bench, "but that's largely because we don't have professional advocates most of the time. It's only when we have the British, as we have quite a lot, that we have really good professional advocates. Then they're very well argued. Most of the time the arguments are conducted on behalf of the government by civil servants who work in their various departments. They have absolutely no experience or skill or qualification as an advocate and it shows. They're very poor at the presentation of the cases." If the parties cannot do themselves justice, judges are, in turn, hindered in their own work. Poor advocacy can thus act as an impediment to the optimal functioning of an international court.

Criticisms of the advocates who come before international criminal tribunals are even stronger. These tribunals have an office of the prosecutor, complete with an extensive and generally competent group of attorneys and legal assistants who are charged with laying out the case against the accused. But who takes care of representing the accused? And are they the equal of those on the prosecution side? Observers have noted that the side of the defense in international criminal proceedings suffers from three weaknesses. First, it starts from a politically disadvantaged position because, by the very creation of the tribunal before which the defense is appearing, the international community has already determined that crimes have been committed and "someone needs to pay." Second, the defense is materially disadvantaged, because it doesn't have the same resources as the prosecution. And, third, there is not yet a sufficient number of defense advocates who are skilled enough to plead in criminal trials before international courts or tribunals, which are sometimes radically different from domestic ones.

Indeed, the defense counsel chosen or retained for those standing trial for crimes in the Balkans and Rwanda have often been characterized as "uneven" in quality, by both judges and observers. They may be inexperienced and/or unfamiliar with the tribunals' procedures; there have even been cases where the tribunal has found defense attorneys in contempt of court for making agreements with their clients to share the fees authorized by the court. But not all international defense counsel can be painted with the same brush. One ICTY judge remarks on a particularly good defense counsel in a case before her chamber, who "was clearly a young guy on the rise, and you could see his courtroom performance improve almost from week to week in terms of cross-examination. . . . I thought he represented the accused in a highly ethical, proficient way."

The perceived unevenness in the quality of the counsel appearing before international courts has led many to think about how this professional group could be monitored. Some suggest that counsel should demonstrate certain minimum qualifications, or even undergo training, before appearing before the various courts. Others have discussed the possibility of creating an international bar association that would take on this role for the entire international judicial system. One ICTY judge concedes the need for a "supervisory body," but also points out that judges are often inclined to "leave the disciplinary thing to the home countries of the counsel." Pending the creation of a general international bar, the International Criminal Bar (ICB) was formed in 2003 to act as the representative of counsel before the ICC, assure their ability to practice in independence, and guarantee an equitable trial to victims and accused. This represents a systematic attempt to regulate the practitioners coming before international courts.[43]

Beyond a concern with certain actors in the international judicial system, it is abundantly clear that expertise in the field of international criminal justice, in particular, has grown by leaps and bounds since the creation of the ad hoc tribunals. "The ICTR, together with the ICTY, have contributed to a professionalization of international criminal justice," says one leading criminal court judge, "in the sense that ten years ago, there were no international judges, no prosecutors, no defense counsel, no administrators. *There was no one who knew anything!* And now you have fifty judges, hundreds of defense counsel, many, many prosecutors, all with experience from the courtroom, in the international context. That's a *huge* capital that's been created." The ICC benefits directly from this professionalization of the field, as staff with experience in the ad hoc tribunals enter the service of the permanent court. While this is good for international criminal justice in the long term, it has created short term problems for the ICTY and ICTR, which find themselves short of experienced staff as they move toward their completion dates.

If international judges have certain views on the other branches of their courts and the counsel appearing before them, those on the other side of the bench have equally strong views about the judges serving in their institutions. A former highly placed staffer at both the ICTY and the ICC, for example, distinguishes between the judicial performance of former diplomats versus former judges. "Diplomats always go for the compromise, former judges go for the principle." Diplomats are able to perform better at the ICJ, he clarifies, because it basically functions as an "arbitral tribunal," meaning that it puts greater value on the settlement of the dispute as contrasted to the application of the hard letter of the law; but in criminal trials, the counsel can easily lead former diplomats by the nose. One senior trial attorney at the ICTY reports that the staff of the office of the prosecutor have views on how the assignment of particular judges and trial chambers to a certain case will affect both the prosecution of the accused and the atmosphere of the courtroom. The chaos of the Milosevic trial is cited as an example; the presiding judge at the time seemed unable to keep the defendant from turning the courtroom into a circus, which frustrated some of the others working on the case. Those on the side of defense in both the ICTY and the ICTR, on the other hand, sometimes feel that the bench is privileging the case of the prosecution and then, citing time constraints, asks the defense to rush its own case.

Registry staffers may have equally critical things to say about a court's bench. An ICTY official charged with outreach work expresses frustration with how slowly judges prepare statements explaining certain decisions and sentences that can be communicated to the victim community. He attributes these delays to "high-handedness" on the part of judges, to a sense of their own importance. Some judges, he declares, "would like to position themselves in their own narrative, one that stretches from Nuremberg and Tokyo far into the future. They want to make grand statements about humanitarian law." Those who have been involved in the ICJ registry similarly comment on the unassailable status that judges assign to themselves by virtue of their election to this prestigious bench. This can create a less-than-truly-cooperative working relationship between organs of the court. As one experienced international court staff member declares, the hierarchy that exists in some institutions is akin to a "feudal system."

The common perception that judges occupy an exalted status—deserved or not—is held both by observers on the outside of the international justice system and by personnel on the inside. One of the markers of this status is the manner in which members of the bench are addressed with the honorific title of "Judge," or even "Your Excellency," outside of the courtroom as well as in. While this is common practice in many countries, and is generally associated with a judge having embodied the dignity of his or her office, it can sometimes strike an odd note in the context of international courts where there is such a diversity of experience and expertise and where judges are sometimes only part time. In some cases, legal officers may themselves have been judges in their home countries before joining the court and have more experience than the members of the bench. It is also apparent that the same kind of verbal respect is not consistently accorded to high-ranking members of prosecution units or registries, despite their own depth of knowledge and the critical role they play in the international justice structure. A former member of the ICJ registry reports that he felt obliged to address a new member of the bench, who was an old and dear friend, as "Judge" once he had assumed his office. A former member of both the prosecution at the Rwanda tribunal and the defense at the Sierra Leone court speaks of her recognition of the shortcomings of some members of the two courts' benches and her simultaneous incapability of foregoing the most deferential terms of address with them at all times. "They believe that it's important to have that level of dignity and respect," she offers in explanation. While some staff members of international courts and tribunals buck convention by eschewing honorific terms of address, they quickly learn that judges resist such a descent to earth. Most actors in the international justice system thus seem to accept that utter deference needs to be paid to the position of judge, even while recognizing that those who occupy the position may well be fallible and all too human.[44]

While judges are often placed in a distinct category from those "on the other side of the bench," there are many who believe that the best judges are those who have had some experience there. Many judges suggest that while persons with prior judicial experience may be best suited to serve on an international bench, the "ideal" candidate has also worked as a defense counsel or prosecutor as well. "I think what matters is that you know what it is like to plead before a bench," explains a judge at the ICTR, "and that witnesses might say something quite different from what you expected, the client is difficult, the preparations have to be done until midnight every evening. I mean, all these aspects of everyday life for an attorney, you mustn't forget them! So if someone asks for a slight extension, in order to consult with his client, the judges will then usually grant it. It is easier to see the necessity of that if you have been in that role yourself." A UN official concurs, noting the special expertise needed by those who judge in criminal courts. "Sometimes I have a feeling that those who are not familiar with criminal court proceedings may not understand that there's a world of difference. I mean, before the International Court of Justice, it is a case between states. It's political, perhaps highly political, and you have to be very careful. But there, you have polite counsel, sometimes coming in their national regalia. The court is addressed in the most elegant terms, and the arguments are very well prepared, and so, intellectually, this is probably a very stimulating exercise, and I don't think there are many incidents in the courtroom. The proceedings are very, shall we say, well structured, and they follow a fairly regular pattern. Whereas in the criminal court, it's completely different, because there are feelings there, witnesses, tears are shed, and there are people who are accused and who risk being sentenced to life. It's a completely different atmosphere. I think that, in a criminal court, it's important that judges actually *do* have experience of adjudicating criminal cases."

No matter what kind of court a judge serves on or his prior professional experience, a judge's ability to remain neutral is paramount. This position requires not only objectivity, but it also calls for self-reflection on the part of judges about their role within the institutions they serve and how they can best perform their work while recognizing the skills, challenges, and points of view of those on the other side of the bench.

Across the Courts

While international judges are increasingly part of the professional community developing around their unique livelihood, there is still some distance to go before they have a fully united approach to justice. The recent multiplication of international courts, each with a different subject matter, geographic and/or personal jurisdiction, and no formal linkage with one another, is a source of concern to many legal scholars and practitioners. They worry about the transformation of international law into an archipelago of self-contained, specialized legal regimes, each endowed with its own court or dispute settlement system, and the disruptive effects this could have on the ultimate unity and coherence of international law. Some suggest international judges can do a lot to prevent this by building bridges between these formally separated judicial islands.[45]

These bridges can take many forms. Judges from various international courts are beginning to meet regularly, in both an official and unofficial capacity. For instance, since the late 1990s, the president of the European Court of Human Rights attends the opening of the European Court of Justice's judicial year; the two courts are in very frequent contact, have professional exchanges, and cite each other's jurisprudence. The judges of the ECHR, headquartered in France, are in similar contact with those of the human rights court based in Costa Rica. A judge of the ECHR observes that these are their "natural sister courts—we exchange delegations with them, we go and see the Court of Justice practically once a year, and the Inter-American Court a little bit less." Judges of emerging economic courts in Africa have visited the ECJ on several occasions. The criminal courts, facing similar challenges of law, politics, and administration, attend meetings together to share ideas. Opportunities for judges to confer with colleagues across the full spectrum of international judicial bodies are more rare; the Brandeis Institute for International Judges is the only regular forum of this type.[46]

Despite such collegial interactions, there is a general acknowledgment in the international judicial sphere that the judges of the International Court of Justice occupy a privileged status, their court having the longest history and its jurisdiction being worldwide. This sense of importance has sometimes been reflected in the attitudes that the court appears to have about its fellow international courts and their judges. ICJ judges may have social interactions with other judges in The Hague—from the ICTY or the ICC—but professional exchanges or fora on judicial dialogue and cross-fertilization do not seem to be part of the court's strategy for strengthening the international judicial community. At the same time, some ICJ judges and court staff clearly feel that judgments issued by their court should carry a particular weight in the international justice system; it has even been suggested that other courts appeal to the ICJ for advisory opinions. One ICJ judge comments that some members of the bench hold onto their image of the *primus inter pares:* "There are those who say we are the UN's court; we are the primary judicial organ in the UN. It says so in the Charter. And it is helpful and useful for international law that we should all be singing from the same song sheet, even if we're performing different tasks in the field. Others feel that there should be mutual respect, and that those other institutions are going to be dealing with things we haven't, and they'll have some new ideas that can be very valuable for *us,* also." Even the Law of the Sea Tribunal, a court with comparable functions and procedures to the ICJ but focused on law of the sea disputes, has been looked at askance by some at the ICJ. The fact that both courts have relatively few cases on their dockets and that they sometimes compete for cases may well be the source of this institutional tension.

Whatever the current state of relations among international courts, they will more than likely have more contact in the future, if only because of the increasingly interconnected nature of the contemporary world. In the *Bosnia and Herzegovina v. Serbia and Montenegro* case the ICJ found that Serbia has an obligation under the 1948 Genocide Convention to cooperate with the ICTY to secure arrest and transfer of indictees.[47] The various situations currently under investigation by the International Criminal Court may well have significance for or overlap with the new African human rights court or the ICJ as well. At the same time, the complementarity principle that underlies the jurisdiction of the ICC will require increasing connections with domestic judiciaries. The availability of courts' decisions on the Internet and the kinds of meetings and institutes that bring judges of various courts together all facilitate relations among international judges, which will benefit, in turn, the institutions on which they serve.

Like other complex organizations, international courts have their strengths and weaknesses, their ways of responding to challenges, their everyday routines, and even their mind-numbing work schedules. Above all, they are shaped by the undeniable humanness of the individuals who work within their walls. International judges in the beginning of the twenty-first century are serving, for the most part, in new institutions. The parameters of their profession are still being explored and a list of "best practices" is still being compiled. Judges are beginning to constitute a real community, not just through the everyday practice of their profession but in the way they think about it. But this process of community building has clear limits. International judges are a wide-ranging bunch and, indeed, the strength of the international judiciary is founded in this very diversity. The challenge for judges is to take full advantage of what their colleagues bring individually to the international justice enterprise—in experience, training, outlook, cultural perspective, and linguistic understanding—while seeking to maximize the spirit of cooperation that is crucial for both fair and efficient work.

The shared mission of international courts—to mete out justice across borders—is furthermore founded on an acknowledgment that peoples and nations belong to a larger human community that needs to think beyond political, ethnic, or linguistic boundaries for the greater well-being of all. International judges do not just think about this community in an abstract way; their daily work both illustrates and facilitates its very existence. It is the internal operations of international courts, with all their complexities and hierarchies, tensions and contradictions, that bring their external mission within reach.

Thomas Buergenthal,
United States

*Judge of the International
Court of Justice*

In 1995, Thomas Buergenthal[1] began a speech at the U.S. Holocaust Museum with these words:

> *A few days ago, I reread an article about the Death March out of Auschwitz that I had written in 1956, only eleven years after the event. It was all still so vivid for me then: the cold Polish winter, the terrible cold, the exhausting three day march to Gliwice where we were stuffed into open railroad cars, the roadside shootings of those who could not walk anymore, my own temptation to simply sit down and get it over with, how three children—two of my friends and I—evaded being shot with the rest of the small group of children who left Birkenau with us, the tightly packed railroad car that emptied out as the dead were thrown overboard while the train moved towards Germany.[2]*

In his work as an international judge, Buergenthal has not had to imagine how it feels to be the victim of abuse and injustice. His childhood experiences have provided him with a perspective that most of his colleagues will never have on human rights violations and crimes committed by states. His adult convictions have led him to put this perspective to singular use as a member of the international judiciary.

Thomas Buergenthal was born in Lubochna, Slovakia, grew up in the Jewish ghetto of Kielce, Poland, and spent several years in the concentration camps of Auschwitz and Sachsenhausen. After World War II, he was reunited with his mother, from whom he had been separated in Auschwitz, and he emigrated to the United States in 1951. His higher education all took place in the United States, ending with LL.M. and S.J.D. degrees in international law from Harvard Law School. Between 1961 and 2000, he taught law at a number of eminent American institutions, including the University of Pennsylvania, the University of Texas, American University, Emory University, and George Washington University. Buergenthal has served on numerous committees and delegations dealing with the development and promotion of human rights and international law, and he is the recipient of an impressive number of awards and honors.

Buergenthal found himself drawn to the field of human rights law early on, when it was just coming into the consciousness of the legal community in the United States. He comments on the trajectory that was eventually to lead him to the position of judge on the Inter-American Court of Human Rights:

I must say, I had never thought of a career as a judge until it happened. When you're young, when you're a student, you dream you'd love to be on this court or that court, but it wasn't something I really thought of. I got to the Inter-American Court just by what I think was sheer accident.

It all began in 1978 with the entry into force of the American Convention on Human Rights. I was teaching at the University of Texas Law School in Austin at the time. One of the courses I taught was a seminar on international human rights law in which I also dealt with the inter-American human rights system and would regularly point out that, since the United States had not ratified the Convention, the U.S. would not be able to nominate candidates for the Court. Although I would explain that U.S. citizens could nevertheless be nominated by any other State that had ratified the Convention, I seriously doubted that this would ever happen and never missed a chance to say so. As it turned out, I could not have been more wrong.

One afternoon in early 1979 I received a telephone call from a person who identified himself as the Ambassador of Costa Rica to the United States and the Organization of the American States (OAS). His reason for calling, he explained, was the forthcoming election of judges to the soon to be established Inter-American Court of Human Rights ["the Court"]. He went on to say that he was instructed by his Government to ask whether I would allow Costa Rica to nominate me to the Court. Convinced that this was a hoax and that the caller was a student in my seminar, I thanked the caller and asked him for his phone number, ostensibly to enable me to call him back after I had had a chance to discuss the matter with my wife. I still could not quite believe it when the number proved to be that of the Costa Rican Embassy in Washington. A few months later, I was elected to the Court.[3]

Being a founding member of a new international court generated excitement, but also presented unforeseen obstacles.

Once the Court was constituted—it was formally inaugurated in San José, Costa Rica, on September 3, 1979—our work began in earnest. Among our initial tasks was the preparation of a draft Statute for the Court, which had to be approved by the OAS General Assembly. We also had to submit a draft budget to the Assembly.

First, however, we had to overcome an unexpected obstacle. Following the Court's festive inauguration, with all the pomp and ceremony Costa Rica could muster, we faced a sad reality: While our official seat was in that lovely country, its Government had not provided us with a place of our own—not even a suite of offices. As a result, we held our first working session in the bathhouse of the Costa Rican bar association. Here the voices of children swimming and jumping into the association's pool often drowned out our early drafting efforts, hardly an auspicious beginning for those of us who thought of ourselves as modern-day John Marshalls. Some time later, we moved to temporary offices in Costa Rica's Supreme Court building and eventually to permanent quarters.[4]

Buergenthal was a judge with the Inter-American Court of Human Rights from 1979 to 1991 and served as vice president and president for four of those years. It was an exciting if frustrating time to be with the court, as it was just beginning its work and faced many challenges. The first case that came to the court, Buergenthal recalls, was "unique in the annals of international jurisprudence":

Labeled Costa Rica v. Costa Rica, *the most apt description of the case, its official name, is* In the Matter of Viviana Gallardo et al. *Viviana Gallardo was a young Costa Rican woman who, with some other individuals, had been arrested by the Costa Rican police following a shoot-out in which one policeman was killed. Shortly after her arrest, while being held in a police station, Gallardo was shot dead by an off-duty policeman who was a friend of the dead officer. These events caused great consternation in Costa Rica, a country that prides itself—with good reason—on being a democracy committed to the rule of law and human rights. Fearing for Costa Rica's international reputation, the President of Costa Rica, who had earlier participated in the Court's inauguration, concluded that the ideal solution would be to submit the matter to the*

Court. After all, the Court had its seat only a few blocks from the Presidential Palace, so why not take advantage of its presence in the country and put it to work?

Although we appreciated the Costa Rican President's confidence in the Court, we had no choice but to reject the very first contentious case referred to us—assuming it could properly be described as a contentious case. The problem was that, although the exhaustion of domestic remedies requirement provided for in the Convention could in principle be waived, this was not true of the proceedings before the Inter-American Commission, which Costa Rica had also sought to waive. Unlike before the Court, individuals have standing in the Commission to present their case on equal footing with the States Parties. To allow a State to unilaterally waive a right that was designed in part to protect the interests of individuals was, in the Court's view, incompatible with the balance the Convention sought to achieve. The Court therefore ruled the case inadmissible and transferred it to the Commission, but Ms. Gallardo's family refused to pursue the matter there. So much for our first case.[5]

It took some time for important cases to reach the IAHCR. But once they did, they proved to be landmark events. Of these, among the most significant were the so-called Honduras Disappearance Cases, involving more than three hundred people in that Central American nation.

Both the admissibility and the merits phases of the Honduran Disappearance Cases presented many novel legal issues. These were, after all, the first disappearance cases ever to be referred to an international court. One difficult evidentiary issue with which the court had to deal is attributable to the fact that a government is not responsible for a person's disappearance simply because he or she disappeared in the country it governs. Responsibility for forced disappearances is therefore very difficult to attribute to governments, which is precisely why some governments engage in the practice. The court concluded, however, that this evidentiary problem can be overcome if evidence of other disappearances fitting a common pattern points to a general practice. The court accordingly ruled that, if the commission could prove that a practice of disappearances existed in Honduras and if it could show that the people disappearing in that country had engaged in similar activities or had similar backgrounds considered subversive by the government, a rebuttable presumption will have been established linking the practice to the disappearance in the specific case. The burden would then shift to the government to show that it had no part in the specific disappearance.

> *In two of the three cases comprising the Honduran Disappearance Cases—the* Velasquez Rodriguez *case and the* Godinez Cruz *case—the government did not meet its evidentiary burden and was held responsible for the individuals' forced disappearances and likely death. In the* Fairen Garbi *and* Solis Corrales *cases, Honduras successfully rebutted the presumption of its involvement because there was nothing in the backgrounds of the victims—they were Costa Ricans traveling to Mexico to visit a relative—to suggest that the Honduran authorities suspected them of anti-state activities. There was also some doubt as to whether the two Costa Ricans had in fact disappeared in Honduras, rather than in El Salvador or Guatemala. The inquiry on this issue was not helped by the failure of El Salvador and Guatemala to cooperate with the court and by the court's lack of power to compel them.*[6]

The court did find the government of Honduras responsible for the forced disappearances in two of the cases and awarded damages to the families. This was followed by a squabble between the court and the government over the timing and the amount of payments, an indication of the continuing difficulty that some international courts have with respect to issues of enforcement. Indeed, the matter remained unresolved until a former judge of the court, Carlos Roberto Reina, became president of Honduras. "The moral of the story," Buergenthal jests, "is that, when it comes to the enforcement of human rights judgments, it helps when former international human rights judges become presidents of their countries."

As judges on the Inter-American Court serve only in a part-time capacity, Buergenthal continued throughout this period to teach and carry out other professional activities. He served as dean at the American University Law School, among other academic posts. Although Buergenthal has since left the Inter-American Court and joined the bench of the International Court of Justice, he continues to feel a special enthusiasm for dealing with human rights issues.

> *What it means to suffer human rights violations is something I feel in my bones. I don't have to be told what happens in a massacre, what it is like to be disappeared or to be tortured. These are not academic subjects for me.*

The View from the International Court of Justice

In 2000, Buergenthal was working in Switzerland as vice chair of the Tribunal on Dormant (Holocaust) Accounts when he received a phone call.

Stephen Schwebel, the U.S. judge who had sat on the bench of the International Court of Justice since 1981 and was then serving as court president, wished to resign his position after completing two years of his third nine-year term. The United States had begun to consider who might replace him. As an international law expert with experience on international courts, Buergenthal's name was quickly suggested.

> *I received a call from the legal adviser of the State Department, who said to me, "You probably know that we've drawn up a list of people, individuals like you, who might be qualified for the court, but you are the only one who didn't nominate himself. Are you interested in being on the court?" Who would not be interested in being on the court? So I said, "Yes." Well, then I came home to my wife, and I said, "Don't count on it. They'll never name somebody who has not been an employee of the State Department or Justice Department."*
>
> *As time went on, I kept hearing that the list was getting shorter and shorter, and that I was still on it. People were lobbying the State Department for their candidates, and I also had some friends supporting me. Then, I was called to an interview while I was still in Switzerland. I had my first interview by phone with the selection committee, the U.S. national group, and the first question I was asked was, "You know all of the people who are on this list, of course. What distinguishes you from them?" I replied, "Well, I've served on two other international courts before," since I had also served on the Administrative Tribunal of the Inter-American Development Bank* [in addition to serving on the Inter-American Court for Human Rights]. *That helped my candidacy, I think, because it did distinguish me from the others.*

Buergenthal arrived in The Hague to take up his position as a member of the ICJ bench in March 2000. "I thought I knew something about this court and about international law before I came," he recalled in 2005. "But I can tell you that I've learned more international law in the last five years here than I did in the thirty-odd years I used to teach the subject. In teaching, you deal with the problems you like to deal with. Here you have no choice. Something is thrown at you, and you may not know anything about the subject, and you have to immerse yourself in it."

The general experience of serving on the ICJ, the oldest and most prestigious international judicial institution in the world, also strikes a contrast with Buergenthal's time at the Inter-American Court. At the ICJ, one feels the "weight of tradition," which can limit judicial creativity:

> *On the Inter-American Court, you were relatively free to strategize about judicial policy, focusing on the policy implications of a case.*

That is not how the ICJ works. At the Inter-American Court we did not have the large body of precedent that the ICJ has built up over the many decades of its existence and we were therefore freer to be more creative. The ICJ is much more formal and to some extent formalistic in its judicial approach.

At the same time, Buergenthal is enthusiastic about some of the time-honored traditions of the ICJ, like that of "writing notes." This practice requires each judge to write a preliminary opinion after the oral legal arguments have been heard in the case. These opinions are then circulated to all the other judges. The group then proceeds to arrive at a judgment through long and painstaking deliberations, taking each judge's arguments into account. The ICJ is famous for its judgments; cases are decided by a majority opinion, which is often accompanied by several dissenting or separate opinions. The deliberation process, Buergenthal says, "is something that I must say I have been genuinely impressed with."

[W]hen I came here, I thought the whole business of writing notes was a waste of time. But I have come to realize its real value, for it forces every judge to carefully study the case. And that's very important on the world court that the ICJ is. The process has many disadvantages, if only because it takes time for us to render a judgment. But it ensures that the views of all judges from all regions of the world have been taken into account, and that has great value.

Of course, this system also tends to produce many separate or dissenting opinions since it is easy for judges to transform their notes into individual opinions if they feel that the judgment does not fully reflect their particular views in the case. Sometimes I feel that too many such opinions are written and that we should only resort to them when we conclude that important principles were not taken into account in the majority opinion.

Buergenthal's experience with other international courts and his openness to having a dialogue with other international judges are reflected in his recognition of the value of other courts' jurisprudence.

Contrary to what one would think, we at the ICJ do read decisions of other courts that bear on what we are doing. And even though we don't cite them—I've written and said we should cite them, but we don't cite them—we do read them, and we take different views into account when they are relevant. The same is true of important national court decisions. The argument for not citing other court decisions or academic writings is that it avoids criticism that we are influenced by the views of one or the other region of the world. There is always the question, for example, that if we cited the European

Court of Human Rights, somebody from Africa or Asia might say, "Why are they only relying on this European Court of Human Rights as the authority?" We don't cite authors because [people would] say, "How come you cited X and you didn't cite Y?" On the Inter-American Court, we did cite the ICJ and we cited the European Court of Human Rights, and initially we even cited academic authorities. Eventually, though, we decided not to cite academic authorities in order to avoid criticism from a variety of quarters. But in my opinion there is no good reason for not citing the judgments of other international courts.

One of the striking characteristics of international courts is the diversity of the people who work in them. They are of different nationalities, language groups, religions, political systems, and, of course, professional training and experience. Buergenthal comments on the misunderstanding that this diversity sometimes creates in the mind of the public:

The question I get very often, and what I think the public should know, is that what unites international court judges is the fact that we are trained in the international legal system. Contrary to what some people believe, international law is a distinct legal system not unlike the civil law or common law system. That is, we share a common theoretical approach to the legal problems before us. In our analysis of a legal problem, we draw on the doctrines and methodologies of the international legal system. That unites us, regardless of where we judges come from. Moreover, most of my colleagues have studied international law not only in their countries but also in the major teaching centers of our field in the world. That, too, is a unifying factor.

Not the Typical American

Thomas Buergenthal is "the American judge" at the ICJ, and his nationality was noteworthy at the Inter-American Court of Human Rights, since the United States is not a party to that institution. His life story and his experience as a professor and judge have contributed to Buergenthal's deep convictions about the importance of U.S. ideals and the rule of law, but he also brings a distinctly cosmopolitan perspective to his work.

I'm an American in the sense that I love America and feel like an American. We immigrants probably have a greater attachment to America than the native-born Americans. We were taken in by America and we were made part of it. And I am here as an American on this court, and that means a tremendous amount to me because I know there are not many countries in the world that would nominate a naturalized citizen to serve on such a court. At the same time, having been born in Europe, I don't think like an American from the Midwest, the West, or even from New York, for example. It is therefore probably easier for me to understand how my colleagues, who come from different countries, think.

Buergenthal has shown himself willing to speak out boldly on the role of the United States in world affairs—of course, on matters that are not before the court. At commencement at American University in Washington, D.C., in 2002, he offered an unsparing critique of U.S. policy. He recalled that he was in The Hague on September 11, 2001; in the aftermath of the attack on the World Trade Center and the Pentagon, he felt an outpouring of support from the Dutch and other Europeans. This warmth stands, he continued, in stark contrast to the "great disappointment" that followed more recent U.S. policies.

It is a disappointment that I share because I believe that these actions are misguided and not in the interest of the United States. They undermine what I have always believed to be our commitment to a world where the rule of law, the protection of human rights and democracy are the core building blocks of our foreign policy. [These actions] undermine the ideological and moral force of the policies of interest we seek to promote. That is why some of our actions are so difficult for our friends around the world to understand, and why they are so harmful to America's long-term political, economic and social interests.

The most recent example . . . is the administration's announcement two weeks ago withdrawing the United States' signature from the Rome Treaty establishing the permanent international criminal courts.[7] Since we have not ratified this treaty, the withdrawal of our signature is designed to express our opposition to the court in the strongest terms, and what is more significant, to allow us to pressure other countries, particularly those who rely on U.S. aid, not to ratify or to operate with the court, which is the real and professed objective of this action. . . . But our almost messianic and fanatical opposition to the International Criminal Court is a manifestation of a negative unilateralism on the part of the U.S. that hurts our image abroad and prevents us from playing a constructive role in the promotion of international legal norms consistent with the ideals this country stands for. What is so objectionable about this attitude is not necessarily our opposition to this or that treaty provision or collective measure—reasonable people can differ on the need or wisdom of one or the other—what is objectionable is that we are pursuing these policies without giving serious thought to their consequences in undermining the international rule of law. One has the feeling that those responsible for these policies could not care less. This is our new, in-your-face diplomacy. It is bad for the United States and bad for the world, which we are part of whether we like it or not. It is a world that we need as much as it needs us.[8]

Reflecting later about his outspokenness on U.S. policy, Buergenthal traces his depth of feeling to his personal history:

I am very emotional about it because I came to America in 1951, roughly during the McCarthy period, and the country survived it. What followed was this tremendous blossoming of the civil rights movement. And despite or maybe even because of Vietnam, what followed was the implementation of a U.S. foreign policy, for which the Carter administration deserves much of the credit, that gave priority to human rights considerations and gave impetus to the contemporary human rights revolution. And now we're just throwing it away by focusing on the "war" on terrorism without realizing that it cannot be won if we do not safeguard the human rights of our adversaries.

Buergenthal addressed U.S. policy again in 2004 in a commencement address at George Washington University. "Unlike in the past," he said, "American lawyers can today no longer afford to leave matters relating to international law and international relations to diplomats, political scientists or politicians. . . . America has much to give to the world and much to learn from it, and we lawyers have an important role to play in the process. It is critical, therefore, that America not weaken its commitment to the rule of law, to human rights, to democracy, to tolerance, and its compassion for the suffering of others."[9] Buergenthal's outspokenness on that occasion was of particular note because it came just a year before the process of his reelection to the ICJ was slated to begin. He was, however, renominated by the Bush administration, and then reelected by the UN General Assembly and Security Council in November 2005. His term on the ICJ continues until 2015.

4 ☘ International Judges and International Law

A Matter of Interpretation

Judges and Justices are servants of the law, not the other way around. Judges are like umpires. Umpires don't make the rules, they apply them. The role of an umpire and a judge is critical. They make sure everybody plays by the rules, but it is a limited role. Nobody ever went to a ball game to see the umpire. Judges have to have the humility to recognize that they operate within a system of precedent shaped by other judges equally striving to live up to the judicial oath.[1]

So John Roberts began his statement at the Senate Judiciary Committee hearings in 2005 to confirm his appointment to the pinnacle of the U.S. judicial system. Although the baseball metaphor is a distinctly American turn of phrase, Roberts echoed an age-old judicial posture on the value of neutrality. In the early 1600s, another chief justice, this time of the King's Bench (England), Lord Edward Coke, made a similar declaration: "It is the function of a judge not to make but to declare the law, according to the golden mete-wand of the law and not by the crooked cord of discretion."[2] The philosopher Francis Bacon, who, not being a judge, perhaps did not feel the need to profess absolute objectivity and fidelity to the letter of the law, promptly rebutted, "Judges must beware of hard constructions, and strained inferences; for there is no worse torture, than the torture of laws."[3] The two Englishmen's statements perfectly epitomize the poles of a debate that has gripped minds for centuries: is there is such a thing as a truly objective judge, one who can simply apply existing laws, without adding, subtracting, or changing them? If so, is such a machine-like judge desirable?

The law is the space within which a judge of any kind and at any level has to operate; no actor in the field, regardless of background or ideology, will disagree. Unless the judge is expressly requested to set the law aside to employ meta-legal criteria like equity and fairness to decide the case (what lawyers call "deciding *ex aequo et bono*"), the judge must situate the case and the judgment within the boundaries of the law, lest the decision be illegitimate and even unlawful. Application of the law to the facts ensures the formal correctness of the judgment. Before any law is applied, however, it needs to be interpreted, and this is where agreement stops.

Despite the efforts of generations of legal scholars and all the resources found in libraries of legal theory and jurisprudence, the interpretation of law remains more an art than a science. There has always been a certain mystique about judges and the arcana of "making the law speak," but the process of interpreting laws is not arbitrary. General principles put limits on how loosely a given law may be interpreted. A statute, for example, must be interpreted so as to be internally consistent. Lists are intentionally to the exclusion of what is not included in the list. General law shall not derogate from specific law. These principles, among many others, are drilled into young minds at law schools around the world.

General principles, however, leave ample room for maneuvering and ideological battles. To simplify grossly, at one end of the spectrum there is "judicial activism," which results in, or does not exclude, some form of lawmaking role for the judiciary in interpreting the law. At the other end lies "judicial restraint," which explicitly rejects a lawmaking role for judges. In the United States, the debate is notoriously lively, especially as concerns federal and state constitutions, but all countries experience variations of the same dilemma. In one corner of the ring are the strict formalists and constructivists, whose theories are known as "textualism," "originalism," or "strict constructionism," emphasizing careful adherence to the text of laws as that text would have been understood by those who adopted it. In the opposite corner are those embracing the theory of the "living constitution," which claims that a statute is organic and must be read so as to keep it consistent with the prevailing values of a society at the time the judgment is rendered. Between these extremes lie a plethora of more nuanced theories and positions.

Wherever one's position on the spectrum from activism to constructionism, the debate is always framed within the context of the law. To decide a case, any judge, domestic or international, applies two bodies of law. "Procedural law" refers to the mechanics of the legal process; that is to say, the body of rules and practice by which justice is administered. "Substantive law" is the set of rules that determines rights and duties in general under the law; (for example, the right to a piece of land, the right not to be tortured, and so on).

Yet, this legal space in which judges operate is substantially different at the national and the international levels. International judges, and particularly the members of the current generation of judges, face somewhat different problems from their national peers. Unlike national judges, international judges do not inherit courts of law; they need to build them. The credibility and legitimacy of their courts cannot be relied upon, but must be established. International judges are keenly aware that while their decisions can be sweeping and influential, they work in fragile institutions.

As compared to their national peers, international judges have a wider margin of maneuver, because the legal boundaries that frame their actions are often less clearly demarcated, and perhaps less patrolled. International lawmaking is still a prerogative of states, directly by way of treaties or indirectly through international organizations. Therefore international judges do not have, on the face of it, much room to participate in the lawmaking process. Yet, in reality, international law tends to be more fluid and less precise than most national laws, thus creating significant opportunities to push the law in new directions.

As the number of courts increases and as those courts produce an impressive volume of decisions, the claim that international judges do not make international law is increasingly anachronistic. In one sense every international court is a world unto itself, but in another, each court is an island in the same sea of international law. Significant evidence indicates that, lack of formal coordination notwithstanding, courts are engaged in a sort of jurisprudential dialogue whose grammar still needs to be deciphered.

Procedural Law

As every lawyer knows, procedure is substance. This is perhaps truer for international courts than domestic courts, since the range of issues regulated by international courts' rules of procedure is much larger—albeit not necessarily deeper—than that of national procedural laws. Rules of procedure of an international court do not merely address matters of internal organization of the court, like judges' terms, precedence, status, disciplining and removal of judges, election of the president and registrar, and deliberations. They also govern issues directly affecting the parties, like institution and conduct of proceedings (oral/written phase and incidental proceedings), representation of the parties, evidence, admissibility, and judgments (both interpretation and revision). In international criminal courts, rules of procedure might even regulate such crucial issues as conduct of investigations, transfer and detention of suspects, rights of suspects, assignment and appointment of counsel, indictments, orders and warrants, production of evidence and disclosure, depositions, motions, and rules of evidence, to name only a few.

Considering the breadth and importance of international procedural law, it is remarkable that international judges have the last word on much of it. Indeed, with very few exceptions, after lengthy negotiations on the structure and jurisdiction of the court, which are set in the statute and other constitutive instruments, governments prefer to leave judges to determine for themselves how the court will operate. Once the rules of procedure are adopted, moreover, they still remain the domain of the judges, who can amend them as they see fit. Governmental diplomacy plays little or no role in the process.

In this regard, the process at the national level is significantly different. Although in many countries judges are usually involved in drafting or revising national courts' rules of procedure, generally the government (executive and/or legislature) leads the process. At the international level, governments typically rubberstamp the rules that judges themselves have drafted.

Granted, international judges do not have unfettered power. Rules of procedure, and any other rules, need to be consistent with each court's constitutive instruments and statute, drafted and adopted by governments in diplomatic conferences. A court cannot confer on itself a jurisdiction that the constitutive instruments have not provided for. Yet through the rules of procedure and their implementation, international judges might significantly alter the essential nature of a court in a way unforeseen by the governments that created it. The more concise the constitutive instruments and statute, the greater the margin of maneuver will be. The closer judges get to the limits of lawmaking by expanding the boundaries of their interpretations, the more uneasy will be the governments whose agents or citizens appear before those judges.

Procedure can be tricky political ground, and states are sometimes reluctant to relinquish ultimate control over it. One of the reasons governments often prefer to settle disputes through arbitration rather than submitting to standing international courts is because governments, not judges, control the arbitration procedure. If the parties do not resort to ready-made sets of rules, they may even write the procedure itself.[4]

Wrestling for Control of Procedure

Of all international courts, two provide recent, though dissimilar, examples of the tug-of-war that exists between judges and governments over control of procedure: the WTO Appellate Body and the International Criminal Court. In the first, judges were left ample margin of maneuver, which they used to shape the court in a quite unforeseen way. In the second, states were careful to create unprecedented restrictions on the discretion of the judges to create procedural rules.

In 1994, the World Trade Organization replaced the General Agreement on Tariffs and Trade (GATT) as the legal and institutional framework for world trade.[5] The WTO departs from the GATT in many ways, but one of the most crucial is the way disputes are settled between members. Disputes under the GATT had been settled for almost fifty years through a procedure more like diplomatic conciliation than adjudication. It was a very flexible procedure, one giving parties many options and ways out, should they not be satisfied with the results. The stress was on compromise rather than on adherence to the letter of the GATT.

The WTO Dispute Settlement Understanding (DSU) introduced a new, binding dispute settlement mechanism.[6] WTO members intended to increase the legal discipline of the international trade regime, but they surely did not plan to judicialize it.[7] One significant difference from the past is that rulings of dispute settlement panels can be appealed before a new organ: the Appellate Body.

"Rather than creating an international trade tribunal of last resort," notes the first chief administrator of the Appellate Body (who in other international judicial bodies would be called the registrar), "the negotiators anticipated that the Appellate Body would hear only a few appeals in the first few years and would have time to develop its own procedures and *modus operandi* incrementally over time."[8] The Appellate Body, in the negotiators' minds, was going to be a safety net of last resort, activated only sporadically, in the unlikely event that panels went seriously astray.

Because the Appellate Body was not supposed to be the pinnacle of the dispute settlement system, the negotiators of the WTO agreements did not spend much time working out the details. The founding document, the Dispute Settlement Understanding (DSU), thus provides very little guidance on the functioning of the Appellate Body; only one article of fourteen subparagraphs addresses this topic. In this regard, the WTO AB is very different from other international tribunals, whose statutes are usually the result of lengthy and complex negotiations and are considerably detailed.[9] Because the Appellate Body was also given the power to draft its own rules of procedure[10]—as usually happens among international courts—the first members of the WTO AB were given de facto unprecedented power to shape the very structure of the organization's dispute settlement system. And they used it. The DSU does not provide for oral hearings, for example, but from the beginning the members of the Appellate Body felt compelled to opt for a more courtlike and less bureaucratic approach by listening to the parties' pleadings in the deliberations room.[11]

While some framers of the DSU may have foreseen and desired a certain degree of judicialization, its eventual extent took many WTO member states by surprise. The Appellate Body, far from being a venue of occasional last resort, now decides dozens of cases per year and is widely considered a true international court.[12] "Governments didn't want it to be really a judicial process," says one member of the WTO AB. "The idea was to still have a diplomatic process, but more disciplined. They created the Appellate Body with only the mandate to control the interpretation and application of the law, but once the body started operating, it quickly became obvious that it could not be like that. . . . It has become more businesslike, from a legal point of view."[13]

Many also agree that had the first members of the Appellate Body not been mostly lawyers, but instead diplomats, as in the GATT system, the WTO process would have probably remained much closer to its diplomatic roots. One of the first members of the WTO AB recalls the seminal period when the first group drew up the rules of procedure. "These three weeks probably were the germ," he recalls, "the seed from which the rest then grew. . . . .We were basically a group of pure lawyers. None of us had been involved in the previous system, except our chairman, Julio Lacarte Muró, who had been there since day one of the GATT and thus was an extremely influential man because of his experience, personality, and age. But Lacarte underwent a fundamental change of outlook and was won over by the lawyers' side. Had he said, 'No, all this is impossible and politically unacceptable,' et cetera, we would probably not have gone as far. He would have had, I believe, the authority to say, 'You are totally missing the goal.' We might have done the same thing anyway, but it would have been much more difficult."

WTO member states have not been completely acquiescent to this judicialization, nor have they entirely renounced control over the process. On two particularly important issues, the Appellate Body encountered resistance as it tested the limits of its power to decide how cases are handled. On both issues, the Appellate Body tried to open proceedings to civil society—people and groups other than member states and their representatives. Member states resisted the change, concerned about the lack of control and interference with quiet diplomacy that outsiders might bring with them.

The first issue was the decision to allow private lawyers, rather than just lawyers employed by governments themselves, to represent member states during hearings. That was a significant departure from the previous tradition, which stressed interaction between members through classic diplomatic channels and states' governmental representatives. Again, the change can be explained by the fact that it was mainly lawyers with significant experience outside of the GATT who implemented the new regime. "During the first cases, the lawyers were sitting in the hall, and the representatives were running all the time back and forth to us," recounts one member of the WTO AB. "From the outset, the Appellate Body decided to act as a tribunal and said, 'What is this nonsense? You are free to put in your delegation anyone you want. That's the way it is in international law.'" The participation of private lawyers is now standard practice at the WTO AB.

On a second issue, however, the Appellate Body generated considerable resistance from states. Shortly after its formation, it took the first steps toward allowing submission of amici curiae briefs by nongovernmental organizations. These submissions would bring formally into the WTO AB information on a point of law (or some other aspect of the case) from NGOs with the status of "friends of the court." However, after the WTO AB gingerly tested the waters in a small number of cases,[14] the majority of WTO members issued a rebuke in unusually strong terms (by the very diplomatic standards of the organization), and the Appellate Body was forced to backpedal.[15]

The International Criminal Court provides a second example of how sensitive the drafting of rules of procedure can be and how reluctant governments might be *not* to have the last word in these matters.

The original draft statute of the ICC, prepared by the International Law Commission in 1995, followed the tradition whereby judges draft the rules and states approve them.[16] Subsequent amendments decided by the judges would enter into force by default unless rejected by the states parties.[17] Between 1996 and 1998, however, during the negotiations leading to the adoption of the ICC statute (the so-called Rome Statute), a split emerged between those who wanted the rules to be incorporated as much as possible into the statute, and hence diplomatically negotiated, and those who wanted to leave them to judges. At stake were not only the length and complexity of negotiations, but also the efficiency of the court, the rights of suspects and accused, and ultimately the extent to which states parties, as contrasted to the judges, would determine the procedures by which their agents and those within their jurisdiction would be affected. One faction believed that giving "legislative power" to judges was at odds with the rule of law, while the opposing group felt that this process would promote institutional adaptability.[18] It is likely that the delegates at the Rome conference were concerned by confusions created by the judges' constant tinkering with the rules of procedure of the Yugoslavia tribunal; those rules had been amended fourteen times between 1994 and 1998 alone.[19]

Eventually, those who wished to restrain the judges prevailed. Rather than letting the judges themselves write their rules, the founders of the ICC created an ad hoc diplomatic conference, the Preparatory Commission, which met in New York between 1999 and 2002. The "PrepCom," as it was called, drafted the overarching rules of procedure, while the judges themselves were left the task of drafting the "regulations," a document limited to the internal functioning and organization of the court.[20] The importance attributed by governments to states' controlling the wording of the rules was highlighted by the fact that any state, regardless of whether or not it was a party to the statute, was given the chance to participate fully in the PrepCom. This was motivated partly by public relations reasons (participation in the PrepCom might induce new states to sign onto the court), but also because governments recognized that nonparties, and even those states with no intention of becoming parties, had to be given the opportunity to prevent the court from extending its powers beyond the strict statutory limits.

Breaking New Ground

It is obvious that the first judges to be elected or appointed to a newly established court play a critical role in the history of the body, since they lay its foundations. Typically, they have to adopt not only the rules of procedure, but also a series of other critical legal instruments that regulate the court's functioning, like judicial guidelines and resolutions on practice, working procedures, rules of conduct, and many other documents. Judges who participated in the creation of the contemporary international courts fondly recall those days as exciting, a period of intense and deliberate work and debate with their colleagues, without the strictures and pressures of pending cases.[21] "You realize you are inventing something important—you have to make it work," one judge recalls about the first days at the ICTR. Failure to adopt rules is not an option, and it is better to get them right the first time. Either it is very difficult to change them afterwards—because of natural and institutional inertia, or because an overcrowded docket does not leave time to reconsider the rules—or excessive tinkering might be frowned upon as a violation of the principle of legality, which mandates a certain stability and predictability of laws.

The judges who built the foundations of today's international judicial bodies during the 1990s and early years of the twenty-first century will go down in history as a generation of legal pioneers. Their work is all the more remarkable if one considers that often they had little or no precedent to draw upon. This is very evident in the case of the ICTY, whose judges had to look back as far as the Nuremberg and Tokyo military tribunals after World War II to find another international criminal court. And those models, because of both the different context and the limited rights they accorded to the defense, were not particularly helpful. The rules of procedure of the ICTY had to be pulled out of thin air.

The ICTY has been often criticized for tinkering too much with its own rules of procedure. Since their adoption in February 1994, those rules have been amended thirty-seven times, on average more than three times a year. Admittedly, many of these amendments have been minor—the basic structure laid down at the beginning still exists—but it is undeniable that the ICTY has largely been a trial-and-error exercise. This process might look rather quirky to those accustomed to the stability of domestic procedural law, but the first judges of the ICTY had little alternative. As the first president of the tribunal, Antonio Cassese, explained to the UN General Assembly, "It would have been impossible for the first truly international criminal tribunal to have adopted the first ever international criminal procedural and evidentiary code from a first draft dealing perfectly with all the diverse issues with which the Tribunal has to cope. . . . It would have equally been impossible for the issues . . . to have been perfectly anticipated and solved at the beginning of 1994 [before the commencement of the first proceedings]."22 When judging the legacy of the ICTY and also the ICTR, one has to keep in mind the critical contribution that those two tribunals, and specifically the first bench of each, made to international criminal law. Subsequent criminal courts, like the Special Court for Sierra Leone and the International Criminal Court, have had the considerable advantage of having a template on which they could work and improve.

Whenever useful precedents and templates are available in international justice, cut-and-paste is widely employed. If one were to draw the genealogical tree of the procedural law of international tribunals, one could find countless examples of borrowing. The procedure of the International Court of Justice is basically that of its predecessor, the Permanent Court of International Justice, which in turn was influenced by the rules of procedure of arbitration, particularly those of the Permanent Court of Arbitration. The ICJ rules have inspired those of the International Tribunal of the Law of the Sea. The rules of the European Court of Justice have been studied and mimicked by the courts of many regional economic integration agreements. The rules of the European Court of Human Rights inspired those of the Inter-American Court of Human Rights, and both were used as template for the African Court of Human and Peoples' Rights. Wordings in many courts' rules, on such issues as the qualifications of international judges, the requirement of independence and impartiality, restrictions upon incompatible outside activities of international judges, often mirror one another. The rules on the institution of proceedings and extension of time limits are usually very similar. When neither the constituent instruments nor the rules of procedure nor practice directions address a particular procedural matter, it is only natural for international judges, as well as the parties, to refer to the practice of other international courts to find inspiration to resolve the question.23

Civil Law versus Common Law Approaches to Procedure

The divide between civil law and common law traditions affects debate over procedural law as well. How much a given set of rules is the product of one legal system or another is in the eyes of the beholders, who quickly fix their attention on elements that seem unfamiliar. When considering the same set of rules, judges from common law countries tend to see a lot of civil law, while those with civil law backgrounds tend to see a lot of common law. Former national judges tend to obsess about the origin of international rules of procedure more than others; one such judge casually observes that such rules are not as strict as those in a domestic setting, perhaps suggesting that they might also be less "lawlike." Former diplomats murmur that the rules are too strict, unrealistic, or blind to political realities. Within Europe, lawyers from the United Kingdom or Ireland point out this or that rule as being "very French"; the French suggest the same rule is "very German."

Veteran judges agree that in the day-to-day life of international courts, the "DNA" of any rule of procedure has little or no importance. The rules form a legal system sui generis, a world of its own that must work and satisfy everyone's sense of justice. A judge who helped establish two international courts, the ICTR and the ICC, pragmatically notes, "What you are inventing is a balance of the two legal systems [common law and civil law], but so many things are new. . . . We were each very territorial and arrogant about our own systems. But then you have to agree. You have to make it work. So you accept each other's suggestions. You can live with it. So you don't insist on a 'no hearsay' rule, for instance. We would debate and debate the different procedures and realize, finally, that the principle is the same."

"The conflict between civil and common law is overstated," another judge agrees. "Look at this tribunal. We have no prohibition against hearsay. And that has been stated in the case law ever since the beginning. And some common law lawyers are saying, 'Oh, how can one trust such a system?' But now we have delivered seventeen judgments involving twenty-three accused, and I don't know of *one* example where hearsay evidence has been the only basis for convicting anyone. In other words, everyone would be *so* careful with it! This is more a battle of words than substance."

In the end, the more international courts that are created and the more precedents that they generate, the easier it will be to create new rules. Moreover, the more that courts borrow procedural laws from one another, the faster a common, truly international procedural law will emerge. This will have a doubly beneficial effect. First, it will reduce the significance of the tension between common law and civil law. Second, it will make it easier for a corps of international judicial professionals to emerge, people who are able to rotate with ease between courts. That will go a long way toward transforming the current array of international courts, through informal communication with each other, into a full-fledged international judicial system. How fast that will happen, and whether that can happen only at the behest of judges and without governmental intervention, remains to be seen.

Substantive Law

Having set down the rules of procedure, courts begin to hear cases, make decisions, and rule on concrete issues regarding specific cases and situations. As we have seen, governments largely let international judges write international procedural law, as a matter of expedience. Substantive law, however, is another matter. In this area, states are considerably more reluctant to let judges create law. Yet all laws need to be interpreted; when disputes are brought before international courts, judges are given a chance to clarify and elaborate upon what states originally meant.

Finding International Law

The process of learning what international substantive law actually is often bewilders domestic lawyers. Civil law lawyers are at loss because the great majority of international law is not neatly systematized into ordered codes. Common law lawyers are comfortable with multiple sources, but they are commensurately baffled by the lack of a fail-safe and agreed-upon system to determine which sources and precedents overrule which. Both groups are at a loss when researching international law because one has to look at dozens of sources without ever being certain of having found them all. A few international judges who started their careers as domestic judges share the same hesitancy. Yet the process of finding international substantive law is far from arbitrary.

International law has three main sources, in increasing order of specificity and relevance: general principles of law; custom; and international treaties.

General principles of law are those principles commonly found in the major legal systems of the world.

Customary international law is the product of the consistent practice of a majority of states, supported by the belief that the practice is obligatory. Customary international law is law for all states, regardless of whether they participated in the formation of the custom. A state is bound by customary international law simply by virtue of being a state.

International treaty law is comprised of obligations that states expressly and voluntarily accept between themselves by entering into agreements. Whatever states agree to, that is law as far as their relations are concerned.

Each of these sources presents significant problems. General principles of law are a source of international law in their own right, but they are resorted to rarely, and only when there is no applicable treaty or practice, or when the practice is unclear or inconsistent. Besides, general principles tend to be so generic that their usefulness is limited.

Custom can also be vague, and the process of determining states' practice on a given issue can be esoteric and controversial. Exactly how many states need to behave in a certain way for that behavior to become mandatory? Forty? Fifty? More than half of all states? Two-thirds? Most? Equally distributed around the globe? Is it a matter of numbers or also of *which* states? If 180 states claim a right to have a territorial sea extending 200 miles from the shore (currently, the custom is 12 miles), but the United States, Russia, China, the United Kingdom, Brazil, Japan, Australia, France, Nigeria, Argentina, Chile, South Africa, Canada, and India object and insist on 12 miles, is it still plausible to claim that 200 miles is the custom? For how long does the behavior need to be practiced? One day? One week? One month? One year? One decade? One century? Where exactly does one look to determine how states behave on a certain issue? Is what they say and do more important to this end than what they do not say and do not do? Most of all, how does one know if states act in a certain way because they feel they ought to or simply as a matter of convenience or civility? What weight should be given to a state's objections to a certain emergent rule of customary international law—and does it matter if that state is a major player in world politics? For instance, the United States was, until recently, one of the few countries in the world that insisted on executing criminals for offenses they had committed when they were juveniles.[24] Only a handful of other countries, outliers on human rights like China, Iran, Pakistan, Yemen, and Saudi Arabia, shared this practice. Can we say execution of juvenile offenders is forbidden as a matter of customary international law? These are key issues on which there are no clear-cut answers, at least not as clear-cut as any domestic lawyer might be used to.

The importance of custom in international law has historically decreased; treaties have gradually replaced it as the main source of that law. Understandably, many people feel the need to take uncertainty out of international law by writing it down in a form that is ascertainable, retrievable, and definitive. Throughout the twentieth century, international organizations did much to codify customary rules. The Geneva Conventions on the treatment of prisoners of war and protection of civilians, for example, have largely codified long-standing humanitarian customs.[25]

Codification of custom is an enormous task since, to be effective, it needs to be as consensual as possible. In 1947, the General Assembly of the United Nations created the International Law Commission (ILC), a body of thirty-four international legal scholars, acting as individuals and not as officials representing their respective states, with the purpose of codifying and promoting international law.[26] The ILC has done much during its fifty years of existence, but everyone agrees that it has barely scratched the surface. Moreover, it is not a lawmaking body per se. Sometimes the results of its codification work are transformed by the General Assembly into a multilateral treaty that then needs to be ratified by member states to become law.

While the number of bilateral and multilateral treaties is always on the rise, the body of written international law is still far from comprehensive. The changing nature of international relations and technical developments constantly creates issues that require new or modified international regulations. Yet the international legal system, unlike national systems, does not have a universally accepted lawmaking body. There is no World Congress with legislative authority. The General Assembly of the United Nations passes nonbinding resolutions and, from time to time, adopts draft treaties. Although the Security Council passes binding resolutions, the argument that it is a "legislature" is highly controversial.[27] Legislation through treaties tends to be slow, significantly slower than lawmaking at the national level. Finally, disputes usually arise precisely when there are no treaties or when the meaning of treaties is uncertain. If the issues were perfectly clear, the dispute would probably never have arisen in the first place.

With the exception of trial-level chambers in international criminal courts, and sometimes human rights courts, most international judges spend the greater part of their time not so much ascertaining facts and deciding who did what, but actually deciding whether what was done was consistent with international law. This requires interpreting what international law prescribes in the first place. When the ICJ rendered its advisory opinion on the legality of the Israeli security barrier, it did not have to determine whether a wall had actually been built, and by whom.[28] Rather, it spent most of its energies on determining whether the UN charter gave the General Assembly the power to request the opinion and whether the court could answer it; what international humanitarian law and human rights law prescribe; whether that law is applicable to the Occupied Territories; what is allowed by the rules on self-defense in international law; what customary international law is on "necessity" as a defense for violating international law; and what are the legal consequences of breaches of international law by Israel. In other words, it was all about determining what international law has to say about whether or not the wall, as constructed, was legal.

Nevertheless, international judges, unlike their domestic peers, do not operate in a structured system of checks and balances, where the legislature can easily intervene to modify the repercussions of a judgment. In this context, interpretation and ideological approaches become paramount. Wittingly or unwittingly, judges might turn into legislators, crossing the line between applying the law and making the law. Understandably, this is rather controversial.

The Emperor's New Clothes

Do international judges have international law–making powers? In theory, besides the adoption of procedural rules, they do not. Much like in the case of an arbitral tribunal, a judgment of an international court is law only for the parties concerned, not for anyone else. Rulings of international courts are *not* a source of international law. The received notion is that they are only a "subsidiary means for the determination of rules of law."[29] These rulings are not sources of rights and obligations for the contesting states. Like the writings of the most distinguished legal scholars, they are documentary sources indicating where evidence of the existence of the rules established by the canonical sources can be found.[30] What is more, the judgment is not even law for the court itself, as there is no such thing as a principle of stare decisis in international law; international courts are not bound by precedents, not even their own.

In the highly politically charged advisory opinion, *Legality of the Threat or Use of Nuclear Weapons,* the International Court of Justice went out of its way to make it clear that it is not a legislator of any sort.[31] "It is clear that the Court cannot legislate," the *Nuclear Weapons* judgment asserted, "and, in the circumstances of the present case, it is not called upon to do so. Rather its task is to engage in its normal judicial function of ascertaining the existence or otherwise of legal principles and rules applicable to the threat or use of nuclear weapons. The contention that the giving of an answer to the question posed would require the Court to legislate is based on a supposition that the present *corpus juris* is devoid of relevant rules in this matter. The Court could not accede to this argument; it states the existing law and does not legislate. This is so even if, in stating and applying the law, the Court necessarily has to specify its scope and sometimes note its general trend."[32] In reality, it is exactly when "specifying the scope of the applicable law and noting its trend" that international judges have a chance to play a part in shaping or reshaping, progressively or regressively, international law.

The de facto lawmaking role played by international judges cannot be denied. The European and the Inter-American courts of human rights have put a lot of flesh around the bare bones of the European and American conventions of human rights, far beyond what the original drafters might have conceived. Just to pick two examples out of dozens, consider the decisions of the IACHR in the 1980s on forced disappearances of persons (*desaparecidos*), which paved the way for a reconsideration of the rules on state responsibility, human rights law, and international criminal law.[33] According to the Rome Statute of the International Criminal Court, forced disappearances are now a crime against humanity, which thus cannot be subject to a statute of limitation.[34] Alternatively, consider the decisions of the ECHR on human rights in the private sphere.[35] The European Convention on Human Rights was originally conceived to protect against direct governmental intrusion. However, through constant jurisprudence, the ECHR has gradually established a doctrine of requiring state intervention and responsibility to safeguard the human rights of individuals against violations committed by other individuals.[36]

Without the key contribution of the European Court of Justice, the process of European integration would have stalled repeatedly because of the reluctance of various member states.[37] Landmarks in the ECJ's history are considered to be the *Van Gend en Loos* decision, which established the direct effect of EC laws in the legal system of member states;[38] the *Francovich* case, which established that member states can be held financially liable for losses resulting from nonimplementation of EC directives;[39] and the *Costa v. ENEL* case, which established the doctrine of supremacy, that is to say, the capacity of a norm of European Community law to overrule inconsistent norms of national law in domestic court proceedings.[40] These are just a few among many rulings with which the ECJ considerably expanded the power and reach of EC laws to the detriment of national laws. Unsurprisingly, these are the very same cases that "Euro-skeptics" cite to illustrate the dangers that an activist ECJ might pose to member states' sovereignty.

The ad hoc tribunals for Yugoslavia and Rwanda and the Special Court for Sierra Leone have set the standard for what it means to have a fair trial in an international context. They have also given life to the Geneva Conventions and to the 1948 Genocide Convention.[41] These tribunals have expanded the field of international criminal law enormously. Before the ICTR ruled, in the *Akayesu* case, that widespread or systematic commission of acts of sexual violence against a civilian population is a crime against humanity, international law's position on the subject was rather ambiguous.[42] Similarly, heads of state have historically enjoyed extensive immunity from prosecution under international law, but the SCSL made significant inroads in limiting such immunities when it took the step to indict and try the former Liberian president, Charles Taylor, for crimes he ordered to be committed in Sierra Leone while he was president of Liberia.[43]

The International Court of Justice has led the way in many areas of international law, despite the claims in its *Nuclear Weapons* decision that its lawmaking powers are limited.[44] One 1949 advisory opinion, *Reparation for Injuries Suffered in the Service for the United Nations,* for example, put an end to the idea that international law applies purely to sovereign states and not to international organizations.[45] A 1951 advisory opinion, *Reservations to the Genocide Convention,* led to a reappreciation of the rules applicable to reservations to treaties.[46] In the 1951 *Fisheries* case, the court made a fundamental contribution in maritime delimitation, articulating the doctrine of straight baselines from which the territorial sea should be measured, thus putting an end to much uncertainty and many disputes.[47]

Finally, the Appellate Body of the World Trade Organization has begun developing a consistent jurisprudence, not only filling many gaps in the organization's fundamental treaties but also taking WTO law in unexpected directions. In the *United States — Shrimp* case, the Appellate Body shocked member governments when it ruled that WTO rules should not be interpreted in "clinical isolation" from other bodies of international law.[48] While this was self-evident to most international lawyers, for GATT/WTO diplomats who were used to an extremely self-contained regime and who were suspicious of external influences, this was a historic change.

Granted, sometimes the jurisprudence of international courts is regressive, trailing one or several steps behind the lawmaking activities of states. In 1974, during the *Icelandic Fisheries Jurisdiction* cases, ICJ judges debated whether a fifty-mile-wide exclusive economic zone was consistent with international law, finding eventually that it was not.[49] Simultaneously, however, the members of the UN, gathered at the negotiating table of the Law of the Sea Convention, were discussing the possibility of creating exclusive economic zones extending up to two hundred nautical miles.[50]

When determining the exact meaning of the law established by the canonical sources, such as custom and treaties, the weight of judgments is much larger than it was before the multiplication of international courts. *International Legal Materials (ILM),* a quarterly publication of the American Society of International Law since 1962, strives to ease the pain of identifying sources of international law by publishing the full texts of important treaties and agreements, judicial and arbitral decisions, national legislation, international organizations' resolutions, and other documents. Neatly arranged stacks of *ILM* issues are a fixture in the office of every international lawyer, much as the mustard-and-red *Reporters,* the collections of decisions of U.S. courts, are in U.S. law firms. Traditionally, most of the 250 pages of the average *ILM* issue used to be dedicated to primary sources of international law, such as treaties. Since the late 1990s, however, judgments of international courts, arbitral awards, and, to a lesser extent, rulings of domestic courts take up much of the space, to the point that treaties are a rare find nowadays.

Again, theory and practice differ. The canonical view of international law is that international courts are not bound by their own precedents. As already mentioned, there is no rule of stare decisis, the keystone of common law legal architecture, mandating courts to be consistent with their own precedents.[51] This is so exactly because first, if there were such a rule, it would attribute to international courts significant lawmaking power and, second, it would somehow diminish the capacity of international adjudicative bodies to settle disputes if they were too constrained by settled jurisprudence. But international courts have evolved far beyond the mere dispute settlement function. They have begun to operate as true courts of law, which implies that they have a strong tendency to remain faithful to their own previous rulings unless there are cogent and legally valid reasons to depart from them.

In practice, then, international judges tend to rule consistently with their own previous rulings. Furthermore, they are inclined to quote each other, thus reinforcing the precedential value of the initial judgment. The echo effect can be significant. While in theory international judges cannot make international law, in the end they achieve lawmaking effects through repeated self-reference.

Professor Alain Pellet, who could be considered the dean of the invisible and unofficial ICJ bar, having litigated more cases at that court than any other counsel in the past three decades, notes that the World Court has always followed the practice of referring to its previous rulings, suggesting that sometimes it might even exaggerate. "Just to give two recent examples, in *Kasikili/Sedudu,* the Court cited seven previous cases in order to make the rather obvious point that the subsequent practice of the parties is relevant to interpreting treaties, and in only three printed pages of its 2004 *Wall* advisory opinion it made not less than twenty-eight cross-references to its previous decisions."[52] Other international courts refer equally to their own precedents, although not all can rely on more than eighty years of jurisprudence, as the World Court can.

Because of the tension between theory and practice—between the need to follow the law as it is written and the need to interpret law so as to effectively carry out the mission entrusted to them—international judges tend to approach precedent both boldly and gingerly at the same time. They are reluctant radicals. "We often have the chance to reconsider our jurisprudence," says a judge on the European Court of Justice, "but I have to say that we are very reluctant to take it. There's a very strong movement in the court to abide by its own jurisprudence for the sake of juridical security. There are fields, of course, where it doesn't much matter what the decision is. What is important is that the decision is kept, so that people know and can regulate their affairs, particularly in business affairs." If decision makers do not like the result, he points out, they have the power to make a new law or directive. Also, he continues, "You don't want to keep on arguing the same point again and again. If you've considered something a year ago, there really isn't much point in raising the same matter again. We are very reluctant to say that an earlier decision was wrong, very reluctant to do that. But you will find the court's decisions gradually depart from an earlier decision and when one looks back after ten years one sees that the earlier decision has just quietly disappeared." An advocate general of the same court, on the other hand, laments that "one of the problems we've had with the past case law is not the court going too far, but the court not going far enough. By not answering very specific questions in very specific terms, it provokes more very specific questions later on. You get a series of judgments, laying down maybe different guidelines going in different directions, instead of a judgment based on a principle."

Reluctance to change is not only a matter of proper judicial policy. "Apart from the general desire for security," continues the ECJ judge, "it seems to me there's actually an institutional inertia pushing to follow case law, which in some ways is worlds stronger than even in a common law jurisdiction in which one is actually bound by precedent. This came to me as rather a surprise, that in many ways we act as though we are bound by precedent in a much stronger way than I had supposed before I came here. It is not only a matter of policy, of *jurisprudence constante*. It is also a sheer matter of mechanics." Diligent clerks, he adds, often turn up precedents that help judges persuade their brethren during the process of deliberation.

A Jurisprudential Dialogue

International judges pay attention not only to the jurisprudence of their own court but also to that of other courts. Granted, since most courts are self-contained worlds and have different jurisdictions (subject matter, personal, geographic, or other), it does not happen often that judges have a formal reason to consider one another's rulings. Yet, from time to time, courts seem to use rulings to engage in a sort of jurisprudential dialogue. The dynamics of this dialogue are variable, but a few patterns do exist. First, it seems to be far from egalitarian. There is an informal and unconscious but tangible pecking order among international courts and tribunals. Some courts prefer talking—or, worse, lecturing—to listening. And when it comes to listening, the level of attention depends on which court is doing the talking.[53]

Then, some have closer relationships than others, which inevitably instigates more intense exchange. For instance, the ad hoc tribunals for Yugoslavia and Rwanda are Siamese twins, connected by the head, as they share the same appellate chamber. The Special Court of Sierra Leone pays great attention to the judgments of these two courts. The International Criminal Court, once it starts to issue decisions, will likely consider the rulings of these courts, too. The European Court of Justice and the Court of the European Free Trade Agreement are also linked, as the agreements creating the EFTA Court require it to follow the jurisprudence of the ECJ.[54] The ECJ and the European Court of Human Rights, having some area of overlap, especially for what concerns individual freedoms, are engaged in a regular dialogue.[55] Their judges meet once a year for an informal one-day seminar and brief each other on pending cases that might be of mutual interest. The ECHR and the Inter-American Court of Human Rights, both being involved in the application of human rights conventions that contain many similar, if not identical, provisions, closely read each other's judgments, although the massive case law of the ECHR gives the Strasbourg court a louder voice than the one in San José.

The role of precedent across international courts has not yet been thoroughly studied, since it is only recently that the number of international rulings of most courts has become sizeable.[56] Of course, policies (always tacit, never explicit) might vary from court to court, and each judge might have a different attitude, but it seems that a few elements of a sort of "theory of precedent" are gradually emerging.

First, no international judge seems to feel bound by the jurisprudence of another court. This is unsurprising given the fact that courts are not even formally bound by their own precedent, that courts are not hierarchically organized, and all are, with few exceptions, self-contained jurisdictions. However, this also seems to stem from a certain sense of pride and defense of one's own judicial turf. Thus, jurisprudence of other courts is taken into consideration only when one's own court has no useful precedents. Although some judges might be more willing then others to cite, citing is generally done sparingly, selectively, and grudgingly. Relying too much on other courts' jurisprudence is tantamount to abdicating one's own role. As a veteran judge says, "Referring to and even quoting a judgment of another court does not make it a formal source. It is just as an example of one proposed solution, a solution which was adopted by the colleagues of another international court."

Second, if, on a given point of law, judges of one court feel differently than those of another court, out of judicial comity they will simply omit to take cognizance of judgments that do not support the reasoning chosen. Citing to say "they got it wrong" is generally avoided, even severely frowned upon.[57] A judge of the Sierra Leone court comments that in the case on the immunity of Charles Taylor,[58] a relevant ICJ case[59] was cited profusely, but "we did not follow it because one was able to distinguish it. So that's how we proceed. We try to be independent in our thinking without showing disregard to earlier thinking of the other courts. We show them the utmost respect."

Third, the formal nature of a judicial finding does not matter. Judges consider decisions of other international courts regardless of whether they are final or preliminary judgments, orders, nonbinding advisory opinions, or anything else. What they look at is the jurisprudence rather than any specific case; what ultimately seems to matter is only that the reasoning that led the other tribunal to a given conclusion is legally sound and persuasive. As one judge admits, "I'm not certain that there is much great practical difference between a decision that is binding, and one that is not binding but persuasive."

In the judges' minds, international courts seem to be divided between generalists (like the ICJ) and specialists (all others), and between regional courts and the so-called universal courts, that is to say, those whose jurisdiction is not restricted to any particular geographic area. This means that, fourth, specialized courts will consider, quote, and defer to the ICJ on matters of general public international law. As a WTO Appellate Body member admits, "I think we would never take on the ICJ. Whenever there is a reference, it is a reference as an authority." Arguably, this should also imply that the ICJ will defer to specialized tribunals concerning matters over which they have special knowledge or competence, but, to date, the ICJ has not done so.

Fifth, "universal" courts might consider, but will refrain from quoting, regional courts. This stems from the need not to attribute particular value to the jurisprudence of certain regions in determining the content of rules of international law which have universal reach. One ICJ judge expresses the concern that "if we cite the European Court of Human Rights, somebody from Africa might say, 'Why are they relying on this European court as the authority?'" The judge points out, however, that in the *Wall* case the ICJ did cite the United Nations Committee on Human Rights. "And there we had no problem because it is a UN body, thus representative of the world, not a particular region." Regional courts, on the other hand, do not seem to have any qualms considering and quoting universal courts, if needed.

Relying on the jurisprudence of national courts seems to be more problematic. Much like the case of international rulings, they are a documentary source that can be used to provide evidence of a rule generated by one of the primary sources. Yet, their impact on substantive international law is limited by several factors.

Domestic courts rarely pronounce themselves on rules of international law; they are rather a more useful source when it comes to searching for general principles of law. Additionally, they seem to be considered a last resort, to be looked at only when international sources do not help. "National case law will come into play mostly when international sources don't give an answer," one judge explains. "For example, when there is a matter of what is impartiality, there is no need to go to a Canadian or German supreme court and find out what impartiality is when you have established case law at the global and regional level. So it becomes more subsidiary. But when it comes to, say, the question of a rather procedural issue that has never been dealt with in human rights case law, and which is very criminal law–oriented, then, why not look at the national level and try to distill, to find out what is the common denominator here, or what is the best solution, even if it is not the common denominator?"

Attitudes toward national case law vary from court to court, and from judge to judge. The civil law/common law divide might play a role in this variation. The Special Court for Sierra Leone, for example, felt free to draw upon the decision of the British House of Lords regarding Chilean dictator Augusto Pinochet when considering matters of immunity.[60] Similarly, it referred to both U.S. and British decisions in a case that came before the appeals chamber regarding judicial independence.[61] "We go wherever we can find a suitable decision with principles that we agree with," says one SCSL judge. "Sometimes where possible, where it's relevant, we go to the jurisprudence of civil law courts. We don't use civil law doctrine and jurisprudence much because, even within the civil law, there's not the degree of harmony that people thought. German civil law is different from the French civil law. And there is so much variation and if you are not a civil lawyer, you do have to leave that side alone. But where we get a clear pronouncement which we understand, then we use it."

Other courts and judges are much more cautious. For instance, the European Court of Justice rarely cites national judgments. One judge explains that his colleagues do sometimes look to the U.S. Supreme Court on matters such as antitrust law or questions of discrimination, but "making the direct acknowledgement could be politically awkward or undesirable. If you do that, then you should be, in principle, open to do that also with, say, the Supreme Court of Somalia. You sort of open up something. We wouldn't necessarily like to have a practice where we would only cite the U.S. Supreme Court but no other national courts, and it also has to be noted that we don't cite our own national courts, either, except of course when they ask us for preliminary rulings. That you can't avoid, but otherwise we wouldn't cite national courts."

Soloists in the Choir

Regardless of the merits of an individual judge's views, "you have first to sell it to your colleagues, because this is a collective decision," as one judge remarks matter-of-factly. International courts are collegial bodies. Decisions are taken by the majority. But, at the same time, courts are composed of remarkable individuals with well-developed ideas, an awareness of their own value, and, very often, pride. Formation of consensus, and the dialectics of the deliberation room, might pose a challenge to men and women used to being themselves the voice of authority.

There is no uniform practice regarding whether judges are allowed to express publicly their disagreement with their court's judgment in a particular case or to explain individually their own legal reasoning. Among the thirteen major international courts, most permit dissenting and individual opinions and declarations, but one of the exceptions, the European Court of Justice, has a large caseload and extensive impact and influence.[62] At the WTO Appellate Body, dissents are discouraged but not forbidden, and the practice in this regard is in a state of flux.[63]

By "dissenting opinion" is usually meant a reasoned statement of a judge who feels unable to agree with the majority of the court as regards the operative part of the decision in question. An "individual" or "separate opinion" is given by a judge who concurs with the majority on the operative part but disagrees with the grounds on which the decision is based. A separate opinion usually provides alternative or supplementary reasons supporting the ruling of the court. Finally, in some courts, like the International Court of Justice, there is also the practice of judges' "declarations," which are statements made for a variety of purposes, like highlighting certain passages of the decision, expressing general dissent without explaining why, explaining a vote, or even expressing feelings.

The issue of dissenting and individual opinions is one of those where the rift between common law and civil law traditions is most evident. The concept of entitling members of a collegiate judicial body to give their personal opinions on the legal questions presented is rooted in the Anglo-Saxon legal tradition, where the judgment is conceived as the sum of the decisions of the individual judges. Conversely, the traditional civil law stance on the issue is that a court is a uniform entity taking decisions by a majority that remains anonymous after deliberating in camera. One reason why the ECJ (and its twin, the EFTA Court) do not allow opinions is believed to be that the founding members of the European Community, which also created the court, were all countries of civil law tradition.[64]

Judges are divided on the merits of formal individual opinions. In the case of concurring individual opinions, it is argued that they enrich the judgment because, having usually been drafted by a single judge only, they show a higher degree of inner logic and consistency than the majority opinion. In the case of dissenting opinions, by letting dissenters go their way, the judgment of the majority looks less like a patchwork of various opinions and a compromise solution. Dissenting opinions may also help the defeated party accept the verdict because they signal that the court gave full consideration to the arguments presented. Pragmatically, in courts that do not routinely operate in chambers, and where cases are decided by groups of ten judges or more, judges argue that opinions might be the only alternative to impossibly protracted deliberations. As a president of a court admits: "We try to avoid dissent, but sometimes it's very difficult to do that, and entirely time consuming, so it's better to have a dissent sometimes."

Some argue that judges are human beings and thus are entitled to their own freedom of speech. Opinions are an essential safeguard of judicial independence and ensure greater transparency and accountability. They allow judges the opportunity to explain their votes and thus prevent speculation and erroneous attribution, particularly when the bench taking the decision is made of a few judges. In the case of the WTO Appellate Body, they are allowed, but discouraged.[65] The result is a compromise solution whereby they are included in judgments but they are not attributed. Yet, since decisions are taken by a chamber of three members, usually everyone involved knows who has authored the opinion. A member of the EFTA Court, where opinions are not allowed and where, likewise, there are only three judges to decide cases, voices his unease: "I think that we should be more honest and introduce a dissenting opinion system, particularly in a court of three, since rumors are going around. We would be much more protected by a dissenting opinion system. Then dissents would be official. Otherwise, they are just floating around."

Judges critical of dissenting and separate opinions argue that far from ensuring independence, they might actually undermine it, particularly in those courts where judges can be reelected or reappointed. This view carries special force at the European Court of Justice, where there is no real competition between states to get their nominees elected, so states de facto decide who their judges will be. Collective judgments, in other words, allow judges more freedom, because their individual role in the decision is hidden from public view. Dissenting opinions, on the other hand, expose judges to the scrutiny of their governments. An ECJ judge observes that "because no opinions are allowed, and it is not said who voted in favor or against, there is no way in which a government would know which way a judge voted on something or another. By the same token, the advantage of not having dissenting opinions is that there is no opportunity for a judge to signal to the boys back home, 'Look what a good boy am I.'"

Allowing opinions places judges in a series of ethical dilemmas, as another ECJ judge explains. "You would have the situation where judges start writing opinions before their mandate expires or before they are asked to resign. Whatever you do then is wrong: if you go against the government, because now you are just doing it in order to show that you're independent. And if you go for the government, it's because you want to be reappointed. It opens up all these sorts of nasty speculations."

Critics of opinions also argue that dissents, or alternate bases for reasoning, weaken the authority of a court. At the WTO, where the Appellate Body is composed of three-person divisions, one member asks, "What's the authority of the decision which is supported by only two?" Manifest dissent jeopardizes the uniform interpretation of the law. In international criminal tribunals, separate or dissenting opinions have the danger of undermining the perception that the accused has been found guilty beyond reasonable doubt. In other contexts, dissents might stir and provide fuel to internal conflicts between institutions and organs and between states and institutions, an anathema particularly for the building of the European federalist project.

This is also why the ECJ, unlike all other international courts, has advocates general. They are full members of the court, but they are not judges and they do not take part in the court's deliberations.[66] Their role is to give the court, in complete independence, a reasoned opinion on the pending case, weighing pros and cons and the likely impact of the judgment on the overall legal system. It is a sort of "institutionalized opinion," one that comes from someone close enough to the court to compensate for the fact that opinions are not allowed at the ECJ, but separate enough not to undermine the court.

General debate about the advantages and drawbacks of opinions aside, everyone agrees that the use and misuse of opinions is largely a matter of an individual's culture and background, self-discipline, and the capacity of the president of the court to mediate. As one judge puts it, "It's a question of disposition. You have to have the discipline not to do that as a breaking exercise. Your colleagues rapidly know if you are going for the common good and try to polish things up and get it a bit better." Another judge echoes those words: "It shouldn't be an avenue for you to portray yourself, or indulge your ego. It's such a disservice to the people who put you there." A judge of the ICJ elaborates on good uses and bad uses of opinions: "The purpose of the opinion is not to criticize a judgment, it's to let your opinion be known, which is not exactly the same thing. There are good uses and not-so-good uses. For instance, in the *Kosovo* cases, a majority of the court—a slight majority—decided that there was no jurisdiction because Yugoslavia was not a member of the United Nations at that time.[67] However, there was a strong minority thinking that there was no jurisdiction for quite different reasons.[68] I think it was quite justified in this case to make an opinion because these might have an impact on the *Bosnia-Herzegovina* case we have now."[69] Unsurprisingly, academics-turned-judges have a particularly bad reputation when it comes to their capacity for team play and for keeping the purpose of the exercise well in focus.

No matter how hard a court tries to find a common ground and no matter how skilled and patient a president might be, certain personalities simply cannot be corralled. Shigeru Oda, the former Japanese judge of the ICJ, has probably most taken advantage of the possibility of speaking his mind.[70] In twenty-six years at the World Court (1977–2003), he authored no fewer than fifteen declarations, twenty-three separate opinions, and fifteen dissenting opinions. Others, like the Sri Lankan Christopher Weeramantry, will probably go down in the history of the court as the author of the lengthiest opinions, often exceeding the length of the judgment itself and resembling veritable treatises of international law in their own right.[71] Recalling the seminal *Tadić* case, decided by the ICTY/ICTR Appeals Chamber, a judge notes, "There was even one judge, the Pakistani judge, who said, 'I write my own judgment.' And he wrote the separate opinion, which was in reality a veritable separate judgment. He just didn't participate!"

All together, opinions of judges of international courts form a very bulky corpus. Numbers at the ICJ alone are staggering: in over sixty years of activity, it has accumulated 1,017 opinions (262 declarations, 406 separate opinions, 349 dissenting opinions) in slightly more than 100 cases.[72] Whether concurring or dissenting, opinions do have a decided but unquantifiable impact on international law. First, international law is shaped by multiple factors that are difficult to unbundle. Second, the exact value of subsidiary sources in the shaping of international law is quite unclear. Third, although parties do frequently cite opinions, they are rarely expressly cited in decisions of international courts themselves, even where that might have been useful or appropriate. Be that as it may, one can find numerous examples in international legal scholarship, especially that of the eldest standing international court, the World Court, of opinions that eventually have altered the course of international law or the subsequent development of the given court's case law.[73]

At one extreme, one might say that opinions are merely equal to the writings of the most distinguished scholars of international law. That is to say, they are just another subsidiary source that can be examined when determining the content of the law as established by the primary sources.[74] At the other extreme, one might say that their practical value approximates that of decisions of a whole court, particularly when well written and reasoned. Regardless, it seems that if, as we saw, lawmaking by international courts is not readily admitted, lawmaking by a *single* judge should arguably be considered even more problematic.

The Limits of Lawmaking

While international judges are undoubtedly playing a lawmaking role much larger than is officially recognized, there are clearly three main limits: formal, political, and structural. The *formal limit* is, once again, the fact that their rulings are not a source of international law per se. They can fill lacunae and, through interpretation, can transform international law, but they can never squarely contradict law as it has been decided by states. There is a dynamic interplay between governments and judges. Judges test the waters more or less gingerly, hoping to convince governments that their rulings indicate the right way forward for the law and are not usurpations of states' exclusive prerogatives.

Then there are *political limits,* which vary from court to court. Some courts can be bolder than others. Many observers agree that the European courts can get away with so much lawmaking because they have the tacit acquiescence of the majority of member states. Courts are able to impose law when political consensus cannot be obtained between member states. "How could you have an internal market if the Danish or French parliament could at any time just pass a law derailing it?" a member of the European Court of Justice comments. "If you accept the supranational idea, then you need to buy the principles of primacy and direct effect that were articulated by this court. It really boils down to acceptance of the very logic behind the union and if you accept it, a lot comes as an automatic consequence." As for the ECJ rulings expanding European law, "I don't find these famous judgments shocking or radical or anything. I think they are more kind of almost necessary." The imperative of the ad hoc tribunals to fulfill the specific mission assigned to them within a short time period created a similar situation, where the judges were necessarily pushed into uncharted legal waters, and their capacity to creatively interpret existing laws to achieve the assigned goals was tested to the limit.

Other courts must tread much more lightly, as they might have no implicit mandate to pioneer. States might be more jealous of their lawmaking prerogatives, and the political backlash for pushing the envelope might be significantly stronger and louder. This is the case at the World Trade Organization and the International Court of Justice. A veteran of the ICJ expresses his anxiety about the subject: "It's always the same problem for the judge. You must apply the law. You have some freedom in applying the law because you are not a machine, but you must be careful to be just where you must be, which requires being both imaginative and prudent. . . . When you look at the history of the court, you'll see that it has been very cautious not to invent new rules, and many of the opinions—dissenting opinions coming from some judges—are criticizing the court on that count. It seems to me that international criminal courts have been way less cautious. One must be careful with taking liberties with the law."

A member of the WTO Appellate Body distinguishes between the "basic function" of the system, which is to settle disputes, and the "ancillary function," which is to clarify. "Now clarification can be interpreted in many ways. I mean, clarifying can be also rationalizing, making it more coherent, et cetera. How far can you go into that, away from simply settling the disputes?" This question, he says, is unanswered in the founding document. It is true, he goes on, that member states expect judges to refrain from expansive interpretation, "but, of course, this is a very primitive way of looking at the function of judgment, and it has not worked this way. . . . You cannot really fulfill even the settlement of dispute function without having some leeway. There is, of course, a kind of an incremental development, but it is being kept to a minimum in order not to shock."

If international judges have gradually, and de facto, become legislators, their lawmaking activities are always subordinated to that of governments. Courts do not necessarily have the last word. States can alter the systemic consequences of a judgment by agreeing to change the law. They exercise, in other words, an ex post facto control over international judges' lawmaking activities—provided that they can agree. "I think it's one of the major weaknesses of the [WTO dispute settlement system] that the politics is not able to correct what the judiciary has gotten wrong," says another Appellate Body member.[75] "After all, we are human beings, and we can always make mistakes. It's one of the major problems. Normally, in constitutional systems around the world, there is somebody who can correct the judges. In Geneva, that is not possible." In a large and cumbersome multinational organization like the WTO, the process of passing new legislation is slow and often unsuccessful. "It's appalling," the member continues. "The judges should not be blamed for that. It is the consensus principle that underlies WTO decision-making that does not work anymore, now that the membership of the WTO has expanded to almost 150 states. There are people, highly respectable people, who say—particularly in the United States—'Cut back on the judicialization of international law!' That's not the right response. Don't cut the rule of law back, make the political decision-making process more efficient."

Third, there are *structural limits* on lawmaking. While individual judges might have their own preferences, the nature of international courts makes it difficult for "judicial policies" to be articulated. When the court has a full docket, it is difficult to find time to sit down and discuss theoretical issues and approaches. In courts with a light docket, judges tend to work only part time, thus reducing the time for brainstorming outside the framework of a specific case. Moreover, calling a meeting on an issue of such a nature might be too formal, inducing judges to retreat to their own ideological positions, rendering the whole discussion sterile. The more judges a court has, the more difficult having such a discussion is. "You see," a judge on the ECJ remarks, "sometimes—indeed, quite often—the outside world wonders 'What is the policy of the court on this, that, or the other?' We don't have any policies, really. This is important to appreciate. We basically judge particular affairs and respond to the challenges of that week's caseload, as it were. We don't take time off and have a discussion on, 'Should the court be activist or not activist?' 'What sort of attitude should the court adopt?' We do have these discussions, but always in the context of particular affairs and particular problems. You see, it's very different from the politicians in that sense. There are so many potential problems that can arise that to try and regulate all of them in advance would mean you'd have no time actually to solve the problems that have arisen. As a judge brought up in the common law tradition, I think that it's not a bad way forward to make your law in the face of particular facts that highlight the decision that you have to make. Then, next time, there's another set of facts, and gradually you build up a jurisprudence."

In court, judges do not discuss jurisprudence in the abstract. They might do that outside the court in academic seminars and conferences, but issues of confidentiality and impartiality make them reluctant to do so. It is essentially a case-by-case process. Yet the nature of international courts is such that international judges do not have control over their docket. Typically, international courts are required to hear every case that is presented to them. Not even international criminal courts escape this rule, as it is the prosecutor who decides who is to be indicted and tried, not the judges. Granted, some cases might fail in the early stages for lack of jurisdiction or on matters of admissibility. Sometimes, a court might be able to extricate itself from a particularly undesirable case on a technicality, like the ICJ did in the case of the French nuclear tests in the South Pacific.[76] Like U.S. district courts and the courts of appeals, international courts generally do not have the power, as a matter of discretion, to deny considering a case. It is the caseload that drives them, not the other way round.[77]

Reluctant Lawmakers

International judges sometimes unconsciously overestimate their power to contribute to international lawmaking. They have the very human desire to be the ones who lead the dance, to put their signature on an important development of international law, forgetting that perhaps they have merely detected a change that was already underway in states' practices, or that they are sometimes mere instruments of larger forces. A member of the WTO admits that "the main users of the WTO dispute settlement system, the United States, the European Union, and even Japan, have a strategic view of cases, and, for that matter, also Canada, Australia. These are regular customers who think long and hard about what implications filing a certain case might have and try to steer international law through our medium in a direction they like. They think strategically and they obviously use us."

Martin Shapiro famously wrote that judges are by definition political actors who are forced by the enterprise of judging to make law, and who serve as a tool of social control for the powerful.[78] In this, national and international judges are very much similar. The context, however, is different. A national judge engaging in lawmaking beyond the formally established limits in a democracy will be criticized, chastised, and even made subject to disciplinary action. Yet, once the straying judge has been corralled or removed, the court lives on. However, international judges who, knowingly or inadvertently, cross the line between interpreting the law as is and writing law, put at risk the future of the court itself, if not the whole edifice of international law. They are more likely to see themselves as compelled to break new ground by circumstance, rather than seeking opportunities to make their mark by developing new law.

Historically, governments have sought to reserve international lawmaking powers to themselves. Some might feel threatened by the multiplication of international courts. Some, like the United States, have a de facto policy of engaging with courts as little as necessary. But it is a fact that the lawmaking capacity of the large international organizations is very limited, given the enormous difficulties of achieving political consensus in groups with 150 or more countries as members. Given this state of paralysis, perhaps greater attention should be paid to how the lawmaking potential of international courts could be better harnessed.

States may be wary of entrusting the helm of the ship of international law to such willful and unpredictable captains as international judges, but those judges have demonstrated a striking ability to make progress through stormy waters over the last two decades. It is true that they have sometimes charted new routes and sometimes undertaken excursions that seemed to go beyond the limits of their formal orders. But they have by and large done so with deep respect for the traditions of their profession and the prerogatives of the governments that have launched their voyages. Acknowledging more frankly their lawmaking role, while clearly demarcating its limits, might be a productive alternative to the political stalemate that is increasingly gripping the key international organizations of the contemporary world.

Georges Abi-Saab, Egypt

Member of the World Trade Organization Appellate Body

Law was not Georges Abi-Saab's first choice of career. But over the last four decades, he has become an eminent figure in the field of international law, both as a professor and as a practitioner. He has also had the opportunity to serve on the bench of three different international courts: the International Court of Justice, the International Criminal Tribunal for the former Yugoslavia, and, most recently, the World Trade Organization Appellate Body. His experience in international justice is thus both deep and broad. But of all the roles that Abi-Saab has played in his field, the one that expresses his essence is that of teacher— a teacher who has from time to time been "borrowed" by the international bench.

Egyptian Beginnings

Abi-Saab's educational career acts as a window onto his intellectual acuity and enthusiasms. Born into a Christian, French-speaking family in Egypt, his first experiences were in a Jesuit-like institution. He eventually left it for a public school attended by a broader spectrum of the Egyptian population, a transition he now considers as significant in his life.

> *That change was very important for me because it gave me the occasion to be with people from other social strata, and other backgrounds — not only social but also cultural and religious.*

As Abi-Saab approached the end of his secondary school studies, he realized that what attracted him most was philosophy. But his father convinced him that law, in the French tradition, serves as a kind of "public philosophy," so it would be an appropriate field of study for the young Abi-Saab, who was thinking vaguely of an intellectual career. He thus entered the Faculty of Law at the University in Cairo but continued to attend lectures in philosophy at the Faculty of Arts as well.

Thus began Abi-Saab's long and remarkably diverse years of higher education. He loved both economics and Islamic law as well as the general theory of law (jurisprudence), topics that were part of his first-year curriculum. In his second year, he was introduced to international law by a young Egyptian professor, Abdullah el-Erian, who had recently completed a doctorate at Columbia University and had a pedagogical approach that was new and fresh to Abi-Saab and his fellow students.

> *The professor created a society of international law where, he said, there would be no membership fees. The only dues were to undertake a small research project. That was revolutionary, in 1951. At the time, undergraduate students didn't go to the library or do research—they just listened to what the professor said, read the book, and took the exam. I chose as a subject for my paper the status of the Universal Declaration of Human Rights, adopted earlier, in December 1948—is it binding or not? So I went to the library and found a book by Hersch Lauterpacht, later a great judge on the ICJ. Then I went to the UN information center in Cairo, where I looked into the documents. Then I made the presentation. The professor was very happy with it and afterwards took me to the faculty room and introduced me to the other professors, saying, "This young boy has done a paper like the ones that graduate students do at Columbia!"*

This auspicious introduction to international law did not, however, result in Abi-Saab's single-minded pursuit of it afterward. Although he did study public international law for a short while in Paris after graduating from Cairo University, he was soon enticed by a scholarship to the University of Michigan, where he enrolled instead in a doctoral program in economics.

Abi-Saab continued at Michigan for two years, during which time he also attended the international law lectures of Professor William Bishop at the law school, much as he had continued to pursue philosophy while studying law in Cairo. Professor Bishop invited him to attend a weekend colloquium on Middle East law, and he found himself correcting the speakers on points about the region that he felt they had misunderstood and on various aspects of Sharia law. A short while later, he was handed a letter by Professor Bishop. To his surprise, it contained an invitation by

Professor Milton Katz, of Harvard Law School, who had been impressed by Abi-Saab's contribution to the colloquium discussions, inviting the young Egyptian to join the newly established international legal studies program he was directing at Harvard. This turn of events was to lead Abi-Saab definitively away from economics and toward what was to become his lifelong calling, international law.

By this time, Abi-Saab's peripatetic approach to his studies was firmly established. He moved from Michigan to Harvard, then on to Cambridge with another fellowship, where he did research for his Harvard doctoral thesis in law. From there he moved on to Geneva, where he was granted yet another fellowship to pursue a second doctorate at the Institut Universitaire de Hautes Etudes Internationales (Graduate Institute of International Studies). This last fellowship was part of a program designed for promising scholars from the Third World, a need that was recognized in the immediate postdecolonization period. Future UN Secretary General Kofi Annan was among Abi-Saab's peers in the same program.

On the verge of turning thirty, Abi-Saab realized that student fellowships would now become scarcer. He did not intend to settle abroad, but he wanted to get some international practical experience before returning home to teach. He considered taking a variety of jobs—with the UN in the Congo and with the International Atomic Energy Agency in Vienna, and he applied for a lectureship in the sociology of international law at the London School of Economics—but none of these positions seemed a perfect fit with his interests or skills, however. As he walked along Lake Geneva one day, contemplating his future, he ran into the director of the Graduate Institute. When asked why he looked so serious, Abi-Saab recounted his dilemma about the various directions in which his life could now turn. The director responded, "How about teaching here for a year while you sort things out?" This "one-year job" turned out to run for thirty-seven years, from 1963 until Abi-Saab's retirement in 2000.

Practitioner on the Side

The constant of Abi-Saab's professional life has been teaching, and he considers it his true calling. One often reads reference to the brilliant general course on international law that he gave in The Hague in 1987. After the final lecture, so delighted were his students that they gave Abi-Saab a standing ovation lasting a full fifteen minutes, a first in the history of the academy. He has worked with countless students over the years; the devotion with which many speak of him is a testament to his ability to act as a mentor. One has only to peruse the enormous volume dedicated to his work and ideas, published in 2001, and to which many of his former students contributed, to gain a sense of the influence he has had on several generations of legal scholars.[1]

Abi-Saab has not confined his work to the academic world, however. He has made equally significant contributions to the field of international law through his practice as an international lawyer and judge, even if these contributions have served only as a complement to his life's work. His first foray into "applied" law was in 1969, when he conducted a study for the United Nations, titled "The Respect of Human Rights in Armed Conflict." Soon afterward, he prepared another report concerning similar issues in the context of wars of national liberation. In the years to follow, Abi-Saab participated in various diplomatic conferences and scientific meetings on related issues and eventually became recognized as an expert in the field of international humanitarian law. This experience was to prove very important years later when he was elected as a judge to the first bench of the International Criminal Tribunal for the former Yugoslavia.

His initial work in international courts was not, however, as a judge but rather as counsel. Through teaching as a visiting professor in Tunisia in 1974, Abi-Saab became acquainted with the Tunisian legal community. This resulted, in 1978, in his being chosen as counsel to represent Tunisia in its case against Libya before the International Court of Justice.[2] When he made his pleading before the bench, it was his first formal appearance before an international court. Yet he already was acquainted with many of the well-known players in international justice, a cosmopolitan group who constituted an "invisible international bar" that can be retained by states in need of experienced international lawyers.[3] This group included Sir Robert Jennings, Abi-Saab's former Cambridge professor, who was soon to become a member and then president of the ICJ bench and who was also on the Tunisian team. The Tunisians were shocked when opposing counsel representing Libya approached Abi-Saab after his pleading and congratulated him warmly.

> The Tunisians thought that I had really given away the case. They didn't understand. But my first pleading went down very well. The judge ad hoc for Libya, Eduardo Jimenez de Arechaga, a very-well-known Uruguayan jurist and former president of the ICJ, told me at the end of the pleadings, "You know, the judges give an Oscar for oral pleadings; there were three nominees, but you got it!" So that was my first case.

Abi-Saab did not seek to join the cadre of international lawyers who appeared repeatedly in cases before the ICJ in the late twentieth century. But he did serve as counsel in five or six major cases and then had the opportunity to serve twice as judge ad hoc on the ICJ: the first time in 1983 for Mali in a frontier dispute with Burkina Faso,[4] and the second time in

1990 for Chad in a territorial dispute with Libya.[5] When asked how appearing before the ICJ bench was different from actually sitting as a judge, Abi-Saab remarks,

> *I came out of the experience as a judge more respectful of the court than I had been when I saw it from the outside. Because I saw that there is a kind of a collective wisdom that prevails there and that transcends the sum of the wisdom of its individual members. A collective wisdom in spite of the fact that the court sometimes fudges issues or finds flimsy ways to get out of awkward corners. But you understand why they do it. They try to find solutions that satisfy both sides at least minimally. This is what I call "transactional justice." But it should not be at the expense of the best legal reasoning. The court has to act as an organ of the international legal system and not merely as an arbitral tribunal in the hands of the parties. It has a duty to safeguard the integrity of the system while settling the dispute before it.*

This early judicial experience at the ICJ was to stand Abi-Saab in good stead for his later work on international courts. Perhaps the most challenging judicial work he carried out was during the early days of the ICTY. He had not intended to be an international criminal court judge and had not even known that he was nominated until another nominee asked Abi-Saab to put in a good word for him with the UN Secretary General at the time, Boutros Boutros-Ghali, a fellow Egyptian and friend of Abi-Saab's, as well as a friend of the Egyptian ambassador's to the UN. When he did so, the response of the latter was, "Why are you helping a competitor? Don't you know that the Egyptian government is thinking of you for the same position?"

Abi-Saab's immediate reaction was that he was not qualified for such a position, as he had no experience in criminal law. But the ICTY bench was to include experts in international humanitarian as well as criminal law; Abi-Saab had a wealth of experience in the former. After his election to the bench in 1993, his primary task was to sit on the Rules of Evidence and Procedure Committee. Abi-Saab explains:

> *I worked very hard because I was coordinating the main work, that of the Rules Committee. And the rules are one of the tribunal's greatest achievements because it is the first detailed code of international criminal procedure. First, we had to combine elements of the adversarial [common law] and inquisitorial [civil law] systems.[6] Secondly, we had to adapt them to the international level. And, thirdly, we had to integrate into the rules the entire UN codex of human rights. So, it was not an easy job.*

Abi-Saab did not remain long on the ICTY bench. After two years, he returned to teaching full time in Geneva, where he had never left off his supervision of student theses. He is pleased to have participated as an appeals judge in what he considers one of the ICTY's most, if not *the* most, significant decisions, that of the interlocutory appeal on jurisdiction in the *Tadić* case of October 2, 1995.[7] This case made history, as it was the first to be dealt with by the ICTY, giving place to the first interlocutory judgment and to the first appeal. Tadić's attorney tried all possible objections to the tribunal's jurisdiction, questioning the very legality of the establishment of the tribunal by the Security Council under the UN charter, as well as the applicability of war crimes in the armed conflict in question. These pleas raised issues that went to the very core of international humanitarian law and the constitutional law of the UN. Abi-Saab comments on the Appeals Chamber judgment,

> This judgment authoritatively decided two fundamental, though — until then — highly controversial questions. The first related to judicial control over the legality of Security Council acts, a highly sensitive matter, particularly in the wake of the ICJ evasive attitude on that issue in the Lockerbie case. The Trial Chamber considered the matter to be beyond its jurisdiction, and that, in any case, it was a nonjusticiable political question.
>
> The Appeals Chamber reversed it on both these grounds, asserting its power to examine the question of the constitutionality of the establishment of the tribunal — which is a legal matter, though with political ramifications — not as a principal cause of action, but as an incidental preliminary question whose prior determination is necessary for the establishment by the court of the existence and ambit of its principal jurisdiction over international crimes. The larger significance of this affirmation, that Security Council action is not above the law or beyond judicial review, needed no demonstration. The other jurisdictional plea of the accused was that the alleged crimes took place in the context of an internal conflict, and that war crimes, according to international law, can only take place in the context of an international armed conflict.
>
> The prosecutor, followed by the trial chamber, considered that the Security Council had classified the armed conflicts in the former Yugoslavia as international in character and that they were bound by this legal characterization. The Appeals Chamber considered that as a court of law, it had to undertake its own legal characterization, and after an exhaustive examination of customary international law, it came to the conclusion that it is already established under general international law that serious violations

of international humanitarian law committed in noninternational armed conflict are punishable as war crimes. This means that the classification of the armed conflict as international or noninternational is immaterial for that purpose, thus opening a very big wedge in the legal wall separating these two types of armed conflicts.

On both these issues, the judgment, by its thorough and tight legal reasoning, made a contribution to the clarification of the law on fundamental, but highly sensitive issues, which makes it one of the major judicial decisions of recent times.

An Advocate for the Periphery

After his retirement in 2000, Abi-Saab remained in Geneva, the city where he has spent most of his professional life. He was elected member of the World Trade Organization Apellate Body (AB) that same year and was reappointed for a second four-year term in 2004. The AB is charged with hearing appeals against judgments, or "reports," as the WTO calls them, in disputes brought by WTO members and already decided by a panel of the organization's Dispute Settlement Body.

The WTO is an interesting vantage point from which to consider one of Abi-Saab's long-standing concerns, that of allowing the voices of the developing world to be heard in international law. Abi-Saab is widely recognized as an advocate of the position that inequalities between "core" countries and those on the "periphery"—to use the terminology of Wallerstein's world-system theory[8]—should be narrowed. And he is well aware that international law has historically privileged the former and disadvantaged the latter. After all, this body of law derives largely from European public law, which had perhaps its most powerful expression at the Berlin Congress of 1885, where the "civilized" powers of Europe summarily carved up Africa, each taking the territories it wanted to exploit. The two ICJ cases on which Abi-Saab served as judge ad hoc were, in fact, a product of this same Berlin conference; they concerned disputes over territorial lines randomly drawn by European powers during the colonial era.[9] In response to the question of how developing countries can become players in the sphere of international law, Abi-Saab responds,

Well, they already participate in a way. The International Criminal Court is a good example—sometimes the big boys don't always get the final say. We had great hopes, my generation, about the Third World progressing, creating elites that can participate effectively in the construction of a universal world order. My experience is that if you have good people who know the subject, any country can exert some influence. And, after all, these are negotiations; they are not fights. So, if you can make a good argument, a good case for your position, some of the others may not end up signing the treaty, as with the ICC, but you can still get what you want. India has very good and stubborn negotiators. They usually leave their mark. The problem with the Third World is that it has lost a lot of time and a lot of clout. People are disillusioned. But the world is moving on. I mean, I don't lose hope when I see that China and India are moving ahead. They are getting their place in the sun, and they constitute a very large part of what used to be called the Third World, or the non-Western world.

Despite his concern for the plight of the Third World, and in particular the African continent, Abi-Saab is not an apologist for certain patterns that have emerged there, nor does he accept the exaggerated claims of cultural relativism. But while he supports the notion that non-Western countries should help shape the direction of the "international community" by subscribing to its universal values, he also believes that local identities need to remain strong. Abi-Saab has this to say about the balance that needs to be sought between international criminal justice processes and more local processes that respond to conflicts on the African continent:

The territorial judge is the natural judge. Because he is closer to the dramatis personae, to the evidence, to the environment, and to the social perception of the legal standards that are supposed to have been violated. So, obviously, he has the best capability to judge. But the question is whether he is able and willing to do so.

This is the question that will be answered by the International Criminal Court, an institution that has been able to draw upon the experiences of the ICTY and the very rules that Abi-Saab and the other shapers of contemporary international criminal justice formulated with little or no guidance from earlier experience.

A Tale of Three Courts

As an academic, Abi-Saab has found himself somewhat frustrated by his work at the Appellate Body. He feels that the role of the judge at both the ICTY and the ICJ gives greater scope for interpretation and for the development of international law. This was particularly the case at the ICTY in its early days.

In order to be consistent with the law, with the principle of legality, we had to apply general international law as it existed at the time of the commission of the crimes, not merely an ex post facto definition of crimes given to us in the statute. Anyway, these definitions were not necessarily completely right. So we had to interpret boldly general international law and the statute to make them coincide. The idea was that we were creating something new, pioneering international criminal justice when everybody thought it had withered away after Nuremberg.

Of course, the ICJ was much more. . . . I wouldn't say cautious, but more restrained. Still, there was ample room for interpretation, rationalization, and elaboration of legal reasoning.

Here at the Appellate Body, the judicial policy of interpretation is strict constructionism, insisting heavily that we must remain very close to the text, even the words, of the agreements, and not add to or diminish from the rights and obligations of the contracting parties, not fill any gaps, et cetera. In a small article I wrote about the AB's method of interpretation, I said that it reminds me of the definition of "sedentary species" in the law of the sea, those species that are immobile on or under the seabed, or, if they move, they are in constant contact with the seabed—the lobster walk, if you like. The AB's approach to interpreting the text, or rather the words of the agreements, is a little bit like that!

You can see that there is a great difference among those three fora. But they have something in common: on whichever you sit, you are exercising the same function, the judicial function. The judicial function has its own requirements, and it is the same everywhere. However, it is like living in different houses. The rules of architecture are the same, but you feel the environment is very different. That is the judicial policy that varies from organ to organ. But judicial policy has to remain within the parameters of the judicial function.

The wide experience in international law that Abi-Saab has had both on and off the bench provides him with a unique perspective on the differing characters of various international courts, the way they work and feel and operate. He does not hesitate to name his favorite:

The International Court of Justice is where I feel most at home. Why? Because, first, it is an animal I have studied throughout my life. My first published book, in French, was about the procedure of the International Court. I know thoroughly the people inside and the people around it, and they deal with subjects I have been teaching and practicing.

The Yugoslavia tribunal was a new creation. I managed to get along very well with the colleagues who were internationalists. But the criminal law judges and lawyers were a little bit alien to me. However, as it was a new thing and we were the founding fathers, I didn't feel estranged because we were all doing pioneering work and everyone was doing what he could.

Here at the Appellate Body, I came into an area that I hadn't really explored in depth before. I had worked on international economic law, but from a very different perspective—on the new international economic order, on the right to development, et cetera—subjects that had a progressive dimension. While the WTO, like its predecessor, the GATT, was perceived as a rich man's club, rather conservative and neoliberal. And the type of law that developed within it is a very specialized type of detailed, not to say tortured, law that I had not been following very closely. Moreover, because of the restrictive judicial policy, there is not much room for legal reasoning and theorizing.

But as I said, the essence is the judicial function. We act in the AB on that basis. Moreover, I meet and work with some interesting people who are different from my familiar international law fauna. There is usually one, sometimes two, international lawyers on the AB. But there is no general conviction that we should open up to general international law or inject a Third World sensibility into our interpretation. Things have developed a little bit, and I feel they are moving in the right direction, but from a certain starting block that you cannot change. If you act as a judge, you cannot tamper with rules. You have to interpret them within the permissible margin for interpretation. But as the AB has this restrictive judicial policy, it reduces even further that margin. Still, however narrow the margin we are left with, it can be used for pushing things in the right direction.

So I feel I am doing a good job. But I am not swimming in my own waters.

Georges Abi-Saab has not followed the usual paths leading to the international bench. Unlike some other international judges who have definitively left academia, the diplomatic service, or a domestic judicial position to serve on an international court, Abi-Saab has never been enticed by the song of that siren. He has preferred to remain, above all, a professor and mentor; "these other experiences have simply irrigated the main channel, which is teaching."

The Inter-American Court of Human Rights, San José, Costa Rica. *(Courtesy of the IACHR)*

The Inter-American Court of Human rights in session. *(Courtesy of the IACHR)*

The bench of the International Court of Justice, June 2006. *(Courtesy of the ICJ. Photography: Hadewych Weys)*

The Peace Palace, housing the International Court of Justice, The Hague, the Netherlands. *(Courtesy of the ICJ. Photography: PE foto)*

The International Criminal Tribunal for the former Yugoslavia, The Hague, the Netherlands. *(Courtesy of the ICTY)*

The judges, registrar, and deputy registrar of the International Tribunal for the Law of the Sea, November 2006. *(Courtesy of ITLOS. Photo: Stephan Wallocha)*

The International Tribunal for the Law of the Sea, Hamburg, Germany. *(Photo: Hans Georg Esch)*

The Special Court for Sierra Leone, Freetown, Sierra Leone. *(Courtesy of the SCSL)*

Trial of Samuel Hinga Norman (second from right in white cap), charged with crimes against humanity and serious violations of international humanitarian law, at the Special Court for Sierra Leone. *(Courtesy of the SCSL)*

A trial in session at the International Criminal Tribunal for Rwanda. Judges are seated on the left in front of the United Nations seal; the translation booth is in the background. *(Courtesy of the ICTR)*

The entrance to the International Criminal Tribunal for Rwanda, Arusha, Tanzania. *(Courtesy of the ICTR)*

5 ✑ Between Law and Politics

The Fiction of Seclusion

Even in the most established democracies, judges live under the threat of intrusion by political forces. By their very nature, judicial decisions are bound to disappoint large numbers of people; inevitably some of those people seek to achieve their ends by undermining the authority and the legitimacy of the courts. This process is magnified in the international arena, where the very legitimacy of law itself is still a matter of debate. Caught between powerful global actors, international courts are fragile institutions, vulnerable to both overt and subtle attempts to sway or undermine their work. International judges cannot afford to turn a blind eye to this aspect of their professional environment.

In an ideal world, the judge sits aloof from the tainted world of politics. His court constitutes a world unto itself, where the inhabitants speak their minds, fight their battles, and play their roles according to a tightly ordered set of rules. In this insulated universe, the outside interests of men and women do not matter. Their loyalties, their convictions, their attachments are irrelevant. This applies most of all to the man behind the bench, who owes allegiance neither to man nor to God, but to a timeless abstraction, the formidable figure of The Law. If politics will enter this sacred realm, it will enter as a mere subject to the law's dominion. The judge, if the case before him compels this, will cleanse and clarify the messy world of politics, but that world will never touch him.

This idealized portrait is an exaggeration, of course, but in fact a great deal rests upon it nevertheless. The rule of law depends on public confidence and credibility, and a judge's real and perceived independence from political prejudices and pressures is vital. Absent that condition, the courtroom becomes simply another venue for the enactment of naked power, or, nearly as bad, it comes to be seen that way by a jaded citizenry. Nations can survive public cynicism about politicians, bureaucracy, interest groups, and even the guardians of public safety—but cynicism about the law itself strikes a fatal blow at the very foundations of a just society. In this sense, the ideal, though unattainable in its purest form, serves as an ennobling aspiration.

Yet the very purity of the ideal is in some ways unhelpful as well. In the first place, no judge really lives in such splendid isolation. Even in the most open and democratic societies, judges are usually chosen by an overtly political process, often involving appointment by an executive, then confirmation by a legislative body—or sometimes direct election by the citizenry. When their tenure is limited, their actions on the bench cannot escape the scrutiny of an interested electorate. Even when a judge holds a lifetime appointment, his work will often be the subject of commentary by politicians and intense debate in the media; judges may avert their eyes from the glare of the spotlight, but they cannot avoid it altogether, at least not without detaching themselves physically and psychically from the communities where they live and work. Furthermore, under even the best of conditions, judges depend for their salaries and the resources for their courts on the whims of the politicians or bureaucrats who establish their budgets and the conditions for court administration. Under these circumstances, the ideal of political purity can lead to inevitable disappointment.

In less open societies, the conditions and compromises can be much worse. In many countries, judges conduct their work in an atmosphere of threat and intimidation. At the "minor pressures" end of the scale, judges work in an atmosphere of unspoken hints from political leaders who have the power to remove them from office. At the more extreme end of the scale, in some circumstances judges become the targets of direct violence, committed by deranged individuals, political partisans, or even by the government itself. The ideal of the apolitical judge is both helpful and unhelpful to judges in these circumstances. It can serve as a rallying point for those who wish to put pressure on government leaders to support judicial independence; but by seeming always out of reach, the ideal can serve to discredit hardworking men and women of integrity who are making necessary compromises as they seek to improve the rule of law in undemocratic circumstances.

Courts are, after all, inextricably part of political systems, and in some ways it might just be better to acknowledge and identify the ways in which judges are a part of that system and to work for their independence within that framework. The role of the judge is defined by a political process; the court's efficacy is determined in part by the cooperation and the competence of other branches of government. This relationship is reciprocal: in an open society, one crucial function of the courts is to limit and define appropriate actions of political leaders. So even in the best of domestic circumstances, judges are constantly playing an important, though unique, role. They are guardians of The Law within their courtrooms, and also, through their actions and behavior, crucial contributors to the health and well-being of the larger political system of which they are a part.

In international courts, the situation is even more complicated. The public interest in judicial independence from political interference is just as crucial, but the interplay between law and politics is, if anything, more complex. After all, judges who serve on international courts are part of an evolving system, with no common structure to link all the courts, no constitution, and few reserves of public confidence built on a system of shared political values and understandings. In a domestic system, the judge's role is defined by a constitution, by legislation, and by tradition; the international judge works with a much thinner layer of founding documents established by diplomats and political leaders. Under these circumstances, it is easy for outsiders to interpret judicial decisions as "political" rather than "legal." With no military or police force at their disposal, and given the uncertainties of funding in the international arena, international judges must rely on the goodwill and cooperation of states both to enforce their orders, and for their livelihoods.

Even more importantly, international courts serve a function where the legal and the political are intimately conjoined. Some are established with the explicit mission to adjudicate disputes between political bodies, whether states or intergovernmental organizations. In other cases, they provide a venue of last resort for individuals or organizations to hold their own national governments accountable to human rights and other legal standards. Even the international criminal courts, which address individual responsibility for major crimes, have been constituted in order to play an important role in persuading governments to take action to prosecute and prevent crimes against humanity.

Like it or not, international judges are intimately involved in the global political order: politicians and diplomats are deeply involved in the process of establishing the courts, choosing the judges, deciding which cases to bring before them, enforcing judicial decisions, and determining their resources. "On the international plane," writes a judge of the tribunal for the former Yugoslavia, "the political environment in which international courts, especially international criminal courts, function brings greater attention to the credibility of the institution, and the performance of the international judge as an independent and impartial arbiter is constantly under scrutiny."[1]

For critics of the international courts, this intimate association with global politics is a fatal weakness. "International law is not law but politics," claims Robert Bork, a former United States federal judge and a long-time critic of international courts. "For that reason, it is dangerous to give the name 'law,' which summons up respect, to political struggles that are essentially lawless." States, according to Bork, will cooperate with courts only when it suits their interests, so judges are reduced either to puppets (when the states approve) or impotents (when the states choose not to cooperate).[2] Former U.S. secretary of state Henry Kissinger comes to a similar conclusion, for exactly the opposite reasons. For Kissinger, it is not law that needs to be protected from politics, but politics from the law. He warns that international adjudication "is being pushed to extremes which risk substituting the tyranny of judges for that of governments; historically the dictatorship of the virtuous has often led to inquisitions and even witch hunts." Far better, Kissinger believes, to allow political matters to take their course in the arena of diplomacy or even conflict, than to allow the intrusion of "unaccountable" judges into the domain of the diplomats.[3]

In a world where states and individuals acted purely on the basis of power, perhaps Bork and Kissinger would be right that international courts are at best frivolous and at worst destructive. But, in fact, international courts have taken their place alongside a host of institutions that have created new and innovative forms of global politics, where nongovernmental actors work alongside powerful governments, where symbolic action plays as prominent a role as military might, where persuasion can substitute for coercion, and where governments have a stake in reining in their own excesses if it also means reining in the excesses of their neighbors and enemies.

For international judges, these considerations mean that it can be more difficult to consider their job as purely "legal" than for their domestic counterparts. They recognize the special challenges to judicial independence that arise in international settings and the extralegal functions that their courts are expected to play. Some cling fiercely to the ideal of the apolitical judge, seeking the maximum detachment and the maximum authority for the rule of law in its highest and most abstract sense. But most take a different tack. They recognize that politics and the law go hand in hand, so it is better for judges to be aware, involved, and strategic about the political engagement of their courts, rather than to pretend that those political implications do not exist. The best protection of judicial independence and the rule of law is transparency—an open recognition of politics and forthright discussions of the strategies that judges use to preserve the law and minimize interference. Transparency, in other words, may be a better guardian of the law than an artificial and unattainable ideal of purity. Maintaining such an ideal runs the risk of judicial complacency and passivity in the face of political threats. If a judge is going to live in a world of politics, better to be aware, involved, and shrewd in the service of the law.

Conflicting Loyalties

The most visible intersection between law and politics for an international judge is the question of nationality. In a domestic court, the judge serves as a citizen of his country. He swears to uphold the law of the land, and his personal allegiance to nation is aligned with his professional allegiance to serving as a guardian of the nation's laws. The international judge, however, faces at the very least a potential conflict between national loyalty and the application of the law. What if the interests of his country and the judge's interpretation of the law come into conflict?

This tension is most obvious in the courts where states themselves are the contending parties. The International Court of Justice adjudicates cases brought by member states against one another. With fifteen judges serving in plenary on most cases, the permanent judges more than occasionally sit in judgment on the pleadings of their own country. The same is true at the Law of the Sea Tribunal, and at the World Trade Organization Appellate Body, where many of the cases involve a small number of powerful countries, this happens frequently.

In the early days of international courts, the participation of judges in cases involving their own countries was actually thought of as an asset to the administration of justice. The Permanent Court of International Justice (and later the International Court of Justice) made explicit provision for judges to sit on cases involving their own countries. The architects of the court reasoned that states would be much more likely to have confidence in the court and therefore more incentive to bring cases before it and follow its judgments if each contending party had a judge on the bench.[4] While this judge would not serve as a "representative" of his country, he would nevertheless have a kind of special knowledge and openness to his nation's perspective, and could convey this in discussions with his colleagues.[5]

To honor this principle and to instill a measure of fairness some courts ensure that every state that comes before them has the right to have a judge of its nationality on the bench. At the ICJ, states have the right to choose an ad hoc judge to serve on a case in which they are a party, if they do not already have a national on the bench.[6] The ad hoc judge, who does not necessarily have to be a citizen of the country that chooses him, serves as a regular voting member of the court for that case.[7] The ECHR has a different system to the same end. Since most ECHR cases involve a citizen taking action against his own country, only one state is involved in any particular case. The judge from that country generally serves as the *rapporteur* on the seven-member panel for that case, meaning that he will take the lead in organizing the documents and proceedings.[8] In part, this is a matter of simple practicality. Although French and English are the official languages of the court, many of the documents in particular cases are in the language of the country involved. A judge *rapporteur* from that country is able to play a part in bringing the full range of evidence, specificities of national law, and cultural considerations to his colleagues on the panel. In other courts, such as the European Court of Justice or the Appellate Body of the WTO, the assignment system is random, so judges may happen to serve on cases involving their own nations, but not systematically.[9]

For the international criminal courts, this situation is less common. For reasons discussed in chapter 2, no one from the former Yugoslavia or from Rwanda has served as a judge in the tribunals for those countries. Situations can arise, however, involving third parties. A criminal panel may be faced with a request by the defense or the prosecution, for example, that a country turn over intelligence information as evidence in a case; such a situation could involve a judge from the state in question.[10]

Overall, then, many judges serving on international courts will sit on cases involving their own countries; the majority of cases involving states as parties will create this potential conflict. The desire to instill states' confidence in the court, the practicalities of language, and the perception of fairness have encouraged the architects of the courts to encourage this practice, but there are at least three potential problems. First, judges may feel direct pressure from their own states. Second, even without overt pressure, judges may consciously or unconsciously compromise their own judicial values in favor of national loyalty. Third, even if states do not apply pressure and judges are scrupulously neutral, the presence of judges sitting on a case involving their own countries may create the appearance of bias.

Judges tend to view the problem of direct pressure by states as serious, but rare. "I have never experienced nor heard any other judge talk of any pressure or effort from either his government or one of the parties or anything of that kind," says a veteran of one of the European courts.[11] "As far as my own government is concerned," says another European judge, "I am in a most felicitous situation of being able to say I have never had a phone call from my government nor did I have any phone calls from the attorneys of the applicants. That's really very comfortable." Judges acknowledge that their peers from countries with a less firm establishment of judicial independence—in Eastern Europe, or in Africa—may run greater risks in this regard. But they are inclined to believe that even in cases where an individual judge may be compromised, the threat to the institution in a panel system is diluted. One respondent, indeed, believes that in some cases judges may be inclined to be tougher on their own countries, pointing to ways that Eastern European judges on the ECHR have often been unusually heavy-handed when it comes to assessing state and police crackdowns on human rights in their home countries.

While they do not dismiss the possibility of conscious or unconscious national prejudice, most judges likewise feel that this threat is not serious in ordinary, day-to-day situations. Every judge faces some sort of competing loyalties. When these loyalties are direct or personal, then recusal is in order. In other circumstances, objectivity is simply a matter of being a good judge. There are, however, some circumstances, such as when a judge is nominated for reelection, where this problem becomes more acute.

The matter of perception, however, presents a problem of a different order. In the early years, proponents of international courts wished to strengthen the credibility of those courts in the eyes of states by ensuring some form of national "representation." In the twenty-first century, however, the notion of representation has become a liability; courts are now under the scrutiny not only of states but of the media, the academy, and nongovernmental organizations and watchdog groups armed with the power of the Internet. With these considerations in mind, Judge Thomas Buergenthal of the ICJ has called publicly for his court to reverse its policy and to replace it with a system where no judge sits on a case involving his own country. Buergenthal himself has voted several times against his own country (the United States) at the ICJ, but he has come to believe that justice would be better served by eliminating the practice of national and ad hoc judges sitting on their countries' cases.[12]

Observers of international courts are divided over how much of an influence nationality has on voting patterns. One recent study contends that judges at the ICJ tend to favor the interests of their own country and other countries with a comparable level of affluence.[13] But another detailed look at the historical record suggests that the majority of judges are right, that critics' concerns about "judicial nationalism" are by and large overblown, arguing that a long-term analysis of voting patterns at the ICJ has shown that nationality has traditionally been a poor predictor of how a judge will vote in a particular case, and that the trend has been toward even greater independence in recent decades. "The changing nature of nationality, international action, and especially international disputes," writes Adam M. Smith, the author of this study, "has made citizenship an imprecise instrument of analysis and potentially an anachronistic tool with which to analyze independence."[14] Nevertheless, the study echoes the judges' concerns about problematic perceptions. With increasing questions about these perceptions from state and nonstate actors, Smith worries that the effectiveness of international courts will be diminished if they "remain mired in increasingly dubious questions of nationality, citizenship, and consequent doubts about judicial 'independence.'"[15]

The Influence of States

The process of choosing judges is one of those "increasingly dubious questions." As we have seen, in almost every case judges ascend to the international bench through a process that begins with nomination by their own country and continues through a diplomatic and electoral process deeply rooted in politics.[16] In some courts, such as the European Court of Justice, where every country is represented on the bench, the approval process following the country's nomination is more or less a formality. But in the courts under the auspices of the United Nations, elections often involve an extensive campaign, complete with campaign literature, meet-the-candidate parties in New York, and backroom deals between members of diplomatic missions.

For some international judges, this process is distasteful and "incompatible with the dignity of the judicial function," as Judge Theodor Meron of the ICTY puts it. "I have thought at times that a ban on direct electioneering by judges might well be attractive," Meron says. "It would certainly raise some practical problems—for example, campaigning by judges might simply be replaced by proxy campaigns by national governments—but, in principle at least, keeping judges at one remove from the political process might benefit both the perceived impartiality of courts and the efficiency and effectiveness of individual judges."[17] It might be noted, however, that campaigns conducted by governments rather than individual judicial candidates might even further strengthen the advantage already held by powerful countries, like Meron's United States. While U.S. candidates can count on the leverage of their own country's weight, candidates from less powerful countries can use the force of their own personalities and experience to compensate for their own sponsor's comparative weakness in the system.

A surprising number of judges, even those with the greatest sensitivity to issues of impartiality and independence, have come to the conclusion that the campaign system, despite its limitations, serves a healthy and important function. "We are being done the honor to represent the legal systems of the UN as a whole and to be the UN's court," says one ICJ judge, "and I can see that it's not unreasonable for them to want to know something about us, feel comfortable with us." While stressing that he keeps discussions of the court's docket strictly off-limits, another judge feels that a refusal to engage with diplomats in the UN system "would show an arrogance that I think is inappropriate." A criminal court judge argues that the campaigning at least allows the judges to put their best foot forward and to make the process more transparent; without that chance, he argues, "you would have just the [political] exchange between the countries without even seeing the people at all." And another UN judge points out that the alternative—an appointment process presided over in all likelihood by the Secretary General—would have problems of arbitrariness and public perception of its own.[18]

While relatively few judges are deeply troubled by the initial election process, many are concerned about the real and perceived threats to judicial independence posed by the process of reelection. Most international courts—the ICJ, ITLOS, ICTY, ICTR, ECJ, and ECHR, among others—have terms ranging from four to nine years, with the possibility of at least one additional term through reelection. Judges standing for reelection run the obvious risk that their decisions on the bench could be scrutinized by their own governments or other states involved in the electoral process. International judges tend to assert, like one European judge, that "I have never during my work at the tribunal thought about my reelection when I decided [matters] in respect to some of the cases," but they are keenly aware of the potential dangers, for others if not for themselves. One judge acknowledges that the principal problem is one of "self-restraint," a retreat to caution at election time that "could not be excluded by the system." In the European Court of Justice, there has been at least one well-publicized case in which governments declined to renominate a sitting judge, leading to charges of political interference.[19] However, as we have seen, the prospect of such interference is limited, in the case of the ECJ, by the fact that there are no dissenting opinions, so that the outside world cannot know with certainty what views any particular judge expressed during deliberations.

The most commonly proposed solution to the reelection problem is to appoint judges for longer, nonrenewable terms. Claus-Dieter Ehlermann of the WTO AB, for example, has called for replacing his body's four-year renewable term with a single term of eight years.[20] One judge on the ICJ suggests that his court would be better served with a single twelve-year term, instead of the renewable nine-year terms currently in force.

Even those judges most inclined to support changes in the process, however, are realistic and sanguine about the politics of the selection process. They recognize that the success of the courts depends on the support of states. The election process provides an invaluable opportunity for judges not only to win support for their own candidacy, but also to emphasize the courts' importance to key decision-makers within their own governments and in the international community. The courts do not operate in a vacuum. In the end, most believe that a transparent political process is preferable to other modes of selection that would hide but not eliminate the presence of political considerations.

Even if judges feel relatively secure that, as individuals, they can resist the wishes of governments, they remain conscious of the pressures that states put on their courts as institutions. Judicial independence, as one judge puts it, "is pretty obvious at home," but in international courts, with the intensity of the spotlight and the absence of settled traditions, "maybe sometimes other circles need to be reminded of it. In other words, I don't think there are any problems inside the organization, but sometimes people need to be reminded of the principles." Governments, in other words, can sometimes regard international courts as yet another international institution, vulnerable to the push and pull of diplomacy and politics.

Cases of direct interference are rare but not unheard-of. One judge recounts the story of a phone call from the office of the president of a large country giving instructions on how to rule on a particular case. "It was combined with a blackmail," the judge recalls, "but I nevertheless said it was totally unacceptable." The blackmail involved not the judge's personal life, but the institutional life of the court; the government threatened to issue damaging statements about the court's efficacy and credibility if the case did not come out in the desired fashion.

Smaller courts are particularly vulnerable to direct and indirect pressure. Whereas the influence of governments will inevitably be diffused in a larger court, some international courts involve as few as three member states and the same number of judges. In these instances, a judge of a smaller court points out, it can be difficult to protect the anonymity of judges' opinions, even if there are no public dissents, and the influence of any one member state on the appointment process and the budget of the court is disproportionately large. The Caribbean Court of Justice has devised a novel way to get around such concerns, by creating the CCJ Trust Fund, which is administered by the Regional Judicial and Legal Services Commission (RJLSC). Each member state makes an initial contribution to the fund, which is then administered by the RJLSC. Investment of the trust fund's resources is undertaken by the RJLSC, rather than state governments, and the return on these investments is used to finance the CCJ. This system helps to avoid situations in which more powerful states can exert undue influence on the court by withholding funds.[21] Some observers are unconcerned with these pressures, and indeed believe that in some ways they should be more formal and institutionalized so as to represent states' interests more directly. The American law scholars Eric Posner and John Yoo have advanced the controversial argument that courts should be "simple, problem-solving devices" and should therefore be less independent and more *dependent* on the disputing states. Such bodies, the authors claim, will be more effective at dispute solving between parties and will not impose solutions that will encourage governments to withdraw from the jurisdiction of the courts.[22]

International judges, as we have seen, reject this line of reasoning, arguing that their independence is central to their own integrity and the courts' credibility. But they are willing to concede that they are not blind to political considerations in certain aspects of their work. They follow closely, for example, the strategies that states pursue in making use of the courts. They are aware that states frequently prefer to settle disputes through private arbitrators rather than submitting to adjudication by an international court; after all, governments feel more in control of the arbitration process, where the players are indeed completely "dependent" because they are chosen by the states themselves. They recognize that states frequently use courts to mandate actions that a government would find politically unpopular to initiate itself. And they are conscious that governments are likely to resist reforms that make the institution too unpredictable and too insensitive to political realities.

So while emphasizing the importance of independence, judges are willing to acknowledge political considerations in thinking about ways in which those judgments should be implemented. One consideration is the timing of the public delivery of judgments. "We want to have a judgment delivered publicly as soon as we possibly can," says one human rights court judge, "although if I were in complete control of this and I knew that there was a hostage crisis going on in a country, I think I probably wouldn't deliver a judgment against that country that week. I think common sense would tell you, if not a sense of decency, to hold your horses for a little while, you know. Less a conspiracy, I think, than a matter of pure pragmatism." Another consideration is the macrolevel impact on the political and economic system. At the European Court of Justice, one judge acknowledges, the financial impact of decisions on governments and on the European Community as a whole is an important factor for some of those on the bench, particularly those from poorer countries. Such considerations "should be considered in the proper way—not to change the result, the logical reasoning—but to be open to limiting the consequences" of the decision. This kind of flexibility, says the judge, might be called "politically judicial reasoning."

One reason for this kind of flexibility is that the courts are in fact peculiarly dependent on governments, not only for their support in an abstract sense, but for their cooperation in implementing their judgments. This is most obvious and dramatic in the case of the international criminal courts, bodies which have neither military or police force at their disposal to apprehend suspects nor permanent prisons in which to house convicted criminals. These courts do have extensive prosecutors' offices to conduct investigations and bring evidence to the courts, but even those efforts require the cooperation of countries in the form of access, technical support, and the availability of key documents. The Rwanda tribunal required the cooperation of "nearly every country in Africa" when it came to apprehending and transferring suspects who had fled to every corner of the continent and beyond. The Yugoslavia tribunal conducted delicate negotiations with NATO and with the government of Serbia for the transfer of Slobodan Milosevič and other high-level indictees.[23] The president of the International Criminal Court, Phillipe Kirsch, points out that many of criminal courts' activities have taken and will take place in situations of armed conflict, creating a major challenge to the court's effectiveness. For the criminal courts, governments are partners in the process in that their support is essential for the courts' effectiveness. He adds, however, that while the International Criminal Court will necessarily have to engage government assistance to carry out its activities, it nonetheless remains a purely judicial institution.

For the courts involving states as parties, questions often arise about how often and how fully governments will comply with their judgments. This situation varies considerably from court to court. In Europe, compliance with decisions of the European Court of Justice is a matter of European Community law. Judgments of the ECJ have "direct effect" in national courts, so domestic judges can implement its judgments as a matter of domestic law.[24] In addition, the ECJ can impose hefty fines on countries that do not comply, although in practice such fines are relatively rare and used more as a threat than a punishment. When Italy, for example, took several years to implement a judgment aimed at providing fair compensation for foreign language assistants in Italian universities, the European Commission asked the ECJ to impose a penalty of more than three hundred thousand Euros per day. The Italian government moved hastily to implement the judgment, and the court declined to penalize Italy for its foot-dragging in the matter.[25]

The European Court of Justice and the European Court of Human Rights function in many ways more like domestic courts than international courts, since they are binding agents in an integrated continental system, and the member states have a considerable stake in the process of cooperation. The ECHR, with its broader membership and far larger number of cases, has less leverage in the matter of compliance than the ECJ, though it, too, has the power to impose monetary awards to compensate victims.[26] Still, good standing in the larger European community is an important incentive for states to cooperate. The pressure may be most effective regarding countries that are parties to the European Convention on Human Rights, but who have not yet been able to join the European Union. An ECHR judge points out that the compliance with court judgments in Turkey, Serbia, Romania, Bulgaria, and other EU-aspirant nations has increased significantly as those countries ratchet up their campaigns for membership. In this case, the judge points out, political pressure is being applied *by* the court, rather than against it.

Outside of a regional system, however, the complicated structure of "membership" in the courts makes enforcement more difficult.[27] In the end, the only real incentive to cooperate is a state's general desire to be a member in good standing of the international community. This means that courts like the International Court of Justice have a stronger record of compliance with smaller states than among the major powers, which can often either refuse to participate in cases before the ICJ or insist on reservations or limitations to its jurisdiction in their particular cases.[28] The United Kingdom, for example, is the only permanent member of the UN Security Council that has made an open-ended declaration of acceptance of the compulsory jurisdiction of the court.[29] All others accept case by case, if ever.

The Role of Presidents

At the center of the courts' push and pull in the world of international politics are the court presidents. The precise definition of the president's role varies from court to court, but there are some common themes and responsibilities. In most cases, the president serves at least four distinct functions: judge, administrator, public spokesperson, and diplomat. The last involves the president in direct and frequent contact with governments: reporting on the work of the courts, securing funds and other resources, seeking assistance in apprehending suspects, and, in the case of the ICC, making the case for states to sign on as parties to the court. The president is not only the leader of the judicial process, but also the builder of the institution in its younger days and its caretaker as the institution matures. His role requires the most delicate balance between the judicial and political functions of the court. Striking this balance is somewhat at odds with the judicial temperament; perhaps this is why the post of president has often been occupied by men and women with backgrounds as diplomats and academics.

The president's role has been particularly crucial over the course of the last twenty years, during the difficult birthing process for several international courts. In those early years, presidents have been called upon to bring a diverse group of people together to build an international institution, while at the same time maintaining a complex set of external relations in order to secure the credibility and future of the court. During his first years in office, Phillippe Kirsch, the first president of the International Criminal Court, traveled frequently to such countries as China, India, Russia, Lebanon, Syria, Mexico, and the United States—where he undertook considerable efforts to try to soften opposition to the court's work in often hostile political environments.

The president embodies the institution of the courts, poised between pure justice and pure politics. It is he who most directly absorbs the states' pressures upon the courts as institutions; it is he who most directly applies whatever leverage the courts may have with governments when it comes to securing assistance, respect, and cooperation. Yet he must remain first and foremost a judge, writes Judge Theodor Meron of the ICTY, striking the delicate balance between securing cooperation and protecting his institution against the undermining influence of state encroachment.[30]

Money and Resources

Judicial independence may be the cornerstone of justice, but every international court is highly dependent in one crucial respect: the money and resources that it takes for it to function.[31] International courts are complicated, expensive endeavors, and they depend for their budgets on the annual largesse and the goodwill of governments and intergovernmental organizations. The courts, moreover, operate in a larger institutional context, in many cases as part of large bureaucracies with rules and regulations that are not always consistent with the smooth functioning of a judicial organization. Caught between the uncertainty of resources and the arcane rules of the bureaucracy, judges frequently find the already measured pace of justice to be almost unbearably slow, and they worry that resource issues will compromise their effectiveness and their credibility.

Money issues are most salient in the criminal courts, by far the most expensive enterprises in the international justice system. Since its establishment in 1993, the ICTY spent over $1.2 billion by 2006; its budget for the two-year period of 2006–2007 was more than $276 million.[32] The ICTR has nearly kept pace: by 2007, the tribunal will have consumed more than $1 billion, with an annual budget just behind that of its sister court.[33] Meanwhile, the International Criminal Court, still a fledgling institution, had an annual budget of $82 million in 2006, when its first proceedings were just getting under way.[34]

Critics of the international courts have been merciless on the subject of costs, with public attacks coming even from within the Office of Legal Affairs at the United Nations itself.[35] Millions of dollars have been spent on a relatively small number of trials. As of 2006, the ICTY had secured forty-seven convictions, the ICTR just twenty-five.[36] Examined in that light, the criminal tribunals look like bloated, self-serving organizations, siphoning much-needed funds away from other enterprises that would more directly touch the lives of people in need. In 2006–2007, the criminal tribunals together commanded approximately 7 percent of the regular budget of the United Nations, providing nearly twenty-two hundred jobs between them.[37] Even a judge on the International Court of Justice, which occupies Andrew Carnegie's opulent Peace Palace in The Hague, cannot help remarking that the criminal tribunals seem to be "awash in money."

The criminal court judges, however, are quick to point out that the complexity of their trials and their unprecedented nature make the cost of justice inherently expensive. For one thing, the ICTY, the ICTR, and the ICC are not simply courts where cases are heard. They are also the home of enormous investigative operations (under the auspices of the offices of the prosecutors), they are victim and witness protection organizations, and they operate their own detention facilities. The costs associated with the judges, their staff, and the courtroom procedures themselves are a relatively small part of the operation. At the ICTY, the prosecutor's office alone employs hundreds of staff members engaged in investigations, preparation of cases, and caring for witnesses. Security costs related to detention facilities, protection of witnesses, and the court buildings themselves consume millions of dollars. Furthermore, high-profile trials are simply expensive; the Oklahoma City bombing trial, conducted in the United States, is estimated to have cost U.S. taxpayers over $80 million in two years.[38]

The international nature of the courts adds no small burden to the costs. Both ad hoc tribunals are headquartered hundreds of miles from the jurisdiction where the crimes took place. This may be an advantage for the administration of impartial justice and security, but it makes for an expensive process in terms of travel and accommodation costs for investigators, witnesses, and even the judges themselves, for whom a "site visit" in the course of a trial can be a time-consuming and costly process. Translation into multiple languages, both of documents and of courtroom proceedings, consumes hundreds of thousands of hours of labor each year. And an international court means an international staff, entitled to return trips to their home countries as a matter of course and as a fixed part of the courts' budgets.

So while observers in the international community have hammered away at the cost of the criminal tribunals, the judges themselves experience a sense of continual shortage and frustration that their critics have little understanding of the challenges of conducting the trials. One criminal court judge cites "economic independence for all the tribunals" as a key priority, noting that some national systems allot fixed percentages of their budgets to the judiciary in order to cultivate predictability and reduce the influence of politics. "What I don't like is the idea to have this burden every year to beg for the money."

The ad hoc tribunals face a special set of challenges as organizations operating with the United Nations system. As UN organizations, the tribunals are bound by rules regarding hiring, pay structure, and expense accounting that are more appropriate to civil service bureaucracies than to the specialized requirements of a court. The UN umbrella adds overhead costs, and it reduces the flexibility and therefore the efficiency of the courts' administration. One court president, though proud of the record of his tribunal, cites the inflexibility of the UN hiring regulations as the one thing that he would change about the court if he could. While the court presidents have sometimes managed to negotiate exceptions, they tend to share the widespread perception that the UN system hampers innovation and efficiency.

For Navanethem Pillay, the chief frustration was the enormous time expended in getting the "little things" done during her tenure as president of the ICTR. Working in Arusha, Tanzania, in facilities barely adequate to their function, her "endless, endless problems with the UN" came to be symbolized for her in a battle with the UN administration over something as trivial as windows. When the court moved into its new facility, UN maintenance workers unaccountably bricked up all the available windows, substituting bits of wire netting as the only air passages in the courtroom. "We just sweated in those courtrooms," Pillay recalls. The first president of the ICTR wrote to the UN secretary general about this several times during the tribunal's first four years, without receiving a response. When Pillay became president, she continued to lobby. "So windows became a big priority for me as president. Finally, in the fifth year, they broke down the walls and put in the windows. The windows were ordered from Nairobi and took nine months to arrive."

With the pace of trials a continuing problem and costs mounting, the UN has in turn put pressure on the ad hoc criminal tribunals to develop a "completion strategy" for wrapping up their trial work by 2008 and their appeals work by 2010.[39] Judges understand that there are good reasons for establishing a time frame; aside from the costs, justice has a diminishing return when trials are held fifteen or more years after the commission of the crimes. But they are also wary that pressures for completion may require sacrificing key principles.[40] "Go for the completion strategy," says one ICTY judge, "but the only thing we cannot do is to reduce the human rights guarantees. This I think we cannot do."

While the criminal tribunals face unique resource and time challenges, other international courts face similar situations. As we have seen, at the European Court of Human Rights the problem is not with lengthy cases, but with sheer volume. As a court of last resort for forty-six countries across the continent, the ECHR allows individuals to file cases once they have exhausted domestic remedies. The process began slowly, but it has snowballed in recent years, to the point that in 2006 the court had a backlog of more than seventy thousand cases.[41] The number is misleading: tens of thousands of those cases will eventually be ruled as inadmissible, but each still needs to be considered in some fashion by the court's registry and disposed of (often in batches) through an appropriate process. Even though the ECHR's budget doubled between 1998 and 2004 in response to the growing backlog, the registrar of the court notes that he would have to double his staff just to keep up with the incoming cases, much less to begin to reduce the backlog.[42]

One ECHR judge notes that states are taking advantage of this situation to try to divert the court from its principal purpose: checking the human rights abuses of governments. "In view of that backlog," says the judge, "there is enormous pressure coming on the court to increase the turnover of cases. Everyone, from the Russians, who I think are certainly enthusiastically backing this idea for us to do more cases, to the Secretary General [of the UN], who seems to have fallen for this line as well, think that this is their real duty: get the court to do more cases. But, of course what they really mean is: have the court occupied with inadmissible cases. That's the only way you can get your numbers up. As long as you're clogged up doing inadmissible cases you can't concentrate on the cases where you *actually* find a violation. In short, don't do the cases that really need to be done. Do only the cases that don't need to be done." Resource challenges, in other words, provide an opportunity for states to seek ways to reduce the effectiveness of the court, without making blatantly aggressive moves against judicial independence.

The situation in the ECHR's counterpart, the Inter-American Court of Human Rights, is even worse. In 2003, the part-time court doubled the length of its working sessions to accommodate an increased caseload, but the Organization of American States was unable to increase the funds available. The situation triggered a "virtual mutiny" among the judges, causing the court to complain to the OAS that "[we] must be candid and express with total clarity that the system is on the verge of collapse. The old adage 'justice delayed is justice denied' is at the point of becoming reality in our own Inter-American System."[43]

For all their problems, the ad hoc tribunals and the human rights courts do at least have regular sources of funding. Not so the Special Court on Sierra Leone, which was established with the expectation that it would be funded by "voluntary contributions" from states and private organizations around the world. This situation put its first president, Geoffrey Robertson, in the undignified position of traveling to world capitals to "sell" his fledgling institution, confronting him with uncomfortable choices about which financial arrangement might compromise the independence, or the perception of independence, of the court. Eventually, Canada, the United States, and other countries stepped forward to finance the SCSL, but resource shortfalls have hampered its operations.[44] The situation is, perhaps, even more dire in the case of the special chambers being established in Cambodia, also funded by voluntary contributions. As of 2006, no trial of a Khmer Rouge leader had yet begun, partly because of political problems with the current Cambodian regime, partly because funding for the court has been fitful at best.[45]

Nevertheless, legitimate questions will persist about the "value" for the dollars spent on international courts. The criminal courts have sometimes been targeted unfairly; but even if their costs are well understood and accounted for, some observers will inevitably wonder whether formal court proceedings represent the best way to spend hundreds of millions of dollars in a search for postconflict justice. Among the noncriminal courts, expansion has led to the creation of new institutions like the International Tribunal for the Law of the Sea, which has a very small caseload; with an annual budget nearly two-thirds that of the much busier International Court of Justice, the ITLOS might well be an example of "judicial overkill."[46] This type of example makes it difficult for judges on the more financially pressed courts to make the case for their resource needs.

The United States' Shadow

When it comes to the intersection of international law and politics, no issue is more important or more sensitive than the role of the United States. The recent hostility of the world's richest and most powerful nation not only toward specific decisions of international courts but to the very idea of international law itself poses a significant threat to the effectiveness of justice on a global scale. International judges follow U.S. actions and rhetoric quite closely, aware of the present and potential impact of such on their work. But they are surprisingly patient and philosophical about U.S. objections, taking a long view that stretches into the past and the future.

American critics object most vociferously to what they consider the "loose cannon" qualities of international courts. John Bolton, a state department official who later became United States ambassador to the United Nations, took the lead in this effort in the early years of the George W. Bush administration, focusing his ire on the International Criminal Court. President Bill Clinton signed the United States onto the ICC at the very end of his presidency, but the U.S. commitment was never ratified by the Senate, and the Bush administration went so far as to withdraw the country's signature.[47] "The ICC is an organization that runs contrary to fundamental American precepts and basic Constitutional principles of popular sovereignty, checks and balances, and national independence," Bolton charged. "Subjecting the United States to this treaty, with its unaccountable prosecutor and its unchecked judicial power, is clearly inconsistent with American standards of constitutionalism."[48] Bolton and other members of the administration argued that these "unaccountable" agents of international justice would bring political motives to their work and would use the ICC to carry out an anti-American agenda by targeting U.S. personnel. U.S. soldiers, they charged, would be constantly vulnerable to being hauled before the bar of justice, since any military mission might be portrayed as a war crime by unscrupulous representatives of the ICC. As a result of these fears, the United States has pressured many members of the court into signing bilateral agreements with the United States, promising not to bring charges against U.S. citizens.[49]

While the ICC has been the critics' principal target in recent years, similar charges have been leveled at the international courts more broadly. Henry Kissinger, as we have seen, believes that international courts simply provide a cover for political maneuvering, and hence are more deceptive and more dangerous than naked power politics practiced traditionally and transparently. Robert Bork has gone even further, charging that international courts provide an opportunity for a global radical intelligentsia to ride its values roughshod over the traditions, practices, and values of sovereign nations and their citizens. "As the culture war has become global," Bork writes, "so has judicial activism. Judges of international courts—the International Court of Justice, the European Court of Human Rights, and, predictably, the new International Criminal Court, among other forums—are continuing to undermine democratic institutions and to enact the agenda of the liberal Left or New Class. Internationally, that agenda contains a toxic measure of anti-Americanism."[50] In other words, international courts are inherently subversive, and a direct threat to U.S. autonomy and to the integrity of the U.S. Constitution.

It has not always been this way. The United States played a supportive role in the formation of international judicial bodies, beginning with the push for the Permanent Court of International Justice in the wake of World War I.[51] Such support echoed Wilsonian ideals and rhetoric about U.S. leadership in promoting democratic societies and justice around the world. After World War II, the United States drove the process behind the establishment of the Nuremberg and Tokyo trials, which for all their difficulties laid the foundation for international criminal law as we know it today. The United States was likewise an early supporter of the establishment of the International Court of Justice as the "principal judicial organ" of the United Nations, and Americans played a leading role in the development and adoption of the Universal Declaration of Human

Rights.[52] More recently, the United States has been an active participant in the dispute settlement process of the WTO, accepting both defeats and victories for its interests in the Appellate Body's final decisions. With regard to the criminal courts, the Clinton administration, led most publicly by Secretary of State Madeleine Albright, took a principal role in the establishment of the Yugoslavia tribunal. In the case of the International Criminal Court itself, Americans played a visible role in the 1998 Rome conference where the ICC was adopted, even though participation in the court has not to date been ratified by the U.S. Senate. In some cases, critics have impugned U.S. motives—skeptics argued that U.S. support for the ICTY, for example, was designed to paper over Western failure to halt the ethnic cleansing and bloodshed in the Balkans—but the steady involvement of U.S. diplomats and leaders in the establishment of international courts is undeniable.[53]

On the other hand, U.S. commitment to international legal institutions has consistently been undercut by its politicians' commitment to U.S. autonomy and freedom of action. As with the League of Nations, the United States was never a party to the Permanent Court of International Justice. Even though it joined the ICJ when it was established after World War II, the United States was one of the leaders of the unsuccessful fight to make the jurisdiction of the court voluntary in all cases. When that battle was lost, the United States Senate insisted on a formal reservation—the Connally amendment—that gave the United States the right to withdraw from the jurisdiction of the court for any case which its own leadership determined was a matter of domestic law.[54] The effect of the Connally amendment was not only to restrict significantly the circumstances under which the United States would submit to international law, but it also gave other countries the option to evade United States suits in the ICJ under the principle of reciprocity.[55] Even this reservation was not enough when Nicaragua brought suit against the United States in the ICJ in 1984, charging U.S. interference in its domestic affairs through the training and arming of the "contras," who sought to undermine the Sandinista government.[56] The United States did not invoke the Connally amendment, but when, in 1986, the ICJ found in favor of Nicaragua in the jurisdiction phase of the case, the United States took the formal step of withdrawing altogether from the compulsory jurisdiction of the court.[57] In addition, the United States has never become a party to the Inter-American Court of Human Rights statute, unwilling to provide a venue for domestic laws and decisions of U.S. courts to be challenged formally in a regional legal setting.[58]

These opposing tendencies underscore longstanding tensions in American political life: between unilateralism and an eagerness to lead the way in international cooperation, between U.S. sovereignty and an abstract commitment to the rule of law, between "messianism" and "chauvinism" of U.S. leaders.[59] In today's period of hostile rhetoric about the international courts, these tensions remain in play. Despite its formal reservations, the United States—under both Presidents Clinton and George W. Bush—agreed to participate in controversial cases before the ICJ involving the rights of foreign nationals on death row. These cases, involving citizens of Germany, Mexico, and Paraguay, revolved around the obligations of the United States under an international treaty to provide access to inmates on death row to the consulates of their home countries.[60] Following one such case, where the prisoners were executed even after an ICJ judgment ordering a stay, the court went so far as to re-assert its authority to issue binding decisions.[61] The refusal of a powerful democracy to honor the court's decisions represents a significant threat to the credibility of the law—though whether it is a threat to the credibility of the international courts or to U.S. democracy itself depends on the perspective of the observer. Yet even in defiance, the U.S. government began to make gestures toward respect for the law, embarking on an education campaign to train state law enforcement officers about international obligations and in some cases encouraging the commutation of death sentences of foreign nationals by governors and parole boards.[62]

International judges pay careful attention to U.S. attitudes and actions, and they are keenly aware of a U.S. government ambivalence that sometimes verges on institutional schizophrenia. They are quick to criticize the United States as a kind of "free rider" in international law, choosing the venues and cases where legal mechanisms suit national interests. But they also recognize that on the global spectrum, the United States has a relatively strong record of respect for international law. They note, for example, that the United States is by far the most frequent participant in proceedings before the WTO Appellate Body, and its record of compliance with those decisions is satisfactory. The cyclical nature of world politics remains much on their minds. "Things have worsened in the last years," says one European judge who has taught at an American university. "I mean, the U.S. has not always been as skeptical as it is now towards international law. I think it's just the consequence of being the last superpower. [Americans] think, 'We can reach our goals more easily by unilateral mechanisms than by transferring sovereignty to international courts.'"

Judges find most of the U.S. arguments against the International Criminal Court, in particular, to be specious, and they also detect mixed motivations even among U.S. opponents that may provide opportunities for more U.S. involvement over time. "I do understand better why the United States would want to protect itself on new developments on the use of force," says one diplomat-turned-judge, "particularly if they are conservative, particularly if they confirm the traditional rules governing the use of force. But in the case of the ICC, it's all, all imaginary." As long as the crime of aggression has not been defined, the civilian and military leaders of a country cannot be brought to task simply for initiating military conflict.[63] There are, moreover, several layers of protection against "unaccountable prosecutors." The prosecutor is, in fact, accountable to a three-judge pretrial chamber, which must affirm any indictment that he wishes to bring.[64] Among other things, the prosecutor must show that the state whose citizens are being charged is either unwilling or unable to bring war criminals to justice using its own justice system.[65] This principle of "complementarity" is designed to encourage governments to address these issues domestically, with the ICC available only as a last resort. The possibility of indictments against American citizens in the ICC certainly exists, but the safeguards in place would reserve such an action for extreme and probably unprecedented circumstances.

The effectiveness of the ICC, argues one judge of the court, depends less on U.S. ratification than on U.S. willingness to cooperate quietly. He notes that the Bush administration has gone on record as labeling the situation in Darfur a "genocide" and calling for action against its perpetrators. The ICC represents the best possible avenue for bringing those perpetrators to justice. "Will [the Americans] cooperate or will they not cooperate?" he wonders. "I don't believe that legislation in place prevents them from cooperating. If they do cooperate, if they do reinforce—they do strengthen—the ICC, they won't like that. But if they do not cooperate, there's no consistency between the stated purpose of bringing punishment and blocking the ICC, so I think this is going to be very interesting to watch." In the long term, in other words, it may not matter whether the United States ratifies the ICC or not, as long as its opposition becomes more muted. "What I would like to see is a level of cooperation, less animosity, a level of cooperation that develops incrementally."

Whenever the United States has decided to participate in an international court, its citizens have been amply represented as judges. Four Americans have served over the years on the Permanent Court of International Justice (even though the United States was not a party to the court), and six have served as permanent judges on the ICJ.[66] Stephen Schwebel served as president of the ICJ from 1997 to 2000. Three Americans have served on the ICTY, including two of its presidents, Gabrielle Kirk MacDonald and Theodor Meron.[67] Two, James Bacchus and Merit Janow, have served on the WTO Appellate Body. Thomas Buergenthal, now a member of the ICJ, served for twelve years as a judge of the Inter-American Court of Human Rights, to which the United States is not even a party; Buergenthal, as we have seen, was nominated to the post by Costa Rica, which clearly hoped that the presence of a U.S. judge might persuade the U.S. government to join the body.

International judges from the United States are clear-eyed about the faults of the international courts, but they are also deeply concerned about the impact of U.S. hostility toward their institutions. One U.S. judge acknowledges that the courts that adjudicate between states (like the ICJ) do allow ample opportunity for political posturing and maneuvering, especially because, he believes, the politicized selection process leads to unqualified appointments to the bench; other judges are more generous about the qualifications of their colleagues. But the U.S. judges seem to be of one mind about what one calls the "screwball diplomacy" of U.S. hostility to the ICC. September 11 and the "war on terror" have led to a weakening of support for human rights generally in the United States, one judge complains, to the point that "we're weakening international institutions and we don't give a damn." Opposition to the ICC goes hand in hand with the restriction of civil rights and human rights within the United States, he believes, and now his country is simply "throwing away" decades of achievements in these areas. Despite his anger, he points out that one source of U.S. indifference to international human rights issues is, ironically, the relative effectiveness of U.S. justice institutions. The citizens of most other countries in the world have often been victimized by their own governments, he points out, so they have had perforce to rely on international institutions as a last resort and as a corrective. U.S. citizens, on the other hand, have had many more opportunities to work for change within their own system. When it comes to understanding oppression, he says, "we just don't have that common experience," an experience that is often vital to building support for international courts.

Overall, however, the record suggests that U.S. hostility has slowed but has not crippled the functioning of the international courts. The ICC has well over a hundred states parties, and although it has had to do without the financial resources of the United States, it brought its first indictments and commenced its first proceedings in 2006. One judge even argues that the United States' public criticism of the ICC helps generate useful publicity and attention for the court. When it was proposed in 2006 that the Security Council refer potential war crimes in the Darfur region of the Sudan to the ICC prosecutor, the United States abstained rather than vetoing the measure, thereby tacitly permitting the work of the court to move forward.[69] The ad hoc criminal tribunals have benefited from considerable U.S. participation, not only on the bench but also through the work of lawyers and investigators in the prosecutors' offices. Even though U.S. compliance with ICJ decisions is far from complete, the United States continues to participate in the court by nominating judges and appearing before the bench. Despite their charges of anti-Americanism and criticism of certain decisions, U.S. critics of the courts have little evidence to back up their allegations of persistent and systematic bias against their country. Indeed, there is considerable evidence that only a handful of cases in international courts have any bearing—much less impact—on matters of U.S. sovereignty.[69] The judges do worry about U.S. influence—a judge from another country claims that three senators took unsuccessful action to oppose his reelection after he participated in decisions that went against the United States—but they tend to see U.S. attitudes and actions as part of an evolving and sometimes cyclical process, recognizing that U.S. opposition is consistent neither across the political spectrum nor over time.

Public Pressures

Seclusion from politics, as regards the ideal type of the judge, also means seclusion from the pressures of the public and the media. For all the U.S. talk of "unaccountable" judges, the United States and most other democracies have attempted to ensure that judges are protected from the swirling winds of public opinion. Insulation from public opinion is, in some ways, basic to the work of the judge, whose first duty is to the law rather than to an electorate. In practice, judicial seclusion from public pressure has proved less than perfect. In the United States, for example, legislatures and other political bodies have tried numerous times to coerce judges to be more responsive to majority sentiment, and the public examinations of Supreme Court candidates have become a regular ritual of political scrutiny.[70] But direct attempts to influence judges represent clear violations of a longheld standard of detachment.

It could be argued, however, that the international courts have in some ways the opposite problem. To the extent that their long-term success depends on their credibility as international institutions, these courts *need* public attention. They need to establish their relevance, their integrity, and their effectiveness. To do so, they need to be seen and heard, not just by the legal and diplomatic communities, but also by a broad cross-section of the citizenry of the countries that support them. Legal scholars Lawrence Helfer and Anne-Marie Slaughter have argued that international courts ignore this larger constituency at their peril. They point out that "individuals and their lawyers, voluntary associations, and non-governmental organizations are ultimately the users and consumers of judicial rulings," and that "an appreciation of the relationship between these social actors and the institutions of state government opens the door to deploying them as forces for expanding the power and influence of international tribunals. Just as an international tribunal may align its case law with the independent incentives facing some national courts, it can also address itself to the individuals and groups who are likely to be the ultimate beneficiaries of the enforcement of international norms and instruments."[71] Without that visibility, the courts run the risk of indifference, leading inexorably to a drop in the support and cooperation from states that are so vital to their success.

This need for public recognition puts international judges in an awkward position. How can they solicit public attention without creating public pressures for particular outcomes? How far should international judges go in making conscious efforts to reach a broader audience? What dangers to their independence and effectiveness might arise in making such efforts?

Some members of the international bench maintain traditional judicial caution about public statements. "As a matter of principle, personally, I don't talk to the press," says one judge who has served as a court president. "But if the head of the public affairs section says I should talk, then I talk." Others prefer to let the official documents speak for themselves, except in unusual circumstances. "Obviously, for a judge who decided a case, especially as one of several judges, to interpret judicial decisions to the media would seldom be wise, and in certain circumstances might be inappropriate," says one judge. "But in case of egregious error or gross misrepresentation by the media, a correction by the judge cannot be entirely excluded. Helping journalists report notable judicial decisions accurately so that the public becomes better informed increases appreciation of the importance of our work and is a legitimate public relations function."[72] One court president is willing to reach out to specific constituencies, such as ministers of state or national judges, and concedes that press releases by themselves are "obviously not enough"; however, he still thinks that "it would be dangerous for the courts through the president to try to explain the judgment."

A growing number of judges, particularly from the criminal courts, see the dangers but still believe that the courts must be more proactive in establishing strong relationships with the media. "We really need to create closer links with the media to inform them," says one judge, "because it's the only way for the people to know what's going on here." By maintaining a judicial silence, warns another judge, courts run the risk of letting interested parties "own" the story. "There should be a much greater attempt to explain the purpose of the court and to keep the public apprised," she argues; otherwise, the court's work is interpreted either by inexperienced members of the press or by NGOs who have an interest in giving it their own spin. Another judge recalls that in the early days of the Inter-American Court of Human Rights, judges were prevented from making "any but the blandest pronouncements" about cases before them. "Judgments of international human rights courts that are not adequately publicized are much easier for governments to disregard," he notes.[73]

With greater efforts in public outreach, however, come increased and sometimes specific public expectations. These expectations are clearest for the criminal courts, to the extent that those courts are seen not as instruments of impartial justice but as mechanisms for punishment or even revenge. "'You know, they're all guilty anyway,'" is how one judge characterizes a commonly held public sentiment. "These are the people that in the international sphere are pushing for convictions and long sentences. They get furious—I'm overstating it—if you don't give a life sentence to everybody that comes down. So there is a switch and the pressure is on to convict, by and large, over there." For judges with a human rights background, this pressure comes with a considerable irony. Many of them spent earlier parts of their careers protecting the rights of *defendants* in national courts, holding military organizations, police departments, and justice systems accountable for their violations of fairness and justice. But as judges on international criminal courts, they can find themselves pressured by erstwhile colleagues to give primary attention to the rights of victims, rather than those in the dock.

The president of the International Criminal Court, Philippe Kirsch, understands that "expectations have always been extremely high" for the ICC. "While the ICC will do everything it can to fulfill its role effectively, it is simply not possible to meet all of the expectations," he continues. "An accurate understanding of the court is important to ensuring sustained, effective—and necessary—support. This is why, when speaking about the court, I explain not only its potential, but also the limitations of the court's jurisdiction, the complexity of situations in which it operates in the field, and its dependence on external support, for example in the execution of arrest warrants." A constant frustration is that the ICTY and the ICC, with jurisdiction over places where fighting has been ongoing, have little ability directly to bring an immediate end to bloodshed.

Nongovernmental organizations play a key role in intensifying media and public scrutiny, a role that international judges consider a mixed blessing. One criminal court judge calls NGO involvement a "healthy development" because activists call attention to "real burning issues" that judges, by habit of professional detachment, tend to set aside. But she argues that NGO involvement "really has to be controlled—they mustn't come here to argue one side of the thing. We're not [only] in the business of convictions." Another judge points out that NGOs, by their nature, are maximalists: "[M]ost of them aim at 100 per cent success and if they don't get that, then there is something wrong." This passion means that they can be of considerable assistance to the courts in providing advice and information, but that their methods are sometimes at odds with the judicial temperament of balance. When it comes to relations with NGOs, "Dialogue, yes, but control, no," says one judge.

The noncriminal courts, too, find themselves under pressure to prove their relevance; judges on these courts concede that they keep one eye on public concerns. At the International Court of Justice, for example, one judge points out that the court is under pressure to issue decisions backed by a large majority in politically sensitive cases such as territory disputes, "where having a pretty united bench is thought pretty important to stop the fighting on the ground." Even though the ICJ's presidents have traditionally maintained considerable reserve, the court as an institution has taken a series of steps to better accommodate the press, including renovations to the press room, increased staff, and video coverage of proceedings. But it is still difficult to get attention for the ICJ's work. "The truth of the matter is that the press at the moment thinks that international crimes are sexy, but that law that's not criminal is boring." Another ICJ judge notes that states parties themselves are adept at using the media for their own ends; for the state's representatives, sometimes the outcome of the court's decision is secondary to the opportunity to prove to the domestic public that they have defended their country's interests before an international institution.

Regional courts like those in Europe face the challenge of communicating a continental perspective through domestic media that inevitably filter the courts' work through their national self-interest. "Most of our decisions are decisions where its direct and immediate impact is on a small, concentrated group of people," says one judge on the European Court of Justice, and that impact is usually negative. "For example, opening a national market, requiring a member state no longer to give protection to its nationals regarding economic support of the state. And instead the benefits are diffused through all the other nationals of the European Union, for example. And who is going to focus on this case? Well, the newspapers of the state it is in and not the other ones." In that situation, "this means that we are a court whose individual decisions will normally, because of asymmetries of costs and benefits, tend to have a risk of lacking popular support. So it is very important that we try to make people understand in terms that our legitimacy comes from the system." The situation is aggravated because affected governments speak readily to their own press, fanning the flames. In one case, an ECJ judge reports, officials of a member state used the press to threaten withholding financial support for the court if a particular judgment was unfavorable; such a use of the media, he says, "is an illegitimate form of pressure."

On occasion, however, the international courts feel an obligation to bend their rules and procedures in the face of national or international opinion. "Sometimes," says a member of the International Court of Justice, "you're quite convinced that the law requires X, but if dreadful things are going on in a particular country, you know, then there is the discussion of, 'How will the world see it if we say we can't hear this, or that they've not complied?'" or if there are "procedures" that interfere with a case being heard. The judge cites the case involving the wall between Israel and the Palestinian territories. Even though "there was no basis" in the court's usual procedure for allowing a nonstate entity—the Palestinians—to appear as a party, "yet every single one of us thought— 'they've just got to be here.'" Part of this, of course, is a calculated effort on the part of the courts to prove their relevance on matters of import. One WTO Appellate Body member bemoans the fact that laymen fail to distinguish between the WTO as an organization and the dispute settlement mechanism, where concerns about institutional priorities can be aired. The public tends to believe, he argues, that the Appellate Body itself "is there to further globalization, to serve the interests of the multinationals, to serve the big powers against the small." Outsiders have the opportunity, he says, to "master the machinery" and further their interests within the system by using the dispute settlement mechanism, "rather than throwing stones from the outside."

Defenders of the ideal of the secluded judge will view the increasing openness of the international courts to the media and the public as a loss for judicial integrity. But there is every reason to come to the opposite conclusion. In a world where public scrutiny of failure is inevitable and public attention to success is scant, the courts as institutions must seize every opportunity to explain their work from the viewpoint of their institutional concerns. This may present some ethical challenges for judges as individual professionals, as we shall explore in the last chapter. But for the courts as institutions, cautious self-promotion is vital to the exercise of their function. They must participate in the process of shaping realistic perceptions of their work; otherwise, they become more vulnerable to the pressure of uninformed, self-interested public expectations. They do not operate in splendid isolation from political actors and the larger public; to pretend that they do simply damages the prospects for effective justice.

Global Justice, Local Impact

One reason that international judges think so much about public opinion and expectations is that they are concerned about the ultimate impact of their courts at the national and even the local level. After all, most international courts are by definition at a remove from the locale of the cases that they hear, a physical gap that can create a psychological and emotional gap between the dispensers of justice and those to and for whom justice is done. Judges know courts do not operate in a vacuum and that the courts' success will be measured not only by the integrity of their proceedings, but by the impact of their cases on people's lives.

This gap is most conspicuous for the international criminal courts, which often take testimony and hear evidence at a remove of hundreds or thousands of miles from where the crimes were committed. No matter how thorough the trials, no matter how appropriate the sentences, will justice be *felt* by the victims and by the citizens of the countries and regions where crimes against humanity have taken place? The incarceration of a small number of perpetrators, no matter how highly placed, may seem remote and incomplete to people who witnessed and survived the massacre of friends and family. Indeed, researchers in both the Balkans and in Rwanda have found widespread discontent with the work of the international tribunals for exactly this reason. The small number of trials, the large expense, the distance from the site, the antiretroviral treatments provided to those suspected of sexual violence crimes in Rwanda while their victims die of AIDS, confinements of those convicted at the ICTY in relatively comfortable European prisons—these factors have sparked widespread discontent and cynicism about the ad hoc tribunals, as individual citizens come to feel that justice is somehow beyond their reach.[74]

The criminal court judges recognize this problem. "In terms of the impact on local life, of course it would be better to have the tribunals on site," one judge says. "I like the idea of being there," says another, "being where the event occurred and before the eyes and ears of the people for whom it matters." But the trade-offs would be significant. Aside from problems of security, the pressures of the national government and other forces within the society would be difficult to resist, possibly compromising the integrity of the judicial process.

For a small minority of the judges, however, the issues of distance and time have begun to eclipse the accomplishments of the tribunals. "I think that it would have been very much preferable to have established a court in the Balkans," says one ICTY judge. "The cases we are judging are too far removed. I don't think that anybody cares about crimes that were committed ten or twelve years ago, including the victims. Very often, they have moved on with their lives, and they often don't want to be witnesses any longer. They have moved on with their lives, to forget. I think that this has taken much too long, and too far away from the places." The ICTY did eventually give support to the establishment of a war crimes chamber to operate within the Criminal Division of the State Court of Bosnia, but the ultimate success of this effort is still in question. Still, says one ICTY judge active in outreach efforts, "it is my feeling that the case for international justice—but I will say more, in general, the case for international law—is lost if the local, the domestic, judiciary are kept out of this."

The architects of the Special Court for Sierra Leone, established much later than the Yugoslavia and Rwanda tribunals, addressed this problem by creating a mixed tribunal of international and domestic judges located in Sierra Leone itself.[75] From the point of view of the local population, says one judge, this was a welcome development, depending, of course, on whether one's friends or one's enemies were before the bench. One ICTY judge suggests that the international community might have tried a modified version of this with the Yugoslavia tribunal by appointing judges from the Balkans to The Hague bench once the conflict there had ended. This would not have solved the problem of distance, but having representatives of their region on the bench might have provided a sense of connection and fairness to citizens of the former Yugoslavia. The problem, however, as the judge points out, is that the tribunal might have been forced to appoint judges from all different sides of the conflict, creating a complex appointment system that could have compromised the tribunal's work.

The ad hoc tribunals were established under chapter 7 of the United Nations Charter, which meant that one part of their mandate was to contribute to reconciliation between the warring parties in the aftermath of the conflicts.[76] Judges have differing opinions about what "contributing to reconciliation" means and the extent to which their courts should be directly involved. For some, the criminal tribunals serve this purpose best simply by conducting their trials properly and holding the highest-level war criminals accountable for their actions; the trials, in this way of thinking, make local efforts at reconciliation possible. One judge on the Rwanda tribunal remarks that reconciliation "is something we want to contribute to, but it is clear that reconciliation must come from the inside, not from outside. You cannot sit back and expect an international court—not in Kigali [Rwanda], but in Arusha [Tanzania], about one-and-a-half hours' flying distance—to do the job of reconciliation."

Others believe that the courts must be more directly visible and involved in the regions, especially in the interests of establishing domestic justice on a firm footing for the future. The tribunals have conducted modest outreach programs in the Balkans and in Rwanda, mostly with the intent of creating public awareness and understanding about the courts and their work.[77] But over the long run, says one judge, the key will be to strengthen local systems of justice. The International Criminal Court, he points out, will never be able to handle all of the world's major crimes. "The case for international law is lost," he argues, "if the domestic judiciary is kept out of it. . . . How can this group of eighteen judges [at the ICC] deal with all the international crimes that are committed?" A strong consensus exists that the ad hoc tribunals had neither a forceful enough mandate nor enough resources to make significant progress in strengthening local justice in the Balkans and Rwanda. The hope is that the ICC, with its principle of complementarity, will eventually provide both the encouragement and, to some extent, the resources and expertise to strengthen weaker national justice systems. But it is not clear whether the will and means to do this will be available.

Judges from the regional courts and from courts serving states parties face these problems in a less dramatic way, but they, too, often think strategically about how to maximize their courts' impact in relation to larger social and political circumstances. There is a long-running debate about the role of judges on the European Court of Human Rights and the European Court of Justice in promoting an agenda of European unity.[78] A high-ranking official of the ECHR says frankly and unapologetically that the heart of the court's work is "the idea of a European unity—a common European identity, an approach based on certain shared values." Even a judge who rejects the idea of a trans-European "policy" concedes that he and his colleagues are constantly faced with "delicate and difficult matters" that challenge them to consider, "What is the function of the court?" Should the ECJ simply apply the law, or take a more active role as a key institution in establishing European unity? "Is it just to hold the ring or is it sometimes to give the lead? But we don't discuss it in abstract terms, we tend to discuss it in the context of a particular case. That said, I suppose the form that the discussion takes may very well be led by a particular discussant's personal view as to how much should be left to the politicians and how much is to be left to law. And sometimes you will find people taking the view, 'Well, this may be intellectually untidy, but this is the messy political field.'"

For some observers, a calculated effort at "incrementalism" is the key to the widespread acceptance of the ECJ throughout Europe, and it provides a model of the ways that judges can take into account political considerations without becoming pawns of the political process. When the ECJ first started, write Lawrence Helfer and Anne-Marie Slaughter, "the forms and language of law insulated an emerging legal community from the political realm. Again, this is not to suggest a strict divide between law and politics, but rather a mediated interaction. The overall boundaries for the ECJ are set by the political institutions of the Community, above all the member states. If the Court pushes teleological interpretation of the treaty—a mode of interpretation biased toward achieving the ever closer union described in the Treaty's preamble—too far too fast, the member states can act to curtail its jurisdiction or urge their national courts to disregard its judgments."[79] The judges may indeed be dealing in the first instance with matters that are brought before them, but the record suggests that they have remained conscious of the larger context of their work.

Control of the docket is essential, if not a prerequisite, for a court to be able to strategize and develop a coherent jurisprudence and maintain a consistent policy. "I am not sure that we can bring about dramatic changes in international law with this court," one ICJ judge admits. "We can do things in a very slow way, by accretion. We can change our procedures sufficiently, and our internal communication, to have an impact on what is happening and what is coming to us. But changing international law will depend still on what is coming in." Lack of control of what issues are brought before the court has various undermining effects. First, it might put the court at the center of a very heated political dispute, but one that the court lacks the power to settle, like the question of the legality of nuclear weapons.[80] Other times, it might push courts to seize the occasion to develop jurisprudence on a given issue because it cannot be sure that a similar case will later arise.

Some courts, however, at a certain point in history, might have an empty or light docket, little or no tradition to preserve, and a small group of judges who have a similar outlook on law. One judge recalls fondly the first few years at the Inter-American Court of Human Rights: "The IACHR was a court where you could say, 'Let's plan a little, let's think about a strategy.' There were seven of us. So even with five, six, you could get together and say, 'Let's think a little bit about how we deal with this. What are the political implications?'" The situation provided the opportunity to strategize about how to convince countries to bring significant matters to their dockets. "We went out and looked for things," he recalls, "and we would talk to governments and get [them to request] advisory opinions . . . otherwise we would have gone out of business." Such direct strategizing is more characteristic of a fledgling institution; the judges at more tradition-bound institutions like the ICJ are conscious of the extent to which their court is used and respected in all corners of the world. One ICJ judge notes with satisfaction that a number of decisions of the court against major Western powers like the United States have helped encourage non-Western countries to trust it and bring cases before it.[81] He notes that, at the court's instigation, the UN has established a fund to enable poorer countries to afford legal counsel before the ICJ. He says that this support has made possible at least three recent cases that would otherwise have been beyond the resources of the parties.[82]

That international judges would think consciously about the impact of their work on individual citizens and the effectiveness of their institutions within the global political context is exactly what concerns their critics. "History shows," writes Robert Bork, "that the citizens of individual nations have been unable and unwilling to resist the depredation of their national courts. There is no reason to expect they will be able to resist courts that are sitting in foreign countries, composed of judges of several nationalities, and operating under vague humanistic standards to which their own nations have, however ambiguously, pledged allegiance."[83] For

Bork, the "depredations" of international courts represent direct threats to the autonomy of individuals and nations.

For the judges, however, there is nothing "vague" or even "humanistic" about the standards that they apply; and their consciousness about domestic and local circumstances, rather than undermining autonomy, ultimately strengthens local capacity. Their courts face misunderstanding, suspicion, and distance—enormous hurdles that can interfere with their credibility. Rather than pretending that their courts can operate in complete isolation, international judges, at their best, have chosen to inspire "allegiance" through persuasion and transparency. Rather than imposing themselves on hostile communities, they have striven to create a more cooperative, mutually beneficial relationship with their constituencies.

ॐ PROFILE

Cecilia Medina Quiroga, Chile

Judge of the Inter-American Court of Human Rights

A Pragmatic Route to the Law

When Cecilia Medina Quiroga reflects on what put her on the path to her current position as international judge, she immediately evokes her upbringing.[1] Medina was born in the south of Chile, but after an earthquake her family moved north to Santiago, the city where she was raised and has lived most of her life. Medina characterizes her family as "progressive":

> *They had very strong ideas about equality. For example, my mother and my aunts all went to university. My mother was born in 1905, so you can imagine that this was not the common standard. So it was my mother who had a university degree, not my father. My father had had to work as he had been fatherless since boyhood, and he had seven brothers and sisters to help. So I grew up in this home where you were always encouraged to talk, to explain, to discuss. Spanish was a very important thing in my house. And books, obviously. We would be having lunch and somebody would use a word in the wrong manner and we would be told to get up and get the dictionary and see what we were saying. This is the kind of family I grew up in.*

Medina came from a family with few resources, and this reality shaped her ideas of what she wanted to do as an adult. She recalls that her economic situation made her first choices of livelihood difficult to pursue. Law was chosen for very pragmatic reasons.

My first inclination was to study engineering. But engineering was a man's profession. I wasn't told not to do it, but my friends all joked about it. And then there was a major problem of money, because you could not possibly study engineering and work at the same time. And I felt responsible not to put any burden on my family. So I decided to study law—the classes were from 8:30 to 1:00 and afterward I could work. If I look back I think that actually this was the right choice for me. I took a job as a secretary in a cement factory; by then I could speak English. I had gone to the Chilean British Institute since I was twelve because I was very keen on languages. So three times a week I went for an hour to this institute, and by the end of five years I could manage quite well. So at the factory, they discovered that I could write in English, and they started asking me to answer letters.

Medina's next job was as assistant to the secretary of a court of first instance of Chile, which, at the time, had only a single judge. She continued in this position until her fifth year of law school, after which she worked furiously to complete her degree and her six months of practical training. Medina was anxious to become a "proper lawyer" and open her own practice. She did this in the north of Chile, where she had relocated with her first husband. She found the practice of her profession disappointing, however.

I realized that I didn't like to be a practicing lawyer. I was good at it, I really was quite good at it, but I couldn't keep detached from my clients. And I had a fatal attraction to poor people in very terrible situations. I would assist them all, and I never had the courage to charge them anything because I thought they had such terrible problems. Was I going to add another burden by saying that they had to pay me? So it was impossible because I didn't have money, and I had to live. I also did not like to assist people whose motives I didn't think were the right ones. I was not a good lawyer in that sense, because as a lawyer, you have to be able to defend any client to the best of your ability. I wasn't able to do that and therefore I didn't take certain people as clients.

After she separated from her husband, Medina found herself back in Santiago with children to support, and with no money and no work. She approached a former classmate, who was a professor at the law faculty at the University of Chile, about a position, and she was offered a low-ranking instructorship teaching constitutional law. Although she at first felt unqualified to teach students, Medina soon realized that she was wrong.

I had a good sense of law and juridical thought, and I started read-
ing and learning. I think I have the capacity to teach. I like teach-
ing and I seem to be clear when I explain. So that compensated
probably for my lack of knowledge at the beginning. I started
moving up in the ladder from the lowest rank of assistants and
went up. I submitted myself to examinations and competitions in
order to advance.

By this time Medina had remarried; her new husband was a fellow law
professor, someone who was to become an important supporter of the Allende regime, which came to power in 1970. When this government fell
to a coup d'état in 1973, led by Augusto Pinochet, Medina's husband
went into hiding and eventually left the country—reluctantly, as he was
worried for his family. Medina had, in the meantime, become a *rappor-*
teur at the Constitutional Court of Chile, in addition to working as a professor. This court was officially abolished upon the takeover by the military regime, which put Medina in a potentially dangerous position.

I was working at the university and at the Constitutional Court.
The court was abolished, and we were summoned one day at the
law school and told that anybody who thought himself to be a sym-
pathizer of Allende had to leave. So I stood up to go. And some-
body said "No, no!" and I said "Yes, yes! That is what I'm going to
do." Then I left the room, and I was then submitted to a trial at the
law school. I was so angry that I requested a copy of the charges,
which were not being given to anybody. But I was so upset that the
man didn't dare refuse. The charge was that I had a certain "tem-
perament," that I might use my position to indoctrinate students. In
other words, I was charged with a crime that I might commit in the
future! And then we left Chile. So I never knew how that trial
ended. I just left.

Discovering a New Niche Abroad

At this point began a long period of exile from her native country. Medina and her children rejoined her husband; the family first spent a period
in East Germany, an experience that she found very difficult due to the
constraints put on her movements and the lack of professional opportunities. Then came an opportunity to relocate to Washington, D.C., in
part through the efforts of Orlando Letelier, a Chilean diplomat from the
former Allende government who had taken up residence in Washington
after running afoul of the Pinochet regime.

Letelier arranged for me to get an academic visa to the United States. But there was no way that I was going to find a place in an American university. I spent months looking for a job in Washington. My husband was earning something like $700 per month, and there were five of us. I remember we paid $450 per month for rent. But finally I found a job that started my career again. Somebody told me that there was an opening in a place called the Institute for the Development of Indian Law. It wasn't an academic opening, but since it was a research institute, I thought they might give me something that would fit my visa. I went there, and they said they needed a fundraiser. And I said, "I cannot do this." And they said, "Well, what can you do?" I said, "I am a lawyer, and I used to teach constitutional law, and I was the undersecretary and rapporteur of the Constitutional Court," and I produced my CV. They took a look at the CV, and I knew they didn't believe me. I just knew. And I said, "Look, I know Americans are not in the habit of asking for references and certificates, but I have all my papers translated and authorized." Three days later, they called me and asked if I could write background papers for the first International Conference on Aboriginal Peoples, organized under the auspices of the UN, which took place in 1977. And it was 1976. And I said, "Yes, this I can do. I am no expert in indigenous rights, but I can do this." So my job was to select a few countries and see how the law treated indigenous people.

This was Medina's real introduction to international human rights. She carried out research every day on indigenous rights at the Library of Congress, which eventually led to work on a library project in the Hispanic Law Division. Finally she was starting to find her professional niche. Her desire to help people could be developed in the field of human rights, she realized. And approaching these rights from an international perspective encouraged Medina to believe that what appeared unreachable within the limits of a single state could be accomplished if pursued jointly by many peoples and individuals.

The peregrinations of Medina's family, however, were not yet at an end. In 1976, Letelier was killed by a car bomb, a crime that many believe was perpetrated with the complicity of the CIA. By sheer luck, Medina's husband was not with him that day; Medina's daughter had also been in the ill-fated car the day before the explosion. Her family decided that they had had enough of the United States. In the meantime, the Dutch government had established the Institute for a New Chile, which aimed to restore democracy in her native country, and Medina was recruited to work there. The family relocated once again, this time to the Netherlands. Medina realized how hard these frequent moves were becoming for her children, who had to face not only another new country but also another new language. Medina had difficulties also, this time with her new job. The Chilean men who were running the institute assigned her responsibilities based on gender rather than on her talent and experience.

> *I wasn't happy. . . . I was the only woman and, therefore, I ended up as a secretary. Although I had an academic training and was capable of writing, of researching, and of doing anything intellectually challenging, I nominally was the secretary. And I had to take care of the coffee and so on. I was back at the bottom. I remember telling someone once that it was like Sisyphus—I'd carry the rock up to the top, only to have it roll all the way back down. That's been the story of my life, actually.*

Medina eventually ended up in Utrecht, teaching courses on international organizations—the IMF, the World Bank, the GATT, and so on. She worked with an expert on human rights, Pieter van Dijk, who suggested that it would be interesting to work on the inter-American human rights system. Medina decided to pursue her doctorate in Utrecht, undaunted by the fact that she was over fifty years old and already a grandmother. She chose the inter-American system as the topic of her dissertation, which placed her in a good position down the line to serve as a judge on the Inter-American Court.

Member of the Human Rights Committee

In 1990, Medina returned to Chile, as soon as the Pinochet regime ceded power through democratic elections. The new minister of foreign affairs was Enrique Silva Cimma, who had been her superior at the law school while she was teaching in the 1960s. She immediately went to him and said that she would like to be nominated to serve on a United Nations committee related to human rights. She wished to pursue her idea that human rights in Chile could be dramatically improved if international law could be brought to bear.

> *In those days, we were about to become a party to the Inter-American Convention on Human Rights. So Cimma said, "Certainly!" He wrote a little letter and I went to the Multilateral Relations Department with my CV and my letter and I said, "Well, I'm interested in really any committee dealing with human rights. I just want to have the United Nations experience." They took a look and*

*said, "It's the Human Rights Committee for her!" So I suppose my
career, what I had done before, was in that sense decisive about
which committee to send me to.*

The election procedure to gain a seat on the committee was not as easy as
that first step, however. It was at this time that Medina realized how political the election process was, and how her background may have been
less important, in some peoples' eyes, than other factors.

*They organized meetings with me. I had to go to New York. Meet-
ings would occur in the lobby at the UN. And it was really funny
because I would be introduced and I would smile and the member
of the Chilean embassy would start saying that I was such a good
candidate. Then they would exchange views about whom Chile
could vote for in order to reimburse my vote. And then they would
say goodbye and I would smile again. I would never say a word. It
was a bit humiliating, to be honest. Although I think that this procedure should be improved, I have to say that in spite of it, the
group I found myself with on the committee was impressive. There
were many professors and former judges of the highest rank.*

Medina served for eight years on the Human Rights Committee, an
experience she characterizes as extremely fruitful for her professional development and the most valuable she has had so far. The high qualifications of the members, and the fact that they came from different regions
of the world and different legal systems, allowed her to expand her own
knowledge of law and to fine-tune her approach to human rights problems. On the committee, she also met individuals from across the globe
with similar concerns and a similar approach to the ailments of the world,
all making his or her own contribution, however small, to improve the
situation of human beings. Medina feels that she is now having a comparable experience at the court; she also feels the comfort of doing this
for Latin America, which she considers "her" world.

A Woman on the Inter-American Court of Human Rights

Medina's election to the Inter-American Court of Human Rights, which
took place in 2003, struck a contrast with her election to the Human
Rights Committee a dozen years earlier. She was interviewed by representatives of other parties to the American Convention on Human Rights,
the treaty that created the court, and, this time, a real exchange of opinions took place during the meetings. The Caribbean states, in particular,
were curious about her views on certain topics.

*They were especially interested in the topic of the death penalty.
And I told them my position, which was probably different from
the one held in many Caribbean countries. Other interviews dealt
with other problems with which certain countries were concerned,
so the persons who were interviewing me had the opportunity to
find out the way I looked at human rights and how I understood
my role in the court should be carried out.*

Medina was the second woman to be elected a judge of the Inter-
American Court. In 2006, two more women were elected to the court.
With three women out of seven members, the IAHCR became the international court with the highest ratio of women to men.[2] This increasingly
even balance was due in large part to the efforts of civil society, in particular to human and women's rights groups and NGOs that have written to
foreign ministries in American states, requesting that they nominate
women to the position of judge. When asked whether it is important to
have women on the court, Medina responds affirmatively:

*Well, if you ask me if it is important to have women, just women, I
would say, "Yes," because it shows that equality is respected. Why
on earth not have women if we are half of the world? So it is important from a symbolic point of view for women to see other
women on the court. And it is important for democracy, because it
shows that women are not discriminated against. But it is also important in the sense of making progress for women's rights. For
this, you not only need a woman on the court, you need one who is
sensitive to the problems of being a woman and who is sensitive to
doing whatever it takes to make people see that some of the situations that women undergo are actually violations of human rights.*

Medina is particularly proud of a hearing where her perspective as a
woman brought out certain aspects of human rights violations that
might have been ignored in her absence. The hearing involved a massacre in Guatemala, where rape and other violations were committed. A
psychologist was called as an expert witness to talk about the effects of
the massacre on victims and how they might guide the determination of
reparations.

*At the end, judges had the right to put questions to the expert. And
she had mentioned the fact that women were raped. I asked,
"Could you please explain to me what is the additional suffering of
a woman who has been raped in a case such as this?" I knew the
answer, but I wanted it on record. And she answered, "Well, there
is an additional suffering because not only have these women been
raped, but they are later repudiated by their husbands if they are*

married or they cannot find a husband if they are single. They have
to leave the community. So they are punished twice." I said, "I
think this is important for reparations." And I thought, "I'm glad I
was here today and asked my question!"

Medina has a special interest in the human rights of women. She has
written on the subject and she organizes postgraduate courses for Latin
American lawyers to train them in international human rights law with
the aim of defending women's human rights at the national and international levels. During her years on the Human Rights Committee, she participated actively in mainstreaming the gender perspective into its work,
an effort that culminated in the adoption by that organ of General Comment 28 on the right of women and men to equal enjoyment of human
rights.[3] Her dedication won her the 2006 Women's Rights Prize of the
Peter Gruber Foundation.[4]

Medina, along with the other judges of her court, is not able to devote
herself entirely to the important work she carries out. Unlike some other
international courts, the Inter-American Court operates only part time. It
generally meets four times a year, for two weeks at a time, at its headquarters in San José, Costa Rica. Outside of these meetings, most judges
pursue other professions, often on a full-time basis. Medina still works at
the University of Chile, where she codirects the Human Rights Center at
the law school, a center that is engaged in research and teaching in the region. The part-time schedule of the court is especially problematic, as it
has a heavy and ever-increasing caseload. Judges are required to work
between sessions—as *rapporteurs* on cases, for example—yet they are not
compensated for their work unless the court is in session.

> *It certainly poses a problem of dedication. I don't know whether*
> *we need a permanent court, but certainly a court that could meet*
> *more often. And a court that would pay the judges an amount that*
> *would allow them to work less outside the court to earn their liv-*
> *ing! All judges are concerned with the lack of time and the enor-*
> *mous responsibility of judging cases for the region.*

Like other regional courts around the world, the Inter-American
Court functions in a particular sociopolitical context that, in turn, influences the work it does. This is particularly evident when one looks at
the question of compliance with the court's decisions. Whereas the
record of compliance with the decisions of the European Court of
Human Rights is very good—a fact which many believe comes from
linking compliance with admission into the European Union—its inter-
American counterpart has had less success in getting states to respect all
aspects of its judgments. Medina ties the failure of states to respond

faithfully to the court's decisions at least partially to the political climate that exists in Latin America and the kinds of abuses that states have historically committed.

> *We have a good record of compliance with parts of our judgments. And all the cases remain open while we monitor compliance. Most of them are open because of something that states almost never do—investigate, prosecute, and sanction in cases of disappearance, in cases of summary executions, and in cases of torture. Usually these requirements are not complied with. And so the cases are left open. But, for example, compensation is almost always complied with. And states don't just pay. For example, in all the cases of massacres, what do they do? As a matter of course, states will make a public act of regret. They will publish the judgment of the court, which is part of the reparations they make. They will put up a plaque in memory of the people that have disappeared. They will name a square or a street. States will always do this. What they will not do is prosecute and punish.*
>
> *But at least the court has broken ground. I think what the court is aiming at is to start building up deterrence. So the court is trying to tell the states to beware, and to let the people who are thinking about staging a coup d'état, and thinking about torturing and disappearing people, that such crimes will have to be prosecuted, that no matter what, no matter how many commissions on truth and reconciliation a state establishes, this prosecution is an international obligation. In this sense, for example, the court has consistently said that some crimes can have no statute of limitations. There is a treaty on this that has not been ratified by many states. Even though it could be said that this treaty is a crystallization of a customary rule, some states are reluctant to commit to it so explicitly. The Inter-American Court is helping by clearly stating that this obligation holds even if family members of the victim are not interested in pursuing it. In other words, prosecution of such crimes is an international obligation to the world at large.*

There are other disappointments in Medina's job, too. She is sometimes frustrated by the repetitive nature of the cases she hears—there are definite patterns to the violations that come before the court. Her frustration comes mainly because the nature of the cases speaks to the inability or unwillingness of states to solve the problems of the past within the boundaries of their own legal orders without individuals being forced to resort to the inter-American system. But these violations are starting to appear in other parts of the world, and the Inter-American Court now finds itself a model of how to deal with them judicially.

Well, it is very disappointing to keep receiving cases of the same sort. That is very disappointing. And to get the odd case here and there of states that try to disguise what they have done, which is something that you notice, or resort to legal arguments in order not to be responsible for the terrible things they have done. It is also disappointing to see that, after so many years, we are still dealing mainly with violations of the rights to life and personal integrity because you realize that states have not done their job with regard to past violations.

Medina notes that the European Court of Human Rights has had increasingly to deal with the same kinds of violations in recent years, with the addition of new members from the central and eastern parts of the continent:

I already foresaw that when I was defending my dissertation in the 1980s. One of my committee said to me that he was surprised that I had written this book and I had taken almost nothing from the European system. And he wanted to know how Europe could help the inter-American system. And I said, "Well, at this moment, I think the question should be just the opposite, what can Latin America do for you because you are in for cases that will be 'Latin American style.' You have had three coups in Turkey. You have had a coup in Greece. You have not dealt with these problems, but we are experts in dealing with them!" And it was a premonition, because that's why the Europeans are now looking at the jurisprudence of the Inter-American Court.

Despite the challenges that arise in getting states to comply with all aspects of a decision or in respecting international norms, Medina is very clear about the importance of the work she is carrying out with the court; she believes that it is critical to the political evolution of the Western Hemisphere. But traces of her early difficulties with the legal profession—her inability to detach from her clients—are detectable in her reactions to judging.

What has given me the most satisfaction, and the most pain at the same time, is to listen to the victims in a hearing and their joy at being able to tell their story and be taken seriously for it. That is for me the greatest satisfaction I have had—when a victim comes and he says, "Finally I am being heard by a serious group of people, by a court, and I am taken seriously and I am seeing that there is somebody who thinks that what these people have done is wrong!" That has been for me the most satisfactory of all. But it is very painful. I often cry, right in court. But we are a bit far away so I hope it doesn't show. But tears will come to my eyes. So I take a drink of water—because it is terrible what you hear! Not only it is terrible what you hear, but it is terrible the way it is told, the emotions that are there. I don't know whether it is good or not to be so affected, but I think if you work in human rights, you have to be able to withstand this. But it is very, very difficult for me. I can't help reacting. What I can do is not let it show. I don't think it has shown in court, how painful this is for me. But it is terrible. In spite of that, you have to keep your emotions at bay in order to fulfill your role as an impartial judge. This is something that one also does when writing. My doctoral dissertation was on the handling of gross, systematic violations in the inter-American system and one of the cases I analyzed was that of Chile under General Pinochet. In that instance I had to curb my passion and let reason speak.

It is a great satisfaction, says Cecilia Medina Quiroga, to see states come to the Inter-American Court of Human Rights, recognizing their responsibility, and asking pardon of the victims who have come to testify. She looks back over the trajectory of her career—her pragmatic decision to pursue the law, her discovery of the field of human rights thousands of miles from her native country, her pathbreaking elections to the UN Human Rights Committee and the Inter-American Court—and she feels, "This is worth something!"

6 ✒ Tests of Character

Earning Respect

The caustic social critic H. L. Mencken once defined a judge as "a law student who marks his own examination papers."[1] The bite of the remark draws on widespread public perception that judges make the rules for themselves as well as for everyone else.

As young and fragile institutions, the international courts depend even more than other legal institutions on the ethical standards and the perceived integrity of their judges. Issues of judicial accountability have been prominent in the United States in recent years, as interest groups from across the political spectrum have accused judges of putting personal opinions and/or political motives before fidelity to the law. But domestic courts in open societies benefit from a common commitment to the rule of law and from the common presumption that strong legal institutions are a public right. If a small number of judges in domestic courts betray high professional standards, their personal careers, more than the legal system itself, are in jeopardy. In the international courts, however, with so many doubts around the world about the viability and appropriateness of the institutions themselves, lapses of ethics and character on the bench threaten a more far-reaching effect. Instances of dishonesty or incompetence can taint the entire network of international courts and tribunals, and they can provide openings for powerful actors to undermine their work. "What, then, is necessary to ensure the independence of the judiciary?" asks ICTY judge Theodor Meron. "While there are many necessary elements, one of the most crucial in my view is public respect for the courts and the judge's conduct."[2]

Unfortunately for the international courts, a series of highly publicized incidents involving judges has served as a lightning rod for criticism of their work. These public incidents are not the stuff of outright dishonesty or corruption; they are, instead, lapses of character or judgment. They are more about arrogance, neglect of duty, or insensitivity than they are about willful sabotage of the law. But in an atmosphere of scrutiny, they are no less damaging to the courts and tribunals than more flagrant offenses. They contribute to a public perception of international judges as callous, incompetent, arrogant, or all of those combined. The judges themselves are concerned and embarrassed by these incidents, though they tend to consider them aberrations in the system, the result of colleagues' reacting poorly under conditions of considerable stress.

These lapses of character, however, reveal two larger sets of problems that face international courts in the area of ethics and conduct. The first is that the international arena presents new and unfamiliar types of ethics challenges for judges; it can be difficult even to define ethics problems, much less to resolve them. With so many different types of career paths and experiences behind them, judges have no common set of ideas about which of their earlier positions or actions constitute grounds for recusal. Rules regarding ex parte communications—discussions outside the courtroom with one or more of the parties in a case—are relatively clear, if very different, in both common law and civil law legal systems; in a mixed system, however, the guidelines are no longer so clear. With customs varying from nation to nation, it can be difficult to determine whether and when it is appropriate for judges to take on professional responsibilities outside their work on the bench. And the length, complexity, and stress of some of the trials are extraordinary tests of character for judges, who have no relief from their central and critical role in the proceedings.

The second problem is the weakness of the institutional mechanisms of accountability. Even in domestic systems, the priority of judicial independence creates challenges for appropriate oversight of the work of judges; it is a delicate matter to create structures and processes for monitoring the ethics of the judiciary while at the same time protecting the judges from outside pressure and influence. In the international arena, this is even more difficult, even when courts are part of a political system like the European Union or the United Nations. The formal guidelines governing the conduct of judges tend to be vague where they exist at all, and enforcement, such as it is, is generally left to the judges themselves. While courts have provisions for the removal of judges for egregious behavior, they have few mechanisms for regulating less serious but more common incidences of misconduct. The relative informality of this approach can leave the courts powerless when judges misbehave; it also makes it difficult for the courts to take preventive action by identifying and codifying the emerging ethical challenges in the distinctive role of the judge.

Issues of character go beyond these formal issues of ethics and conduct. The work of the international courts is determined not only by how judges act, but also by who, in a fundamental way, they *are*. The act of judging requires individuals to detach themselves from their personal experiences in order to follow the law and to practice objectivity. But wisdom, common sense, and empathy—essential to good judgment—are the products of personal experience; so good judges, whether they acknowledge it or not, inevitably draw on their own backgrounds in exercising their professional duties. How judges negotiate the simultaneous exercise of detachment and self-examination is one of the key tests of character on the bench and essential to the effectiveness of their institutions, especially in a setting where the backgrounds are so diverse.

Character is also not only an individual matter; at stake as well is the collective character of the bench. It is a commonplace of human experience that group action diffuses individual responsibility, that people will make errors collectively that no individual would make on his or her own. The collective work of international judges brings great strengths to their institutions, as colleagues learn from and guide one another in the give and take of consultation and deliberation. But close working relationships in a closed system has its dangers as well, as colleagues learn to ignore one another's shortcomings and become insensitive to their collective blind spots. Ultimately, the effectiveness of the international courts depends on successful and enriching collaborations among judicial colleagues and on limiting the human tendency to confuse collective wisdom with what is right.

Canons and Codes

Every profession develops rules and guidelines to try to strengthen the integrity of its practitioners; but with the judiciary, the stakes are higher. Misconduct by a judge does not merely harm the interests of particular individuals or classes of people—it threatens the credibility of the rule of law.

Over the past twenty-five years, codes of conduct for judges have been developed and refined in domestic court systems all over the world. In the United States, there is an extensive web of codes, not only at the federal level but throughout the fifty states. Domestic codes of conduct cover a wide variety of topics, but they boil down to two key areas: conflict of interest and the maintenance of visibly high standards of professional conduct.[3]

Just as a judge needs a measure of protection from powerful actors in order to preserve his independence, so does the public need assurance that a judge approaches each case without a personal interest in its outcome. The common conception of this as an effort to eliminate judicial "bias" overstates the case. Many judges, as we shall see, argue that no thinking, feeling human being can (or should) enter the courtroom as a blank slate, entirely void of preconceptions. But no one can have confidence in the reasoning and decisions of a judge who has a stake in the outcome, for reasons of his associations, his pecuniary interests, or his personal commitments. The establishment of this confidence for member states is crucial as well, especially in regions where domestic judiciaries have a record of corruption or incompetence.[4]

Conflict-of-interest concerns make some choices obvious: judges are required to recuse themselves when they have a personal association with someone involved as one of the parties in a case. But other forms of association create grey areas. To what extent can a judge perform work for pay outside his primary occupation as a judge, and will those outside activities compromise his work on the bench? Can a judge exercise his commitments as a citizen, taking part in activities that are intended to lead to social or political change? Do political commitments or public statements made before a person joined the bench disqualify him from taking part in cases that touch on the matters involved? The codes of conduct vary widely in their specificity on these questions. Some codes try to define "conflict of interest" as precisely as possible. Others rely on general language, anticipating that no broad-based document can possibly capture all of the possible circumstances. Inevitably, conflict-of-interest considerations become matters of interpretation and contestation.

Standards of professional conduct are in some ways easier to define, in part because here appearances matter a great deal. While codes and practice treat matters of diligence and competence, few things take precedence over "decorum," the outward projection of detachment, serenity, and integrity. The work of judges is measured not only by what they accomplish, but the manner in which they accomplish it. Decorum applies not only to judges' work on the bench, but to their behavior as members of the larger community; judges are required to uphold the reputation of justice, so to speak, even when off-duty. Standards of professional conduct also include more specialized topics such as confidentiality, especially regarding matters of deliberation among judicial colleagues, and the specific interactions of judges with witnesses, prosecutors, attorneys, and others involved with their cases.[5]

In comparison with domestic courts, the elaboration of codes of conduct for judges at an international level is still quite primitive. While *The Code of Conduct for United States Judges* is a lengthy text (with detailed commentary on situations and circumstances under the heading of seven primary "canons"),[6] among the international courts, standards of conduct for judges are generally treated formally only in a few lines in the courts' founding documents.[7] Over the course of seventy-nine pages in the rules of the European Court of Human Rights, for example, judicial conduct receives only two brief mentions: under rule 3, judges are required to swear an oath of secrecy regarding deliberations, and under rule 4, to refrain from any outside activity "which is incompatible with their independence or impartiality."[8] Article 4 of the statute of the International Court of Justice requires judges to swear to perform their duties "honourably, faithfully, impartially and conscientiously," but the document declines to provide definition for those adverbs.[9] At the International Criminal Tribunal for Rwanda, the judges adopted a thirty-two-page document elaborating standards of conduct for defense counsel, but they declined to adopt a similar document to govern their own behavior.[10] The founding statutes of international courts generally have language addressing basic issues, such as recusal and confidentiality, in very general terms; judges have been reluctant to adopt more specific subsequent language.

Few international courts have adopted a formal code of judicial ethics. Exceptions include the International Criminal Court and the Caribbean Court of Justice.[11] The eleven articles of the ICC code highlight the key topics, but still provide little detail or specific guidance. Under article 4, "Impartiality," for example, the two provisions call upon judges simply to "be impartial and ensure the appearance of impartiality in the discharge of their official functions," and to "avoid any conflict of interest, or being placed in a situation which might reasonably be perceived as giving rise to a conflict of interest." The language on "integrity," "confidentiality, "diligence," and other topics reveals a similar level of generality. Lest any judges feel too threatened even by this sweeping language, article 11 emphasizes that the principles of the code are only "guidelines" and are "advisory in nature and have the object of assisting judges with respect to ethical and professional issues with which they are confronted."[12] The Caribbean Court of Justice's *Code of Judicial Conduct* is more detailed; twenty-four separate clauses address the topic of "propriety" alone.[13]

Why are judges reluctant to address these issues more directly and formally within their courts? Cynics will answer that judges do not wish to live within the kinds of constraints that they impose upon others. Judges themselves, on the other hand, are understandably wary of documents that might inadvertently threaten their independence by empowering outside actors to supervise their work.[14] One legal scholar, surveying the minimal development of codes in international courts, explains this reluctance as a matter of judicial temperament. "It is characteristic of many legal professions in their earlier years," Detlev Vagts writes, "that they feel no need for formal rules and institutions to guide and control the behavior of judges and lawyers. There are only a few persons in the profession and they know what they are supposed to do. In the rare case that somebody is tempted to lapse from grace, the prospect of disapproval by one's peers is deterrence enough."[15] Collegiality, in other words, substitutes for formal process—at the very heart of a rules-based profession.

Commitments, Conflicts, and Recusal

The paucity of formal language does not mean, however, that judges themselves are unconcerned with issues of ethics and conduct. Indeed, public and private contemplation of such questions touches the very essence of their work, in no area more dramatically than that of recusal.

Most of the time, recusal is a relatively routine matter, involving personal association of the judge with some aspect of the case that is coming before him. In the International Court of Justice, the recusal process has, by and large, been steady but sometimes puzzling over the court's history, in part because the judges have often recused themselves without giving public reasons.[16] In some cases the reasons are obvious: with so many of the ICJ judges having served as lawyers and diplomats in the international arena, judges have often recused themselves because of their prior involvement as a representative of one of the parties, of a government, or of the United Nations. In other cases, however, judges have continued to sit on cases even though their previous work brought them in some way in contact with the dispute at hand. The French judge, for example, sat on the case that New Zealand brought against his country over the resumption of nuclear testing, even though he had previously served as a legal advisor to the French foreign ministry.[17] "Basically the recusal thing works okay," says one ICJ judge.[18] For one thing, the sheer size of the ICJ bench—fifteen judges strong—mitigates against concern that the participation of any one judge will have an undue influence. Another source of the relative relaxation about recusal is the historical attitude, addressed earlier, that there is actually some advantage to some extent of "partiality" in the ICJ process, since states are more comfortable with a judicial proceeding when one of their own nationals is on the bench.[19]

The specific circumstances and relative newness of international courts mean that the issue of recusal is still being defined and warmly debated. The development of the issue is illustrated in situations that have come before three of the international courts in recent years. All three instances focus, in different ways, on whether views and opinions expressed by international judges *before* they were on the bench disqualify them from hearing particular cases.

In 2003, the International Court of Justice agreed to render an advisory opinion regarding the legal consequences of the barrier that the state of Israel was constructing in and around parts of the West Bank.[20] Early in 2004, the government of Israel wrote to the ICJ requesting that Judge Nabil Elaraby be excluded from hearing the case. Judge Elaraby, Israel pointed out, had served for many years as a legal advisor to the Egyptian government and as such had been intimately involved in aspects of the

Middle East peace process involving the Israelis and Palestinians. In that capacity, Israel charged, Elaraby had "previously played an active, official,
and public role as an advocate for a cause that is in contention in this case."
How could Elaraby objectively view the case of the wall, when he had
played a prominent part in efforts to address the Israeli/Palestinian conflict?

This request was considered by the remaining fourteen members of the
ICJ (excluding the judge in question), and two weeks later the majority
ordered that Israel's request be denied. The ICJ statute, the majority said,
does indeed bar the participation of a judge from a case when he has
acted "as agent, counsel, or advocate for one of the parties." In this instance, however, Judge Elaraby performed his duties "in his capacity of a
diplomatic representative of his country" at a time well before the wall at
the center of the current case was even contemplated, much less constructed. The order follows the ICJ's historical reluctance to impose recusal on one of its members because of prior government service, unless
that service relates in a visible and direct way to the case in hand. The
subtext here is that, in a court with members of extensive national experience, the recusal process could quickly get out of hand if the relevant article of the statute is interpreted too liberally.

In this case, however, the potential tensions over the recusal issue became public. Judge Thomas Buergenthal issued a strong dissent, focusing
on a different aspect of Israel's request. Buergenthal agreed with the majority that Elaraby's words and actions while in government service did
not disqualify him in this case, since opinions he expressed in that capacity "were not Judge Elaraby's personal views, but those of his Government
whose instructions he was executing." Buergenthal was more troubled,
however, by an interview that Judge Elaraby gave to an Egyptian newspaper in August 2001, after he had left the service of the Egyptian government and two months before he was elected to the ICJ. Elaraby was
quoted as criticizing Israel for perpetrating "grave violations of humanitarian law," for committing "atrocities" on the Palestinian civilian population, and for occupying Palestinian territory "against international law."
Buergenthal argued that these sentiments—offered at a time when Elaraby
was a free agent and not speaking on behalf of his government—constituted a threat to the perception of impartiality. He rejected what he called
a "formalistic and narrow construction" of the relevant provision of the
statute, arguing that he was most concerned about "the appearance of
bias," and not the personal integrity of Judge Elaraby, "for whom I have
the highest regard not only as a valued colleague but also a good friend."

Buergenthal's dissent brings into the open the delicate question of how
the bare facts of judges' biographies influence the perception of justice on
international courts. On highly charged matters, as in the case of the
wall, such scrutiny is inevitable, as parties contend for advantage in the

court of public opinion. Indeed, the perception of the impartiality of Judge Buergenthal himself became an issue later. When the ICJ issued its advisory opinion in 2005, Buergenthal was the lone dissenter from an opinion that was harshly critical of Israeli actions; the judge's dissent argued that the court had taken insufficient notice of Israel's legitimate security concerns.

The distinction between opinions offered while in government service and opinions expressed in the free marketplace of ideas has surfaced in the criminal courts as well. Anzo Furundzija appealed his conviction in the Yugoslavia tribunal on the grounds that Judge Florence Mumba, one of the three judges on his trial panel, had served as a member of the United Nations Commission on the Status of Women (UNCSW) before her appointment to the bench. Furundzija was convicted, among other charges, of inciting and permitting the mass rape of Bosnian women. His lawyers argued that Mumba's association with UNCSW—and particularly her public statements in that capacity about the need to identify rape as a war crime and to bring perpetrators to justice—constituted a threat to the perception of her impartiality. Among other things, they called attention to the facts that the authors of one of the amicus curiae briefs in the case had served with Mumba at the UNCSW and that a member of the prosecutor's team had attended a conference on war crimes issues at which Mumba was present.

The ICTY appeals chamber thoroughly rejected Furundzija's argument. Judge Mumba, the chamber pointed out, was appointed to UNCSW by her home country of Zambia, and was simply serving as a representative of her government. The appeals judges pointed out that previous experience in international humanitarian law and human rights is, under the ICTY statute, one of the essential qualifications of members of the bench, and that Florence Mumba's participation in UNSCW was one of the very activities that made her eligible to serve as an international judge. "It would be an odd result," the appeals chamber concluded, "if the operation of an eligibility requirement were to lead to an inference of bias." The chamber took the occasion to go even further, pointing out that that the law begins with the presumption of impartiality of a judge, and developed the principle that it is up to those who question that impartiality to prove that there is a strong basis for their concerns.[21]

At the Special Court for Sierra Leone, however, the public statements of a judge before he came onto the bench became the subject of a bitter battle with major consequences. In 2005, the defense counsel for Issa Sesay, an indictee at the SCSL, filed a motion requesting the permanent removal of Geoffrey Robertson, the president of the court, not only from sitting on his case but from the bench altogether. At issue was a book published in 2002, shortly before Robertson was named to the SCSL, called *Crimes against Humanity*.[22] One section of that book was devoted to what Robertson described as the outrages committed by the Revolutionary United Front (RUF), one of the rebel groups in Sierra Leone, whose actions were at the very heart of the later proceedings in the SCSL. In the book, Robertson described the RUF as "guilty of atrocities on a scale that amounts to a crime against humanity [which] must never again be forgiven." Citing these statements as evidence of, if not bias itself, at least the appearance of bias, Sesay's lawyers asked that either Robertson remove himself from the case or the Appeals Chamber of the court disqualify him.

Robertson refused to withdraw, offering the curious explanation that giving in to this demand would constitute a threat to judicial independence. But his fellow judges on the appeals chamber came down hard on him. Robertson's charges in *Crimes Against Humanity,* his fellow judges said, constituted sufficiently explicit and specific opinions so that there was "no doubt that a reasonable man will apprehend bias, let alone an accused person."[23] Robertson's colleagues on the appeals chamber disqualified him not only from the case in hand, but from all cases involving alleged members of the RUF. While the appeals chamber declined to remove him permanently from the court (saying that they could do so only if a judge is "palpably unfit"), the court as a whole then adopted a procedural change that had the result of ending Robertson's tenure as court president.

The highly specific and unambiguous nature of Robertson's writings gave his fellow judges little choice but to disqualify him. Indeed, it seems surprising that it would never have occurred to Robertson himself that these words would escape the attention of defendants at the SCSL. It is equally surprising that the book, published during the very year that Robertson was being considered for the bench, could have escaped the attention of those considering his qualifications for election. In any case, it is telling that it requires so flagrant an instance of prejudgment to set the wheels in motion to disqualify a judge who has not himself opted for recusal. While there has been concern about the appearance of bias in the WTO dispute settlement system, in most instances judges on international courts tend to view a variety of previous commitments as an *asset* to their work, not as a public liability.[24]

The International Judge as Moonlighter

The instances regarding Elaraby, Mumba, and Robertson involved actions taken and statements made *before* they were named to the bench, but what kinds of activities are appropriate for judges to undertake *while* they are members of international courts? Every court has language barring judges from work and actions that conflict with his or her work on the bench, but the texts are in most cases general and leave the judges themselves with considerable latitude, as long as the activity they undertake is not overtly "political" in nature.[25]

Historically, this flexibility has been necessary because of the inconsistent nature of the workload of the international courts and because of their public mission. For many years, the International Court of Justice had a relatively light caseload; while its judges were technically full time, the schedule permitted outside commitments without placing an undue burden on the work of the court. These outside commitments could be construed as beneficial to the court and to the emerging field of international law. When members of the court spoke or taught at universities, or even when they performed work as arbitrators in private disputes, they lent their authority to the spread of knowledge about—and participation in the development of—international law.

In other courts, judges serve on a part-time basis, so it is a given that they will be working in universities and in private practice, often on a full-time basis. The judges of the International Tribunal for the Law of the Sea and of the Inter-American Court of Human Rights are required to be in Hamburg and San José, respectively, only a few weeks a year; while the members of the Appellate Body of the WTO have a somewhat more intensive commitment in Geneva, they, too, are not considered full time and have ample additional professional activities. Many of the International Criminal Court judges began their service on a part-time basis, though once the trial and appeals courts are fully in operation, all eighteen judges there will be full time.

At the other end of the spectrum, the ad hoc criminal tribunals and the European Court of Human Rights are under pressure to speed up their proceedings and (in the case of the ECHR) reduce their backlog, so their judges have many fewer opportunities for outside commitments. The ECHR designates particular weeks each year when its sessions are suspended, encouraging its judges to undertake speaking or other engagements exclusively during those periods. Indeed, its court president actively encourages judges to speak in their own countries during these intervals, in the hopes of promoting knowledge and understanding of the court's work.

Speaking, teaching, and private arbitration are the most common outside activities. Many members of the international bench served as academic and public figures before becoming judges, and they relish the opportunity to continue their public engagement. Most seem untroubled by the potential for breaches of confidentiality or conflicts of interest; they take a commonsense attitude that they will not discuss cases on their courts' dockets, or matters likely to come before them; they tend to speak and teach on matters of international law more broadly. They can generally accept honoraria for their speaking engagements (and salaries when they teach, if they are not full-time judges), with the general expectation that the remuneration involved does not pose a threat to their independence on the bench.

The involvement of many judges—particularly from the ICJ—as arbitrators, however, raises more troubling questions. This work, often involving transactions between major multinational corporations, is very lucrative for the arbitrators, and as such raises the question of where judges' priorities lie. It is not so much that the private arbitrations raise direct issues of conflict of interest, as that the knowledge that judges are being compensated generously for outside work undermines confidence that the judges' priorities lie with the court. "It is different from other professions, because of the sensitivity, the need for impartiality, and independence," says Hans Corell, the UN's former undersecretary general for legal affairs. "I'm not suggesting that those who are serving there can't perform as arbitrators, but I am concerned, for example, that the judges in the International Court of Justice seem to be engaged in other business. . . . In my view, if you hold a position so august as judge of the International Court of Justice, that should be your business. Well, of course you can give lectures. You can write a book if you want. But you should not be engaged in other adjudicative activities." Some members of the ICJ itself have reservations about this particular activity. "My own view has been that I personally feel uncomfortable with the idea of a judge here continuing with arbitrations in which international law is not the heart," says one judge of the court. "I mean, I think we are regarded as really the top international lawyers; we should be devoting our life to that. If, occasionally, very occasionally, there's some state arbitration. . . . it might be okay. But it should be, in my opinion, heavily self-regulated."

Even if judicial independence were not an issue, outside activities threaten in some cases to disrupt the schedules of increasingly busy courts. Court presidents are often inclined to accommodate their busy colleagues, but the cost to efficiency can be high. One member of a court at The Hague complains that some European judges are, in effect, commuters, spending half of the week in their home countries, an hour or two by plane from Schiphol Airport. Others point out, however, that those colleagues busiest with outside activities are sometimes simply the most efficient workers. "Although some have more outside activities than others," says one criminal court judge, "it does not mean that those who have more activities outside are making fewer contributions. Exactly the opposite—some simply work more. They are used to working more."

Some of those "used to working more" wish to continue their involvement after they leave the bench, raising ethical questions involving the activities of judges who have retired or moved into a different stage of their professional career. At what point, for example, is it appropriate or ethical for a former judge to appear as a counselor before a court on which he served? In some cases, he could be advising clients on the same types of matters on which he ruled when he was sitting on the bench. The special knowledge of the court's workings and his personal relationships with his former peers would appear to give an ex-judge a special advantage. But as one ECJ judge points out, it is difficult to establish firm rules about such matters in the international arena, because the national traditions are very different; common law systems, he points out, tend to be much more restrictive about judges appearing before their former courts than civil law jurisdictions. Another European judge proposes a two-year "cooling-off period," "maybe just to make sure that the person has never been involved in the case that he is then presenting to us." Judges seem reluctant to consider hard-and-fast rules in this area, underscoring the intimate nature of a relatively small pool of major players in the international law field.

As the business of international courts continues to increase, however, more courts may eventually have to resort to the stricter set of general rules regarding outside activities like those adopted by the ECHR. Even when outside commitments pose little threat to judicial independence, they can create the perception that judges are self-interested, rather than disinterested. While limiting outside activities may indeed punish the most competent judges—those whose services are in most demand, after all—the continued support of the international community for their work may depend upon it.

Competence and Decorum

With widespread skepticism about the mission and purposes of international courts, the standards of international judges' professional behavior come under intense scrutiny. "Some of these judges, even professional judges, do not seem to realize that they are working under a microscope, the microscope of the world," says Hans Corell. "Some of them behave in a manner that I don't think necessarily reflects well on the judicial profession." Some widely publicized incidents involving international judges have compromised the dignity of that profession. These cases can contribute to a perception that incompetence, laziness, and arrogance infect a substantial minority of international judges, threatening the dignity and respect for the international courts as a whole.

The criminal tribunals, whose activities are closely followed by the media and thus are more visible to the public, and where the stress level is exceptionally high, have provided some of the more embarrassing moments for international judges. At the Yugoslavia tribunal, one defendant appealed his conviction on the ground that the presiding judge at his trial, Adolphus Karibi-Whyte, was asleep during substantial portions of the trial; it was alleged that members of the registrar's office and one of his fellow judges frequently had to nudge him to keep him awake. The judges of the appeals chamber reviewed the videotapes of the trial and conceded that the tapes did indeed "demonstrate a recurring pattern of behaviour where Judge Karibi-Whyte appears not to have been fully conscious of the proceedings for short periods at a time," but in the end they rejected the argument that these brief periods of unconsciousness constituted "substantial portions of the trial." The judges reprimanded their colleague for his conduct; if his somnolence was due to medical conditions over which he had no control, then he should have removed himself from a case to which he could not devote his full attention, they said. But they decided that the appellant had failed to prove that Judge Karibi-Whyte missed anything "essential" or "crucial" during the trial proceedings.[26]

If the "sleeping judge" exposed the criminal tribunals to ridicule, the case of the "laughing judges" at the Rwanda tribunal occasioned outrage.[27] During a lengthy cross-examination of a witness testifying about her rape during the period of the genocide, two of the three judges on the bench were seen to be sniggering, apparently laughing at the incoherence of the witness's account. The judges tried to explain later that they were laughing at the incompetence of the examining attorney, not at the witness herself, but the damage was done.[28] The press had caught this laughter on camera and the footage was aired repeatedly around the world, including in Rwanda. The effects of this press coverage were devastating to the tribunal. The ICTR judges were pilloried as callous to the sufferings of victims, insensitive to the solemnity of the proceedings, and incapable of meeting the challenge of controlling themselves, much less their courtroom.[29]

Incidents like these have exposed international judges to a broadbrushed critique of their competence and character, sometimes even from their peers and colleagues. Arrogance is an occupational hazard in the judiciary, and it could be argued that it is reinforced at the international level, with its array of special privileges. With so many perks and their diplomatic status, says a staff member at the registrar's office at the ICTY, the judges tend to become "little popes," thinking of themselves as infallible, insensitive to the concerns of others around them. "People begin to think of themselves as very important," says one ICJ judge, with a touch of self-deprecation. "And you begin to assume that you're having a tremendous impact on the world." Arrogance can lead, in some cases, to sheer laziness, a willingness to leave the details and the brunt of the work to others. As we have seen, judges at the criminal tribunals are frequently criticized for leaving much of their judgment writing to their legal assistants; sometimes the judges have been criticized by their peers for their inability to handle many of the difficult legal challenges before them. Patricia Wald was particularly blistering on the subject of her colleagues after she left the bench of the ICTY. She complained in print that the UN election process allowed incompetents to be appointed, leaving "a cluster of hardworking, experienced judges to bear the laboring oar for the substantive work of the Tribunal, particularly the writing of judgments." Wald went on to bemoan unnecessary "reversible errors," "inappropriate questions," and "uninformed rulings" on the part of her colleagues, though she says that she "saw no case in which the fundamental rights of the accused were impugned which did not eventually get righted. It was more a case of efficiency than ultimate fairness."[30]

Observers agree that this litany of complaints applies only to a minority of judges, and one might see a similar range of competence and similar expressions of self-importance in any high-ranking profession. So the pressing question for the international courts remains: what are the means for holding judges accountable, once they are elected, in the instances where they do cross the line or fail to meet a standard?

"Corporate Solidarity"

Every international court specifies a procedure for removing a judge for egregious misconduct. Most frequently, the court's statute provides that the judges of a court may remove one of their peers from the bench if they decide unanimously that he or she has not lived up to the requirements of service.[11] The statutes provide broad flexibility for making that decision; they do not lay out a series of precise circumstances under which judges can or should remove their fellows. It is obvious, however, that it would take an extraordinary situation—one where the misconduct was flagrant and beyond doubt—for all of the other judges on a court to agree to such drastic action. No judge has ever been removed "for cause" from an international court or tribunal.

Most misconduct, however, falls far short of the kind of blatant greed or incompetence that would lead to removal, and the statutes provide little guidance for what to do in situations that call for less dramatic corrective action. There are procedures for assessing the necessity for disqualification from individual cases, in instances when judges do not recuse themselves. But beyond recusal, the courts have precious few mechanisms for regulating the behavior of judges, especially in the harder-to-measure areas that fall under the category of "professional ethics."

In the absence of formal mechanisms for monitoring the performance of judges, the president of the court plays an important role. In practice, court presidents tend to have little actual authority over their fellow judges, but the president is the chief administrator of the judges' business, and disciplinary matters end up in his domain. As in a national court, says one court president, "the president normally has no disciplinary powers over his judges, so you're trying to reason with the judges and some will at once accept that." The president may find himself trying to convince a judge to recuse himself in a particular case, rather than be disqualified by his peers. He may try to persuade a judge to tone down the recriminations toward his colleagues in the draft text of a dissenting opinion. Or he may have to take a judge aside and urge him not to speak so openly about the court's business to the media. "It's much more pleasant to do the work if you have a nice climate," the court president continues. "I think it enhances the credibility of the court to the outside world if you prevent clashes from being made public." But his power is limited. "If that happened when [judges were calling] each other fools and idiots and irresponsible or nonpatriotic and all the rest I would certainly come in and say, 'You can't do that,' but I can't guarantee, I have no veto right or disciplinary powers." Presidents also have the option of using backdoor political channels to put pressure on underperforming colleagues. The president of a UN court, one judge points out, could theoretically urge the secretary general to speak quietly to the government of a bad judge, putting pressure on him to resign. It's not a perfect method, the judge concedes, but "there may be no other way to cure it."

These examples suggest how large a premium many judges place on keeping disciplinary matters internal and quiet. This is a matter not only of shielding individual colleagues from the glare of the public spotlight, but also of protecting the reputations of the institutions. However, if maintaining credibility takes precedence over uprooting misconduct, the integrity of the courts is bound to suffer.

As in domestic courts, the accountability of the international judiciary is largely a matter of conscience and collegiality. "Accountable to God, is an old-fashioned way of putting it," says one judge. He does not even see himself as accountable, exactly, to fellow judges. "I have to live with my colleagues," he says, "and it is a feature one prefers, to be well-thought-of by one's colleagues rather than to be thought a pain in the neck." Another judge emphasizes the power of pride: "If you're associated with something, you want it to be good," she says. "You don't want it to be some kind of sloppy mess kind of thing. And in that sense that's really the accountability kind of thing." Another puts it even more succinctly: "There is no check from the outside; it's only from the inside."

Even if the judges act individually with integrity and dignity, can the courts collectively fail the test of character? We tend to think of ethics in terms of personal decision-making, overlooking the critical aspect of collective responsibility within organizations. Each international court develops its own judicial culture. If we are going to examine judicial ethics and character in the broadest sense, we need to ask whether the judicial culture of international courts nurtures integrity and fairness.

As with any other organization, the greatest threats to the courts' organizational integrity lie in the inherent tendency to self-protection. Internal matters of privilege, power, and advancement within the system create alliances and forces that resist change and marginalize those who bring new methods and ideas. "I was surprised at the amount of politics," says one criminal court judge, speaking of the internal decision-making process of the court. The lack of clear rules regarding the assignment of cases, the intricacies of elections for the officers of the court, the assignment of judges to particular chambers—these internal matters contribute to a sense of expectation that individual judges should stay in line. This has the potential for impact on actual decisions, this judge charges, because those who disagree publicly with the court's leadership can be punished through administrative procedures. "So all this means that the judges are not independent, but not because of external pressure, but because of internal anxiety."

This perception suggests that the risk of what one former international judge calls "corporate solidarity" is high. Gil Carlos Rodríguez Iglesias, who served as a judge on both the European Court of Justice and the European Court of Human Rights, does emphasize that "a judge's personal responsibility should be determined only by a judicial body," but he worries openly that "the need for judicial independence is hard to reconcile with the creation of a system for ensuring responsibility." Corporate solidarity, Rodríguez argues, arises in any situation where peers sit in judgment on one another. Individuals have a natural interest in withholding judgment of their peers, because of bonds of collegiality, because of concerns for the public face of the institution, and because they wish mild treatment for themselves in return. The tendency reflects a potential shortcoming of the "epistemic community" of judges that we have remarked upon previously. Rodríguez does not offer a practical solution to the tension between independence and accountability—indeed, he seems to suggest that the problem may not be resolvable. But he seems to feel that an open discussion of the problem may itself be a form of raising the standards of responsibility.[32]

There are, of course, some good reasons for the relative weakness of the system of accountability for international judges. Strong methods of oversight by external monitors are vulnerable to abuse and raise the specter of interference with judicial independence. Better, perhaps, to run the risk of misconduct by an occasional "bad apple" than to create structures where powerful players can interfere with judicial decision making under the guise of improving professional standards. In practice, the system seems to work reasonably well; judicial misconduct appears to be relatively infrequent and it has not, to date, substantially damaged the work of any of the international courts. But the weak mechanisms of accountability leave the courts vulnerable in two important respects. First, the climate of self-regulation reinforces the arguments of critics who portray international judges as free-floating individuals whose standards of justice are at odds with individual nations and citizens. Second, without stronger processes in place, international courts may be vulnerable to a major scandal whose damage would be widespread.

Circumstance and Experience

Ethics is more than codes and regulations; its most ancient articulation is as the essence of character: what matters is not just what one *does,* but who, in a fundamental sense, one *is.* The ancient Greeks assumed that character was a matter of all the elements that make up a human being—his background, his upbringing, his training, his community, and his own inner will. But by what standard should we assess the character of a judge? Is he more impartial, and therefore more virtuous, if he is able to detach himself successfully from the influences of his past? Or does his excellence depend on his ability to integrate all the disparate strands and teachings that have shaped his life? How much special knowledge can or should an international judge bring to his work?

Not even the strictest insistence on judicial impartiality can separate a judge entirely from his personal circumstances. But there can be a debate over whether a rigorous effort at detachment is desirable. Some see the influences of background as potential biases to be overcome; others see them as potential assets to understanding, which must nevertheless be kept in check.

The circumstances of the international courts lead many judges to seek creative and appropriate ways to allow their life experiences to inform their work. Working alongside colleagues with very different backgrounds, judges find that matters of perspective, informed by personal experience, inevitably play a part in their daily work. In efforts to understand the extreme and dramatic evidence before them, especially in criminal trials, judges find that they need to seek points of reference in their own personal or national experiences. And the relative newness of the legal tradition in the global arena compels international judges to rely more heavily on instinct and intuition than do their domestic counterparts. Judges who embrace the special contributions of background and character to their work are well aware of the dangers of allowing personal experience to outweigh the hard facts of evidence and the text of the law. They point out, however, that the eclectic mix of personalities and nationalities on the international bench provides a strong corrective to the potential for individual bias. The embrace of personal circumstance builds, as we have seen, on the foundation of shared judicial temperament.

One controversial question is whether a judge's race or gender can or should inform the work from the bench. We have already seen that the International Criminal Court provides in its statute for gender balance in the composition of its bench, an explicit concession that men and women bring special and different insights.[33] One ICC judge downplays the issue, calling gender "no more than a starting point," but another claims that her experience in criminal trials has convinced her that, on an issue like the protection of witnesses, women judges are indeed more sensitive to the needs of women and children. "We have to take a very careful approach," she says, "and the female judges can make all the difference." Another criminal court judge attests that gender "does matter. . . . I'm not saying clearly it's a necessity, but I do think it does give you a different insight." She points, by way of example, to the *Srebrenica* case at the ICTY, where what was at stake was whether the mass murder of young men constituted genocide because a generation of women of child-bearing age were deprived of husbands and potential fathers of their children.[34] Citing the "terrible feelings of insufficiency" on the part of the women trying to make a new life for themselves, she cautiously says that, for a judge, "I won't say it helped to be a woman, but I felt I had some insight into it."

International judges are coming to terms with integrating what they already know into their work, but they are distinctly divided when it comes to assessing how important it is to acquire *new* knowledge once they ascend to the bench. Judges on international courts, after all, sit on cases involving countries and cultures far from their own experience, which raises the question of whether their relative ignorance aids impartiality or restricts necessary understanding. For example, the first four cases investigated by the prosecutor of the International Criminal Court all pertain to situations in Africa;[35] how much should ICC judges with limited experience of the continent catch up on African politics, culture, and society? One ICC judge started reading voraciously on Africa as soon as the prosecutor publicly announced his investigations, believing that "you are a better judge if you understand the people involved, from the victim's side, and from the accusing side." Institutionally, the ICC has provided the judges with access to this kind of information, through the president's office, but "it's totally up to the judge to take and to study that, or to simply study penal law, international law, or whatever." But other judges have taken a more hands-off approach, feeling that they cannot possibly catch up on the full complexity of the African background, and that they are better off assessing what is actually brought before them through the court documents and through testimony. One criminal court judge points out that her colleagues tend by force of habit to be resistant to learning, in part from the arrogance that is an occupational hazard on the bench. Against considerable resistance, she has helped to design programs for judicial education ("now we call it 'strengthening judicial capacity' because judges are very important, they are 'superior'"), and she believes that she is making headway in convincing her colleagues that judicial character and competence depend on a spirit of continuous learning. But judges are reluctant to admit their deficiencies, even to one another. "Sometimes," she says, "international judges are afraid to say 'I don't know that.'"

Moral Stature

International judges, then, have begun to find ways to bring the full dimensions of their background and character to their work on the bench, but they are ambivalent about participation in the wider realm of public discourse. As we have seen, international courts depend for their ultimate effectiveness on being *seen*; if their work is invisible (no matter how competent), the larger goal of shoring up public confidence in, and nations' commitment to, international justice will not be met. Since judges are the permanent and public face of the courts, the imperative of visibility would seem to put some pressure on international judges to accept a role as public figures. But judges are cautious about accepting a role that might threaten their integrity and the perception of their impartiality.

Many international judges fall back on traditional judicial caution. "My position is that a judge is not a public person," one criminal court judge states outright. "Everything that he or she has to say should be in the decisions of the court." The more that judges say outside the formal utterances, the more likely they are to be misunderstood or accused of one form or another of bias. Another judge takes a slightly more open position. "My view is that everyone has, of course, freedom of expression and we all have the right to make utterances, including judges at the international level. But I will certainly wish to keep a very low profile as long as I have the present position in order to avoid any misunderstandings. It could complicate your task if you got too involved in polemics, even if it is not your *own* conflict. We are not politicians, we are judges." Judges tend to be more comfortable speaking out about general principles of international law, as long as they "pay extreme attention to not clashing with their own responsibilities."

Others believe that the developing field of international justice requires judges to venture more prominently into the public arena than they might in a domestic setting. There is widespread agreement that judges should be silent about matters before their court, political matters, and specific cases in other courts, but some feel an obligation to become more active on behalf of international judicial institutions in a larger sense. Because international courts are vulnerable to criticism and attack, some judges feel compelled to explain and advocate for their work and their decisions, in a manner that some consider unseemly. But how else, advocates of openness argue, will the larger world understand the significance of important new developments like the formal declaration of rape as a war crime, or convictions for the crime of genocide? Judges, they say, can and should help the media and the larger public understand the work of the courts. Some go even further, arguing that international judges have, in effect, a moral obligation to defend the interests of justice worldwide. This entails using the offices of the international judge to call attention to abuses of judicial independence in domestic settings, even if such a public call runs the risk of interference in the "political" realm. To remain silent about threats to justice and to fellow judges, in other words, presents a graver moral threat than the risk of "speaking out of turn" about matters beyond one's own court. "Some judges may not agree that that's the role of judges," concedes one criminal court judge, "but, particularly in the light of worldwide outrage at the treatment of detainees and torture of detainees, the voice of judges has been very silent and this has been noted in the press. We are the guardians of justice and judicial standards. We shouldn't be seen to be acquiescent with violations."[36]

International judges tend to reject vigorously the idea that they should act as "moral authorities," in the role of what Ronald Dworkin has called the "secular papacy." They recoil from the idea that their own personal values intrude upon their decisions under the law. But judges are more open to expressing what Dworkin calls the judiciary's "political morality"—convictions not about substantive issues (like abortion or monopolies or what constitutes a crime against humanity), but about how decisions should be made, enforced, and respected.[37] It can be argued, in other words, that in the international realm, judges not only can but must turn their traditional reticence on its head, at least when it comes to explaining principles of international justice and the nature of the institutions that enact it. This may require delicacy and tact; in this sense judges on the international bench are called upon to reassess judicial ethics not only in terms of their own actions, but also in terms of their responsibility to the long-term success of their courts.

The increasing acceptance of a broader definition of judicial ethics and character in the international arena will inevitably trouble critics who are concerned that the courts provide opportunities for judges to impose their "personal values" on unsuspecting citizens of nations around the world. But it is impossible to expect the highest standards of integrity and judgment of men and women while at the same time demanding that they separate themselves from the values that underlie their professionalism. Those international judges who think most deeply about this issue believe that self-examination, transparency, and the diversity of their institutions are better guarantors of impartiality and fidelity to the law than the chimera of a value-free judiciary.

John Hedigan, Ireland

Judge of the European Court of Human Rights

Beyond His Borders

John Hedigan has always been what he calls "an internationalist," someone deeply interested in what is happening in the world and a believer in the community of nations.[1] This perspective led him to become involved in human rights early on, during his years of education in his native Ireland. His first awareness of such issues was inspired by events occurring across the Atlantic in the United States.

> *The American civil rights movement was the first way in which I ever remember human rights coming into my consciousness. I was very big into debating societies in Belvedere College, where I went to school. The movement was really beginning to impinge on our consciousness in 1962–63. We used to see on TV all these terrible pictures of dogs attacking black demonstrators and incredible things like that, and the civil rights bill became the topic for discussion in our debating societies.*

This introduction resulted in Hedigan's engagement with human rights at university, this time in a way that went beyond speech-making:

> *When I went to university, a few of us resurrected a branch of Amnesty International, which is still going strong now. I represented the university on the National Executive Committee, and we were doing all sorts of the work that Amnesty still does, taking up the*

case of pretty much forgotten people. One man for whom we campaigned was a dissenter in the Soviet Union. He was imprisoned in a psychiatric hospital. This was not uncommon in those days. The theory appeared to be that one had to be mad to disagree with the great Soviet dream!

During his early years as a barrister in Dublin, Hedigan continued his connection to Amnesty International, eventually becoming the national director of the international campaign against torture. Its motto was "Torture—as unthinkable as slavery!"

When he considers his career as a judge at the European Court of Human Rights, he is gratified by how directly this work has satisfied his lifelong interests.

I find myself in the kind of job I really could scarcely have ever hoped to end up in because of where my interests lie. Practicing as a barrister in Ireland, I had a certain practical experience in the area of human rights, but only on a national level. Then in the 1980s, my wife, who worked in the legal division of Foreign Affairs, became the agent for Ireland at the [European] Court of Human Rights. I started to take a deep interest in Strasbourg because of its international dimension. The court embodies both aspects of the line of interest I had always had—international affairs and human rights. When my wife attended Strasbourg for meetings, I came out here myself whenever I had some free time to study what was going on at the court. I soon developed the idea that I would like to act as counsel in cases on behalf of Ireland before the Court of Human Rights. That's really what I had in mind at that stage. I never thought I would end up here as judge!

But Hedigan did eventually end up on the bench of the ECHR. He now decides cases brought against the forty-six member states of the Council of Europe, including, if rarely, his native country.

Hedigan considers his appointment to the ECHR as, to a certain extent, a matter of being in the right place at the right time. In 1998, the ECHR changed its status from a part-time to a full-time court, and the Irish judge who had been serving for many years was retiring.

The Irish government, in October 1997, if my memory serves me correctly, advertised the job within the legal profession and the judiciary. That was the first time they had ever done so. They advertised within the profession because judges in Ireland are only appointed from among the ranks of practicing lawyers. The government was obliged to submit to the Council of Europe a list of three names as candidates for the post of judge of the new court. In the

end, they picked three people and they put the list in order of pref-
erence, which was the way they used to do it then—they're not sup-
posed to do it that way now—and I was the first preference. The
candidates had to appear in Paris in January 1998 before the Ad
Hoc Committee on Legal Affairs and Human Rights of the Parlia-
mentary Assembly of the Council of Europe. The committee, hav-
ing interviewed the three Irish candidates, recommended my name
and I was elected subsequently by the Parliamentary Assembly. So
that's how I ended up here.

In addition to his full-time work on the bench, Hedigan has worked
tirelessly to change the conditions of work for ECHR judges so that they
have more security. Unlike many international judges, those of the ECHR
do not receive a retirement pension or the other benefits normally accom-
panying a professional position. Thus, there may be little incentive for a
supreme or high court judge to abandon a secure position on a national
bench and venture into the uncertainties of such a judgeship. This is particularly true for judges and other legal professionals who are years away
from retirement age.

The conditions of work here are extremely poor for the judges, de-
spite the fact that, like most people at international level, they get a
fairly high salary. Unlike all other persons working in the Council
of Europe, ECHR judges have no social protection at all. Indeed,
they are treated almost as though they are nonpersons! This has
been a major issue for the court since its creation. The president of
the court has repeatedly and publicly called for the rectification of
this state of affairs, but to no avail. As chair of the Committee on
the Status and Condition of Judges, together with my colleagues, I
have worked to ameliorate this deplorable state of affairs. Unfortu-
nately we have not, despite strenuous effort, been able to persuade
the Council of Europe governments to meet these basic obligations
to their judges. It is an extraordinary and anomalous situation.

The lack of security attached to his position was daunting for Hedigan, who had to essentially close down his practice as barrister upon his
appointment to Strasbourg. He thus had to forego the opportunity of advancing his lifelong profession, with only the certainty of a six-year term
as an international judge in return.

It was a little intimidating because I was required to give up my
practice. Most people who practice at the bar in Ireland have had
much the same experience of practically starving for the first few
years when they have little or no work. So, having survived that
period and been in practice for twenty-two years, it was a little bit

intimidating to just pull the shades down on it all and say good-bye, because God only knew what was around the corner. Still, it was an irresistible opportunity.

Hedigan was reelected for a second six-year term in 2004.[2] He is unsure about what he will do when he eventually leaves the court. His decision to leave Ireland for Strasbourg was a definitive moment in his professional life, probably eliminating the possibility of his ever practicing again as a barrister.

I think it's very unlikely that somebody in my position could go back to Ireland and take up his practice. Time moves on, and so do the main actors in the legal profession. In our system, a barrister depends upon solicitors for work. Those who are away, like myself, are quickly forgotten and replaced by others. Normally, people who become judges in our system remain so for the rest of their lives, so they are not looking for work after serving on the bench.

Human Rights in the "New Europe"

Like many of his fellow judges, Hedigan feels that the importance of the work he performs at the ECHR outweighs the many disadvantages that come with professional insecurity. The last fifteen years have seen momentous changes in Europe, and the court feels them firsthand. The expansion of the European human rights regime to include most of the countries of the former Soviet Union has, in particular, been both encouraging and challenging for the ECHR. When the court became a permanent body in 1998, the European Human Rights Commission, which had functioned alongside the court as a body for filtering cases, was abolished. The rationale for this move was that the commission was no longer necessary, since the shift from part time to full time would allow the court itself to handle all types of human rights complaints in the future. This has since proved to be far from true.

The commission and the part-time [European Court of Human Rights] were to be replaced and one full-time, permanent [ECHR] was to be established in their place. Some of the reasons that were advanced at the time were that it would save a great deal of money. This was quite unrealistic. It was not credible that it would cost less money to process the cases that were already increasing in number by quantum leaps. Throughout the 1980s, the workload was increasing at an extraordinary rate. And then the Berlin Wall fell in 1989 and suddenly there was a vast new reservoir of potential violations.

All these East European countries, former Soviet countries, all wanted to join the Council of Europe. In practical terms, it was probably unwise to allow them in, or at least to require them to ratify the convention immediately. But for political reasons, which I think were correct, it was very important to get them all inside the democratic tent, to grasp this moment in history and not to let it slip away. It was probably the right thing to do.

But allowing this, I think the process should have paused in relation to the negotiations for the creation of a permanent court. The impact of absorbing so many countries with little protective mechanisms for protecting human rights was likely to be enormous on the workload of the new court. Instead of just abolishing the commission in order to avoid duplication of work with the court, according to the rather dubious logic of the time, it would have been better had they reformed the commission and provided that its function would be to decide on the admissibility of the cases—no opinion to be produced, just to decide admissibility. The new, full-time court might then have been established to do the kind of work that had made its reputation earlier: the production of important judgments of high jurisprudential value, well reasoned, well researched, and accurate in factual matter. In the context of the current vast caseload, this is a real challenge for the court now: how to maintain the highest standards in its case law while dealing with an unmanageable caseload.

The court continues to campaign for the creation of a separate, quasi-judicial filtering body. I would like all who apply to Strasbourg to have an answer, even if for 90 percent of them it will be "no"—that is, their cases will be deemed inadmissible. But it is totally unacceptable that tens of thousands must wait in an unending queue to receive this answer.

There are currently two other regional human rights courts in the world, the Inter-American Court of Human Rights, whose first judges were elected in 1979, and the African Court of Human and Peoples' Rights, whose first judges were elected in 2006. Both of the regional bodies that created these courts decided, unlike the Council of Europe, to preserve their human rights commissions. The Inter-American Commission of Human Rights works as a screening body for the IACHR, which then only receives those cases that are most significant. Hedigan bemoans the fact that his own court has no such screening body, the result being an ongoing caseload of daunting proportions:

Last year the court delivered 30,000 decisions, and 1,560 judgments. Consider that the United States Supreme Court has never, if I am correct, exceeded 100 cases a year. It puts things in perspective.

Moreover, these numbers are increasing inexorably year by year. The fact that the vast majority of those decisions are decisions of inadmissibility doesn't matter. Cases don't all come with a big sign on them saying, "Inadmissible." Someone has to read them. Some judicial formation here has to decide.

Despite the breadth of its geographic jurisdiction and the wide cultural and historical differences among its member states, the ECHR has an excellent record of compliance with its decisions. One reason is that membership in the European Union is now linked with compliance, and countries that are anxious to come under the umbrella of the European Union make great efforts to implement the court's judgments. Hedigan points out that the issue of compliance is not the responsibility of the judges:

The judgments are notified to the Committee of Foreign Ministers of the Council of Europe countries or, in reality, to the Committee of Ambassadors here in Strasbourg, who are their deputies. Once a judgment against a country is notified to them, it goes onto their agenda and it keeps coming back up with a request to explain what action has been taken to comply with the judgment. Perhaps the most classic example would be Turkey. You know that Turkey is very anxious to join the European Union, and the European Union has indicated that it is prepared to talk to them about it. It's a very controversial issue in Europe as to whether they should or should not be allowed to join. Among many other different things, they have to comply with the judgments of the Court of Human Rights. Consequently, they have been implementing the judgments with considerable vigor for a number of years, and this has helped Turkey to meet perceived European standards in relation to human rights protection and the rule of law.

There are inevitably problems with some of the "newer recruits." However, it is not just countries of the "New Europe" that may have difficulty in implementing judgments of the court. Hedigan recalls the difficulty that Ireland had in complying with one of the ECHR's judgments.

In Ireland, when the Norris v. Ireland *judgment was produced— which condemned Ireland for not having decriminalized the laws against homosexuality—I think there was a kind of broad consensus that it was predictable. But there was also a very strong sense that nothing was going to happen for quite a long time, if ever, because no one in Ireland, no politician, was going to introduce a bill in the parliament decriminalizing homosexuality. And so about five years passed, if I'm not mistaken. Norris even threatened to bring another action against the country. Then, finally, a very formidable woman was made the minister for justice. Perhaps there was a sense that a woman might do what a male politician dared not. In any event, she introduced the bill and Ireland ended up in compliance with the judgment of this court.[3] In every other respect, however, Ireland's record of compliance with our judgments has been very good.*

Another country of the "Old Europe" that has run afoul of the ECHR repeatedly is Italy. Most of the judgments against it are for violations of article 6 of the European Convention of Human Rights, which guarantees the right to a trial within a reasonable time. Despite considerable political pressure, the Italian government has not made the judicial reforms necessary to bring its trial system into line with its peer nations.

Italy is coming under great pressure from the Committee of Ministers, and from the court as well, and there has been much criticism of their apparently clogging up the caseload of the court. Italy is one of the most successful countries in Europe, so this problem should be solvable. Action has been taken by Italy in this regard— they have introduced a law, called the "Pinto Law," which provides a domestic remedy, in Italy, whereby persons who are the victims of delay in proceedings, which would be a violation of article 6, may sue in the Italian courts for their damages. The court here has held that that is now a domestic remedy that must be exhausted before parties can come to Strasbourg.[4] Unfortunately, the implementation of this law by the Italian courts has caused some difficulty, but hopefully this problem is on its way to resolution.

The Wisdom of an International Regime

It might be asked why a regional judicial body is better suited to consider and rule on issues of human rights than a domestic court. Why should the bench of an international court make difficult decisions about the way a society conducts itself—such as how it balances freedom of religion with freedom of expression when it comes to wearing the Islamic veil in public schools, or balances the right to individual privacy with freedom of the press—rather than the judges who are members of that same society? Hedigan has thought deeply about this issue, outlining both the rationale for and his personal vision of the international human rights regime.

The whole system is based on the proposition that the protection of human rights at the national level doesn't work. World War II and apartheid were the two most convincing proofs of that. You have to have collective responsibility. A domestic government under threat may be tempted, indeed even terrorized, by attacks against its people to take action that is inappropriate in a democracy and contrary to the rule of law. In such a situation, everyone loses—the government loses its moral authority, the people lose precious rights that took decades, if not centuries, to achieve. A domestic government attempting to subvert the democratic order may also be unrestrainable at the national level, for many reasons. In these circumstances, an international supervision may be the only forum to which the citizen may go to claim his government is violating standards to which his country is committed.

That is the idea that gave birth to this court. It is worth noting that no part of the world has had to struggle more against terrorism than Europe in the last fifty years. Many times, this court has been obliged to condemn governments for their actions in trying to meet these threats. To their credit, governments have abided by these decisions, and the terrorist threat has largely been successfully met. Think of Ireland, the United Kingdom, France, Germany, Italy. In the agony of these terrible threats, no institution is more valuable than an independent court to adjudicate on the actions of governments. It provides a forum for the victim and both guidance and support for the governments. Central to this function is the creation of universal standards of human rights protection. If you ask whether domestic courts could not come to proper decisions in relation to some of these matters, yes, I have no doubt that they could. But in relation to matters that are quite specifically set for our court, where we are trying to establish a common standard for forty-six countries, how could one of the individual countries achieve that? How could the Irish Supreme Court decide what was correct for forty-six countries? It couldn't; it could only decide for itself. So if you want to set an across-the-board standard for forty-six countries, which is what we are doing, you have by definition got no alternative but to have an international court of some sort. At the moment, it happens to be us.

But I think that going towards a more global solution to human rights issues would be the ideal. A global human rights court, to which people would have a right of individual petition and whose judgments would be complied with, would be ideal. It's unfortunately not going to happen anytime soon. We have hopes for the new African Court of Human and Peoples' Rights. The Inter-American Court of Human Rights has its limitations, at the moment because it doesn't have U.S. backing. Asia apparently is showing no signs of having a court of human rights. That just about covers everyone. So the prospects for a global court are not great right now.

But who would have thought about a European Court of Human Rights sixty years ago? Sixty years from now, the world will be a very different place. Hopefully, it will be a better place and maybe there will be a place for a global court of human rights. As far as human rights protection is concerned, it is already a considerably better place as a result of the institutions that have been established.

The idea that the rights of individuals can best be protected through international efforts is, indeed, a recent development, one that has emerged from a complex dynamic between historical events and reactions to those same events. Hedigan sees this development as unquestionably positive and is proud of the role his court plays in ensuring the centrality of human rights in both the thinking and behavior of European states.

I think that the individual is the most precious form in society. The relationship between the state and the citizen—the individual—lies at the very heart of civilization. That they're treated with decency and respect, can stand up and say their piece whenever they want, that they're not going to be tortured, or abducted, or imprisoned for their views or their religion—these are precious and vulnerable rights. I think the court is spreading those standards all over Europe. The things that are happening in this regard, and that have happened in Europe over the last half a century, are remarkable.

The European Court of Human Rights has contributed to rising expectations regarding the protection of rights across the continent. John Hedigan finds himself torn between pride in the accomplishments of his court and frustration with its inability to reach its full promise.

Conclusion

Toward an Uncertain Future

Most international judges have not inherited institutions of law. They have built them, brick by brick, law by law. Thomas Buergenthal arrived in Costa Rica to discover that he and the other members of the first bench of the Inter-American Court of Human Rights were to meet in an abandoned bathhouse. Navanethem Pillay, as president of the Rwanda Tribunal, established by the Security Council of the United Nations, found herself in battles for window screens and air conditioners. Georges Abi-Saab remembers with fondness the exhilaration of surveying the "green fields" of the uncharted legal landscape in the first years of the Appellate Body of the World Trade Organization. Other, older institutions, like the European Court of Human Rights (active since 1959), have undergone dramatic processes of reinvention, which are still not complete. The expansion of Europe has dramatically altered the character of the ECHR, bringing new judges and new languages, and increasing its annual caseload by tens of thousands. Even the oldest institution, the International Court of Justice (active since 1946), is arguably transforming. Once a venue primarily for disputes between a limited number of developed countries and between developed and developing countries, in recent years it has become a truly global court, settling disputes between a much larger and more diversified constituency on an increasingly diverse range of issues. This process of invention and reinvention has forced judges on international courts and tribunals to create a new professional role, combining the remote erudition of the scholarly jurist with the political savvy of the international civil servant.

What is the future of the work of the international judge? In twenty years, in fifty years, will the world have a more settled, more coherent system of international legal institutions? Will those institutions command widespread respect? Will international judges serve more as guardians and less as builders?

The trajectory is far from clear. On the one hand, as we have seen, the number and scope of international courts has increased substantially in the last years of the twentieth century and the first years of the twenty-first. Projected forward, this expansion suggests a trend toward a prolife-ration of courts and a firmer establishment of the rule of law in the inter-national sphere. Some envision a world where the international rule of law hinges on an integrated network of international courts that bring in-creased predictability and accountability to matters of economy and crime, war and peace.

On the other hand, other signs point toward a slowdown. Judicializa-tion has made significant advances in some areas, such as international criminal law, but other significant areas of human activity, such as migra-tions, the environment, financial relations, and telecommunications, are scarcely touched by international courts. Resistance to the increasing ex-panse and authority of the international courts by some of the world's major powers raises the possibility that even if international courts con-tinue, their work could become marginalized or trivialized. Although international judicial bodies have continued to function in the face of hostility from large countries like the United States, China, and Russia, their relevance to the major social and political problems of the world could be eroded over time, with courts continuing to exist as a pale shadow of their former selves.

Even if the international courts do continue to develop and expand, this increased presence will not necessarily lead to greater coherence and stability. Proliferation could be a recipe for legal chaos, as courts struggle with overlapping jurisdictions, an uncertain hierarchy, unclear relation-ships between international and domestic law, and the occasional dishar-mony between legal systems. Indeed, states may find good reasons to sup-port proliferation for exactly this reason: the more courts, the more opportunities for "forum shopping," as governments seek legal bodies that will be friendly to their interests.

This uncertain future hinges in important ways on three principal trends in the international courts and tribunals. First, the development of a worldwide community of international judges has the potential to stim-ulate innovative legal thinking and to enhance the stability of interna-tional law, but this global network has significant limits to its extent and also carries the threat of stifling innovation. Second, the controversial role of international judges as builders—not merely interpreters—of the law has contributed to significant advances in the clarity and scope of international law; carried too far, this trend could undermine the whole system by upsetting the delicate balance between states and courts. Third, the fragility of international judicial bodies—in terms of resources, public respect, and reliance on governments acting in concert—casts doubt upon the future of the strength and independence of these courts. Each of these trends contains both seeds of promise and of doubt.

The Future of the "Invisible College"

As we have seen, the community of international judges is partly a matter of common patterns of education, partly a matter of common professional experiences in the world of law, academia, and diplomacy, and partly a matter of increased opportunities for meaningful interaction and dialogue among the various courts. There was once a time when the "invisible college" of international judges consisted of a small band of men, principally Europeans, clustered tightly in The Hague.[1] Today's more extensive network has much more diversity in terms of geography, race, and gender, but the common bonds across space and time and the universal understanding of the judicial function often minimize those differences. Training in a relatively small number of key universities ensures significant commonalities in the legal mindset of international judges, shaping attitudes and philosophies. The career paths for many international judges intersect in international courtrooms and at academic and diplomatic conferences, allowing personal relationships to develop that can carry over to the bench. And the growing number of judicial conferences has created new opportunities for previously scattered international judges to sit together and compare ideas about such topics as the use of precedent, independence and accountability, the writing of judgments, and the problems of enforcement.

The development of this community has had a profound effect on the work and role of international judges. The major differences in legal method and practice between the civil law and common law systems appear to pose challenges for international courts, but judges insist that a fidelity to basic principles developed through their networks tends to minimize this conflict. The community has also created important restraints on the threat of fragmentation in the international legal system, as judges read and take into consideration the judgments of their peers on other courts, even if they do not always cite or rely upon them. In the criminal field, men and women with experience in the ad hoc tribunals are now playing a key part in the development of the permanent International Criminal Court, bringing rules, practices, and procedures with them. International judges cannot rely for authority and consistency on an extensive body of history, tradition, and documents, as can their counterparts in the strongest national systems; the "invisible college" of international judges goes a long way toward mitigating the relative paucity of those crucial bulwarks. In many ways it appears that the international community of judges both takes advantage of and contributes to trends toward globalization by building on communications networks and by making legal interpretations that break down barriers between nations and peoples.

Two important cautions, however, should temper faith in the extension of the trajectory of this community's development. First, we should be careful not to exaggerate its closeness and consistency. The growing "epistemic community" of judges[2] may help close some anticipated gaps, like the differences between civil law and common law, but other breaches remain. One such breach has to do with how much judges and courts should rely explicitly on dialogue and community itself; when it comes to how much international courts should cite one another's judgments, and who should cite whom, there is considerable disagreement. Perhaps more importantly, the veneer of cosmopolitanism cannot entirely hide the presence of national perspectives on the international bench, as political divides subtly but inevitably intrude (just as they do in domestic jurisdictions) into judicial practice and decision making.

The second and more important caution is that the development of a judicial community could nurture stagnation as easily as vitality. To the extent that international courts increasingly represent a collection of men and women who have trained and worked in similar institutions, thinking and practices can become ossified, and the pace of change and innovation can decelerate. As we have seen, some people who work for judges in international courts fear that this has happened to some extent already, as judges wrap themselves in a mantle of infallibility that comes with the privileges of office. Others fear that the development of a global community threatens to institute an artificial construct of global values that blurs or masks healthy differences of national or local perspective. As judges and courts become more intertwined, there is always the risk that individual judges are more likely to put the interests of their prerogatives and institutions ahead of larger considerations of justice.

It seems likely that the international judicial network will continue to grow and expand—at least on the surface. But this development will not lead inexorably toward a healthy combination of coherence and innovation. Fifty years from now, the invisible college of international judges is likely to be more visible, but whether its impact will be superficial or profound remains to be seen.

New Law, New Problems

International judges have become "reluctant radicals," driven by necessity, as they see it, to fill in the gaps in the law in order to render judgments in uncharted legal terrain. What impact will this trend have on the future of international courts and tribunals? Once again, the verdict is uncertain.

The judges' willingness to step into the breach has a significant impact both in enhancing the law and in enhancing the authority of their courts.

The European Court of Justice has played a pivotal role in the advancement toward an ever-closer union by extending the spirit of the treaties founding the European Communities into a predictable and specific set of judicial practices that go well beyond the expectations of the original drafters of those treaties. The ad hoc tribunals have broken new ground in international criminal law, in applying the generic categories of crimes against humanity to specific situations, such as mass rape, hate speech, and ethnic cleansing. The Appellate Body of the World Trade Organization transformed itself from a marginal afterthought into a crucial judicial body in the arena of trade disputes. U.S. Chief Justice John Roberts, as we have seen, has compared judges to umpires, as straightforward interpreters of the rules; but when a complex game is being played with a short rulebook, the referees have to make on-the-spot decisions according to the spirit of the game. As we have seen, these developments have cheered some observers for their boldness, while alarming others who see them as an encroachment on the prerogative of sovereign nations.

Despite international judges' temperamental reluctance "to fill in the law's gaps," some version of this pattern is likely to persist, if for no other reason than that most judges, like other professionals, want to promote the relevance and the authority of their institutions. This pattern indicates that judges, whenever they have a chance, will address directly problems that states and intergovernmental organizations are either unable or unwilling to tackle through the political process—and will continue to do so. When organizations like the WTO are too divided and unwieldy to make improvements via the political process, a strong and able judiciary offers an alternative route to change. When states are reluctant for political reasons to hold men and women accountable for war crimes, the International Criminal Court can step into the breach. When states can reach consensus only at the highest level of abstraction in a treaty or convention, the judicial process offers a more direct route to filling in the details.

Yet there are good reasons to hope that the lawmaking tendencies of international judges will be curbed—or become less necessary—in future years. What may be necessary and productive in the early years could become a dangerous habit as judicial institutions reach their maturity. Depending, as they do, on the cooperation and goodwill of individual states, international judges cannot, in the long run, afford to be seen as unpredictable and unrestrained. Some critics of the international courts have already attacked the courts on these grounds, seeking to undermine their viability. A long-term pattern of radicalism, however reluctant, could ultimately empower and embolden the courts' nationalist opponents.

Equally importantly, international judges themselves generally do not want to be in the role of lawmakers. They insist that they would much prefer to base judgments on a rich and specific set of legislative documents, rather than relying on imprecise law, or worse, on customary international law and principles of law. From their point of view, their own lawmaking tendencies will automatically be circumscribed if states themselves can improve the political processes through which international treaties and conventions are developed. In this sense, their most far-reaching decisions often seem implicitly designed to try to provoke regional or international organizations into adopting new international law that reflects the will of the constituents. Up to this point, however, there is little evidence that judges have been consistently successful in stimulating a more efficient political process in the international arena.

This dynamic suggests that the "necessary evil" of judicial lawmaking may be present in future configurations of international courts, even long after the expiration date of the rationalization that the courts are still young. This could lead to continued innovation, to institutional irrelevance, or to an extension of the uneasy combination of both.

Fragility and Independence

The largest threat to the development of the role of international judges remains the fragility of the institutions in which they work. This fragility takes many forms.

The most obvious and tangible is relative lack of financial resources. Some international courts operate on the verge of bankruptcy and are in the undignified and potentially compromising position of having to beg for funds from states and other donors. Even the ad hoc tribunals, which have received large and stable outlays of funds from the United Nations, are stretched to the breaking point by the scope of their mandate and by the logistics of investigation, security, and translation. The European Court of Human Rights staggers under the weight of its case backlog, with insufficient staff even to process the cases, much less to act on them in a timely manner. Uncertain funding mechanisms reflect the ambivalence of the states and organizations toward their judicial creations. So the courts are fragile, too, because of the variety of ways in which they must depend on governments: for enforcement of their judgments, for providing top-quality members for their bench, and sometimes for providing the physical spaces in which they operate. The fragility of legal institutions and threats to judicial independence are pronounced for judges at the national level, also, but these factors are exacerbated for international judges by the tendency of states to acknowledge their respect for international law only when it favors their interests.

These factors would limit the effectiveness of any professional, but they are particularly alarming for judges because they threaten to compromise the cornerstone of their work—their independence. Although, as we have seen, direct pressure on international judges is rare, the judges work in an environment where subtle dangers lurk on all sides. This begins with the selection process, as candidates try to elude the diplomats' probing questions about their views and philosophies. Once on the bench, judges are often tempted to augment their incomes with outside commitments; moreover, their independence may be compromised through self-censorship if they face reelection campaigns. Even if a judge feels that he as an individual is immune from pressure, he may believe that the work of his court as an institution is manipulated by the outside actors who control the purse strings. Of course, judges themselves have contributed at times to the fragility of their institutions, through all-too-human weaknesses that have exposed their courts to ridicule, criticism, and vitriol.

A fragile present implies an uncertain future. Although several international courts have permanent mandates, they are nevertheless at the mercy of states for the resources and respect that they require to be effective.

What could impel states to provide more regular and whole-hearted support for international courts as institutions? Here it is possible that the answer lies in an element that judges are traditionally loath to cultivate: the respect and support of the public at large. In many counties, the public currently has scant idea of the role that international courts play, or even the potential benefits of a stable, authoritative worldwide rule of law.

One exception is the regard in which Europeans hold their court of human rights. The fact that the ECHR is accessible to individual petition, for all the problems that this causes, helps to establish a direct bond between the court and its public constituency. The court is now even exploring the possibility of Web-casting its public hearings, so that people in the far-flung corners of Europe can follow its activities and feel that they are part of the Council of Europe body that protects human rights. Such a relationship is not reproducible in courts that adjudicate only between states, however, or in those that prosecute the largest-scale crimes.

The Role of the National Judge

A critical dynamic that could affect all three of these factors is the relationship between international judges and their brethren who serve as national judges. In our own time, these particular connections tend to be personal and haphazard, but in the future they may well determine whether international courts succeed or whether they wither away as relics of the post–Cold War era. Many of the most significant judgments of international courts have bite and impact only when national judges cooperate—by implementing judgments locally, by speeding up extraditions, and by issuing injunctions against their own governments to comply with orders or to issue compensation to plaintiffs. International courts, when national courts ignore or dismiss their rulings, are reduced to little more than wishful thinking. Absent the power of an international police force, international courts depend on the recognition by domestic judges that the rulings of international courts have local force. The success of the European Court of Justice and the European Court of Human Rights have been made possible by deep and sincere cooperation from national benches across the continent.[3]

Mutual recognition (and proper respect and consideration) between international and domestic courts can be imposed by law. For instance, a national constitution might enshrine international law, including international decisions, as the supreme law of the land, superior to the constitution itself; in such circumstances, national judges are obliged to recognize the jurisprudence of international judicial bodies.[4] The great majority of national constitutions, however, are much less sweeping, so decisions about how much to recognize and follow the rulings of international courts come down to the discretion of individual judges. In many instances, national judges have considerable leeway in deciding how far they want to follow their international peers. They have incentive to do so, because in some circumstances the rulings of international courts may give them grounds for bolder and fairer judgments.

The engagement of national judges could have a profound effect on all three of the factors that will influence the ultimate success of the work of international judges. An extended global judicial community that includes national and international judges together has the potential for greater innovation and limits the dangers of exclusivity. Dialogue between international and national jurisdictions can help temper the lawmaking tendencies of international judges and synchronize their efforts with the developments within individual countries. And visible respect for international institutions on the part of national judges could make a large difference in increasing government and public support to strengthen international judicial bodies.

Phillip Rapoza, chief justice of the Court of Appeals of Massachusetts, served for eighteen months as a judge on the Special Panels for Serious Crimes in East Timor.[5] He believes that his experience on an international court has influenced not only his view of the importance of such institutions but also his entire perspective on being a judge. "It broadened my perspective in many ways," Rapoza says. "When you go to a society like East Timor, you come face to face with what justice is all about. What do we do as judges? What is the purpose of the judicial process and how can it best be served? At home, the answers to such questions are rooted in our established legal culture, which has developed over a long period of time. But when you work not only in the international environment, but also in the developing world, you realize that in many ways you are beginning at step one. You find yourself in a position where you are part of an institution that is, for the first time, establishing the mechanism and means for justice to be done. When you serve on such a tribunal, helping to give it form and substance, you become very aware of the importance of what it is that you do as a judge."

As judges, Rapoza continues, "we know that we must be fair and impartial, but those concepts take on an added dimension in the international context. Service on the Special Panels exposed me to cases of widespread and systematic criminal activity on a scale that I would never have experienced in my home court. In cases of such magnitude, where the entire civilian population is victimized, you see even more clearly the importance of the rule of law in all its aspects. For example: for the accountability of perpetrators to be properly and credibly established, it is vital that the integrity of the judicial process be beyond question. This point is even clearer when the court on which you serve is located within the very society where such crimes occurred. Crimes against humanity and related offenses arise in the context of a particular social or political conflict and serving as a judge in the same country where those events took place brings the whole experience into sharp focus. The basic principles of justice and fairness with which you are already familiar still apply, but they are taken to a level where their significance becomes all the more vivid to you as a judge. It's something you already know, or *should* know, but you feel it inside in a very powerful way."

National judges do not have to serve in international courts themselves in order to appreciate the enhanced perspectives that the work of these institutions can provide to judiciaries at all levels. A variety of institutions have begun to stimulate and nurture the development of these connections between the international and the national judiciary, and such efforts are bound to multiply in the coming years. The success of the next phase of the work of international judges may depend upon the depth and continuity of those links and the mutual sympathy and support that judges around the world develop for one another.

Ultimate Purposes

Asked what their institutions are ultimately *for,* judges give a variety of answers. Despite the many differences among the types of courts they sit on and cases they hear, their responses fall into three areas: the establishment of a community of law, the preservation of the dignity of the individual, and the prevention of violence and war.

Law substitutes rules for power. It is easy to forget how novel this axiom of modern societies is in the international arena. International courts seek to extend this principle from domestic spheres into relations between nations, not only providing new mechanisms for resolving conflicts, but changing the nature of the ways that states interact with one another. "I've always thought that the most important thing that this court has been able to do in Europe is the idea of a community of law," says a member of the European Court of Justice. "Conflicts are not solved by the power of the member states but by law. And that means by law applied in a manner that is equal to all. I think the court has through its history remained quite faithful to it . . . the idea that you know that the rules are the same for everyone. You know that those rules are based actually as much as possible on the status of the protection of individuals and not member states necessarily. That is important. And I think that's probably the most important function of the court that people can understand."

The European courts have the advantage of helping to create a community of law in the context of an increasingly strong transnational political community; courts with worldwide jurisdiction face a greater challenge in extending this principle globally. Yet when it comes to law and politics, the national and regional differences are somewhat exaggerated. As we have seen, international judges, for better and for worse, share a great deal in terms of background, education, and faith in universal principles of law, even if they come from very different societies and legal traditions. These common elements of background make the prospect of a worldwide community of law—established not by fiat but by judicial dialogue—an imaginable enterprise. To some, the increasing number of international courts is the key to this community, though judges have argued among themselves about this. "Why are you so concerned about the proliferation of international courts?" one ICJ judge reports asking another. "My approach has always been the more, the better. From my experience . . . there is this very important interaction between the courts—the creative interaction, which leads to new decisions by other courts, and that's how our common law has developed."

For international judges, the establishment of a community of law is a critical foundation for the protection of the rights and the dignity of individual human beings. "The whole system of international law was based on the proposition that the protection of human rights at the national level doesn't work," says a human rights court judge. "World War II and the development of apartheid in South Africa in the late 1940s were the two most convincing proofs of that. You have to have collective responsibility." Domestic governments, including those in the most open and democratic societies, have frequently abdicated their responsibilities to protect individual rights, even those guaranteed in their own constitutions or other founding documents. Judges, even those with warm feelings for U.S. ideals and values, point to the challenges to civil liberties and rights within the United States in the early years of the twenty-first century as an example of how democracies can fail their own citizenry. International judges do not see their courts as a substitute for the protections offered by domestic courts, but rather as part of a global network that provides mutual sustenance between and among judicial institutions. Overwhelmed as they are by thousands of backlogged cases, the judges on human rights courts take some pride in the idea that their institutions provide one source of hope and an avenue for action for individuals.

The dignity of the individual is no less essential for the international criminal courts. Pathbreaking developments in law—the trials for the crime of genocide; the establishment of rape as a war crime; the legal liability of those whose speech provokes violence—these are not abstract triumphs for the field, but definitions that restore meaning to individual lives. The International Criminal Court has given extensive attention to the rights of victims to participate and speak in its trials, a recognition not only of the importance of victim testimony to the process of collecting evidence, but also of the courts' responsibility to help empower and restore voice to survivors of mass violence. But the judges recognize that the work of their courts does not begin and end with trials; their ultimate success must be measured in the creation and strengthening of institutions of justice and civil society that build on the international tribunals to fortify human agency and dignity over the long run.

In the end, however, no ultimate purpose of the international courts and tribunals is more important than the prevention of violence and warfare. For many of the courts, this is an explicit part of their mission, as expressed in their founding statutes and documents. Many of the cases before the International Court of Justice have involved border disputes, the kind of territorial squabble between nations that is often settled on the battlefield. More recent cases at the ICJ have addressed the means of war, as nations have sought limitations, for example, on the legal use of nuclear weapons. No judge pretends that the international courts can be a cure-all for warfare, but they argue passionately that they are one essential institution among many that offer alternatives to military action.

How effectively can the international courts deter future violence? The early record is not encouraging, even for the criminal courts. The conflict in the Balkans continued to rage, and leaders on all sides encouraged and perpetrated crimes against humanity, even after the establishment of the Yugoslavia tribunal in 1993. The threat of arrest and prosecution by the International Criminal Court did not appear to be having a salutary impact on a series of bloody internal conflicts raging across Africa in the years following 2002, when the court's statute came into force. But judges point out that the world is only at the very beginning of this particular phase of international justice. At the level of specific deterrence, one criminal court judge points out, convictions in the tribunals have indeed taken a number of dangerous individuals out of circulation, where they can no longer wreak havoc on civilian populations. As for the larger idea of general deterrence, "Well, that is an interesting question. We have now, for somewhere between four hundred and twelve hundred years, used punishment as deterrence against crime at the national level. And all states believe in it, on all five continents. And if that is the situation at the national level, what would then be the argument that this cannot work at the international level? I can't see that there is any distinction there. If you first believe in punishment, there is no reason to distinguish and say that this belief is only applicable at the national level and not the international level, provided that the message is clear and repeated frequently enough." The criminal courts are young, he continues: "Don't expect too much from such a fledgling bird, not only to rise from the ashes but to start flying." Another judge uses a different metaphor: "I never considered the ICC as instant coffee."

Whether trying individuals, providing an avenue for redress of individual grievances, or settling disputes between nations, judges make direct, sometimes even sentimental connections between their work and the establishment of peace. "A hundred years ago, my grandparents on both sides were just young, married people," says John Hedigan of the European Court of Human Rights. "They were not very-well-off people, but they were comfortably off, middle-class Irish. They must have looked forward to the twentieth century with tremendous optimism; everything was happening, inventions, whatnot, great developments in social justice, and so on. And nobody could have foreseen the catastrophes that were going to befall Europe in the first half of the century. If we succeed in spreading our gospel across the whole of Europe, convincing people about the importance of the rule of law, the rights of citizens as individuals, not as members of communities, it becomes more and more difficult for governments to manage to persuade their people to go to war with each other. That's ultimately, for me, the main aim of the whole thing."

John Hedigan received his legal training at a time when the position of the international judge was an unusual and rarified role, principally a European phenomenon—by and large at the margins of law schools, much less in the public eye. The grandchildren of today's international judges, on the other hand, will come of age in an era when the position of the international judge is an established global phenomenon, an unavoidable presence for those who cast an eye on the international arena.

Will international judges contribute to "the main aim of the whole thing," to a reduction of conflict and violence? In the long run, their effectiveness will likely depend on the degree of public support they receive.

The negative consequences of the deterioration of the worldwide rule of law are palpable, at least to those who prefer that conflicts be addressed without resort to arms. Yet it is difficult to convince citizens of any nation that their country is better off entrusting some portion of its sovereignty to an international body. The ultimate success of international judges, however, may depend on the extent to which citizens around the world are willing to make this commitment.

Appendixes

Appendix A

Basics of International Courts

Name	Founded in; active since	Constituting instrument	Location	Organ of which international organization	Number of states party to the court's statute
International Court of Justice (ICJ)	1945; 1946	Charter of the United Nations, concluded in San Francisco, June 26, 1945, entered into force on October 24, 1945, *UNTS,* vol. 1, at 16, arts. 7.1, 36.3, and chap. 14 (arts. 92–96)	The Hague, the Netherlands	United Nations (one of the six principal organs of the organization)	All UN members (192), plus any other non-UN member state who acepts the court's jurisdiction
International Tribunal for the Law of the Sea (ITLOS)	1982; 1996	United Nations Convention on the Law of the Sea, concluded in Montego Bay, Jamaica, December 10, 1982, entered into force November 16, 1994, U.N.Doc.A/CONF.62/122 (1982), *ILM,* vol. 21, 1982, at 1261	Hamburg, Germany	United Nations	152 states are parties to the Law of the Sea Convention
International Criminal Tribunal for the former Yugoslavia (ICTY)	1993; 1993	Security Council Resolution 827 (1993), of May 25, 1993, *ILM,* vol. 32, 1993, at 1203, and subsequent amendments	The Hague, the Netherlands	United Nations	All UN members (192)

Number of judges	Jurisdiction (compulsory vs. optional)	Kind of disputes	Judicial activity (1990–2003)	Budget	Web site
15 (plus one or two ad hoc judges)	For the court to exercise jurisdiction states must have explicitly accepted it	Any disputes between states raising issues of international law	30 judgments, 45 new cases filed, 3 advisory opinions	$34,956,900 (biannual 2006–2007)	http://www .icj-cij.org
21 (plus one or two ad hoc judges)	In general, for the court to exercise jurisdiction states must have explicitly accepted it, but on certain limited issues it has compulsory jurisdiction	Disputes arising out of the implementation of the Law of the Sea Convention and related agreements	12 cases, 11 judgments	€17,214,700 (biannual 2007–2008)	http://www .itlos.org/
9 trial judges, plus 7 appeals judges (shared with the ICTR), plus 9 ad litem judges	Compulsory	International crimes committed in the territory of the former Socialist Republic of Yugoslavia since 1991	75 public indictments, 18 completed cases, 11 judgments in various stages of appeal	$276,474,100 (biannual 2006–2007)	http://www .un.org/icty/

Appendix A: *Basics of International Courts* (continued)

Name	Founded in; active since	Constituting instrument	Location	Organ of which international organization	Number of states party to the court's statute
International Criminal Tribunal for Rwanda (ICTR)	1994; 1995	UNSC Resolution 955 (1994) of November 8, 1994, *ILM*, vol. 33, 1994, at 1598, and subsequent amendments	Arusha, Tanzania	United Nations	All UN members (192)
International Criminal Court (ICC)	1998; 2003	Statute of the International Criminal Court [hereinafter: Rome Statute], concluded in Rome, July 17, 1998 (A/CONF.183/98, July 17, 1998), *ILM,* vol. 37, 1998 at 999	The Hague, the Netherlands	Self-standing international organization, which is supported by the United Nations	104 states
Special Court for Sierra Leone (SCSL)	2002; 2003	Statute of the Special Court for Sierra Leone, January 16, 2002, 2178 *UNTS* 145	Freetown, Sierra Leone	Self-standing international organization, which is supported by the United Nations	Sierra Leone and the United Nations
European Court of Human Rights (ECHR)	1950; 1959	European Convention for the Protection of Human Rights and Fundamental Freedoms, concluded in Rome, November 4, 1950, entered into force on September 3, 1953, *UNTS,* vol. 213, at 221; *European TS,* vol. 1, at 4; as modified by subsequent protocols	Strasbourg, France	Council of Europe	46

Number of judges	Jurisdiction (compulsory vs. optional)	Kind of disputes	Judicial activity (1990–2003)	Budget	Web site
9 trial judges, plus 7 appeals judges (shared with the ICTY), plus 9 ad litem judges	Compulsory	International crimes committed in the territory of Rwanda between January 1, 1994 and December 31, 1994	58 cases in progress, 17 completed cases	$269,758,400 (2006–2007)	http://www .un.org/ictr/
18	Compulsory	International crimes (i.e., war crimes, crimes against humanity, crimes of genocide, and crimes of aggression)	No final decisions yet; first pretrial hearings took place in 2006; several ongoing investigations	€88,871,800 (2007)	http://www .icc-cpi.int/
11	Compulsory	War crimes and crimes against humanity committed in Sierra Leone after November 30, 1996	11 indictments proceeding, 2 withdrawn due to death	$25,539,700 (biannual 2005–2006)	http://www .sc-sl.org/
46	Compulsory	Violations of the human rights guaranteed by the European convention	8140 cases deemed admissible, 3940 judgments	€44,189,000 (2006)	http://www .echr.coe.int /ECHR/

Appendix A: *Basics of International Courts* (continued)

Name	Founded in; active since	Constituting instrument	Location	Organ of which international organization	Number of states party to the court's statute
Inter-American Court of Human Rights (IACHR)	1969; 1979	American Convention on Human Rights, concluded in San José, Costa Rica, November 22, 1969. *UNTS*, vol. 1144, at 123	San José, Costa Rica	Organization of American States	24 states to date have accepted the IACHR's jurisdiction
World Trade Organization (WTO) Appellate Body	1994; 1995	General Agreement on Tariffs and Trade: Multilateral Trade Negotiations Final Act Embodying the Results of the Uruguay Round of Trade Negotiations, concluded in Marrakech, April 15, 1994, *ILM*, vol. 33, 1994, at 1125, annex 2 of the Final Act, Understanding on Rules and Procedures Governing the Settlement of Disputes, pp. 1226–1247	Geneva, Switzerland	Self-standing international organization	150
Court of Justice of the European Communities (ECJ)	1952; 1952	Treaty Establishing the European Coal and Steel Community, concluded in Paris, April 18, 1951, *UNTS*, vol. 261, at 143, entered into force July 25, 1952, and subsequent amendments	Ville de Luxembourg, Luxembourg	European Union/European Communities	27

Number of judges	Jurisdiction (compulsory vs. optional)	Kind of disputes	Judicial activity (1990–2003)	Budget	Web site
7	For the court to exercise jurisdiction, states must have explicitly accepted it	Violations of the human rights guaranteed by the American convention	95 judgments, 8 advisory opinions, 146 orders for provisional measures	$1,391,300 (2006)	http://www .corteidh .or.cr/
7	Compulsory	Appeals against reports of dispute settlement panels arising out of disputes on the interpretation and implementation of the WTO and GATT trade agreements	304 disputes formally initiated, 59 appellate rulings, 115 panel reports	CHF 4,726,000 (2006)	http://www .wto.org/ english/ tratop_e/ dispu_e/ appellate_ body_e.htm
27	Compulsory	Interpretation and implementation of the EC/EU agreements and secondary Community legislation	1580 infringement cases by Commission, 3048 cases referred by national courts; figures for the European Court of First Instance: 1823 decisions from 2507 cases filed	€250,338,602 (2006)	http://www .curia.europa .eu/en/

Appendix A: *Basics of International Courts* (continued)

Name	Founded in; active since	Constituting instrument	Location	Organ of which international organization	Number of states party to the court's statute
European Free Trade Agreement (EFTA) Court of Justice	1992; 1994	Agreement on the European Economic Area and Agreement between the EFTA States on the Establishment of a Surveillance Authority and a Court of Justice, concluded in Oporto, Portugal, May 2, 1992, no. 94/L344/1, *O.J.*, of December 31, 1994, vol. 37, p.1	Ville de Luxembourg, Luxembourg	European Free Trade Association	3
Court of Justice of the Andean Community	1979; 1984	Treaty Creating the Court of Justice of the Cartagena Agreement, concluded in Cartagena, May 28, 1979, *ILM*, vol. 18, 1979, at 1203 as modified by subsequent protocols	Quito, Ecuador	Andean Community	4

Number of judges	Jurisdiction (compulsory vs. optional)	Kind of disputes	Judicial activity (1990–2003)	Budget	Web site
3	Compulsory	Interpretation and implementation of the EFTA agreements	59 opinions (2003)	Not available	http://www .eftacourt .lu/
4	Compulsory	Interpretation of the Cartagena Agreement and its protocols and additional instruments, and secondary Community legislation	29 nullifications, 94 infringement cases, 550 preliminary rulings regarding interpretive questions	$1,580,000 (2005)	http://www .tribunaland ino.org.ec/

Appendix A: *Basics of International Courts* (continued)

Name	Founded in; active since	Constituting instrument	Location	Organ of which international organization	Number of states party to the court's statute
Caribbean Court of Justice	2001; 2005	Agreement Establishing the Caribbean Court of Justice, signed on February 14, 2001	Port of Spain, Trinidad and Tobago	Caribbean Community	15

Note: Data compiled by the authors, based on the best information available and updated visiting the Web sites of the various international courts and the organizations they belong to as well as scholarship where available.

Judicial activity (1990–2003) : In the case of courts that have become operative after 1990, of course, the figures indicate judicial activity since they started operating.

Source: Alter, Karen J. "Private Litigants and the New International Courts." *Comparative Political Studies* 39, no. 1 (2006): 22–49.

Number of judges	Jurisdiction (compulsory vs. optional)	Kind of disputes	Judicial activity (1990–2003)	Budget	Web site
7	Compulsory	a) Interpreting the Revised Treaty of Chaguaramas, which establishes the CARICOM Single Market and Economy (CSME), b) Act as a final court of appeals against rulings of courts of those states which have accepted this jurisdiction (at the moment, Guyana and Barbados)	1 decision in 2005, 4 decisions in 2006	Financed through a $100 million trust fund through the Caribbean Development Bank	http://www .caribbean courtof justice.org/

Appendix B

Judges Interviewed for This Book

Following is a list of judges interviewed for *The International Judge,** along with their country of origin, gender, and the court on which they served at the time of the interview or have served on in the past.** Additional international courts on which they have served are noted in parentheses.

1. Georges Abi-Saab, Egypt, M, WTO AB (ICJ as ad hoc judge, ICTY)
2. Emmanuel Ayoola, Nigeria, M, SCSL
3. Carl Baudenbacher, Liechtenstein, M, EFTA
4. Dennis Byron, St. Kitts and Nevis, M, ICTR
5. Thomas Buergenthal, USA, M, ICJ (IACHR)
6. Claus Dieter Ehlermann, Germany, M, WTO AB
7. Gudmundur Eiriksson, Iceland, M, ITLOS
8. Gilbert Guillaume, France, M, ICJ
9. Mehmet Guney, Turkey, M, ICTY
10. John Hedigan, Ireland, M, ECHR
11. Rosalyn Higgins, UK, F, ICJ
12. Francis Jacobs,*** UK, M, ECJ
13. Hassan Jallow, The Gambia, M, SCSL (ICTR as chief prosecutor)
14. Philippe Kirsch, Canada, M, ICC
15. Egil Levits, Latvia, M, ECJ (ECHR)
16. Luís Miguel Poiares Pessoa Maduro,*** Portugal, M, ECJ
17. Cecilia Medina Quiroga, Chile, F, IACHR
18. Erik Møse, Norway, M, ICTR
19. Tafsir Malick Ndiaye, Senegal, M, ITLOS
20. Elizabeth Odio Benito, Costa Rica, F, ICC (ICTY)
21. Navanethem Pillay, South Africa, F, ICC (ICTR)
22. Fausto Pocar, Italy, M, ICTY
23. Phillip Rapoza, USA, M, East Timor
24. Allan Rosas, Finland, M, ECJ
25. Konrad Schiemann, UK, M, ECJ
26. Stephen Schwebel, USA, M, ICJ
27. Vassilios Skouris, Greece, M, ECJ
28. Anita Usacka, Latvia, F, ICC
29. Budislav Vukas, Croatia, M, ITLOS

30. Patricia Wald, USA, F, ICTY
31. Inés Weinberg de Roca, Argentina, F, ICTR (ICTY)
32. Luzius Wildhaber, Switzerland, M, ECHR

---

* A description of the interview process is provided in the introduction.

** Many other court staff members were also interviewed, but they are not identified.

*** Advocate general of the European Court of Justice. Advocates general are full members of the court but they are not judges. They do not take part in the court's deliberations, yet they assist with each case and deliver their opinions on questions. It is the role of the advocates general to propose to the court, in complete independence, a legal solution to the cases for which they are responsible.

Appendix C

Commonalities and Differences between the Civil Law and the Common Law Legal Traditions

In various places throughout this book, reference has been made to differences (actual or just perceived) between how judges trained in different legal systems think and operate. A few words are necessary to clarify the differences between the main legal traditions.

"Legal traditions," or "legal families," are a "set of deeply rooted, historically conditioned attitudes about the nature of law, about the role of law in the society and the polity, about the proper organization and operation of a legal system, and about the way law is or should be made, applied, studied, perfected, and taught. The legal tradition relates the legal system to the culture of which it is a partial expression. It puts the legal system into cultural perspective."[1]

The main legal traditions are the Romano-Germanic, also known as civil law tradition, and the Anglo-Saxon, also known as common law tradition. Other legal traditions include legal systems based on religious beliefs, such as Islamic law, Hindu law, Jewish law, and various customary laws, such as Chinese law, African tribal laws, but many of these traditions have been supplanted or buried under one of the two main traditions as Europeans colonized the world between the sixteenth and nineteenth centuries. In certain countries, one can find elements of more than one tradition coexisting, as in Canada and Israel, in which case scholars talk about "mixed jurisdictions."

Common law and civil law legal traditions belong to the larger Western law family, as they share similar social objectives (e.g., the stress is more on personal rights, as opposed to the rights of the group/family/tribe), thus setting them apart from other legal traditions, current and past. Indeed, distinctions between common law and civil law approaches to law and courts are often overdrawn, as both civil law and common law ultimately descend from Roman law. Nevertheless, at a very general level of abstraction, some distinctions between how judges and courts of law operate in the two traditions can be made.

One of the main differences is the role of judges in lawmaking. In the civil law tradition, the function of the legislator is to legislate, and the functions of the courts is to apply the law. There is little or no room for judges to create law. Common law, on the other hand, gives judges large lawmaking powers.

In common law systems, judicial opinions are a primary source of law, and prior judicial decisions are binding in subsequent cases. The stare decisis principle requires that a decision of a court on a point necessary to the decision in the case, consonant with reason, and in harmony with the spirit of the times should not be departed from by that court or any court subordinate to it in the judicial hierarchy of that jurisdiction. The starting point of judicial reasoning is past decisions, which are binding by reason of authority. The approach is rather empirical.

Conversely, civil law legal systems are based upon detailed legislative codes rather than judicial precedents. These codes are a comprehensive, authoritative collection of rules covering all the principal subjects of law. Civil law codes are often developed by legal scholars and academics and then enacted by legislative bodies. They are based on philosophy, theory, and abstract principles. Courts' previous decisions are no more than a source that can be used to clarify the content of the law, not a real source of the law per se. Civil law judges must cite at least one statutory provision as a basis for each decision. A decision based solely on case precedent will be reversed for "lack of legal basis." Judgments have only the "authority of reason." Commentary on the law by scholars plays a much greater role in civil law systems than in common law systems.

From these overarching distinctions, more follows. First, judgments in civil law systems tend to be written in a more formalistic style than judgments of courts in common law countries and tend to be shorter. Common law judgments extensively expose the facts, compare or distinguish them from the facts of previous cases, and decide (if not create) the specific legal rule relevant to the present facts. Civil law decisions first identify the legal principles that might be relevant, then verify if the facts support their application. Thus, only the facts relevant to the advanced principle are usually stated.

In civil law jurisdictions, laws tend to be general (short) and abstract. In common law traditions, they are longer and rather more detailed. In civil law systems, to interpret ambiguous law judges tend to focus on the intention of the legislator. They examine the legislation as a whole, including the *"travaux préparatoires,"* as well as the provisions more immediately surrounding the obscure text. The code purports to be comprehensive and to encompass the entire subject matter, not in the details but in principles, and to provide answers for questions that may arise. In other words, there are no lacunae and, if necessary, the judge can resort to "general principles of law" to resolve the question before him or her. In common law jurisdictions, statutes have to be read against a case law background. Thus, statutes are to be objectively constructed according to certain rules (e.g., an enactment must be read as a whole; special provisions will control general provisions, so as to meet the subjects' reasonable understandings and expectations; and so on).

In civil law systems, professors of law command great respect and deference by legislators and judges. In common law systems, generally the practicing lawyer and judge are at the apex of the legal world. Moreover, while in common law countries judges are usually recruited from among experienced practitioners and sometimes elected by the people, in civil law countries judges are appointed fresh from specialized schools or after having taken cumbersome national exams. In civil law countries, judges start in the profession in their mid to late twenties, soon after graduation from law school, and remain judges throughout their lives.

There are other differences relating to the way courts operate and trials are held. The common law trial style is usually called "adversarial," while the civil law trial is called "inquisitorial." This reflects a big difference in the role of the lawyers in both legal systems.

For instance, since civil law systems tend to be more synthetic than analytical, more abstract than empirical, rules of evidence tend to be much less detailed than in common law systems, and documentary proof is preferred over witness testimony, with the latter receiving very little weight. On these matters, the judge has greater discretion. Second, in civil cases, while common law countries often resort to juries, in civil law systems typically there is neither a trial nor a jury. Civil law court proceedings in civil cases consist of a series of isolated hearings, with no formal "pretrial" discovery. Third, in many civil law countries the decision comes down as "decision of the court," without an indication of its author, a concurring opinion, or a dissent. In the common law countries, individual judges' opinions are clearly stated and cited as such. Finally, in civil law legal systems, courts of appeals as a general rule review de novo both issues of fact and law, whereas in common law countries only the law is reviewed, subject to the "clearly erroneous" rule.

In criminal law cases, under the civil law system, lay judges (i.e., lay people appointed as judges), might sit on the bench, together with professional judges, to decide the case. In most cases in common law systems, there is one judge, whose role is that of an impartial referee between the parties to make sure they comply with procedural requirements. Civil law systems are different, first, because it happens more often that a case is heard before a bench made of multiple judges and, second, because judges, or at least some of them, are actively involved in determining the facts of the case. In many civil law systems, both the judge and the prosecutor are judges, and in some cases they can switch roles.

To know more about differences between civil law and common law traditions, see:

- http://www.droitcivil.uottawa.ca/world-legal-systems/eng-monde.php. This is the Web site of the University of Ottawa, Faculty of Law, Civil Law section.
- David, René, and John E. C. Brierly. *Major Legal Systems in the World Today: An Introduction to the Comparative Study of Law,* 3rd ed. London: Stevens, 1985.
- Glenn, H. Patrick. *Legal Traditions of the World: Sustainable Diversity in Law.* 2nd ed. Oxford and New York: Oxford University Press, 2004.
- Grilliot, Harold J., and Frank A. Schubert. *Introduction to Law and the Legal System.* 5th ed. Boston: Houghton Mifflin Company, 1992.
- Merryman, John Henry. *The Civil Law Tradition: An Introduction to the Legal Systems of Western Europe and Latin America.* 2nd ed. Stanford, Calif.: Stanford University Press, 1985.
- Tetley, William. "Mixed Jurisdictions: Common Law vs. Civil Law (Codified and Uncodified), Part I." *Uniform Law Review* 4, no. 3 (1999): 591–619.
- ———. "Mixed Jurisdictions: Common Law vs. Civil Law (Codified and Uncodified), Part II." *Uniform Law Review* 4, no. 4 (1999): 877–906.

Acknowledgments

A book with three authors may not be three times better than a volume penned by a single individual, but there are three times as many people to thank for their varied contributions.

First, we benefited from the invaluable assistance of the thirty-two sitting and former international judges, listed in appendix A, who each gave us several hours of their time for face-to-face interviews. Their generosity, their openness, and their trust truly made this book possible. We are especially grateful to the five sitting judges—Navi Pillay, Thomas Buergenthal, Georges Abi-Saab, Cecilia Medina Quiroga, and John Hedigan—who permitted us to write profiles of their lives and work.

Beyond the judges, many individuals gave us the benefit of their special insights, expertise, and information about the world of international courts and tribunals. The registrar of the International Tribunal for the Law of the Sea, Philippe Gautier, as well as former registrars Eduardo Valencia Ospina of the International Court of Justice and Paul Mahoney of the European Court of Human Rights, provided the invaluable perspective of the courts' chief administrators. Staff members and scholars, currently or formerly associated with various courts, were equally helpful, including: Fatou Bensouda, Sam Muller, and Hirad Abtahi about the International Criminal Court; Liam McDowall, Fredrik Harhoff, and Dan Saxon about the Yugoslavia tribunal; Simone Monesabian about the Special Court for Sierra Leone; Suzanne Chenault about the Rwanda tribunal; David Aaron about the Caribbean Court of Justice; Olger Gonzalez and Thomas Antkowiak about the Inter-American Court of Human Rights; and Stephanie Cartier about the World Trade Organization Appellate Body. Arlene Pacht of the International Association of Women Judges and Ana Uzelac of the Institute for War and Peace Reporting provided helpful background information.

For help with the preparation of the manuscript, we are indebted to a number of people at our host institutions. Lindsay Raub, at New York University Law School, and Sharon Carroll, now at Cleary Gottlieb Steen and Hamilton, assisted with research and copyediting of the early drafts of our chapters. At Loyola Law School Los Angeles Daniel Kelly and Jennifer Varjabedian helped prepare the footnotes, while Laura Cadra at the library provided information for the appendix on civil law and common law. At Brandeis University, Christopher Moore did yeoman's work editing the manuscript, and he also organized the process of collecting and annotating the illustrations.

In the fall of 2006, our manuscript underwent intensive revisions in response to comments by readers who took time away from their busy schedules to provide detailed and thoughtful responses to our draft. Our thanks to Karen Alter, Linda Carter, Allison Danner, Paul Davison, Sylvia Fuks-Fried, Richard Goldstone, Ruth Mackenzie, Joost Pauwelyn, and Georgene Vairo for correcting errors and providing constructive suggestions for improvement. Beyond these readers, a number of individuals have been mentors and guides to our broader work with international judges. Four board members at the International Center for Ethics, Justice and Public Life—Hans Corell, Richard Goldstone, Margaret Marshall, and Theodore C. Sorensen—have been particularly helpful on this topic to Dan Terris and Leigh Swigart. Linda Carter and Gregory Weber of McGeorge Law School have played a key part in the development of our Brandeis Institute of International Judges. At the Project on International Courts and Tribunals, Cesare Romano has benefited from the patronage of Philippe Sands and Shepard Forman. We are grateful to Judge Sonia Sotomayor for agreeing to write the foreword to this volume, and to Robin Kar, of Loyola Law School, for putting us in touch with her.

Our work has profited from considerable institutional support from near and far. The JEHT Foundation provided the bulk of the funding for our research, and Garth Meintjes has been unflagging in his enthusiasm. Marty Krauss, the provost of Brandeis University, has encouraged and supported the work of Dan Terris, Leigh Swigart, and the International Center for Ethics, Justice and Public Life. The Center on International Cooperation at New York University (led by Shepard Forman and Bruce Jones, respectively the director and deputy director); the Centre for International Courts and Tribunals of the Faculty of Law, University College London; and Loyola Law School have provided, at various times, intellectual and physical homes for Cesare Romano's work. We are grateful to the professional editorial assistance of Phyllis Deutsch at the University Press of New England, and of John Louth and Rebecca Smith at Oxford University Press.

Photographs of the judges profiled in this book are reproduced courtesy of the individual judges. The photograph of Georges Abi-Saab on page 131 is courtesy of Olivier Junod-Chen, Numeric World.

Finally, our families have put up with our travel schedules, conference calls, deadlines, and other inconveniences of authorship while still managing to offer support, guidance, and a strong dose of realism. Our greatest debts, therefore, are to Peter, Alex, and Marcus Glomset; to Francesca Guerrini and Emma and Leo Guerrini Romano; and to Maggie Stern Terris and Ben, Eli, Theo, and Sam Terris. We owe you one—and we're sure you'll collect!

Dan Terris, Cesare Romano, and Leigh Swigart
Waltham, Massachusetts / Los Angeles, California, March 2007

Notes

Introduction (pages x–xx)

1. See, for example, José E. Alvarez, "The New Dispute Settlers: (Half) Truths and Consequences," *Texas International Law Journal* 38, no. 3 (2003), 405–444. For more works on international courts, see the bibliography.

2. See chapter 5 for a discussion of these issues.

3. For more information on the BIIJ, see http://www.brandeis.edu/ethics/international_justice.

4. For information on PICT, see http://www.pict-pcti.org.

5. On the Burgh House Principles, see chapter 6 and *The Burgh House Principles on the Independence of the International Judiciary* (London: Study Group on International Courts and Tribunals of the International Law Association, 2004); see *Law and Practice of International Courts and Tribunals* 4, no. 1 (2005), 247–260.

6. See, for example, the discussions in Robert Badinter and Stephen G. Breyer, *Judges in Contemporary Democracy: An International Conversation* (New York: New York University Press, 2004); Martin Mayer, *The Judges* (New York: St. Martin's Press, 2004); see also Ronald Dworkin, "The Judge's New Role: Should Personal Convictions Count?" *Journal of International Criminal Justice* no. 1 (2003).

7. Many international judges have contributed their "voices" to the academic literature on international law, but almost always in their capacity as scholars, rarely in their capacity as judges.

8. The names of those interviewed appear in appendix B.

9. On occasion, we have asked permission from interviewees to identify them by name for selected specific quotations.

10. See chapter 2 for more detailed statistics.

11. See chapter 2 for a breakdown by region of international judges.

12. See chapter 1.

13. For a fuller explanation of the terminology and the institutions we call "international courts" and tribunals, see chapter 1.

14. In the case of those judges we singled out for profiles, we had an initial interview and then one or two follow-ups. The interviewees have read and approved the versions of the profiles as they appear in this volume.

Chapter 1: International Courts (pages 1–14)

1. Sometimes the parties will each choose two arbitrators, with the four together choosing a fifth, to make up a panel of five.

2. Treaty of Amity, Commerce and Navigation, 19 November 1794, U.S.–Gr. Brit. 8 Stat. 116 (52 Consol. T.S. 243).

3. Treaty of Washington, 8 May 1871, U.S.–Gr. Brit. 17 Stat. 863 (143 Consol. T.S. 145).

4. The PCIJ is often called the first international court, but in reality the title should go to the Central American Court of Justice, a regional court created in 1908. Unlike the PCIJ, however, the Central American Court of Justice had only limited geographic jurisdiction and was short-lived, as it ceased to operate after 1918.

5. Statute of the Permanent Court of International Justice, art. 9, 16 December 1920, 6 L.N.T.S. 380, PCIJ series D, no. 1 (1926).

6. Charter of the United Nations, art. 92, 26 June 1945, 59 Stat. 1031.

7. See Cesare P. R. Romano, "The Proliferation of International Judicial Bodies: The Pieces of the Puzzle," *NYU Journal of International Law and Politics* 31, no. 4 (1999), 713–723. See also Christian Tomuschat, "International Courts and Tribunals with Regionally Restricted and/or Specialized Jurisdiction," in *Judicial Settlement of International Disputes: International Court of Justice, Other Courts and Tribunals, Arbitration and Conciliation; An International Symposium* 285–416 (Heidelberg: Max-Planck Institut Für Ausländisches Öffentliches Recht und Völkerrecht, 1987).

8. That is to say, their existence must be independent of the vicissitudes of a given case, but not necessarily of a given situation, like the genocide in Rwanda or the war in Yugoslavia. This criterion eliminates arbitral tribunals, which are adjudicative bodies created by the parties to settle a given dispute and which are disbanded after the award is rendered.

9. Directly by treaty, or by an international legal act deriving its force from a treaty, such as a Security Council resolution.

10. At times, international courts might apply, besides international law, other bodies of law. E.g., hybrid international courts, like the Special Court for Sierra Leone, also apply the criminal laws of the country in which they have been set up.

11. In certain limited cases, the parties might have some limited control over they way the court proceeds. For instance, in the case of the International Court of Justice, if they agree, the parties can have the case heard by a selected group of judges (a "chamber," in ICJ jargon) rather than the full court. In ad hoc international arbitration, however, the parties have complete control over which rules of procedure the arbitral tribunal will apply. They can use ready-made sets of rules or draft them for each case.

12. All international courts share this feature, which sets them apart from quasi-judicial bodies, like commissions and committees that issue only findings and recommendations. However, certain international courts, besides issuing binding judgments, sometimes have the power to act nonbindingly. For example, the International Court of Justice can issue advisory opinions, which are not binding.

13. We also interviewed Judge Phillip Rapoza of the Special Panels for Serious Crimes in East Timor, which is a hybrid criminal court.

14. A more complete list of less active or not yet operational courts also includes the Benelux Economic Union Court of Justice, and the Common Market of Eastern and Southern African Court of Justice.

15. For a comprehensive listing of international adjudicative bodies see the synoptic chart in Romano, "The Proliferation of International Judicial Bodies," 718–719. An updated version (third edition) is available at http://www.pictpcti.org/publications/synoptic_chart.html.

16. José E. Alvarez, "The New Dispute Settlers: (Half) Truths and Consequences," *Texas International Law Journal* 38 no. 3 (2003); and José E. Alvarez, *International Organizations as Law-Makers* (Oxford and New York: Oxford University Press, 2005).

17. Kenneth W. Abbott, Robert Keohane, Andrew Moravcsik, Anne-Marie Slaughter, and Duncan Snidal, "The Concept of Legalization," *International Organization* 54, no. 3 (2000).

18. The Caribbean Court of Justice is unique because it has both original and appellate jurisdiction. In its original jurisdiction, like the ECJ, the CCJ is responsible for interpreting the Revised Treaty of Chaguaramas, which establishes the Caribbean Community (CARICOM) Single Market and Economy. See http://www .sice.oas.org/trade/ccme/protocol1.asp. Yet it also has appellate jurisdiction, as it acts as the common final court of appeal for those states that have accepted its jurisdiction (at the moment, Guyana and Barbados). This hybrid structure is unique among international courts.

19. The differences between hybrid courts and fully international criminal courts are that the former are composed of a mix of international and local judges, and to decide cases they apply a mix of local and international procedural and substantive laws. Some are more domestic courts, with various international elements grafted on, like the internationalized panels in Kosovo; others approximate international courts but retain some domestic elements, like the Special Court of Sierra Leone. On hybrid criminal tribunals, see generally, Cesare P. R. Romano, André Nollkaemper, and Jann K. Kleffner, *Internationalized Criminal Courts and Tribunals: Sierra Leone, East Timor, Kosovo, and Cambodia,* International Courts and Tribunals Series (Oxford and New York: Oxford University Press, 2004); and Cesare P. R. Romano, "Mixed Criminal Tribunals," in *Max Planck Encyclopedia of Public International Law,* 3rd rev. ed. [in press].

20. The Seabed Disputes Chamber of the International Tribunal for the Law of the Sea is open, in some circumstances, to state enterprises and natural or juridical persons. UN Convention on the Law of the Sea, art. 187 and art. 189 (10 December 1982), 1833 U.N.T.S. 397.

21. In this book, when we refer to the ad hoc tribunals, we are generally referring to the International Criminal Tribunal for the former Yugoslavia (ICTY) and the International Criminal Tribunal for Rwanda (ICTR), the two oldest, largest, and most prominent among these bodies.

22. Those who want to have more specific information about the various courts—their powers, composition, jurisdictions, and so forth—will find it in appendix A, "Basics of International Courts."

23. For some explanations of why international courts have proliferated, see, in general: the issue of *International Organizations* on the topic "Legalization and World Politics" (vol. 54, no. 3, summer 2000); Alvarez, "The New Dispute Settlers"; and Romano, "The Proliferation of International Judicial Bodies."

24. *Jerusalem Post,* July 16, 2004.

25. The International Court of Justice exercises two kinds of jurisdiction: contentious, where it issues binding rulings on disputes; and advisory, where it provides, at the request of certain UN organs and some of its agencies, clarifications as to what international law requires in a given situation. Advisory opinions of the ICJ are not binding but are widely regarded as authoritative restatements of international law.

26. Associated Press, May 4, 2005.

27. *New York Times,* December 9, 2005.

28. *USA Today,* March 21, 2005.

29. *Washington Post,* June 21, 2006.

30. "Cheese law a feta accompli," *Daily Telegraph* (Sydney, Australia), October 27, 2005; "Protecting feta won't make it betta," *Herald Sun* (Melbourne, Australia), November 5, 2005.

31. "King of 'chaos'; Belgian Jean-Marc Bosman opened the lid on free agency, and the sport hasn't been the same," *San Diego Union-Tribune,* December 21, 2005; "Football faces 'second Bosman' as clubs take on Fifa," *Observer* (London), October 23, 2005. Insiders put the possible cost of a ruling in favor of the plaintiff at the staggering figure of about 860 million euros ("Judges may again play major role in game's future," *Irish Times* (Dublin), May 16, 2006).

32. December 14, 2005.

33. *International Herald Tribune,* July 8, 2004.

34. May 13, 2005.

35. There are many more examples of high-profile rulings from the ECHR, like a ruling upholding a ban against Islamic headscarves imposed by the secular Turkish government ("Turkish student loses legal battle over Islamic headscarf," *Financial Times,* November 11, 2005), or the decision against Russian authorities for having committed serious breaches of human rights during military offensives in Chechnya ("Court condemns Russia over Chechnya deaths," *Financial Times,* February 25, 2005; "Russia ordered to pay for Chechen deaths," *Guardian,* February 25, 2005).

36. Cf. Kathryn Sikkink and Ellen Lutz, "The Justice Cascade: The Evolution and Impact of Foreign Human Rights Trials in Latin America," *Chicago Journal of International Law* 2, no. 1 (2001).

37. In the 1990s, the creation of an International Court for the Environment was proposed but has never been realized. See http://www.icef-court.org/icef /about.htm; and Alfred Rest, "Need for an International Court for the Environment? Underdeveloped Legal Protection for the Individual in Transnational Litigation," *Environmental Policy and Law* 24, no. 4 (1994); and Amedeo Postiglione, *The Global Environmental Crisis: The Need for an International Court of the Environment* (Florence: Giunti, 1996).

38. E.g., Iran, North Korea, Vietnam, Laos, and Belarus are some of the countries that are not party to any treaty providing for compulsory adjudication through a regime-based judicial body. If one also considers the international judicial bodies that exist only on paper (e.g., the tribunals of the Arab Maghreb Union or the Organization of Arab Petrol Exporting Countries), or are active at very minimal levels (e.g., the Court of the Commonwealth of Independent States), then one could add to the list also Syria, Kazakhstan, and Uzbekistan.

39. *Certain Questions of Mutual Assistance in Criminal Matters (Djibouti v. France),* http://www.icj-cij.org/icjwww/idocket/idfj/idjfframe.htm.

40. *Avena and other Mexican Nationals (Mexico v. United States of America),* 2004 Rep. ICJ 12 (31 March 2004), http://www.icj-cij.org/icjwww/idocket /imus/imusframe.htm.

41. *European Communities—Regime for the Importation, Sale and Distribution of Bananas* (WT/DS27), Request for Consultations by Guatemala, Honduras, Mexico, and the United States (4 October 1995).

42. *United States—Measures Affecting the Cross-Border Supply of Gambling and Betting Services* (WT/ DS285/1), S/L/110, Request for Consultations by Antigua and Barbuda (27 March 2003).

43. For a comprehensive overview of international courts operating in Africa, see http://www.aict-ctia.org.

44. This is how the genocide in Darfur has come under ICC investigation despite the fact that Sudan is not a party to the statute of the International Criminal Court. S.C. Res. 1593, U.N. Doc. S/RES/1593 (31 March 2005).

45. E.g., Joost Pauwelyn, "The Transformation of World Trade," *Michigan Law Review* 104, no. 1 (2005), 1–65.

Chapter 2: International Judges (pages 15–37)

1. In the fall of 2006, the Centre for International Courts and Tribunals, Faculty of Laws, University College London, launched a comprehensive three-year project on the process and legitimacy in the nomination, election, and appointment of international judges. See http://www.ucl.ac.uk/laws/cict/index.shtml? judicial-selection.

2. Of the courts on which this book focuses, only a few provide on their Web sites comprehensive biographical information on their judges, including name, nationality, date of birth, education, career background, publications, and extracurricular activities. The most detailed (sometimes exceedingly detailed) information can be found on the Web sites of the ICJ, ITLOS, and WTO. A notch below that level of detail is the data on the ICC Web site, and sparser still are the biographical profiles on the Web sites of the ICTY, ICTR, Special Court for Sierra Leone, ECJ, CCJ, and IACHR. The European Court of Human Rights started posting information on its judges only recently, and it is rather generic. More information on the ECHR judges can be found only if one digs deep into the records of the Council of Europe, but that is hardly accessible to the public. The EFTA Court of Justice does not post any judicial information on its Web site at all.

International judges' biographies do not provide any information on questions one might like to know about, like race, dual or multiple nationalities, political orientation, or religion—factors that play a great role in debates about judges in domestic courts. At the international level, concerns about diversity and representativeness are couched in terms of geographic diversity. Finally, there is no common format for biographies, making comparison and aggregation of data particularly problematic. Hence, a group portrait of international judges is necessarily sketchy and surely cannot claim absolute fidelity and completeness. The information here has been compiled with data collected in January 2006.

3. As indicated in chapter 1, one could define this group more broadly. The full list, from the 17 courts that meet our adopted criteria of what an international court is, includes 245 judges. If we were to expand the focus even further to encompass all other international courts that operate more intermittently, then the total would exceed 300, and if several other quasi-judicial control and implementation bodies existing in the world were counted in, it would easily exceed 500. These figures do not take account of judges sitting only for a particular case (i.e., ad litem judges at the ICTY and ICTR, alternate judges at the SCSL, ad hoc judges at the ICJ or ITLOS, and panelists of the WTO panels) or the judges of the newly established European Union Civil Service Tribunal, which is an administrative tribunal and, as such, belongs to a different order altogether. The figures also do not include the advocates general at the European Court of Justice, who have the status of judges but do not take part in deliberations (8). At the time of this writing, in January 2006, the number of permanent members of the thirteen

major courts we identified is 215, divided as follows: ECHR (46); ECJ (25); CFI (25); ICTY/ICTR (25); ITLOS (21); ICC (18); ICJ (15); SCSL (11); CCJ (7); IACHR (7); WTO AB (7); EFTA Court (3); CACJ (5).

4. They are Thomas Buergenthal at the ICJ, Theodor Meron at the ICTY, and Merit Janow at the WTO AB.

5. The ECJ together with its Court of First Instance(50), the EFTA Court (3), and the ECHR (46).

6. The civil law/common law divide and implications for international courts are discussed at length in chapter 4. An overview of the main distinctions between common law and civil law can be found as appendix C.

7. Of the 215 judges sitting in January 2006, only one did not have a degree either in law or international relations: Arumugamangalam Ganesan, member of the WTO Appellate Body, who has an MA and MS in chemistry (University of Madras, India). He has gained his experience and knowledge of the legal aspects of international relations through a life in national and international civil service.

8. Complete information on educational backgrounds is not available for all of the judges.

9. Some have degrees from multiple institutions. Other U.S. schools where international judges studied are NYU (3), UC Berkeley (2), U Illinois (Chicago) (2), Notre Dame (1), St. Johns' NY (1), Tufts (1), UC Los Angeles (1), New School (1), U Michigan (1), Bethany College (1), Cornell (1), Duke (1), Georgetown (1).

10. Others are Edinburgh U (2), London School of Economics (2), Glasgow U (1), King's College (2), Kent at Canterbury (1), Nottingham (1), Leeds (1), Newcastle (1). Several did their barrister training at Gray's Inn.

11. Others are the École nationale d'administration (ENA) (3), Strasbourg (2), Aix-Marseilles (1), Nancy (1).

12. It is noteworthy, however, that this judge, Rosalyn Higgins, was elected president of the ICJ by her peers in February 2006. Two ad hoc female judges are Susanne Bastid and Christine Van den Wyngaert.

13. Judge Olga Navarrete Barrero was the president of the Andean Court of Justice at the time of this writing.

14. The first was Sonia Picado Sotela, who served from 1989 to 1994.

15. In addition to having a high percentage of female judges, the ICC also had the only openly gay judge on an international court: Sir Adrian Fulford. The *Independent,* online edition, "Gay Power: The Pink List," 18 December 2006, http://news.independent.co.uk/uk/this_britain/article1153578.ece.

16. There are exceptions. For instance, at the ICJ; Pieter Hendrik Kooijmans was from 1993–1994 foreign minister of the Netherlands. He was also vice chairman of the Dutch Evangelical Party (merged in 1980 with two other parties into the Christian Democratic Party), chairman of the Foreign Affairs Committee of the Christian Democratic Party. At ITLOS: Jean-Pierre Cot was member of the European Parliament (1978–1979 and 1984–1999); president of the Budget Committee of the European Parliament (1984–1989); president of the Socialist Group of the European Parliament (1989–1994); vice president of the European Parliament (1997–1999); between 1981 and 1982 he was a member of the French government (minister of cooperation and development). At the ICTY/ICTR: Mohamed Shahabuddeen was first deputy prime minister and vice president, Guyana (1983–1987). At the ICTR: Jai Ram Reddy has been a member of the House of Representatives and leader of the opposition in the Fijian Parliament (1977–1984, 1992–1999). At the ICC: Karl T. Hudson-Phillips, member of Parliament for Trinidad and Tobago (1966–1976); Elizabeth Odio

Benito was minister of justice, and once candidate for prime minister, of Costa Rica. At the ECHR: Volodymyr Butkevych, member of the Ukrainian Parliament; Andras Baka, member of the Hungarian Parliament (May 1990–April 1991) and deputy chairperson of the National Assembly (1991–1994); Antonella Mularoni, member of the Grand and General Council of the Republic of San Marino (since May 1993). At the ECJ: Antonio Mario La Pergola was elected to the European Parliament (1989–1994). At CFI: Irena Pelikanova, member of the Legislative Council of the Government of the Czech Republic (1998–2004); Ingrida Labucka, member of Parliament (2002–2004). At the IACHR: Sergio Garcia-Ramirez has been member of the Institutional Revolutionary Party (PRI) (since 1961); occupied different positions under the PRI regime; served in the cabinet of President José López Portillo as secretary of labor and then in the cabinet of President Miguel de la Madrid as attorney general; in 1988 he lost his bid to be the PRI's presidential candidate against Carlos Salinas de Gortari.

17. This last distinction is particularly imprecise as often someone might serve in an international organization on behalf of his own government.

18. Rome Statute of the International Criminal Court, art. 36.5, 17 July 1998, U.N. Doc. A/CONF.183/9, 37 I.L.M. 1002, 2187 U.N.T.S.

19. About twenty-six judges, at some point in their career, had ambassadorial appointments.

20. Unattributed quotations in this chapter are from judges interviewed for this book in 2005 and 2006. See the methodology section of the introduction and the list of judges interviewed, in appendix B.

21. In this regard, things have not changed much since 1944 when Manley Hudson wrote; "The role is not one offering a career for which men are, or can be, specially trained." Manley Ottmer Hudson, *International Tribunals: Past and Future* (Washington, D.C.: Carnegie Endowment for International Peace and Brookings Institution, 1944), 32.

22. Coalition for an Effective African Court on Human and Peoples' Rights, "The Election of Judges to the African Court on Human and Peoples' Rights," Press communiqué, Khartoum, 16–25 January 2006.

23. Ibid.

24. A notable exception is the Caribbean Court of Justice. Whether or not regional governments put forward suggestions for candidates, it should be noted that the CCJ has recently accepted applications from *all* interested parties, regardless of origin. The CCJ placed a call for applications to this effect on its Web site in 2006.

25. One renowned notable exception is Elizabeth Odio Benito. Odio Benito was the only nominee to the ICC not sponsored by her own nation, Costa Rica. First, she was officially presented as Costa Rica's candidate, but President Abel Pacheco later changed his mind and withdrew her name. As both Odio Benito and Pacheco are members of the same political party (Odio Benito once ran as a candidate for prime minister), intra-party feuds might explain the sudden about-face. However, it has also been suggested that Odio Benito's prochoice stance on abortion motivated Pacheco to move against her (http://www.lifesite.net/ldn/2003/mar/03031201.html). Eventually, various women's rights NGOs mobilized to campaign in her support. She was nominated again, but this time by Panama, whose president, Mireya Moscoso, was a prominent activist for women's rights. In the end, she was elected in the first out of thirty-three rounds of voting, indicating strong support from governments around the world.

26. *Judicial Independence: Law and Practice of Appointments to the European Court of Human Rights,* Report from Interights (London: 2003), 18. The report also suggests that there is at least one instance where a government appointed an independent body for the purpose of devising a list of nominees, and then failed to follow the body's recommendation.

27. Parliamentary Assembly, Council of Europe, Recommendation 1429 (24 September 1999, 32nd sitting).

28. Opinion of the European Court of Human Rights on Parliamentary Assembly Recommendation 1429 (1999), 6 March 2000, reprinted in *Judicial Independence,* report from Interights, 48–49.

29. Ibid.

30. Reply from the Committee of Ministers on Recommendation 1429 (1999), adopted at the 72nd Meeting of the Ministers' Deputies, 21 September 2000, Doc. 8835 (25 September 2000), in ibid., 46–47.

31. Ibid.

32. Statute of the International Court of Justice, art. 2, 11 November 2005.

33. Hudson, *International Tribunals: Past and Future,* 34.

34. T. O. Elias, "Does the International Court of Justice, As It Is Presently Shaped, Correspond to the Requirements Which Follow from Its Functions As the Central Judicial Body of the International Community?" in *Judicial Settlement of International Disputes: International Court of Justice, Other Courts and Tribunals, Arbitration and Conciliation; An International Symposium,* ed. Max-Planck-Institut für Ausländisches Öffentliches Recht und Völkerrecht (Berlin, Heidelberg, and New York: Springer, 1974), 21–22. The passage is quoted in E. Valencia-Ospina, "Editorial Comment," *The Law and Practice of International Courts and Tribunals* 1, no. 1 (2002): 8–9.

35. *Judicial Independence,* Report from Interights, 23–24.

36. Ibid., 23–24.

37. According to NGOs observing the process of election of judges of the African Court of Human and Peoples' Rights, out of the list of twenty-one nominees, only nine candidates (one-third) had verifiable experience in the field of international law and human rights. Coalition for an Effective African Court on Human and Peoples' Rights, "The Election of Judges." A study by Jean-François Flauss of the 1998 election of the judges of the European Court of Human Rights noted that: "What is most surprising . . . [i]s that something like one third of the candidates found it virtually impossible to mention any human rights activities worthy of the name in their CVs. While some candidates got around this difficulty by paralipsis, most attempted, more or less cleverly, to save face. Rare were those who simply admitted their lack of experience without beating about the bush." Jean-François Flauss, "Analysis of the Election of the New European Court of Human Rights," *Revue Trimestrielle des Droits de L'Homme,* 9, no. 35 (July 1998), 435–464, reprinted in *Judicial Independence,* report from Interights, 67–83.

38. The main exception is Pierre G. Boutet, at the Special Court for Sierra Leone: military judge (1982); assumed the position of deputy chief military trial judge (1986); was appointed chief military trial judge in 1987, and became the judge advocate general (JAG) of the Canadian Forces (1993), responsible for the provision of legal advice and legal services to the Department of National Defence and the Canadian Forces. Other exceptions: A. Raja N. Fernando, also of the Special Court for Sierra Leone, is judge advocate for the Sri Lankan Navy, rank of commodore; Jacob Wit, of the Caribbean Court of Justice, served as second lieutenant in the Royal Dutch Navy (1976–1978).

39. Georg Nolte, *European Military Law Systems* (Berlin: W. de Gruyter, 2003).

40. In fact, there are a few examples of governments nominating foreigners. For instance, Thomas Buergenthal, a U.S. national, was nominated by Costa Rica (and eventually elected) to the Inter-American Court of Human Rights, not only in recognition of his competence and knowledge of the European human rights system, but also as an attempt to lure the United States into ratifying the Inter-American Convention on Human Rights. The United States never did so and, since Buergenthal's appointment, no other U.S. citizen has been elected to the bench of the San José court. Likewise, in 1921, John Bassett Moore of the United States was elected to the PCIJ on the nomination of the Italian Group, as the United States had not yet joined the League of Nations. See John Bassett Moore, "The Organization of the Permanent Court of International Justice," *Columbia Law Review* 22, no. 6 (1922), 497–526.

41. For an extended discussion of the issue of nationality, see chapter 5.

42. Linguistic issues in courts are addressed in much more detail in chapter 3.

43. See the profile in this volume of Thomas Buergenthal, who served on the IAHCR before his appointment to the ICJ.

44. E.g., Jorda and Odio Benito of the ICTY to the ICC; Pillay of the ICTR to the ICC; Abi Saab of the ICTY to the WTO AB. Also, ICTY ad litem judges Hans-Peter Kaul and Dembele Diarra now are judges at the ICC.

45. Several others have or had honorary appointments or nonjudicial positions in a body such as the Permanent Court of Arbitration.

46. For instance, a judge currently serving at the ICJ, Thomas Buergenthal, was formerly a judge and president of the IACHR (1979–1991) and then judge, vice president, and president of the Administrative Tribunal of the Inter-American Development Bank (1989–1994). At the WTO AB, Georges Abi-Saab has been a member of the ICTY/ICTR Appeals Chamber and an ad hoc judge at the ICJ. At the ICTY, Mohammed Shahabuddeen, a member of the ICTY/ICTR Appeals Chamber, has been a judge at the ICJ (1988–1997), while Christine Van Den Wyngaert has been an ad hoc judge at the ICJ. At the ICC, a larger number of judges has previous experience: Elizabeth Odio Benito served at the ICTY (1993–1998), as did Claude Jorda (1994–2003; president, 1999–2003), while Navanethem Pillay served at the ICTR (1995–2003; president, 1999–2003). Finally, the ECJ has in its ranks four former ECHR judges: Jerzy Makarczyk, Pranas Kuris, Uno Lohmus, and Egils Levits, from Poland, Lithuania, Estonia, and Latvia, respectively.

47. Statute of the International Criminal Tribunal for the Former Yugoslavia, art. 13, (1) (c), S.C. Res. 827, U.N. Doc. S/RES/827 (25 May 1993); Statute of the International Criminal Tribunal for Rwanda, art. 12 (3) (c), S.C. Res. 955, U.N. Doc. S/RES/955 (8 November 1994). For a version of the ICTY Statute incorporating all subsequent amendments, see http://www.un.org/icty/legaldoc-e/index .htm. For a version of the ICTR Statute incorporating all subsequent amendments, see http://www.ohchr.org/english/law/itr.htm.

48. Richard H. Steinberg, "Judicial Lawmaking at the WTO: Discursive, Constitutional, and Political Constraints," *American Journal of International Law* 98, no. 2 (2004), 247–275.

49. ICJ, ICTY, and ICTR (respectively, 15 and 25 [combined ICTY/ICTR] judges out of 192 UN members), ITLOS (21 members out of 152 parties to the Law of the Sea Convention), WTO Appellate Body (7 AB members out of 149 WTO members), IACHR (7 out of 35 OAS members), or the ICC (18 out of 102 parties to the Rome Statute).

50. In hybrid criminal courts, international judges are nominated by the UN secretary general and no elections are held.

51. E.g., ACHPR, ICJ, ICC, ICTY, ICTR, ITLOS, and WTO AB. See, in general, Edward McWhinney, "Internationalizing the International Court: The Quest for Ethno-Cultural and Legal-Systemic Representativeness," in *Essays in Honour of Judge Taslim Olawale Elias*, edited by Taslim Olawale Elias, Emmanuel G. Bello, and Bola Ajibola (Dordrecht, Neth.; and Boston: M. Nijhoff, 1992).

52. The only exception to this was a period between 1967 and 1985, when there was no Chinese member because the political issue of China's representation was contended between the People's Republic of China and Taiwan.

53. For the ICJ, ITLOS, ICC, ICTY, and ICTR.

54. For the WTO AB.

55. For the IACHR.

56. At the International Criminal Court, each state puts forward one nominee. At the International Tribunal for the Law of the Sea, each state can propose a maximum of two nominees, which is also the case at the Yugoslavia and Rwanda tribunals. At the European Court of Human Rights, every state *must* present three nominees, while at the Inter-American Court of Human Rights, *up to* three nominees are allowed. For the ICJ election, National Groups of the PCA can put forward up to four nominees (but only two of them may have the same nationality as the proposing group).

57. The main exception is, of course, the ECHR, since states are required to present three national candidates.

58. E.g., the election campaign of Kenneth Keith of New Zealand at the ICJ in 2005.

59. For a further discussion of how judges see the election process in relation to international politics, see chapter 5.

60. Ireland officially complained, saying that the template is standardized to fit continental (i.e., civil law) careers and is ill suited for common law lawyers. Flauss, "Analysis of the Election."

61. Philippe Sands, "Global Governance and the International Judiciary: Choosing Our Judges," *Contemporary Legal Problems* 56 (2003): 502.

Profile: Navanethem Pillay (pages 39–48)

1. This profile is based largely on an interview conducted on 5 April 2005 in The Hague.

2. Pillay started her law practice in 1967.

3. This situation at the court is also mentioned in chapter 3.

4. *Prosecutor v. Jean-Paul Akayesu* (ICTR-96–4), Judgment (2 September 1998).

5. *Prosecutor v. Ferdinand Nahimana, Jean-Bosco Barayagwiza, Hassan Ngeze* (ICTR-99-52-T), Judgment (3 December 2003).

6. As of January 2007, this case was still on appeal.

7. This rule prohibits judges from discussing a case that is currently awaiting judicial determination.

8. One such sensational incident at the ICTR is discussed in chapter 6.

9. The ICC is not a UN court, unlike the ad hoc criminal tribunals. It is a self-standing international organization. However, the voting for ICC judges has, as

of 2007, twice been held at the UN, where ambassadors for the states that are parties to the Rome Statute vote on behalf of their governments.

10. The code of ethics of the ICC is discussed in chapter 6.

Chapter 3: Inside the Courts (pages 53–90)

1. United Nations Convention on the Law of the Sea, Annex VI, arts. 12–13, 10 December 1982, 1833 U.N.T.S. 397.

2. Convention for the Protection of Human Rights and Fundamental Freedoms, art. 19, 4 November 1950, 213 U.N.T.S. 221, E.T.S. No. 5 amended by protocol 11 to the European Convention on Human Rights, 33 I.L.M. 943.

3. Statute of the Court of Justice of the European Community, art. 4, 298 U.N.T.S. 147, as amended by Council Decision 88/591, O.J. C 215/1 (21 August 1989).

4. Agreement Establishing the Caribbean Court of Justice (14 February 2001); *Protocol to the African Charter on Human and Peoples' Rights on the Establishment of an African Court on Human and Peoples' Rights*, art. 15, 10 June 1988, OAU Doc. OAU/LEG/EXP/AFCHPR/PROT (III) (entered into force 25 January 2004).

5. *Dispute Settlement Understanding,* Article 17:3, sentence 2; Preparatory Committee for the World Trade Organization, Sub-Committee On Institutional, Procedural And Legal Matters, Recommendations (8 December 1994), PC/IPL/13, para. 4.1–2.

6. Organization of American States, *Statute of the Inter-American Court of Human Rights,* art. 22.1, 31 October 1979, O.A.S. Res. 448, 9th Sess., art. 3 (entered into force 1 January 1980).

7. Statute of the International Court of Justice, June 26, 1945, 59 Stat. 1031 (entered into force 24 October 1945).

8. Statute of the International Criminal Tribunal for the Former Yugoslavia, S.C. Res. 827, U.N. Doc. S/RES/827 (25 May 1993); Statute of the International Criminal Tribunal for Rwanda, S.C. Res. 955, U.N. Doc. S/RES/955 (8 November 1994).

9. Unattributed quotations in this chapter are from judges interviewed for this book in 2005 and 2006. See the methodology section of the introduction and the list of judges interviewed in appendix B.

10. Patricia M. Wald, "Running the Trial of the Century: The Nuremberg Legacy," *Cardozo Law Review* 27, no. 4 (2006): 1567.

11. David G. Savage and Joan Biskupic, *Guide to the U.S. Supreme Court,* 4th ed. (Washington, D.C.: CQ Press, 2004).

12. It has been noted by some scholars that the extent to which staff attorneys are involved in decision writing in U.S. appellate courts has, in fact, become problematic as it can affect the quality and even the impartiality of the product. E. A. Thompson and R. S. Thompson, "Research Staff at Appellate Courts: Function, Personalities and Ethical Restraints," in *The Role of Courts in Society,* ed. Shimon Shetreet (Dordrecht, Neth.; and Boston: M. Nijhoff, 1988), 244–270.

13. Lyndel V. Prott, *The Latent Power of Culture and the International Judge* (Abingdon, UK: Professional Books, 1979).

14. Prott, *The Latent Power of Culture.*

15. Information on caseload from http://www.echr.coe.int/.

16. European Convention on Human Rights, art. 35.

17. The *rapporteur* is responsible for managing the case, which includes interacting with registry staff and attorneys on its various aspects, summarizing its points to fellow judges, and so on.

18. The implications of dissenting or separate opinions, and the impact that allowing or disallowing them has on courts and on the nature of international law, is discussed in chapter 4.

19. Harry T. Edwards, "The Effects of Collegiality on Judicial Decision Making," *University of Pennsylvania Law Review* 151, no. 5 (2003).

20. Anne-Marie Slaughter, "Court to Court," *American Journal of International Law* 92, no. 4 (1998).

21. Peter M. Haas, "Introduction: Epistemic Communities and International Policy Coordination," *International Organization* 46, no. 1 (1992).

22. Ibid., 2–3.

23. The idea of an epistemic community has been applied also to human rights practitioners working in the field of transnational justice; cf. Kathryn Sikkink and Ellen Lutz, "The Justice Cascade: The Evolution and Impact of Foreign Human Rights Trials in Latin America," *Chicago Journal of International Law* 2, no. 1 (2001). Lutz and Sikkink point out that this group blends characteristics typical of both epistemic communities and advocacy networks.

24. See chapter 2.

25. This happened with the 2004 enlargement of the European Union to include Cyprus, the Czech Republic, Estonia, Hungary, Latvia, Lithuania, Malta, Poland, Slovakia, and Slovenia.

26. See appendix C, "Commonalities and Differences Between the Civil Law and the Common Law Legal Traditions."

27. The irony is that it was created to try those most responsible for the 1994 genocide; "second tier" leaders of the genocide are tried in the Rwandan national judiciary, where they may receive the death penalty. In October 2006, however, it was reported that Rwanda's ruling party was pushing for a law abolishing the death penalty. This would clear the ICTR and Western countries to extradite genocide suspects to Rwanda for trial in the national judiciary after the mandate of the ICTR is finished.

28. Lars Waldorf, "Mass Justice for Mass Atrocity: Rethinking Local Justice as Transitional Justice," *Temple Law Review* 79, no. 1 (2006).

29. Giorgia Sessi, *Interpreting at International Courts and Tribunals: An Overview* (Bologna: Università di Bologna, 2005), 107.

30. Roseann Dueñas González, Victoria F. Vásquez, and Holly Mikkelson, *Fundamentals of Court Interpretation: Theory, Policy, and Practice* (Durham, N.C.: Carolina Academic Press, 1991), 16.

31. Ibid., 265.

32. Wald, "Running the Trial of the Century," 1595.

33. See, in general, Cesare P. R. Romano, "The Americanization of International Dispute Resolution," *Ohio State Journal on Dispute Resolution* 19, no. 1 (2003).

34. This quote is generally attributed to William E. Gladstone, British statesman (1809—1898). Quoted in John Bartlett's *Familiar Quotations,* 17th ed. (New York: Little, Brown & Company, 2002), 472.

35. D. W. Bowett, *The International Court of Justice: Process, Practice and Procedure,* Public International Law Series (London: British Institute of International and Comparative Law, 1997).

36. European Court of Human Rights, Analysis of Statistics 2005. See http://www.echr.coe.int.

37. WTO, Understanding on Rules and Procedures Governing the Settlement of Disputes, art. 17.5, Annex II, 15 April 1994, 1869 U.N.T.S. 401.

38. European Convention on Human Rights, art. 5.

39. David Wippmann, "The Costs of International Justice," *American Journal of International Law* 100, no. 4 (2006): 873–878.

40. Elizabeth Neuffer, *The Key to My Neighbor's House: Seeking Justice in Bosnia and Rwanda* (New York: Picador, 2001), 268–270. See also *Second Annual Report of the ICTR*, at http://69.94.11.53/ENGLISH/annualreports/a52/9731665e.htm.

41. Allain Pellet, "The Role of International Lawyer in International Litigation," in *The International Lawyer as Practitioner*, ed. Chanaka Wickremasinghe (London: British Institute of International and Comparative Law, 2000).

42. Romano, "The Americanization of International Dispute Resolution."

43. Article 4 of the International Criminal Bar Constitution also states that, "The ICB shall promote and advance: *a.* Ethics for counsel and disciplinary proceedings.; *b.* Professional training; *c.* The development and administration of the legal aid system of the Court.; *d.* The administration of the list of legal practitioners eligible to be appointed by the Court, the development and amendment process of the Elements of Crimes, Rules of Procedure and Evidence, and other relevant instruments of the Court; *e.* General support for counsel before the Court; *f.* The resolution of disputes relating to the professional conduct of counsel and their remuneration; *g.* Other matters relating to the independence and effectiveness of counsel before the Court or the principles of the ICB." See http://www.adwokatura.pl/Pliki/Criminal_Bar_Resolution.doc.

44. This attitude parallels that often found at the national level in relation to judges and thus is not unique to the international judiciary.

45. E.g., Anne-Marie Slaughter, "A Global Community of Courts," *Harvard International Law Journal* 44, no. 1 (2003); Jenny S. Martinez, "Towards an International Judicial System," *Stanford Law Review* 56, no. 2 (2003); W. W. Burke-White, "A Community of Courts: Toward a System of International Criminal Law Enforcement," *Michigan Journal of International Law* 24, no. 1 (2002); Laurence R. Helfer and Anne-Marie Slaughter, "Toward a Theory of Effective Supranational Adjudication," *Yale Law Journal* 107, no. 2 (1997); Anne-Marie Slaughter, "A Real New World Order," *Foreign Affairs* 76, no. 5 (1997): 183, 187 (noting that citing international decisions helps courts "gain legitimacy by linking [themselves] to a larger community of courts").

46. See, http://www.brandeis.edu/ethics/international_justice/biij.html.

47. *Application of the Convention on the Prevention and Punishment of the Crime of Genocide (Bosnia and Herzegovina v. Serbia and Montenegro)*, Judgment, 26 February 2007, para. 8.

Profile: Thomas Buergenthal (pages 92-101)

1. This profile is based principally on published sources and an interview at The Hague, April 28, 2005.

2. http://muse.jhu.edu/journals/human_rights_quarterly/vo18/18.4buergenthal.html. The occasion was the commemoration ceremony of the Auschwitz Death March.

3. Thomas Buergenthal, "Remembering the Early Years of the Inter-American Court of Human Rights," *New York University Journal of Law and International Politics* 37, no. 2 (2005): 260.

4. Ibid., 261.

5. Ibid., 264–265.

6. Ibid., 272.

7. The withdrawal took place on 6 May 2002.

8. Thomas Buergenthal, commencement address at American University, 19 May 2002. Available at http://www.american.edu/media/speeches/buergenthal .htm.

9. Thomas Buergenthal, commencement address at George Washington University, 24 May 2004. Available at http://www.gwu.edu/~newsctr/newscenter /commencement04/buergenthal_remarks.html.

Chapter 4: International Judges and International Law (pages 102-130)

1. Statement of John G. Roberts, Jr., Senate Committee on the Judiciary, *Confirmation Hearing on the Nomination of John G. Roberts, Jr., to be Chief Justice of the United States*, S. Hrg. 109–158, 109th Cong., 1st sess., September 12–15, 2005.

2. Edward Coke, *The Second Part of the Institutes of the Laws of England* (London: E. and R. Brooke, 1797), 51.

3. Francis Bacon, *The Essays* (Harmondsworth, Eng.; and New York.: Penguin Books, 1985), 223.

4. See chapter 1.

5. The WTO was established by the Marrakech Agreement Establishing the World Trade Organization, 15 April 1994, 108 Stat. 4809, 1867 U.N.T.S. 14. General Agreement on Tariffs and Trade, 30 October 1947, T.I.A.S. 1700, 55 U.N.T.S. 187.

6. Understanding on Rules and Procedures Governing the Settlement of Disputes, Annex II, 15 April 1994, 1869 U.N.T.S. 401 (hereafter "DSU").

7. They carefully avoided calling the Appellate Body "a court," its members "judges," its reports "judgments," its working rules "rules of procedure," or its chief administrator a "registrar."

8. Debra P. Steger, "Improvements and Reforms of the WTO Appellate Body," in *The WTO Dispute Settlement: 1995-2003*, ed. Federico Ortino and Ernst-Ulrich Petersmann (The Hague: Kluwer Law International, 2004), pp. 41–43.

9. See, for instance, the Statute for the International Tribunal for the Law of the Sea (41 articles), the Statute of the International Court of Justice (70 articles), and, more recently, the Rome Statute for the International Criminal Court (128 articles).

10. Article 17(9) of the DSU.

11. Other examples: article 17(11) of the DSU, on the decision-making process of the Appellate Body, which was complemented by rule 3 (decision making), rule 4 (collegiality), and rule 6 (division) of the *Working Procedures for Appellate Review* (WT/AB/WP/5, R. 20 [1] January 4, 2005), in contrast with article 29 (majority for decision) and article 35 (composition) of the Statute of the International Tribunal for the Law of the Sea. Article 17 of the DSU does not specify how appellate procedures should be instituted. It is the Appellate Body in rule 20 of the *Working Procedures for Appellate Review* that specified how appeals are to

be commenced, whereas the Statute of the International Tribunal for the Law of the Sea contains an article dealing with institution of proceedings (article 24).

12. Steger, "Improvements and Reforms," 41–43.

13. Unattributed quotations in this chapter are from judges interviewed for this book in 2005 and 2006.

14. *United States—Importation of Certain Shrimp and Shrimp Products,* Report of the Appellate Body, 12 October 1998, WT/DS58/AB/R; *United States—Imposition of Countervailing Duties on Certain Hot-Rolled Lead and Bismouth Carbon Steel Products Originating in the United Kingdom,* Report of the Appellate Body, 10 May 2000, WT/DS/138/AB/R; *European Communities—Measures Affecting Asbestos and Asbestos-Containing Products,* Report of the Appellate Body, 12 March 2001, WT/DS135/AB/R; *European Communities—Measures Affecting Asbestos and Asbestos-Containing Products—*Communication from the Appellate Body, 8 November 2000, WT/DS135/9; *Procedures for Appellate Review,* 8 November 2000, WT/DS135/9.

15. "*Amicus* Brief Storm Highlights WTO's Unease with External Transparency," *Bridges Weekly Trade News Digest* 4, no. 9 (November–December 2000): 1. Since then, in practice amicus briefs are still being submitted, but panels and the Appellate Body do not acknowledge relying on information contained in them to reach decisions.

16. Art. 19(2), ILC Draft Statute for an International Criminal Court, in *Report of the International Law Commission on the Work of its Forty-Sixth Session,* U.N. GAOR, 49th Sess., Supp. No. 10, U.N. Doc. A/49/10 (1994), p. 43.

17. Ibid. at art. (19)(3).

18. Bruce Broomhall, "Article 51: Rules of Procedure and Evidence," in Trifterer, Otto, ed. *Commentary on the Rome Statute of the International Criminal Court* (Baden-Baden: Nomos Verlagsgesellschaft, 1999), 681.

19. It is unlikely, however, that developments at the WTO Appellate Body had any impact on the Rome conference, as changes at the WTO took place very gradually and were largely off the radar screen of anyone who was not a specialist on the WTO.

20. Rome Statute, arts. 51 and 52.

21. "I think that the first period was the best, the most active one," one judge on the Law of the Sea Tribunal recalls. "First of all, we discussed the rules of procedure, which were drafted during the preparatory commission. After the signature of the convention, the preparatory commission and subcommission number four drafted the rules for us on the basis of rules of procedure of the ICJ. But then, starting the work in Hamburg, we had to modify a lot. We worked almost a year on our rules of procedure in order to adopt them to the expectations of the tribunal."

22. Address of 19 November 1996, United Nations Press Release GA/9166, *Bulletin of the International Criminal Tribunal for the Former Yugoslavia* 2, no. 13 (1996).

23. See, generally, Chester Brown, *A Common Law of International Adjudication* (Oxford: Oxford University Press, 2007).

24. In March 2005, the United States Supreme Court ruled that the death penalty for those who had committed their crimes at under eighteen years of age was cruel and unusual punishment and hence barred by the Constitution. *Roper v. Simmons* (03-633) 543 U.S. 551 (2005).

25. See Theodor Meron, "The Geneva Conventions as Customary Law," *American Journal of International Law* 81, no. 2 (1987): 348.

26. See Statute of the International Law Commission, G.A. Res. 174, U.N. GAOR, 2nd Sess., art. 1(1), 2(1), U.N. Doc. A/519 (1947).

27. See, e.g., Stefan Talmon, "The Security Council as World Legislature," *American Journal of International Law* 99, no. 1 (2005): 175; Frederic L. Kirgis, "The United Nations at Fifty: The Security Council's First Fifty Years," *American Journal of International Law* 89, no. 3 (1995): 506; Eric Rosand, "The Security Council as 'Global Legislator': Ultra Vires or Ultra Innovative?" *Fordham International Law Journal* 28, no. 3 (2005): 542.

28. *Legal Consequences of the Construction of a Wall in the Occupied Palestinian Territory*, Advisory Opinion, 2004, ICJ Rep. 136 (9 July 2004). However, it did look at the path followed by the wall.

29. ICJ Statute, art. 38 (1) (d).

30. Ibid. at arts. 38, 59.

31. *Legality of the Threat or Use of Nuclear Weapons*, Advisory Opinion, 1996 I.C.J. Rep. 226 (8 July 1996).

32. Ibid. at para. 18.

33. *Velasquez-Rodriguez*, Inter-Am. Ct. H.R. (ser. C), no. 4 (1988); *Fairen Garbi and Solis Corrales*, Inter-Am. Ct. H.R. (ser. C), no. 6 (1989); *Godinez Cruz*, Inter-Am. Ct. H.R. (ser. C), no. 5 (1989), respectively.

34. Rome Statute of the International Criminal Court, 17 July 1998, art. 7(1)(i), 29, U.N. Doc. A/CONF.183/9 (1998).

35. See, generally, Andrew Clapham, *Human Rights in the Private Sphere* (Oxford: Oxford University Press, 1993).

36. See, e.g. *Von Hannover v. Germany*, 40 Eur. Ct. H.R. 1 (24 June 2004), wherein the ECHR found Germany's courts in violation of Princess Caroline von Hannover's right to privacy under article 8 of the European Convention on Human Rights and Fundamental Freedoms by failing to protect her from the publication of several photographs depicting her and her family in their private lives.

37. See, generally, Karen J. Alter, *Establishing the Supremacy of European Law: The Making of an International Rule of Law in Europe*, Oxford Studies in European Law (Oxford and New York: Oxford University Press, 2001); Alec Stone Sweet, *The Judicial Construction of Europe* (Oxford and New York: Oxford University Press, 2004).

38. *Van Gend en Loos v. Nederlanse Administratie Der Belastingen*, Case 26/62 (1963) ECR 1, C.M.L.R. 105.

39. *Francovich and Bonafaci v. Italy*, joined cases C-6/90 and C-9/90 (1991) ECR I-5357.

40. *Costa v. ENEL*, Case 6/64 (1964) ECR 585.

41. *Genocide Convention; Geneva Convention for the Amelioration of the Condition of the Wounded and Sick in Armed Forces in the Field*, art. 3, 12 August 1949, 6 U.S.T. 3114, 75 U.N.T.S. 31; *Geneva Convention for the Amelioration of the Condition of Wounded, Sick, and Shipwrecked Members at Sea*, art. 3, 12 August 1949, 6 U.S.T. 3217, 75 U.N.T.S. 85; *Geneva Convention Relative to the Treatment of Prisoners of War*, art. 3, 12 August 1949, 6 U.S.T. 3316, 75 U.N.T.S. 135; *Geneva Convention Relative to the Treatment of Civilian Persons in Time of War*, art. 3, 12 August 1949, 6 U.S.T. 3516, 75 U.N.T.S. 287.

42. See David S. Mitchell, "The Prohibition of Rape in International Humanitarian Law as a Norm of Jus Cogens: Clarifying the Doctrine," *Duke Journal of Comparative and International Law* 15, no. 2 (2005): 219.

43. *Prosecutor v. Charles Ghankay Taylor,* Case No. SCSL-2003–01-I, Decision on Immunity from Jurisdiction, 31 May 2004 (*Prosecutor v. Taylor*).

44. *Legality of the Threat or Use of Nuclear Weapons,* at para. 18.

45. *Reparation for Injuries Suffered in the Service of the United Nations,* Advisory Opinion, 1949 ICJ Rep. 174, 179 (11 April 1949), stating that the UN has international personality and is a "subject of international law and capable of possessing international rights and duties, and that it has capacity to maintain its rights by bringing international claims."

46. *Reservations to the Convention on the Prevention and Punishment of the Crime of Genocide,* Advisory Opinion, 1951 ICJ Rep. 15 (28 May 1957).

47. *United Kingdom v. Norway,* 1951 ICJ Rep. 116, 142 (18 December 1951).

48. WTO Appellate Body, *Report on United States—Import Prohibition of Certain Shrimp and Shrimp Products,* 6 November 1998, WTO Doc. WT/DS58/AB/R.

49. *Fisheries Jurisdiction (United Kingdom v. Iceland),* Merits, Judgment of 25 July 1974, ICJ Rep. (1974), pp. 3–173; *Fisheries Jurisdiction (Federal Republic of Germany v. Iceland),* Merits, Judgment of 25 July 1974, *ICJ Reports* (1974), pp. 175–251.

50. The two-hundred-mile limit was eventually included in the final text of the convention in 1982. United Nations Convention on the Law of the Sea, art. 57, 10 December 1982, U.N. Doc. A/CONF.62/122 (1982).

51. See, e.g., Statute of the International Court of Justice, 26 June 1945, art. 59, 59 Stat. 1031 (entered into force 24 October 1945); Rome Statute of the International Criminal Court, art. 21(2).

52. Alain Pellet, "Article 38," in *The Statute of the International Court of Justice: A Commentary,* ed. Andreas Zimmermann, Christian Tomuschat, and Karin Oellers-Frahm (Oxford and New York: Oxford University Press, 2006), 785.

53. Nathan Miller, "An International Jurisprudence? The Operation of 'Precedent' across International Tribunals," *Leiden Journal of International Law* 15 (2002): 483, 489–490.

54. See, generally, Thordis Ingadottir, "The EEA Agreement and Homogeneous Jurisprudence: The Two-Pillar Role Given to the EFTA Court and the Court of Justice of the European Communities," *Yearbook of International Law and Jurisprudence* 2 (2002).

55. See, e.g., *Bosphorus Hava Yollari Turizm ve Ticaret Anonim Sirketi v. Ireland (Bosphorus II),* App. No. 45036/98 (para. 1, Eur. Ct. H.R. 30 June 2005).

56. Miller, "An International Jurisprudence?" 483–526.

57. However, there are some very notorious exceptions, as when the ICTY chastised the International Court of Justice in the decision of its appeals chamber in the *Tadić* case. In its earlier *Nicaragua* case (*Military and Paramilitary Activities in and against Nicaragua* (Nicaragua v. United States of America) [Merits], Judgment, 1986 ICJ Rep. 4 (27 June 1986), the ICJ had to determine whether a foreign state (the United States), because of its financing, organizing, training, equipping, and planning of the operations of organized military and paramilitary groups of Nicaraguan rebels (the so-called contras) in Nicaragua, was responsible for violations of international humanitarian law committed by those rebels. The ICJ held that a high degree of control was necessary for this to be the case. It required not only that a party be in effective control of a military or paramilitary group, but also that the control be exercised with respect to the specific operation

in the course of which breaches may have been committed. In the *Tadić* appeal decision, the ICTY criticized the "*Nicaragua* test" as not consonant with the logic of international law of state responsibility and at variance with judicial and state practice. *Prosecutor v. Duško Tadić,* Case No. IT-94-1-A, Judgment, 15 July 1999 (ICTY Appeals Chamber), paras. 116–145.

58. *Prosecutor v. Taylor.*

59. *Arrest Warrant of 11 April 2000* (Democratic Republic of the Congo v. Belgium), 2002 ICJ Rep. 3 (14 February 2002).

60. *Prosecutor v. Taylor.*

61. *Decision on Preliminary Motion Based on Lack of Jurisdiction (Judicial Independence), Prosecutor v. Sam Hinga Norman,* Case No. SCSL-2004-14-AR72(E) (Appeals Chamber), 13 March 2004.

62. The EFTA Court also does not permit dissents. See Carl Baudenbacher, "Judicialization: Can the European Model Be Exported to Other Parts of the World?" *Texas International Law Journal* 39, no. 2 (2004): 384, stating that "[t]he main argument against introducing a dissenting opinion system in the Community courts and the EFTA Court is the fear that dissenting judges could be exposed to pressures by governments and their chances to be reappointed could be placed at risk."

63. John H. Jackson, "Dispute Settlement and the WTO: Emerging Problems," in World Trade Organization Secretariat, *From GATT to the WTO: The Multilateral Trading System in the New Millennium* (The Hague: Kluwer Law International, 2000), 71 ("There is no indication of particular authorship of any part of an Appellate Body report and no provision for dissenting opinions"). However, a recent WTO Appellate Body decision may suggest that this is changing. In the *Asbestos* case, one of the panelists wrote a concurring opinion, changing the long-standing practice of writing unanimous opinions. WTO AB Report, *European Communities—Measures Affecting Asbestos and Asbestos-Containing Products,* WTO Doc. WT/DS135/AB/R (12 March 2001).

64. I.e., France, West Germany, Italy, Belgium, the Netherlands, and Luxembourg.

65. See n, 63, above.

66. K. P. E. Lasok, *The European Court of Justice: Practice and Procedure,* 2nd ed. (London: Butterworths, 1994).

67. *Legality of the Use of Force* (Serbia and Montenegro v. Belgium; Serbia and Montenegro v. Canada; Serbia and Montenegro v. France; Serbia and Montenegro v. Germany; Serbia and Montenegro v. Italy; Serbia and Montenegro v. the Netherlands; Serbia and Montenegro v. Portugal; Serbia and Montenegro v. the United Kingdom), 2004 ICJ Rep. 3 (15 December 2004); *Legality of the Use of Force* (Yugoslavia v. the United States), Provisional Measures, 1999 ICJ Rep. 916 (2 June 1999); *Legality of the Use of Force* (Yugoslavia v. Spain), Provisional Measures, 1999 ICJ Rep. 761 (2 June 1999).

68. *Legality of the Use of Force* (Preliminary Objections), Serbia and Montenegro v. France, Joint Declaration of Vice President Ranjeva, Judges Guillaume, Higgins, Kooijmans, Al-Khasawneh, Buergenthal and Elaraby, 2004 ICJ Rep. 3 (15 December 2004).

69. *Application of the Convention on the Prevention and Punishment of the Crime of Genocide (Bosnia and Herzegovina v. Serbia and Montenegro),* Judgment (26 February 2007).

70. See, generally, Shigeru Oda, Edward McWhinney, and Mariko Kawano, eds., *Judge Shigeru Oda and the Path to Judicial Wisdom: Opinions (Declarations, Separate Opinions, Dissenting Opinions) on the International Court of*

Justice, 1993-2003, Judges, vol. 4 (Leiden, Neth.; and Boston: Martinus Nijhoff, 2006).

71. See, e.g., *Gabcikovo-Nagymaros Project* (Hungary v. Slovakia), 1997 ICJ 7 (25 September 1997); *Legality of the Threat or Use of Nuclear Weapons,* Advisory Opinion.

72. Figures as of November 15, 2005. Hofmann and Laubner, "Article 57," in Zimmermann et al., *A Commentary,* p. 1209.

73. See, e.g., *LaGrand (Germany v. United States),* 2001 ICJ Rep. 104 (27 June 2001); *Nicaragua v. United States; Legality of the Threat or Use of Nuclear Weapons; Legal Consequences of the Construction of a Wall in the Occupied Palestinian Territory; Prosecutor v. Akayesu* (ICTR 96–4-T), (2 September 1998).

74. ICJ statute, art. 38.1.d.

75. However, article 3.9 of the WTO *Dispute Settlement Understanding* provides that "[t]he provisions of this Understanding are without prejudice to the rights of Members to seek authoritative interpretation of provisions of a covered agreement through decision-making under the WTO Agreement or a covered agreement which is a Plurilateral Trade Agreement."

76. *Nuclear Tests* cases: (New Zealand v. France), Merits, Judgment, 1974 ICJ Rep. 457; and (Australia v. France), Merits, Judgment, 1974 ICJ Rep. 99 (20 December 1974).

77. The U.S. Supreme Court can pick and choose cases by granting writs of certiorari. In practice, it turns down most submissions and tends to use its time to consider only matters of national or constitutional importance. Thus, by picking and choosing which cases and which issues it will consider, it can decide in what area of law it will make an impact and how. However, the Supreme Court's raison d'etre is to harmonize and establish binding precedents for the inferior courts of appeals, a rationale that is not valid for international courts since they are not organized in a judicial system.

78. Martin M. Shapiro, *Courts: A Comparative Political Analysis* (Chicago: University of Chicago Press, 1981).

Profile: Georges Abi-Saab (pages 134-137)

1. Boisson de Chazournes and V. Goland-Debbas, eds., *The International Legal System in Quest of Equity and Universality/L'ordre juridique international, Un système en quête d'équité et d'universalité, Liber Amicorum Georges Abi-Saab* (The Hague: Kluwer Law International, 2001).

2. *Continental Shelf* (Tunisia v. Libya), Merits, Judgment, 1982 ICJ Rep. 18 (24 February 1982).

3. This "invisible bar" is also mentioned in chapter 3.

4. *Case Concerning the Frontier Dispute (Burkina Faso v. the Republic of Mali),* Merits, Judgment, 1986 ICJ Rep. 554 (22 December 1986).

5. *Territorial Dispute* (Libya v. Chad), 1994 ICJ Rep. 6 (13 February 1994).

6. See appendix C.

7. *Tadić* (IT-94-1).

8. See Immanuel Maurice Wallerstein, *The Modern World-System* (New York: Academic Press, 1974).

9. Pierre-Marie Dupuy, "Libre parcours à travers la richesse d'une oeuvre: Notes de lectures sur les travaux de Georges Abi-Saab," in Boisson de Chazournes and Goland-Debbas, eds., *The International Legal System.*

Chapter 5: Between Law and Politics (pages 149-178)

1. Theodor Meron, "Judicial Independence and Impartiality in International Criminal Tribunals," *American Journal of International Law* 99, no. 2 (2005): 361.

2. Robert H. Bork, *Coercing Virtue: The Worldwide Rule of Judges* (Washington, D.C.: AEI Press, 2003), 21.

3. Henry Kissinger, *Does America Need a Foreign Policy? Toward a Diplomacy for the 21st Century* (New York: Simon & Schuster, 2002), 273.

4. Stephen M. Schwebel, "National Judges and Judges Ad Hoc of the International Court of Justice," *International and Comparative Law Quarterly* 48, no. 4 (1999).

5. Nicolas Valticos, "L'évolution de la notion de juge ad hoc," *Revue Hellénique de Droit International* 50, no. 1 (1997).

6. Statute of the International Court of Justice, 26 June 1945, art. 31, 59 Stat. 1031 (entered into force 24 October 1945).

7. For example, Thomas Franck of the United States served as an ad hoc judge appointed by Indonesia in the Indonesia case: *Sovereignty over Pulau Ligitan and Pulau Sipidan (Indonesia v. Malaysia)*, 2002 ICJ Rep. 625 (17 December 2002).

8. See European Convention on Human Rights and Fundamental Freedoms, 4 November 1950, art. 27(2), 213 UNTS 222 (entered into force 3 September 1953); European Court of Human Rights, Rules of Court, rule 49 (2006).

9. See Rules of Procedure of the Court of Justice of the European Communities of 19 June 1991, art. 11(b)–(c) (OJ L 176); *Understanding on Rules and Procedures Governing the Settlement of Disputes,* art. 17(1), 15 April 1994, 1869 U.N.T.S. 401.

10. See Rome Statute of the International Criminal Court, 17 July 1998, art. 72, U.N. Doc. A/CONF.183/9 (1998).

11. Unattributed quotations in this chapter are from judges interviewed for this book in 2005 and 2006. See the methodology section of the introduction and the list of judges interviewed in appendix B.

12. Thomas Buergenthal, "The Proliferation of Disputes, Dispute Settlement Procedures and Respect for the Rule of Law," *Arbitration International* 22, no. 4 (2006). Buergenthal's U.S. predecessor on the ICJ, Stephen Schwebel, voted eleven times against the United States, though some of these instances involved minor matters. See other cites regarding ICJ voting patterns in Schwebel, "National Judges and Judges Ad Hoc," 893, n.14.

13. Eric A. Posner and Miguel de Figueiredo, "Is the International Court of Justice Biased?" Olin Working Paper No. 234 (December 2004), University of Chicago Law and Economics, http://ssrn.com/abstract=642581.

14. Adam M. Smith, "'Judicial Nationalism' in International Law: National Identity and Judicial Autonomy at the International Court of Justice," *Texas International Law Journal* 40, no. 2 (2005): 222.

15. Ibid., 230. See also, Ruth Mackenzie and Philippe Sands, "International Courts and Tribunals and the Independence of the International Judge," *Harvard International Law Journal* 44, no. 1 (2003).

16. See chapter 2.

17. Meron, "Judicial Independence," 362.

18. The Secretary General has presided over the selection of the "international" members of the bench of mixed tribunals in Sierra Leone and East Timor.

19. This was the case of a judge from Bulgaria, who voted against his country in a case before the court. See Jean-François Flauss, "Analysis of the Election of the New European Court of Human Rights," *Revue Trimestrielle des Droits de L'Homme* 9, no. 35 (1998), 70.

20. Claus-Dieter Ehlermann, "Six Years on the Bench of The 'World Trade Court': Some Personal Experiences as Member of the Appellate Body of the WTO," *Journal of World Trade* 36, no. 4 (2002): 608–609.

21. See "About the Caribbean Court of Justice, Part II: The Appellate Jurisdiction of the Caribbean Court of Justice," available at http://www.caribbeancourtofjustice .org/about2.htm; Jamaica Information Service, "Every Effort Made to Insulate CCJ From Political Influence" (June 12, 2003), available at http://www.caribbeancourtof justice.org/papersandarticles/ccjinsulation.pdf.

22. Eric A. Posner and John C. Yoo, "Judicial Independence in International Tribunals," *California Law Review* 93, no. 1 (2005): 6–7, 27. For a convincing opposing viewpoint, see Laurence R. Helfer and Anne-Marie Slaughter, "Why States Create International Tribunals: A Response to Professors Posner and Yoo," *California Law Review* 93, no. 1 (2005): 899–955, in the same issue.

23. See Marlise Simons and Carlotta Gall, "The Handover of Milosevic," *New York Times,* June 29, 2001, A1; Statement of the Prosecutor, Carla Del Ponte, ICTY Press Release, 29 June 2001, F.H/P.I.S./598e, available at http://www.un.org/ icty/pressreal/p598-e.htm.; Donna E. Arzt, "The Lockerbie 'Extradition by Analogy' Agreement: 'Exceptional Measure' or Template for Transnational Criminal Justice?" *American University International Law Review* 18, no. 1 (2002): 222–225, suggesting that Milosevic's transfer was a product of Yugoslavia's need for economic assistance.

24. See *Da Costa v. Nederlandse Belastingadminstratie,* Case 28–30/62 (1963) ECR 61; and *Srl CILFIT and Lanificio di Gavardo SpA v. Ministry of Health,* Case 283/81 (1982) ECR 3415. See also, Georg Ress, "The Effect of Decisions and Judgments of the European Court of Human Rights in the Domestic Legal Order," *Texas International Law Journal* 40, no. 3 (2005): 374, noting that the ECJ's judgments "have direct effect on domestic legal orders because of the supremacy of European Community law." This direct effect is unique among most international courts, wherein judgments are normally only binding on the parties to the particular case. See also *Amministrazione delle Finane dello Stato v. Simmenthal,* Case 106/77 (1978) ECR 629, wherein the ECJ held that European Community law has supremacy over national law, including national laws subsequently passed.

25. *Commission v. Italy,* Case C-119/04 (2006) OJ C 224/04.

26. See Laurence R. Helfer and Anne-Marie Slaughter, "Toward a Theory of Effective Supranational Adjudication," *Yale Law Journal* 107, no. 2 (1997): 295.

27. See generally Posner and Yoo, "Judicial Independence in International Tribunals"; Helfer and Slaughter, "Why States Create International Tribunals, 899; Helfer and Slaughter, "Supranational Adjudication," 295.

28. See Constanze Schulte, *Compliance with Decisions of the International Court of Justice* (Oxford: Oxford University Press, 2004).

29. See Declarations Recognizing as Compulsory the Jurisdiction of the Court, International Court of Justice, available at http://www.icj-cij.org/icjwww /ibasicdocuments/ibasictext/ibasicdeclarations.htm. The five permanent members of the Security Council are China, France, the Russian Federation, the United Kingdom, and the United States; http://www.un.org/sc/members.asp.

30. Meron, "Judicial Independence," 364–365.

31. For overviews of the financing of international courts and tribunals, see Cesare P. R. Romano, "The Price of International Justice," *The Law and Practice of International Courts and Tribunals* 4 (2003); Cesare P. R. Romano, "International Courts and Tribunals: Price, Financing and Output," in *International Conflict Resolution, Conferences on New Political Economy* (formerly *Jahrbuch Für Neue Politische Ökonomie*) 23, ed. Stefan Voigt, Max Albert, and Dieter Schmidtchen (Tubingen, Ger.: Mohr Siebeck, 2006); and David Wippmann, "The Costs of International Justice," *American Journal of International Law* 100, no. 4 (2006).

32. See the ICTY Web site at http://www.un.org/icty/glance-e/index.htm.

33. See the ICTR Web site at http://69.94.11.53/default.htm.

34. See the ICC Web site at http://www.icc-cpi.int/library/asp/Part_II_-_Proposed_Programme_Budget_for_2006.pdf.

35. Ralph Zacklin, "The Failings of Ad Hoc International Tribunals," *Journal of International Criminal Justice* 2, no. 2 (2004).

36. See the ICTY Web site http://www.un.org/icty/glance-e/index.htm and the ICTR Web site at http://69.94.11.53/default.htm.

37. The "regular budget" of the UN excludes peacekeeping operations and other specialized agencies, such as the United Nations Development Program and UNICEF. If one includes all these UN operations, annual UN spending is closer to $15 billion, putting the criminal tribunals at less than 1 percent of the total. See http://www.un.org/geninfo/ir/index.asp?id=150.

38. Nolan Clay, "McVeigh's defense tops $13 million; attorneys cost over $6.7 million," *Saturday Oklahoman* (Tulsa), June 30, 2001.

39. See Daryl A. Mundis, "The Judicial Effects of the 'Completion Strategies' on the Ad Hoc International Criminal Tribunals," *American Journal of International Law* 99, no. 1 (2005); Report on the Judicial Status of the International Criminal Tribunal for the Former Yugoslavia and the Prospects for Referring Certain Cases to National Courts, UN Doc. S/2002/678 (2002); Completion Strategy of the International Criminal Tribunal for Rwanda, enclosure, in Letter Dated 29 September 2003 from the President of the International Criminal Tribunal for Rwanda Addressed to the Secretary-General, U.N. Doc. S/2003/946 (2003); SC Res. 1534, para. 3 (26 March 2004).

40. Mundis, "Judicial Effects."

41. As of January 1, 2007, there were 89,900 cases pending before the ECHR. See ECHR Survey of Activities 2006, p. 51, available at http://www.echr.coe.int/NR/rdonlyres/69564084-9825-430B-9150-A9137DD22737/0/Survey_2006.pdf.

42. See also Romano, "International Courts and Tribunals."

43. Letter of November 20, 2003, to the OAS secretary general by the Inter-American Court of Human Rights, para. 6. See http://derechos.org/nizkor/costa_rica/doc/oea2.html.

44. See Chandra Lekha Sriram, "Wrong-Sizing International Justice? The Hybrid Tribunal in Sierra Leone," *Fordham International Law Journal* 29, no. 3 (2006); James Cockayne, "The Fraying Shoestring: Rethinking Hybrid War Crimes Tribunals," *Fordham International Law Journal* 28, no. 3 (2005), 629–635; Celina Schocken, "The Special Court for Sierra Leone: Overview and Recommendations," *Berkeley Journal of International Law* 20, no. 2 (2002), 453–455.

45. See Katheryn M. Klein, "Bringing the Khmer Rouge to Justice: The Challenges and Risks Facing the Joint Tribunal in Cambodia," *Northwestern University Journal of International Human Rights* 4, no. 3 (2006).

46. Romano, "International Courts and Tribunals," 205.

47. See U.S. Department of State, Bureau of Political-Military Affairs, "Fact Sheet on the International Criminal Court," 2 August 2002, available at http://www.state.gov/t/pm/rls/fs/2002/23426.htm.

48. John Bolton, "American Justice and the International Criminal Court," remarks at the American Enterprise Institute, 3 November 2003, available at http://www.state.gov/t/us/rm/25818.htm.

49. The United States has made one hundred such agreements ("Article 98 Agreements") to date. See Press Statement, "U.S. Signs 100th Article 98 Agreement," 3 May 2005, http://www.state.gov/r/pa/prs/ps/2005/45573.htm. See generally, Chet J. Tan, Jr., "The Proliferation of Bilateral Non-Surrender Agreements among Non-Ratifiers of the Rome Statute of the International Criminal Court," *American University International Law Review* 19, no. 5 (2004); Diane F. Orentlicher, "Unilateral Multilateralism: United States Policy toward the International Criminal Court," *Cornell International Law Journal* 36, no. 3 (2004).

50. Bork, *Coercing Virtue,* 10.

51. See Benjamin B. Ferencz, *An International Criminal Court, a Step toward World Peace: A Documentary History and Analysis,* 2 vols. (Dobbs Ferry, N.Y.: Oceana Publications, 1980), 27, describing President Woodrow Wilson's involvement in the creation of the League of Nations and his Peace Plan, which proposed a permanent court. See, generally, Mark W. Janis, *The American Tradition of International Law* (Oxford and New York: Oxford University Press, 2004).

52. For example, Eleanor Roosevelt served as chairperson of the Drafting Committee for the Universal Declaration of Human Rights. See Eleanor Roosevelt, "The Promise of Human Rights," *Foreign Affairs* 26, no. 3 (1948): 470–477.

53. See Michael P. Scharf, "Indicted for War Crimes, Then What?" *Washington Post,* October 3, 1999, B1.

54. See "Connally Amendment to the U.S. Reservation to the Statute of the International Court of Justice," 14 Aug 1946, reprinted in *American Journal of International Law* 41 (1947); Margaret A. Rague, "The Reservation Power and the Connally Amendment," *New York University Journal of Law and International Politics* 11, no. 2 (1978); Michla Pomerance, *The United States and the World Court as a "Supreme Court of the Nations": Dreams, Illusions, and Disillusion* (Dordrecht, Neth.: M. Nijhoff, 1996).

55. For a historical overview, see John Francis Murphy, *The United States and the Rule of Law in International Affairs* (Cambridge and New York: Cambridge University Press, 2004).

56. *Military and Paramilitary Activities in and Against Nicaragua* (Nicaragua v. United States of America) Merits, Judgment, ICJ Reports 1986 Rep. 4 (27 June 1986).

57. See "Withdrawal From Proceedings in the Nicaragua Case: Statement Issued By The Department of State," 1985, reprinted in Pomerance, *The United States and the World Court,* 444; Anna Haughton, "United States Accountability for Intervention in the Western Hemisphere and Compulsory Compliance with the International Court of Justice," *New England International and Comparative Law Annual* 8 (2002); Douglas J. Ende, "Reaccepting the Compulsory Jurisdiction of the International Court of Justice: A Proposal for a New United States Declaration," *Washington Law Review* 61 (1986).

58. The United States does host and play an active role in the less intrusive Inter-American Commission on Human Rights, based in Washington, D.C. See, Elizabeth A. H. Abi-Mershed, "The United States and the Inter-American Court

of Human Rights," in *The United States and International Courts and Tribunals,* ed. Cesare P. R. Romano (unpublished ms.).

59. Thomas M. Franck, "The United States and the Historic Idea of a World Court," in *The Role of Courts in Society,* ed. Shimon Shetreet (Dordrecht, Neth.; and Boston: M. Nijhoff, 1988).

60. *LaGrand* (Germany v. U.S.) 2001 ICJ Rep. 104 (27 June 2001); *Avena and Other Mexican Nationals* (Mexico v. United States) 2004 ICJ Rep. 128 (31 March 2004); *Vienna Convention on Consular Relations* (Paraguay v. United States), Provisional Measures Order, 1998 ICJ Rep. 248 (9 April 1998).

61. *LaGrand,* para. 109.

62. Sean D. Murphy, "The United States and the International Court of Justice: Coping with Antinomies," in Romano, ed., *The United States and International Courts and Tribunals.*

63. See Rome Statute, art. 5(2). See, generally, Mauro Politi and Giuseppe Nesi, *The International Criminal Court and the Crime of Aggression* (Aldershot, Eng.; and Burlington, Vt.: Ashgate, 2004).

64. Rome Statute, art. 15(4).

65. Rome Statute, arts. 17(1)(a) and 53(1)(b).

66. Americans who have served on the Permanent Court of International Justice are John Bassett Moore (1922–1928), Charles Evans Hughes (1928–1930), Frank Billings Kellogg (1930–1935), and Manley Ottmer Hudson (1936–1942). On the International Court of Justice, the Americans who preceded the current U.S. judge, Thomas Buergenthal, are: G. H. Hackworth (1946–1961), P. C. Jessup (1961–1970), H. D. Dillard (1970–1979), and S. M. Schwebel (1981–2000).

67. The other is Patricia Wald.

68. John P. Cerone, "U.S. Attitudes towards International Courts and Tribunals," in Romano, ed., *The United States and International Courts and Tribunals.*

69. Karen J. Alter, "The United States and International Courts: Four Varieties of Delegation and Their Implications for Delegating U.S. Sovereignty," in Romano, ed., *The United States and International Courts and Tribunals.*

70. For example, the recent appointments to the U.S. Supreme Court to fill vacancies left by Sandra Day O'Connor and William Rehnquist created heated debate. Harriet Miers went so far as to withdraw herself as a nominee after being subjected to strict scrutiny over her politics and judicial qualifications. For discussion of the recent appointments to the U.S. Supreme Court, see Michael A. Fletcher and Charles Babington, "Miers, Under Fire From Right, Withdrawn as Court Nominee," *Washington Post,* October 28, 2005, A1; David Stout and Timothy Williams, "Miers Ends Supreme Court Bid After Failing to Win Support," *New York Times,* October 27, 2005; Peter Baker, "Alito Nomination Sets Stage for Ideological Battle," *Washington Post,* November 1, 2005, A1; Elisabeth Bumiller and Carl Hulse, "Bush Picks Appeals Court Judge to Succeed O'Connor on Court," *New York Times,* October 31, 2005.

71. Helfer and Slaughter, "Supranational Adjudication," 312.

72. Meron, "Judicial Independence," 369.

73. Thomas Buergenthal, "Remembering the Early Years of the Inter-American Court of Human Rights," *New York University Journal of Law and International Politics* 37, no. 2 (2005): 279.

74. See Eric Stover, *The Witnesses: War Crimes and the Promise of Justice in The Hague* (Philadelphia: University of Pennsylvania Press, 2005). See also "The Challenges of International Justice," a report of a 2004 colloquium of prosecutors

of international courts and tribunals, available at http://www.brandeis.edu/ethics/international_justice/ICTR_Report.pdf.

75. However, when the highest-profile defendant to come before the SCSL, former dictator Charles Taylor, was indicted, the court began preparations to hold his trial in the still-underused facility of the ICC in The Hague, out of fear that his trial, if held locally, could spark conflict in Sierra Leone and surrounding countries.

76. See Charter of the United Nations, chap. 7, 26 June 1945, 59 Stat. 1031, entered into force 24 October 1945; Statute of the International Criminal Tribunal for Rwanda, SC Res. 955, annex (8 November 1994), 33 ILM 1602 (1994); SC Res. 827, para. 4 (25 May 1993), 32 ILM 1203 (1993); Statute of the International Criminal Tribunal for the Former Yugoslavia, U.N. Doc. S/25704, annex, art. 29 (1993), 32 ILM 1192.

77. See Tim Gallimore, "The ICTR Outreach Program: Integrating Justice and Reconciliation," Conference on Challenging Impunity (7–8 November 2006), available at http://69.94.11.53/ENGLISH/challenging_impunity/gallimore.pdf; Kingsley Chiedu Moghalu, "Image and Reality of War Crimes Justice: External Perceptions of the International Criminal Tribunal for Rwanda," *Fletcher Forum of World Affairs* 26, no. 2 (2002). For information on the ICTY's Outreach Program, see International Criminal Tribunal for the former Yugoslavia, "ICTY Outreach Programme: Introduction," available at http://www.un.org/icty/bhs/outreach/outreach_info.htm.

78. Alec Stone Sweet, *The Judicial Construction of Europe* (Oxford and New York: Oxford University Press, 2004).

79. Helfer and Slaughter, "Supranational Adjudication," 315.

80. *Legality of the Threat or Use of Nuclear Weapons*, Advisory Opinion, 1996 ICJ Rep. 226 (8 July 1996).

81. See Cesare P. R. Romano, "International Justice and Developing Countries: A Quantitative Analysis," *The Law and Practice of International Courts and Tribunals* 1, no. 2 (2002); and Cesare P. R. Romano, "International Justice and Developing Countries: A Qualitative Analysis," *The Law and Practice of International Courts and Tribunals* 1, no. 3 (2002).

82. Some observers might argue, however, that three cases in a decade is a relatively low rate of usage.

83. Bork, *Coercing Virtue*, 16.

Profile: Cecilia Medina Quiroga (pages 180–187)

1. This profile is based on an interview conducted September 24, 2006, in San José, Costa Rica.

2. The court with the second-highest percentage of women judges is the International Criminal Court, with seven women on a bench of eighteen as of 2006. The ICC is, furthermore, the only international court that calls explicitly in its founding documents for "a fair representation of male and female judges," Rome Statute, art. 36 (8) (a)(iii).

3. Human Rights Committee, General Comment 28, "Equality of rights between men and women" (art. 3), U.N. Doc. CCPR/C/21/Rev.1/Add.10 (2000).

4. See http://www.scienceinpublic.com/2006/gruber/womensrights.htm. The official citation celebrates Medina Quiroga for "advancing the rights of women through the framework of international law."

Chapter 6: Tests of Character (pages 191–210)

1. H. L. Mencken, *A Mencken Chrestomathy*, 1st ed. (New York: A. A. Knopf, 1949). See http://en.wikiquote.org/wiki/H._L._Mencken.

2. Theodor Meron, "Judicial Independence and Impartiality in International Criminal Tribunals," *American Journal of International Law* 99, no. 2 (2005): 360.

3. Most U.S. states have created codes of judicial conduct based on the "Model Code of Judicial Conduct" developed by the American Bar Association; see http://www.abanet.org/cpr/mcjc/toc.html.

4. For example, the Caribbean Court of Justice established a Regional Judicial and Legal Services Commission (RJLSC) in order to reassure member states, some of whom had faced problems with their domestic judiciaries.

5. For example, canon 3 of the *Model Code of Judicial Conduct* states, "A judge shall be patient, dignified and courteous to litigants, jurors, witnesses, lawyers and others with whom the judge deals in an official capacity, and shall require similar conduct of lawyers, and of staff, court officials and others subject to the judge's direction and control." See http://www.abanet.org/cpr/mcjc/canon_3 .html.

6. *The Code of Conduct for United States Judges* was adopted first in 1973 and revised most recently in 2000. See http://www.uscourts.gov/guide/vol2 /ch1.html.

7. See Dinah Shelton, "Legal Norms to Promote the Independence and Accountability of International Tribunals," *The Law and Practice of International Courts and Tribunals* 2, no. 1 (2003): 27–62.

8. European Court of Human Rights, *Rules of Court* (last modified in July 2006); available at: http://www.echr.coe.int/echr.

9. Statute of the International Court of Justice; available at: http://www.icj-cij.org /icjwww/ibasicdocuments/ibasictext/ibasicstatute.htm.

10. ICTR, *Code of Professional Conduct for Defence Counsel;* available at http://69.94.11.53/ENGLISH/basicdocs/codeconduct.htm.

11. As of late 2006, the European Court of Human Rights was nearing completion of a code of judicial ethics. The World Trade Organization also has "rules of conduct for the understanding on rules of procedure governing the settlement of disputes," destined for those serving on panels, on the Appellate Body, and as arbitrators or experts. These rules address impartiality, independence, and potential conflict of interest, among other pertinent issues. See http://www.wto.org/english /tratop_e/dispu_e/rc_e.

12. International Criminal Court, *Code of Judicial Ethics,* ICC-BD/02-01-05 (3 September 2005); available at: http://www.icc-cpi.int/about/Official_Journal .html.

13. Caribbean Court of Justice, *Code of Judicial Conduct;* available at: http://www.caribbeancourtofjustice.org/codeofethics.html.

14. One substantial recent effort by a study group of the International Law Association, in cooperation with PICT, led to the drafting of the "Burgh House Principles," a document outlining ethical standards for international judges, intended as a template for individual courts to adapt to their own circumstances. See ILA papers, appendix A, for earlier related documents. See *The Burgh House Principles on the Independence of the International Judiciary* (London: Study Group on International Courts and Tribunals of the International Law

Association, 2004); available at: http://www.pict-pcti.org/activities/Burgh%20 House%20English.pdf.

15. Detlev F. Vagts, "The International Legal Profession: A Need for More Governance?" *American Journal of International Law* 90, no. 2 (1996): 250.

16. Gilbert Guillaume, "Some Thoughts on the Independence of International Judges Vis-à-Vis States," *The Law and Practice of International Courts and Tribunals* 2, no. 1 (2003).

17. *Request for an Examination of Situation in Accordance with Paragraph 63 of Court's Judgment of 20 December 1974 in Nuclear Tests* (New Zealand v. France), 1995 ICJ Rep. 288 (22 September 1995).

18. Unattributed quotations in this chapter are from judges interviewed for this book in 2005 and 2006. See the methodology section of the introduction and the list of judges interviewed, in appendix B.

19. See chapter 5. Of course, the parties themselves have frequently been less relaxed. For a bitter assessment of the ICJ in the *Nicaragua* case from the point of view of one of the U.S. participants, see Davis R. Robinson, "The Role of Politics in the Election and the Work of Judges in the International Court of Justice," *Proceedings of the American Society of International Law* 97 (2003): 277–282.

20. *Legal Consequences of the Construction of a Wall in the Occupied Palestinian Territory,* Advisory Opinion, 2004 ICJ Rep. 136 (9 July 2004).

21. *Prosecutor v. Furundzija* (IT-95-17/1-A), Appeals Judgment (21 July 2000).

22. Geoffrey Robertson, *Crimes against Humanity: The Struggle for Global Justice* (London: Allen Lane, 1999).

23. "Decision on Defense Motion Seeking the Disqualification of Justice Robertson from the Appeals Chamber" (13 March 2004), *Prosecutor v. Sesay* (SCSL-2004–AR15-15), 3.

24. Ruth Mackenzie and Philippe Sands, "International Courts and Tribunals and the Independence of the International Judge," *Harvard International Law Journal* 44, no. 1 (2003): 281.

25. Shimon Shetreet, "Standards of Conduct of International Judges: Outside Activities," *The Law and Practice of International Courts and Tribunals* 2, no. 1 (2003): 127–161; Mackenzie and Sands, "International Courts and Independence," 282.

26. *Prosecutor v. Mucic et al.* (IT-96-21), Appeals Chamber, Judgment (20 February 2001), para. 620–650. After leaving the ICTY shortly after the *Celebici* case, Karibi-Whyte was nominated by Nigeria to the International Criminal Court, but he was not elected to the ICC. It should also be noted that all three of the *Mucic* judges came under criticism for failing to manage their courtroom well over the course of a particularly long and difficult case. See Elizabeth Neuffer, *The Key to My Neighbor's House: Seeking Justice in Bosnia and Rwanda* (New York: Picador, 2001).

27. *Butare, Prosecutor v. Nyiramasuhuko et al.* (ICTR-98-42).

28. "UN Judges Laugh at Rape Victim," *Monitor,* December 3, 2001; available at http://www.globalpolicy.org/intljustice/tribunals/2001/0512rwa.htm.

29. See President Navanethem Pillay's December 14, 2001, statement about the incident, at http://69.94.11.53/ENGLISH/PRESSREL/2001/9-3-07.htm.

30. Patricia M. Wald, "Reflections on Judging: At Home and Abroad," *University of Pennsylvania Journal of Constitutional Law* 7, no. 1 (2004): 219–247, 226–227.

31. See, for example, *ICJ Statute,* art. 18.

32. Robert Badinter and Stephen G. Breyer, *Judges in Contemporary Democracy: An International Conversation* (New York: New York University Press, 2004), 302.

33. See chapter 2.

34. *Srebrenica,* Prosecutor v. Nikolic (IT-02-63).

35. *Situation in Democratic Republic of the Congo* (ICC-01/04); *Situation in Uganda* (ICC-02/04); *Situation in Central African Republic* (ICC-01/05); *Situation in Darfur, Sudan* (ICC-02/05).

36. *Complementarity and Cooperation: The Challenges of International Justice,* Report of the 2004 Brandeis Institute for International Judges (Waltham, Massachusetts: Brandeis University, 2004); available at http://www.brandeis.edu /ethics/international_justice/biij.html.

37. Badinter and Breyer, *Judges in Contemporary Democracy,* 71–72.

Profile: John Hedigan (pages 212–218)

1. This profile is based on interviews conducted in April 2005 and November 2006.

2. Under a proposed reform under consideration in 2007, Hedigan's term would be extended by an additional two years and then he would not be eligible for further reelection.

3. *Norris v. Ireland,* judgment of the European Court of Human Rights, 26 October 1988, ser. A, no. 142. See "European Court rules against Irish laws on homosexuality," *Guardian,* October 27, 1988.

4. *Scordino v. Italy,* judgment of the ECHR, delivered 29 March 2006 (Grand Chamber, no. 36813/97, sect. 1).

Conclusion (pages 223–228)

1. Oscar Schachter, "The Invisible College of International Lawyers," *Northwestern University Law Review* 72, no. 2 (1977).

2. See chapter 3.

3. Karen J. Alter, *Establishing the Supremacy of European Law: The Making of an International Rule of Law in Europe,* Oxford Studies in European Law (Oxford and New York: Oxford University Press, 2001).

4. South Africa is one such country.

5. Interview conducted 14 November 2006. The East Timor court is an example of a hybrid court with international judges sitting alongside domestic judges to decide criminal matters. See Cesare P. R. Romano, André Nollkaemper, Jann K. Kleffner, and Project on International Courts and Tribunals, *Internationalized Criminal Courts and Tribunals: Sierra Leone, East Timor, Kosovo, and Cambodia,* International Courts and Tribunals Series (Oxford and New York: Oxford University Press, 2004).

Appendix C (page 248)

1. John Henry Merryman, *The Civil Law Tradition: An Introduction to the Legal Systems of Western Europe and Latin America,* 2nd ed. (Stanford, Calif.: Stanford University Press, 1985), 1–2.

Bibliography

Note: URLs in the endnotes and bibliography were last visited on 17 April 2007.

Abbott, Kenneth W., Robert Keohane, Andrew Moravcsik, Anne-Marie Slaughter, and Duncan Snidal. The Concept of Legalization." *International Organization* 54, no. 3 (2000): 401–419.

Abel, Albert S. "Courts and Tribunals: Partners in Justice." In *Jus Et Societas: Essays in Tribute to Wolfgang Friedmann,* edited by Gabriel M. Wilner. The Hague: Martinus Nijhoff, 1979.

Abi-Mershed, Elizabeth A. H. "The United States and the Inter-American Court of Human Rights." In *The United States and International Courts and Tribunals,* edited by Cesare P. R. Romano. Unpublished manuscript, 2007.

Abi-Saab, Georges. "Whither the Judicial Function: Concluding Remarks." In *International Organizations and International Dispute Settlement: Trends and Prospects,* edited by Laurence Boisson de Chazournes, Cesare Romano, and Ruth Mackenzie. Ardsley, N.Y.: Transnational, 2002.

Address of 19 November 1996, United Nations Press Release GA/9166. *Bulletin of the International Criminal Tribunal for the Former Yugoslavia* 2, no. 13 (1996).

Ajibola, Bola. "Africa and the International Court of Justice." In *Liber Amicorum "in Memoriam" of Judge José María Ruda,* edited by José María Ruda and Calixto A. Armas Barea, 353–366. The Hague and Boston: Kluwer Law International, 2000.

Akhavan, Payam. "Beyond Impunity: Can International Criminal Justice Prevent Future Atrocities?" *American Journal of International Law* 95, no. 1 (2001): 7–31.

Allain, Jean. *A Century of International Adjudication.* The Hague: TMC Asser Press, 2000.

———. "The Role of the Presiding Judge in Garnering Respect for Decisions of International Courts." *Michigan Journal of International Law* 22, no. 3 (2001): 391–421.

Alter, Karen J. *Establishing the Supremacy of European Law: The Making of an International Rule of Law in Europe.* Oxford Studies in European Law. Oxford and New York: Oxford University Press, 2001.

———. "International Courts Are Not Agents! The Perils of the Principal-Agent Approach to Thinking about the Independence of International Courts." *Proceedings of the American Society of International Law* 99 (2005): 138–141.

———. "Private Litigants and the New International Courts." *Comparative Political Studies* 39, no. 1 (2006): 22–49.

———. "Resolving or Exacerbating Disputes? The WTO's New Dispute Resolution System." *International Affairs* 79, no. 4 (2003): 783–800.

————. "The United States and International Courts: Four Varieties of Delegation and Their Implications for Delegating U.S. Sovereignty." In *The United States and International Courts and Tribunals,* edited by Cesare P. R. Romano. Unpublished manuscript, 2007.

Alvarez, José E. "The New Dispute Settlers: (Half) Truths and Consequences." *Texas International Law Journal* 38, no. 3 (2003): 405–444.

————. *International Organizations as Law-Makers.* Oxford and New York: Oxford University Press, 2005.

Amerasinghe, Chittharanjan F. "Judges of the International Court of Justice: Election and Qualifications." *Leiden Journal of International Law* 14, no. 2 (2001): 335–348.

————. "Judging with and Legal Advising in International Organizations." *Chicago Journal of International Law* 2, no. 1 (spring 2001): 283–293.

Arzt, Donna E. "The Lockerbie 'Extradition by Analogy' Agreement: 'Exceptional Measure' or Template for Transnational Criminal Justice?" *American University International Law Review* 18, no. 1 (2002): 163–236.

Askin, Kelly D. "Prosecuting Wartime Rape and Other Gender-Related Crimes under International Law: Extraordinary Advances, Enduring Obstacles." *Berkeley Journal of International Law* 21, no. 2 (2003): 288.

————. "Sexual Violence in Decisions and Indictments of the Yugoslav and Rwandan Tribunals: Current Status." *American Journal of International Law* 93, no. 1 (1999): 97–123.

Badinter, Robert, and Stephen G. Breyer. *Judges in Contemporary Democracy: An International Conversation.* New York: New York University Press, 2004.

Barav, Ami. "The Court of Justice of the European Communities." In *The Role of Courts in Society,* edited by Shimon Shetreet, 390–424. Dordrecht, Neth., and Boston: M. Nijhoff, 1988.

Baudenbacher, Carl. "Judicial Globalization: New Development or Old Wine in New Bottles?" *Texas International Law Journal* 38, no. 3 (2003): 505–526.

Baudenbacher, Carl, Per Tresselt, and Thorgeir Orlygsson. *The EFTA Court Ten Years On.* Oxford and Portland, Ore.: Hart, 2005.

Baxter, R. R. "The Procedures Employed in Connection with the United States Nominations for the International Court in 1960." *The American Journal of International Law* 55, no. 2 (1961): 445–446.

Bedjaoui, Mohammed. "The 'Manufacture' of Judgments at the International Court of Justice." *Pace Yearbook of International Law* 3 (1991): 29–61.

Bell, John. "European Perspectives on a Judicial Appointments Commission." *The Cambridge Yearbook of European Legal Studies* 6 (2003–2004): 35–54.

Bello, Judith Hippler, and Peter H. F. Bekker. "Legality of the Use by a State of Nuclear Weapons in Armed Conflict." *American Journal of International Law* 91, no. 1 (1997): 134–138.

Boisson de Chazournes, Laurence, and V. Goland-Debbas, eds. *The International Legal System in Quest of Equity and Universality/L'order juridique international, Un système en quête d'equité et d'universalité, Liber Amicorum Georges Abi-Saab.* The Hague: Kluwer Law International, 2001.

Boisson de Chazournes, Laurence, Cesare Romano, and Ruth Mackenzie. *International Organizations and International Dispute Settlement: Trends and Prospects.* Ardsley, N.Y.: Transnational, 2002.

Bork, Robert H. *Coercing Virtue: The Worldwide Rule of Judges.* Washington, D.C.: AEI Press, 2003.

Bowett, D. W. *The International Court of Justice: Process, Practice and Procedure,* Public International Law Series. London: British Institute of International and Comparative Law, 1997.

Broomhall, Bruce. "Article 51: Rules of Procedure and Evidence." In *Commentary on the Rome Statute of the International Criminal Court,* edited by Otto Trifterer. Baden-Baden: Nomos Verlagsgesellschaft, 1999.

Brown, Chester. *A Common Law of International Adjudication.* Oxford: Oxford University Press, 2007.

———. "Legal Norms to Promote the Independence and Accountability of International Tribunals." *The Law and Practice of International Courts and Tribunals* 2, no. 1 (2003): 27–62.

Brownlie, Ian. "Politics and Law in International Adjudication." *Proceedings of the American Society of International Law* 97 (2003): 282–286.

Buergenthal, Thomas. Commencement address at American University, 19 May 2002. Available at http://www.american.edu/media/speeches/buergenthal.htm.

———. Commencement address at George Washington University, 24 May 2004. Available at http://www.gwu.edu/~newsctr/newscenter/commencement04/buergenthal_remarks.html.

———. "Human Rights and the U.S. National Interest." *Vital Speeches of the Day* 47, no. 13 (1981): 414–416.

———. "The Inter-American Court of Human Rights." *American Journal of International Law* 76, no. 2 (1982): 231–245.

———. "The Normative and Institutional Evolution of International Human Rights." *Human Rights Quarterly* 19, no. 4 (1997): 703–723.

———. "The Proliferation of Disputes, Dispute Settlement Procedures and Respect for the Rule of Law." *Arbitration International* 22, no. 4 (2006): 495–499.

———. "Proliferation of International Courts and Tribunals: Is It Good or Bad?" *Leiden Journal of International Law* 14, no. 2 (2001): 267–275.

———. "Remembering the Auschwitz Death March." *Human Rights Quarterly* 18, no. 4 (1996): 874–876.

———. "Remembering the Early Years of the Inter-American Court of Human Rights." *New York University Journal of International Law and Politics* 37, no. 2 (2005): 259–280.

Buergenthal, Thomas, and Edwin D. Williamson. "Should the United Nations Establish a Permanent International Criminal Court?" *CQ Researcher* 5, no. 25 (1995): 601.

The Burgh House Principles on the Independence of the International Judiciary. London: Study Group on International Courts and Tribunals of the International Law Association, 2004. Available at http://www.pict-pcti.org/activities/Burgh%20House%20English.pdf and in *The Law and Practice of International Courts and Tribunals* 4, no. 2 (2005): 247–260.

Burke-White, W. W. "A Community of Courts: Toward a System of International Criminal Law Enforcement." *Michigan Journal of International Law* 24, no. 1 (2002): 1–101.

Caflisch, Lucius. "Independence and Impartiality of Judges: The European Court of Human Rights " *The Law and Practice of International Courts and Tribunals* 2, no. 1 (2003): 169–173.

Caldeira, Gregory, and James Gibson. "Democracy and Legitimacy in the European Union: The Court of Justice and Its Constituents." *International Social Science Journal* 49, no. 152 (June 1997): 209–224.

―――. "The Legitimacy of the Court of Justice in the European Union: Models of Institutional Support." *American Political Science Review* 89, no. 2 (1995): 356–376.

Cassese, Antonio. "The ICTY: A Living and Vital Reality." *Journal of International Criminal Justice* 2, no. 2 (2004): 585–597.

―――. "Reflections on International Criminal Justice." *The Modern Law Review* 61, no. 1 (1998): 1–10.

Cassese, Antonio, Paola Gaeta, and John R. W. D. Jones. *The Rome Statute of the International Criminal Court: A Commentary.* Oxford and New York: Oxford University Press, 2002.

Cerone, John P. "U.S. Attitudes towards International Courts and Tribunals." In *The United States and International Courts and Tribunals,* edited by Cesare P. R. Romano. Unpublished manuscript, 2007.

The Challenges of International Justice. Proceedings of the Colloquium of Prosecutors of International Criminal Tribunals, Arusha, Tanzania, 2004. Waltham, Massachusetts: Brandeis University, 2004. Available at http://www.brandeis.edu/ethics/international_justice/publications.html.

Charnovitz, Steve, Debra P. Steger, Peter van den Bossche, and Florentino P. Feliciano, eds. *Law in the Service of Human Dignity: Essays in Honour of Florentino Feliciano.* Cambridge and New York: Cambridge University Press, 2005.

Clapham, Andrew. *Human Rights in the Private Sphere,* Oxford Monographs in International Law. Oxford: Oxford University Press, 1993.

Cockayne, James. "The Fraying Shoestring: Rethinking Hybrid War Crimes Tribunals." *Fordham International Law Journal* 28, no. 3 (2005): 616–680.

Complementarity and Cooperation: The Challenges of International Justice. Report of the 2004 Brandeis Institute for International Judges. Waltham, Massachusetts: Brandeis University, 2004. Available at http://www.brandeis.edu/ethics/international_justice/publications.html.

Complementarity and Cooperation: International Courts in a Diverse World. Report of the 2006 Brandeis Institute for International Judges. Waltham, Massachusetts: Brandeis University, 2006. Available at http://www.brandeis.edu/ethics/international_justice/publications.html.

Coomber, Andrea. "Judicial Independence: Law and Practice of Appointments to the European Court of Human Rights." *European Human Rights Law Review* 8 (2003): 486–500.

Cottier, Thomas, Petros C. Mavroidis, and Patrick Blatter, eds. *The Role of the Judge in International Trade Regulation: Experience and Lessons for the WTO.* Ann Arbor: University of Michigan Press, 2003.

Damrosch, Lori F., ed. *The International Court of Justice at a Crossroads.* Dobbs Ferry, N.Y.: Transnational, 1987.

―――. "The Election of Thomas Buergenthal to the International Court of Justice." *American Journal of International Law* 94, no. 3 (2000): 579–582.

―――. "Ensuring the Best Bench: Ways of Selecting Judges." In *Increasing the Effectiveness of the International Court of Justice: Proceedings of the ICJ/Unitar Colloquium to Celebrate the Fiftieth Anniversary of the Court,* edited by Connie Peck and Roy S. K. Lee, 188–206. The Hague; Boston; and Cambridge, Mass.: M. Nijhoff, 1997.

Darmon, Marco. "The Role of the Advocate General in the Court of Justice of the European Communities." In *The Role of Courts in Society,* edited by Shimon Shetreet, 425–436. Dordrecht, Neth.; and Boston: M. Nijhoff, 1988.

David, René, and John E. C. Brierley. *Major Legal Systems in the World Today: An Introduction to the Comparative Study of Law.* 3rd ed. London: Stevens, 1985.

Delmas-Marty, Mireille. "The Contribution of Comparative Law to a Pluralist Conception of International Criminal Law." *Journal of International Criminal Justice* 1, no. 1 (2003): 13–25.

Dugard, John. "1966 and All That: The South West Africa Judgment Revised in the East Timor Case." *African Journal of International and Comparative Law* 8 (1996): 549–563.

Dworkin, Ronald. "The Judge's New Role: Should Personal Convictions Count?" *Journal of International Criminal Justice* 1, no. 1 (2003): 4–12.

———. *Justice in Robes.* Cambridge, Mass.: Belknap Press, 2006.

Eagleton, Clyde. "Choice of Judges for the International Court of Justice." *American Journal of International Law* 47, no. 3 (1953): 462–464.

Edwards, Harry T. "The Effects of Collegiality on Judicial Decision Making." *University of Pennsylvania Law Review* 151, no. 5 (2003): 1639–1690.

Ehlermann, Claus-Dieter. "Experiences from the WTO Appellate Body." *Texas International Law Journal* 38, no. 3 (2003): 469–488.

———. "Reflections on the Appellate Body of the WTO." *Journal of International Economic Law* 6, no. 3 (2003): 695–708.

———. "Six Years on the Bench of The 'World Trade Court'—Some Personal Experiences as Member of the Appellate Body of the WTO." *Journal of World Trade* 36, no. 4 (2002): 605–639.

———. "Tensions between the Dispute Settlement Process and the Diplomatic and Treaty-Making Activities of the WTO." *World Trade Review* 1, no. 3 (2002): 301–308.

Ehlermann, Claus-Dieter, and Lothar Ehring. "Decision-Making in the World Trade Organization." *Journal of International Economic Law* 8, no. 1 (2005): 51–75.

Elias, Taslim Olawale. "Does the International Court of Justice, As It Is Presently Shaped, Correspond to the Requirements Which Follow from Its Functions As the Central Judicial Body of the International Community?" In *Judicial Settlement of International Disputes: International Court of Justice, Other Courts and Tribunals, Arbitration and Conciliation; An International Symposium,* edited by Max-Planck-Institut für Ausländisches Öffentliches Recht und Völkerrecht. Berlin; Heidelberg; and New York: Springer, 1974.

Elias, Taslim Olawale, Emmanuel G. Bello, and Bola Ajibola. *Essays in Honour of Judge Taslim Olawale Elias.* Dordrecht, Neth.; and Boston: M. Nijhoff, 1992.

Ende, Douglas J. "Reaccepting the Compulsory Jurisdiction of the International Court of Justice: A Proposal for a New United States Declaration." *Washington Law Review* 61, no. 3 (1986): 1145–1183.

Eyffinger, Arthur. *The International Court of Justice.* The Hague: Kluwer, 1996.

Falk, Richard A. "Nuclear Weapons, International Law and the World Court: A Historic Encounter." *American Journal of International Law* 91, no. 1 (1997): 64–75.

———. "Toward Authoritativeness: The ICJ Ruling on Israel's Security Wall." *American Journal of International Law* 99, no. 1 (2005): 42–52.

Ferencz, Benjamin B. *An International Criminal Court, a Step toward World Peace: A Documentary History and Analysis.* 2 vols. Dobbs Ferry, N.Y.: Oceana Publications, 1980.

Fishbayn, Lisa. "Litigating the Right to Culture: Family Law in the New South Africa." *International Journal of Law, Policy, and the Family* 13 (1999): 147–173.

Flauss, Jean-François. "Analysis of the Election of the New European Court of Human Rights." *Revue Trimestrielle des Droits de L'Homme* 9, no. 35 (1998): 435–464.

Franck, Thomas M. *Recourse to Force: State Action against Threats and Armed Attacks,* Hersch Lauterpacht Memorial Lectures. Cambridge and New York: Cambridge University Press, 2002.

———. "The United States and the Historic Idea of a World Court." In *The Role of Courts in Society,* edited by Shimon Shetreet, 366–389. Dordrecht, Neth.; and Boston: M. Nijhoff, 1988.

Gemar, Jean-Claude, and Nicholas Kasirer. *Jurilinguistique: entre langues et droits* [Jurilinguistics: Between Law and Language]. Montreal and Brussells: Thémis/Bruylant, 2005.

Gibson, James, and Gregory Caldeira. "The Legitimacy of Transnational Legal Institutions: Compliance, Support, and the European Court of Justice." *American Journal of Political Science* 39, no. 2 (1995): 459–489.

Glenn, H. Patrick. *Legal Traditions of the World: Sustainable Diversity in Law.* 2nd ed. Oxford and New York: Oxford University Press, 2004.

Goldstone, Richard. *For Humanity: Reflections of a War Crimes Investigator.* The Castle Lectures in Ethics, Politics, and Economics. New Haven, Conn.: Yale University Press, 2000.

González, Roseann Dueñas, Victoria F. Vásquez, and Holly Mikkelson. *Fundamentals of Court Interpretation: Theory, Policy, and Practice.* Durham, N.C.: Carolina Academic Press, 1991.

Graybill, Lyn. "To Punish or Pardon: A Comparison of the International Criminal Tribunal for Rwanda and the South African Truth and Reconciliation Commission." *Human Rights Review* 2, no. 4 (October 2001): 3–18.

Grilliot, Harold J., and Frank A. Schubert. *Introduction to Law and the Legal System.* 5th ed. Boston: Houghton Mifflin Company, 1992.

Gross, Leo, ed. *The Future of the International Court of Justice.* Dobbs Ferry, N.Y.: Oceana Publications, 1976.

Guillaume, Gilbert. "Advantages and Risks of Proliferation: A Blueprint for Action." *Journal of International Criminal Justice* 2, no. 2 (2004): 300–303.

———. "The Future of International Judicial Institutions." *International and Comparative Law Quarterly* 44 (1995): 848–862.

———. "Some Thoughts on the Independence of International Judges Vis-à-Vis States." *Law and Practice of International Courts and Tribunals* 2, no. 1 (2003): 163–168.

Haas, Peter M. "Introduction: Epistemic Communities and International Policy Coordination." *International Organization* 46, no. 1 (1992): 1–35.

Hansen, P.I. "Juridialization and Globalization in the North American Free Trade Agreement." *Texas International Law Journal* 38 (2003): 489–503.

Haughton, Anna. "United States Accountability for Intervention in the Western Hemisphere and Compulsory Compliance with the International Court of Justice." *New England International and Comparative Law Annual* 8, no. 2 (2002).

Helfer, Laurence R., and Anne-Marie Slaughter. "Toward a Theory of Effective Supranational Adjudication." *Yale Law Journal* 107, no. 2 (1997): 273–391.

———. "Why States Create International Tribunals: A Response to Professors Posner and Yoo." *California Law Review* 93, no. 1 (2005): 899–955.

Higgins, Rosalyn. "A Babel of Judicial Voices? Ruminations from the Bench. *International and Comparative Law Quarterly* 55, no. 4 (2006): 791–804.

———. "Non-Identification of the Majority and Minority in the Practice of the International Court of Justice." In *Jus Et Societas: Essays in Tribute to Wolfgang Friedmann,* edited by G. M. Wilner, 134–150. The Hague: Martinus Nijhoff, 1979.

———. "Respecting Sovereign States and Running a Tight Courtroom." *International and Comparative Law Quarterly* 50, no. 1 (2001): 121–132.

———. "The ICJ, the ECJ and the Integrity of International Law." *International and Comparative Law Quarterly* 52, no. 1 (2003): 1–20.

Huber, B. "Human Rights and Criminal Law: The Impact of the European Court of Human Rights on the Administration of Justice of Its Members." *Comparative and International Law Journal of Southern Africa* 14 (1981): 300–314.

Hudson, Manley O. "The Election of Members of the Permanent Court of International Justice." *The American Journal of International Law* 24, no. 4 (1930): 718–727.

———. *International Tribunals: Past and Future.* Washington, D.C.: Carnegie Endowment for International Peace and Brookings Institution, 1944.

———. "The Twenty-Fourth Year of the World Court." *American Journal of International Law* 40, no. 1 (1946): 1–52.

Huntington, Samuel P. *The Clash of Civilizations and the Remaking of World Order.* New York: Simon & Schuster, 1996.

Hurd, Ian. "Legitimacy and Authority in International Politics." *International Organization* 53, no. 2 (1999): 379–408.

Ingadottir, Thordis. "The EEA Agreement and Homogeneous Jurisprudence: The Two-Pillar Role Given to the EFTA Court and the Court of Justice of the European Communities." *Yearbook of International Law and Jurisprudence* 2 (2002): 193–202.

Jackson, John H. "Dispute Settlement and the WTO: Emerging Problems." In *From GATT to the WTO: The Multilateral Trading System in the New Millennium.* The Hague: Kluwer International, 2000.

Jacobs, Francis G. "Judicial Dialogue and the Cross-Fertilization of Legal Systems: The European Court of Justice." *Texas International Law Journal* 38, no. 3 (2003): 547–556.

Janis, Mark W. *The American Tradition of International Law.* Oxford and New York: Oxford University Press, 2004.

Johnson, Timothy Russell. *Oral Arguments and Decision Making on the United States Supreme Court.* SUNY Series in American Constitutionalism. Albany: State University of New York Press, 2004.

Jorda, Claude. "The Major Hurdles and Accomplishments of the ICTY: What the ICC Can Learn from Them." *Journal of International Criminal Justice* 2, no. 2 (2004): 572–584.

Judicial Independence: Law and Practice of Appointments to the European Court of Human Rights. Report from Interights. London: Interights, 2003.

Kaul, Hans-Peter. "Construction Site for More Justice: The International Criminal Court after Two Years." *American Journal of International Law* 99, no. 2 (2005): 370–384.

Keck, Margaret E., and Kathryn Sikkink. *Activists Beyond Borders: Advocacy Networks in International Politics.* Ithaca, N.Y.: Cornell University Press, 1998.

Kelly, J. P. "Judicial Activism at the World Trade Organization: Developing Principles of Self-Restraint." *Northwestern Journal of International Law and Business* 22, no. 3 (2002): 353–388.

Kenney, S. J. "The Members of the Court of Justice of the European Communities." *Columbia Journal of European Law* 5 (1998): 101–133.

Keohane, Robert, and Ruth W. Grant. "Accountability and Abuses of Power in World Politics." *American Political Science Review* 99, no. 1 (2005): 29–43.

Kirgis, Frederic L. "The United Nations at Fifty: The Security Council's First Fifty Years." *American Journal of International Law* 89, no. 3 (1995): 506–539.

Kirsch, Philippe, and John T. Holmes. "The Rome Conference on an International Criminal Court: The Negotiating Process." *American Journal of International Law* 93, no. 1 (1999): 2–12.

Kissinger, Henry. *Does America Need a Foreign Policy? Toward a Diplomacy for the 21st Century.* New York: Simon & Schuster, 2002.

Klein, Katheryn M. "Bringing the Khmer Rouge to Justice: The Challenges and Risks Facing the Joint Tribunal in Cambodia." *Northwestern University Journal of International Human Rights* 4, no. 3 (2006): 549–566.

Lasok, K. P. E. *The European Court of Justice: Practice and Procedure.* 2nd ed. London: Butterworths, 1994.

Lauterpacht, Elihu. "The International Lawyer as Judge." In *The International Lawyer as Practitioner,* edited by Chanaka Wickremasinghe, 125–146. London: British Institute of International and Comparative Law, 2000.

Lavalle, Roberto. "Nationality as a Factor in the Election of the Members of the International Court of Justice, with Particular Reference to Occasional Elections." *Revue Belge de Droit International* 29, no. 2 (1996): 625–632.

Mackenzie, Ruth, and Philippe Sands. "International Courts and Tribunals and the Independence of the International Judge." *Harvard International Law Journal* 44, no. 1 (2003): 271–285.

Martinez, Jenny S. "Towards an International Judicial System." *Stanford Law Review* 56, no. 2 (2003): 429–529.

Max-Planck-Institut für Ausländisches Öffentliches Recht und Völkerrecht. "Judicial Settlement of International Disputes: International Court of Justice, Other Courts and Tribunals, Arbitration and Conciliation; An International Symposium." Proceedings of the Beiträge zum ausländischen öffentlichen Recht und Völkerrecht. Bd. 62, Berlin, Heidelberg, and New York: Springer, 1974.

Mayer, Martin. *The Judges: A Penetrating Exploration of American Courts and of the New Decisions—Hard Decisions—They Must Make for a New Millennium.* New York: Truman Talley Books/St. Martin's Press, 2007.

McNelis, Natalie. "The Role of the Judge in the EU and WTO." *Journal of International Economic Law* 4, no. 1 (2001): 189–208.

McWhinney, Edward. "The International Court as Constitutional Court and the Blurring of the Arbitral/Judicial Processes." In *The Flame Rekindled: New Hopes for International Arbitration,* edited by Sam Muller and Wim Mijs, 81–89. Dordrecht, Neth.; and Boston: M. Nijhoff, 1994.

———. "Internationalizing the International Court: The Quest for Ethno-Cultural and Legal-Systemic Representativeness." In *Essays in Honour of Judge Taslim Olawale Elias,* edited by Taslim Olawale Elias, Emmanuel G. Bello, and Bola Ajibola, 277–289. Dordrecht, Neth; and Boston: M. Nijhoff, 1992.

———. "Law, Politics and 'Regionalism' in the Nomination and Election of World Court Judges." *Syracuse Journal of International Law and Commerce* 13 (1986): 1–28.

McWhinney, Edward, and Paul Martin. *The International Court of Justice and the Western Tradition of International Law.* Dordrecht, Neth; and Boston; Hingham, Mass.: M. Nijhoff, 1987.

Meron, Theodor. "Crimes and Accountability in Shakespeare." *American Journal of International Law* 92, no. 1 (1998): 1–40.

———. "The Geneva Conventions as Customary Law." *American Journal of International Law* 81, no. 2 (1987): 348–370.

———. "Judicial Independence and Impartiality in International Criminal Tribunals." *American Journal of International Law* 99, no. 2 (2005): 359–369.

———. "Revival of Customary Humanitarian Law." *American Journal of International Law* 99, no. 4 (2005): 817–834.

———. "War Crimes Law Comes of Age." *American Journal of International Law* 92, no. 3 (1998): 462–468.

Merrills, J. G. "The Making of an International Judge." In *Judge Sir Gerald Fitzmaurice and the Discipline of International Law.* The Hague: Kluwer Law International, 1998.

Merryman, John Henry. *The Civil Law Tradition: An Introduction to the Legal Systems of Western Europe and Latin America.* 2nd ed. Stanford, Calif.: Stanford University Press, 1985.

Miller, Nathan. "An International Jurisprudence? The Operation of 'Precedent' across International Tribunals." *Leiden Journal of International Law* 15 (2002): 483–526.

Mitchell, David S. "The Prohibition of Rape in International Humanitarian Law as a Norm of Jus Cogens: Clarifying the Doctrine." *Duke Journal of Comparative and International Law* 15, no. 2 (2005): 219–257.

Moghalu, Kingsley Chiedu. "Image and Reality of War Crimes Justice: External Perceptions of the International Criminal Tribunal for Rwanda." *Fletcher Forum of World Affairs* 26, no. 2 (2002): 21–46.

Moore, John Bassett. "The Organization of the Permanent Court of International Justice." *Columbia Law Review* 22, no. 6 (1922): 497–526.

Morgan, D. L. "Implications of the Proliferation of International Legal Fora: The Example of the Southern Bluefin Tuna Cases." *Harvard International Law Journal* 43, no. 2 (2002): 541–551.

Muller, Sam, and Wim Mijs, eds. *The Flame Rekindled: New Hopes for International Arbitration.* Dordrecht, Neth.; and Boston: M. Nijhoff, 1994.

Mundis, Daryl A. "The Election of Ad Litem Judges and Other Recent Developments at the International Criminal Tribunals." *Leiden Journal of International Law* 14 (2001): 851–866.

———. "From 'Common Law' towards 'Civil Law': The Evolution of the ICTY Rules of Procedure and Evidence." *Leiden Journal of International Law* 14 (2001): 367–382.

———. "Improving the Operation and Functioning of the International Criminal Tribunals." *American Journal of International Law* 94, no. 4 (2000): 759–773.

———. "The Judicial Effects of the 'Completion Strategies' on the Ad Hoc International Criminal Tribunals." *American Journal of International Law* 99, no. 1 (2005): 142–158.

Murphy, John Francis. *The United States and the Rule of Law in International Affairs*. Cambridge and New York: Cambridge University Press, 2004.

Murphy, Sean D. "The United States and the International Court of Justice: Coping with Antinomies." In *The United States and International Courts and Tribunals*, edited by Cesare P. R. Romano. Unpublished manuscript, 2007.

Mutua, Makau. *Human Rights: A Political and Cultural Critique*. Pennsylvania Studies in Human Rights. Philadelphia: University of Pennsylvania, 2002.

Neuffer, Elizabeth. *The Key to My Neighbor's House: Seeking Justice in Bosnia and Rwanda*. New York: Picador, 2001.

Newburger, Emily. "The Bus Driver's Daughter." *Harvard Law Bulletin* (spring 2006).

Nolte, Georg. *European Military Law Systems*. Berlin: W. de Gruyter, 2003.

Oda, Shigeru, Edward McWhinney, and Mariko Kawano. *Judge Shigeru Oda and the Path to Judicial Wisdom*. Leiden, Neth.; and Boston: Martinus Nijhoff, 2006.

Oellers-Frahm, Karin. "ICJ: International Court of Justice." In *A Concise Encyclopedia of the United Nations*, edited by Helmut Volger, 281–294. The Hague and New York: Kluwer Law International, 2002.

Orentlicher, Diane F. "Unilateral Multilateralism: United States Policy toward the International Criminal Court." *Cornell International Law Journal* 36, no. 3 (2004): 415–433.

Owens, Lori Jean. *Original Intent and the Struggle for the Supreme Court: The Politics of Judicial Appointments*. Lewiston, N.Y.: Edwin Mellen Press, 2005.

Pasqualucci, Jo M. "Sonia Picado, First Woman Judge on the Inter-American Court of Human Rights." *Human Rights Quarterly* 17, no. 4 (1995): 794.

———. "Thomas Buergenthal: Holocaust Survivor to Human Rights Advocate." *Human Rights Quarterly* 18, no. 4 (1996): 877.

Paulson, Colter. "Compliance with Final Judgments of the International Court of Justice Since 1987." *American Journal of International Law* 98, no. 3 (2004): 434–461.

Pauwelyn, Joost. "The Transformation of World Trade." *Michigan Law Review* 104, no.1 (2005): 1–65.

———. "The Use of Experts in WTO Dispute Settlement." *International and Comparative Law Quarterly* 51, no. 2 (2002): 325–364.

Peck, Connie, and Roy S. K. Lee, eds. *Increasing the Effectiveness of the International Court of Justice: Proceedings of the ICJ/Unitar Colloquium to Celebrate the 50th Anniversary of the Court*. The Hague; Boston; and Cambridge, Mass.: M. Nijhoff, 1997.

Pellet, Allain. "The Role of International Lawyer in International Litigation." In *The International Lawyer as Practitioner*, edited by Chanaka Wickremasinghe. London: British Institute of International and Comparative Law, 2000.

Pocar, Fausto. "The Proliferation of International Criminal Courts and Tribunals: A Necessity in the Current International Community." *Journal of International Criminal Justice* 2, no. 2 (2004): 304–308.

Politi, Mauro, and Giuseppe Nesi. *The International Criminal Court and the Crime of Aggression*. Aldershot, Eng.; and Burlington, Vt.: Ashgate, 2004.

Pomerance, Michla. "The ICJ's Advisory Jurisdiction and the Crumbling Wall between the Political and the Judicial." *American Journal of International Law* 99, no. 1 (2005): 26–42.

————. *The United States and the World Court as a "Supreme Court of the Nations": Dreams, Illusions, and Disillusion.* Dordrecht, Neth.: M. Nijhoff, 1996.

Posner, Eric A., and Miguel de Figueiredo. "Is the International Court of Justice Biased?" Olin Working Paper no. 234. University of Chicago Law and Economics. December 2004. Available at Social Science Research Network: http://ssrn.com/abstract=642581.

Posner, Eric A., and John C. Yoo. "Judicial Independence in International Tribunals." *California Law Review* 93, no. 1 (2005): 1–74.

Postiglione, Amedeo. *The Global Environmental Crisis: The Need for an International Court of the Environment.* Florence: Giunti, 1996.

Prott, Lyndel V. *The Latent Power of Culture and the International Judge.* Abingdon, U.K.: Professional Books, 1979.

Raab, Dominic. "Evaluating the ICTY and Its Completion Strategy: Efforts to Achieve Accountability for War Crimes and Their Tribunals." *Journal of International Criminal Justice* 3, no. 1 (2005): 82–102.

Rague, Margaret A. "The Reservation Power and the Connally Amendment." *New York University Journal of Law and International Politics* 11, no. 2 (1978): 323–358.

Ratner, Steven R. "The International Criminal Court and the Limits of Global Judicialization." *Texas International Law Journal* 38, no. 3 (2003): 445–453.

Ress, Georg. "The Effect of Decisions and Judgments of the European Court of Human Rights in the Domestic Legal Order." *Texas International Law Journal* 40, no. 3 (2005): 359–382.

Rest, Alfred. "Need for an International Court for the Environment? Underdeveloped Legal Protection for the Individual in Transnational Litigation." *Environmental Policy and Law* 24, no. 4 (1994): 173–187.

Robertson, Geoffrey. *Crimes against Humanity: The Struggle for Global Justice.* London: Allen Lane, 1999.

Robinson, Davis R. "The Role of Politics in the Election and the Work of Judges in the International Court of Justice." *Proceedings of the American Society of International Law* 97 (2003): 277–282.

Romano, Cesare P. R. "The Americanization of International Dispute Resolution." *Ohio State Journal on Dispute Resolution* 19, no. 1 (2003): 89–119.

————. "International Justice and Developing Countries: A Qualitative Analysis." *Law and Practice of International Courts and Tribunals* 1, no. 3 (2002): 539–611.

————. "International Justice and Developing Countries: A Quantitative Analysis." *Law and Practice of International Courts and Tribunals* 1, no. 2 (2002): 367–299.

————. "International Courts and Tribunals: Price, Financing and Output." In *International Conflict Resolution,* Special issue of the annual journal, *Conferences on New Political Economy (formerly Jahrbuch Für Neue Politische Ökonomie)* 23, edited by Stefan Voigt, Max Albert, and Dieter Schmidtchen, 189–245. Tubingen, Ger.: Mohr Siebeck, 2006.

————. "Mixed Criminal Tribunals." In *Max Planck Encyclopedia of Public International Law,* 3rd rev. ed., Oxford and New York, Oxford University Press, in press.

————. "The Price of International Justice." *Law and Practice of International Courts and Tribunals* 2, no. 4 (2003): 281–328.

———. "The Proliferation of International Judicial Bodies: The Pieces of the Puzzle." *NYU Journal of International Law and Politics* 31, no. 4 (1999): 709–751.

———. "The Shift from the Consensual to the Compulsory Paradigm in International Adjudication: Elements for a Theory of Consent." *New York University Journal of International Law and Politics* 39, no. 1 (2007): 101–177.

Romano, Cesare P. R., André Nollkaemper, and Jann K. Kleffner. *Internationalized Criminal Courts and Tribunals: Sierra Leone, East Timor, Kosovo, and Cambodia.* Oxford and New York: Oxford University Press, 2004.

Roosevelt, Eleanor. "The Promise of Human Rights." *Foreign Affairs* 26, no. 3 (1948): 470–477.

Rosand, Eric. "The Security Council as 'Global Legislator': Ultra Vires or Ultra Innovative?" *Fordham International Law Journal* 28, no. 3 (2005): 542–590.

Rosas, Allan. "Fundamental Rights in the Luxembourg and Strasbourg Courts." In *The EFTA Court Ten Years On,* edited by Carl Baudenbacher, Per Tresselt, and Thorgeir Orlygsson, 163–175. Oxford and Portland, Ore.: Hart, 2005.

———. "International Dispute Settlement: EU Practices and Procedures." In *German Yearbook of International Law,* 284–322. Berlin: Duncker & Humblot, 2003.

Rosenne, Shabtai. "The Composition of the Court." In *The Future of the International Court of Justice,* edited by Leo Gross, 377–441. Dobbs Ferry, N.Y.: Oceana Publications, 1976.

———. "Elections of Members of the International Court of Justice: Late Nominations and Withdrawals of Candidacies." *American Journal of International Law* 70, no. 3 (1976): 543–549.

———. "International Court of Justice; Practice Directions on Judges Ad Hoc: Agents, Counsel and Advocates; and Submission of New Documents." *The Law and Practice of International Courts and Tribunals* 1 (2002): 223–245.

———. "Sir Hersch Lauterpacht's Concept of the Task of the International Judge." *American Journal of International Law* 55, no. 4 (1961): 825–862.

Ruda, José María, and Calixto A. Armas Barea. *Liber Amicorum 'in Memoriam' of Judge José María Ruda.* The Hague and Boston: Kluwer Law International, 2000.

Russell, Peter H., and Kate Malleson, eds. *Appointing Judges in an Age of Judicial Power: Critical Perspectives from around the World.* Toronto and Buffalo, N.Y.: University of Toronto Press, 2006.

Sands, Philippe. *From Nuremberg to The Hague: The Future of International Criminal Justice.* Cambridge and New York: Cambridge University Press, 2003.

———. "Global Governance and the International Judiciary: Choosing Our Judges." *Contemporary Legal Problems* 56 (2003): 482–502.

———. "The Independence of the International Judiciary: Some Introductory Thoughts." In *Law in the Service of Human Dignity: Essays in Honour of Florentino Feliciano,* edited by Steve Charnovitz, Debra P. Steger, Peter van den Bossche, and Florentino P. Feliciano, 313–322. Cambridge and New York: Cambridge University Press, 2005.

———. *Lawless World: America and the Making and Breaking of Global Rules from FDR's Atlantic Charter to George W. Bush's Illegal War.* New York: Viking, 2005.

Savage, David G., and Joan Biskupic. *Guide to the U.S. Supreme Court.* 4th ed. Washington, D.C.: CQ Press, 2004.

Schachter, Oscar. "The Invisible College of International Lawyers." *Northwestern University Law Review* 72, no. 2 (1977): 217–226.

Scheffer, David J. "The United States and the International Criminal Court." *American Journal of International Law* 93, no. 1 (1999): 12–22.

Schermers, Henry G. "Election of Judges to the European Court of Human Rights." *European Law Review* 23, no. 6 (1998): 568–578.

Schocken, Celina. "The Special Court for Sierra Leone: Overview and Recommendations." *Berkeley Journal of International Law* 20, no. 2 (2002): 436–461.

Schulte, Constanze. *Compliance with Decisions of the International Court of Justice.* Oxford: Oxford University Press, 2004.

Schwebel, Stephen M. "Concluding Observations." In *The Flame Rekindled: New Hopes for International Arbitration,* edited by Sam Muller and Wim Mijs, 177–183. Dordrecht, Neth.; and Boston: M. Nijhoff, 1994.

———. "National Judges and Judges Ad Hoc of the International Court of Justice." *International and Comparative Law Quarterly* 48, no. 4 (1999): 889–900.

———. "The Reality of International Adjudication and Arbitration." *Willamette Journal of International Law and Dispute Resolution* 12, no. 2 (2004): 359–65.

Sessi, Giorgia. *Interpreting at International Courts and Tribunals: An Overview.* Bologna: Università di Bologna, 2005.

Shapiro, Martin M. *Courts: A Comparative Political Analysis.* Chicago: University of Chicago Press, 1981.

———. "'Deliberative,' 'Independent' Technocracy v. Democratic Politics: Will the Globe Echo the E.U.?" *Law and Contemporary Problems* 68, no. 3–4 (2005): 341–356.

———. "The European Court of Justice." In *Judicial Independence in the Age of Democracy: Critical Perspectives from around the World,* edited by Martin M. Shapiro, 273–300. Charlottesville: University Press of Virginia, 2001.

Shapiro, Martin M., and Alec Stone Sweet. *On Law, Politics, and Judicialization.* Oxford and New York: Oxford University Press, 2002.

Shelton, Dinah. "Legal Norms to Promote the Independence and Accountability of International Tribunals." *The Law and Practice of International Courts and Tribunals* 2, no. 1 (2003): 27–62.

Shetreet, Shimon. "Standards of Conduct of International Judges: Outside Activities." *The Law and Practice of International Courts and Tribunals* 2, no. 1 (2003): 127–161.

Sikkink, Kathryn, and Ellen Lutz. "The Justice Cascade: The Evolution and Impact of Foreign Human Rights Trials in Latin America." *Chicago Journal of International Law* 2, no. 1 (2001): 1–33.

Slaughter, Anne-Marie. "Court to Court." *American Journal of International Law* 92, no. 4 (1998): 708–712.

———. "A Global Community of Courts." *Harvard International Law Journal* 44, no. 1 (2003): 191–219.

———. "A Real New World Order." *Foreign Affairs* 76, no. 5 (1997): 183–197.

Slaughter, Anne-Marie, Alec Stone Sweet, and Joseph Weiler. *The European Court and National Courts—Doctrine and Jurisprudence: Legal Change in Its Social Context.* Evanston, Ill.: Northwestern University Press, 1998.

Smith, Adam M. "'Judicial Nationalism' in International Law: National Identity and Judicial Autonomy at the ICJ." *Texas International Law Journal* 40, no. 2 (2005): 197–231.

Solan, Lawrence, and Peter Meijes Tiersma. *Speaking of Crime: The Language of Criminal Justice.* The Chicago Series in Law and Society. Chicago: University of Chicago Press, 2005.

Spender, Jean. *Ambassador's Wife*. Sydney: Angus and Robertson, 1968.

Sriram, Chandra Lekha. "Wrong-Sizing International Justice? The Hybrid Tribunal in Sierra Leone." *Fordham International Law Journal* 29, no. 3 (2006): 472–506.

Steger, Debra P. "Improvements and Reforms of the WTO Appellate Body." In *The WTO Dispute Settlement: 1995–2003*, edited by Federico Ortino and Ernst-Ulrich Petersmann. The Hague: Kluwer Law International, 2004.

Steinberg, Richard H. "Judicial Lawmaking at the WTO: Discursive, Constitutional, and Political Constraints." *American Journal of International Law* 98, no. 2 (2004): 247–275.

Stone Sweet, Alec. *European Integration and the Legal System*. Wien, Aus.: Institut für Höhere Studien (IHS), 2005.

———. *Governing with Judges: Constitutional Politics in Europe*. Oxford and New York: Oxford University Press, 2000.

———. *The Judicial Construction of Europe*. Oxford and New York: Oxford University Press, 2004.

Stone Sweet, Alec, Wayne Sandholtz, and Neil Fligstein. *The Institutionalization of Europe*. Oxford: Oxford University Press, 2001.

Stover, Eric. *The Witnesses: War Crimes and the Promise of Justice in the Hague*. Philadelphia: University of Pennsylvania Press, 2005.

Stover, Eric, and Harvey M. Weinstein. *My Neighbor, My Enemy: Justice and Community in the Aftermath of Mass Atrocity*. Cambridge and New York: Cambridge University Press, 2004.

Talmon, Stefan. "The Security Council as World Legislature." *American Journal of International Law* 99, no. 1 (2005): 175–193.

Tan, Chet J., Jr. "The Proliferation of Bilateral Non-Surrender Agreements among Non-Ratifiers of the Rome Statute of the International Criminal Court." *American University International Law Review* 19, no. 5 (2004): 1115–1180.

Tetley, William. "Mixed Jurisdictions: Common Law vs. Civil Law (Codified and Uncodified), Part I." *Uniform Law Review* 4, no. 3 (1999): 591–619.

———. "Mixed Jurisdictions: Common Law vs. Civil Law (Codified and Uncodified), Part II." *Uniform Law Review* 4, no. 4 (1999): 877–906.

Thompson, E. A., and R. S. Thompson. "Research Staff at Appellate Courts: Function, Personalities and Ethical Restraints." In *The Role of Courts in Society*, edited by Shimon Shetreet, 244–270. Dordrecht, Neth.; and Boston: M. Nijhoff, 1988.

Tomuschat, Christian. "International Courts and Tribunals with Regionally Restricted and/or Specialized Jurisdiction." In Max Planck Institut, *Judicial Settlement of International Disputes: International Court of Justice, Other Courts and Tribunals, Arbitration and Conciliation; An International Symposium*. Max-Planck Institut Für Ausländisches Öffentliches Recht und Völkerrecht. Berlin, Heidelberg, and New York: Springer, 1974.

Trifterer, Otto, ed. *Commentary on the Rome Statute of the International Criminal Court*. Baden-Baden: Nomos Verlagsgesellschaft, 1999.

Vagts, Detlev F. "The International Legal Profession: A Need for More Governance?" *American Journal of International Law* 90, no. 2 (1996): 250–261.

Vajic, Nina. "Diplomatic Settlement or Adjudication? Advantages and Drawbacks." In *The Peaceful Settlement of Disputes between States: Universal and European Perspectives,* edited by L. Caflisch, 17–23. The Hague: Kluwer Law International, 1998.

Valencia-Ospina, Eduardo. "Editorial Comment." *The Law and Practice of International Courts and Tribunals* 1, no. 1 (2002): 1–12.

Valticos, Nicolas. "L'évolution de la notion de juge ad hoc." *Revue Hellénique de Droit International* 50, no. 1 (1997): 1–15.

———. "Pratique et ethique d'un juge 'ad hoc' à la Cour International de Justice." In *Liber Amicorum Judge Shigeru Oda,* edited by Nicolas Valticos, 107–116, 2002.

Voeten, Erik. "The Politics of International Judicial Appointments: Evidence from the European Court of Human Rights." (September 6, 2006). Available at Social Science Research Network: http://ssrn.com/abstract=939062.

Wald, Patricia M. "ICTY Judicial Proceedings: An Appraisal from Within." *Journal of International Criminal Justice* 2, no. 2 (2004): 466–473.

———. "Last Thoughts." *Columbia Law Review* 99, no. 1 (1999): 270–272.

———. "Reflections on Judging: At Home and Abroad." *University of Pennsylvania Journal of Constitutional Law* 7, no. 1 (2004): 219–247.

———. "Running the Trial of the Century: The Nuremberg Legacy." *Cardozo Law Review* 27, no. 4 (2006): 1559–1597.

———. "To 'Establish Incredible Events by Credible Evidence': The Use of Affidavit Testimony in Yugoslavia War Crimes Tribunal Proceedings." *Harvard International Law Journal* 42, no. 2 (2001): 535–553.

Waldorf, Lars. "Mass Justice for Mass Atrocity: Rethinking Local Justice as Transitional Justice." *Temple Law Review* 79, no. 1 (2006): 2–84.

Wallerstein, Immanuel Maurice. *The Modern World-System.* New York: Academic Press, 1974.

Watson, Geoffrey R. "The 'Wall' Decisions in Legal and Political Context." *American Journal of International Law* 99, no. 1 (2005): 6–26.

Watts, Arthur. "The Importance of International Law." In *The Role of Law in International Politics: Essays in International Relations and International Law,* edited by Michael Byers, 5–16. Oxford and New York: Oxford University Press, 2000.

Wedgwood, Ruth. "The ICJ Advisory Opinion on the Israeli Security Fence and the Limits of Self-Defense." *American Journal of International Law* 99, no. 1 (2005): 52–61.

Weiss-Brown, Edith. "Judicial Independence and Impartiality: A Preliminary Inquiry." In *The International Court of Justice at a Crossroads,* edited by Lori F. Damrosch and American Society of International Law, 123–154. Dobbs Ferry, N.Y.: Transnational, 1987.

Wessel, Jared. "Judicial Policy-Making at the International Criminal Court: An Institutional Guide to Analyzing International Adjudication." *Columbia Journal of Transnational Law* 44, no. 2 (2006): 377–452.

Westbrook, Jay Lawrence. "International Judicial Negotiation." *Texas International Law Journal* 38, no. 3 (2003): 567–586.

Wetzel, Joseph R. "Improving Fundamental Rights Protection in the European Union: Resolving the Conflict and Confusion between the Luxembourg and Strasbourg Courts." *Fordham Law Review* 71, no. 6 (2003): 2823–2862.

Wildhaber, Luzius. "Gerichte Und Richter Im Europäischen Verfassungsraum." *Zeitschrift für schweizerisches Recht* 126, no. 1(2) (2006): 93–105.

Wildhaber, Luzius, and Antônio A. Cançado Trindade. "Exchange of Letters between the Presidents of the European Court of Human Rights and the Inter-American Court of Human Rights." *Human Rights Law Journal* 20, no. 12 (1999): 488–489.

Wilson, Richard. *Human Rights, Culture and Context: Anthropological Perspectives.* London and Sterling, Va.: Pluto Press, 1997.

Winkelmann, I. "Groups and Groupings in the UN." In *A Concise Encyclopedia of the United Nations,* edited by Helmut Volger, 158–161. The Hague and New York: Kluwer Law International, 2002.

———. "Regional Groups in the UN." In *A Concise Encyclopedia of the United Nations,* edited by Helmut Volger, 455–458. The Hague and New York: Kluwer Law International, 2002.

Wippmann, David. "The Costs of International Justice." *American Journal of International Law* 100, no. 4 (2006): 861–880.

Zacklin, Ralph. "The Failings of Ad Hoc International Tribunals." *Journal of International Criminal Justice* 2, no. 2 (2004): 541–545.

Zimmermann, Andreas, and the International Court of Justice. *The Statute of the International Court of Justice: A Commentary.* Oxford and New York: Oxford University Press, 2006.

Index

Note: Page numbers in italics refer to photographs.